GENERAL HISTORIES

The Office of the Secretary of the Air Force
1947–1965

George M. Watson, Jr.

**Center for
Air Force
History**

Washington, D.C.

1993

Library of Congress Cataloging-In-Publication Data

Watson, George M.
The Office of the Secretary of the Air Force, 1947–1965 / George M.
Watson, Jr.
        p.   cm.--(General histories)
 Includes bibliographical references and index.
ISBN 0-912799-76-5 (casebound).--ISBN 0-912799-78-1 (perfectbound)
 1. United States. Dept. of the Air Force--History.   I. Title. II. Series.
UG633.W337   1992
353.63'09--dc20

                                                              92-18308
                                                                  CIP

For Sale by the Superintendent of Documents, U.S. Government Printing Office,
Washington, D.C. 20402

Foreword

If power in Washington is often thought of as a zero-sum game, success is best achieved by creating "win-win" propositions. The Secretary of the Air Force, placed at the nexus of several power centers and responsible for fashioning a consensus, reports to the Secretary of Defense, deals with various deputy secretaries as peers, and interacts with the Air Force Chief of Staff, who supervises the service. The Secretary has real but circumscribed influence, yet must, to be effective, move individuals and agencies, with little more than limited or indirect authority over them.

This work traces the history of the Office of the Secretary of the Air Force from its formation in the 1920s (as the Office of the Assistant Secretary of War for Air) through World War II, under Robert A. Lovett. It concentrates on the period from 1947, when the Air Force became independent of the Army, to 1965, when the United States became involved in the Vietnam War. During this time several laws significantly reshaped the U.S. military establishment: the National Security Act of 1947, its amendments of 1949, Reorganization Plan No. 6 of 1953, and the Department of Defense Reorganization Act of 1958. These laws gradually strengthened the Department of Defense and firmly established civilian control over the military services.

Author George Watson details how these laws affected the functioning of the first seven Secretaries of the Air Force, from W. Stuart Symington to Eugene M. Zuckert. The Air Force and its Secretaries struggled over autonomy, roles, and missions; fought the Korean War and the Cold War; procured advanced aircraft, missiles, and other weapons; and wrestled with many issues involving budgets, force size and structure, racial integration, morale, and congressional and public relations.

The Secretaries of the Air Force have each brought unique leadership styles to office. This study provides a context for understanding the complex changes that confronted them as the United States successively moved through the jet, atomic, and space ages. It should prove useful to both civilian and military Air Force policy makers as they operate in a new era in which America's air power has become truly global and unprecedented in influence and reach.

RICHARD P. HALLION
Air Force Historian

Preface

In 1948 Secretary of the Air Force W. Stuart Symington was often referred to as the third most powerful man in the world after the President of the United States and the Secretary of Defense. Yet only thirteen years later, Secretary of the Air Force Eugene M. Zuckert admitted to functioning as little more than a group vice president. Symington could argue on virtually equal terms with Secretary of Defense James V. Forrestal, but Zuckert had to make an appointment merely to converse with the Under Secretary of Defense. Did this erosion of power occur because of Congress, because of the U.S. strategy of limited warfare that led to stalemate in Korea, or because the Air Secretaries lost power to aggressive Air Staffs and successive Secretaries of Defense?

This book focuses on the role and influence of the Office of the Secretary of the Air Force from 1947 to 1965, a critical period in American history. It was a time when the air forces underwent a tremendous amount of expansion and contraction—the military budget had been slashed after World War II, then rapidly increased when the United States went to war in Korea. The Air Force entered the missile age, and Americans began to question the conduct of their military establishment in international affairs.

The era was marked by two major developments. The first was a shift in power from Congress to the President. Following World War II, the executive branch determined strategy and overall level of military effort—the number of wings for the Air Force, divisions for the Army, and ships for the Navy. While the legislative branch could exert some influence over decisions on these matters, it could not initiate military strategy and policy. That power remained with the executive branch.[1] The second major development was the establishment and gradual strengthening of centralized civilian control over the nation's armed forces through the passage of several laws—the 1947 National Security Act, its 1949 amendments, Reorganization Plan No. 6 of 1953, and the Department of Defense Reorganization Act of 1958.

The first of these laws, the landmark National Security Act, passed in September 1947, represented the outcome of many months of comprehensive deliberations among military, congressional, and other governmental leaders. The act instituted supervisory authority over the defense establishment by civilians and close interaction between military and non-military elements of the government.[2]

The National Security Act of 1947 created a Secretary of the Air Force with an under secretary and two assistant secretaries. It outlined no specific duties and thus gave the secretary more or less a free hand in organizing his office. Follow-on legislation—the 1949 amendments, Reorganization Plan No. 6, and the 1958 Reorganization Act—offered no further direction about what Secretaries of the Air Force could do, only what they could not do.

The Secretaries of the Air Force, therefore, rarely if ever operated according to master plans. They reacted instead to problems arising from presidential agendas, the exigencies of events at home and abroad, and the uncertainties of military funding. Priorities tended to change from secretary to secretary so that the significance of procurement, for example, a major issue during Robert A. Lovett's tenure from 1941 to 1945, diminished under Stuart Symington's from 1947 to 1950, when salvaging a minimal force structure became the dominant concern.

Symington had to spend most of his time resisting the austerity-minded Truman administration and its Secretary of Defense, Louis A. Johnson. Thomas K. Finletter, who succeeded Symington and served until 1953 was spared such pressure when military spending soared during America's involvement in the Korean conflict. When President Dwight D. Eisenhower in 1953 honored his promise to end the fighting, he introduced a policy of "security and solvency." That policy, which called for reduced military spending and a stretched out Air Force structure, was, however, quickly reversed when the Soviet Union launched Sputnik, the first space satellite, in 1957.

In times of plenty the Air Secretaries could focus on other than budgetary issues. Harold E. Talbott, who served from 1953 to 1955, concentrated on reenlistment, and Eugene M. Zuckert, who served from 1961 to 1965, promoted weapon systems development and prepared the Air Force to counter a very strong-minded Secretary of Defense, Robert S. McNamara.

The Secretaries of the Air Force, obliged to preserve what they believed to be adequate forces, had often to weigh their loyalty to the administrations that appointed them against the needs of their military departments. At times they disagreed with presidential policies and actively sought congressional support for Air Force positions. Some secretaries were able to help fulfill Air Force requirements by influencing Congress, by smoothly cultivating, even manipulating, the press, and by fostering the interest of private enterprise in air defense objectives. Stuart Symington employed a particularly dynamic and engaging personality in dealing with Congress and military professionals. Robert Lovett remained close to his friends and colleagues from the industries he viewed as vital to the nation's air defenses during World War II.

In addition to giving the Air Force its independence and its own secretary, the National Security Act of 1947 instituted the National Military Establishment, headed by a Secretary of Defense who coordinated three equal military departments—the Army, the Navy, and the Air Force. The act also established three non-military agencies to coordinate national security efforts:

The National Security Council. The council advised the President on the risks and benefits to the country associated with the uses of military power and considered policies of interest to various departments of the U.S. government concerned with national security.[3] The council was headed by the President of the United States and included the Secretaries of State, Defense, Army, Navy, and Air Force, as well as the Chairman of the National Security Resources Board.

The Central Intelligence Agency. The agency was empowered to collect and coordinate all intelligence gathered by other agencies of the Federal government, to analyze it, and to make it available to the President and the National Security Council.

The National Security Resources Board. The board advised the President on strategies to coordinate military, industrial, and civilian mobilization for the best use of the nations's manpower, raw materials, and manufacturing facilities.[4] Its membership was comprised of a chairman and heads of departments and agencies designated by the President.

Under the National Security Act, the Secretary of Defense became the principal assistant to the President in all matters relating to national security. He had, however, only "general direction, authority, and control over the military departments" and was not allowed to maintain a military staff or appoint more than three special assistants from civilian life. He was allowed a war council, made up of the service secretaries and the service chiefs of staff. His most significant authority extended to the supervision, coordination, and preparation of budget estimates on the requirements of the National Military Establishment. However, the military departments could prepare their own budget estimates and present them to the Joint Chiefs of Staff for review. The act permitted the service secretaries to present their views to the President and Congress but required them to inform the Secretary of Defense before doing so.[5]

After the National Security Act took effect, the Secretary of Defense confronted service secretaries who had grown accustomed to operating independently, vying for their particular service interests. It became clear that the Chiefs of Staff were unable to prevent controversies or even to clarify roles and missions as long as they could not overcome excessive allegiance to their own services. The designers of the National Security Act realized that it would require improvements but concluded that despite many shortcomings, it was better than no act at all.

Soon after taking office, James V. Forrestal, the first Secretary of Defense, concluded that he needed a much larger and more independent staff as well as real control over the military departments. His views were shared by the Hoover Commission (led by former President Herbert Hoover), the first commission assigned to review the organization of the executive branch. A number of changes sought by Forrestal and the commission were incorporated into the National Security Act Amendments of 1949. These amendments changed the name of the National Military Establishment to the Department of Defense. The service secretaries lost their executive branch status and their seats on the

National Security Council. They also lost their right of direct appeal to the President and to the Director of the Bureau of the Budget. The Secretary of Defense would speak for all three services on the National Security Council. The Office of the Secretary of Defense was strengthened by the addition of a deputy and three assistant secretaries. The Secretary of Defense also gained more control over the military budget with a departmental comptroller. The service secretaries preserved the right to present their views before Congress relating to military matters after first notifying the Secretary of Defense.[6]

The 1949 amendments did not settle roles and missions which were furiously debated during Secretary of Defense Johnson's tenure (1949–1950) over such issues as strategic bombing, the tactical function, support of ground operations, and the Navy's proposed supercarrier. As President-elect in 1953, Dwight D. Eisenhower called for certain changes within the Department of Defense—clearer lines of authority, better service cooperation, and greater civilian control. Arguing that no function should be performed independent of the "direction, authority and control of the Secretary of Defense," he commissioned a study headed by Nelson A. Rockefeller to assess the department's organization.[8]

The Rockefeller Committee's recommendations formed the basis for Reorganization Plan No. 6 of 1953, which firmly established the doctrine of civilian control with a line of authority from the President as Commander in Chief to the Secretary of Defense. The latter would act through his service secretaries who became his "operating managers" as well as his principal advisors. Plan No. 6 reduced service autonomy even further by eliminating some of its boards and agencies and by tripling the number of Assistant Secretaries of Defense, bringing the total to ten, including the General Counsel.[9]

The Secretary of Defense came to rely on the assistant secretaries to the detriment of the service secretaries. Although the Assistant Secretaries of Defense were not in the direct line of authority, their proximity to the Secretary of Defense—and the chain of command—placed them strategically. The Secretary of Defense began taking their advice, which often contradicted the services'.[10]

Organizational changes within the Department of Defense affected communications between the Office of the Secretary of the Air Force and the Air Staff. In effect, the new Assistant Secretaries of Defense represented a layer of authority between the Defense Secretary and the service secretaries. In late 1947 and 1948 Secretary Symington and his staff routinely coordinated matters with the Air Staff before raising them with the Office of the Secretary of Defense. By 1953 much of the Air Staff was dealing directly with Assistant Secretaries of Defense without first consulting with the Office of the Secretary of the Air Force. Then too, the Office of the Secretary of the Air Force occasionally failed to inform the Air Staff of its dealings with the Office of the Secretary of Defense. Direct and personal communications between the Office of the Secretary of the Air Force and the Air Staff began to diminish and were replaced by a new triangular relationship between those offices and the Office of the Secretary of Defense.

Between 1953 and 1958 there were many proposals for further centralization of authority within the Department of Defense. They were furthered by rapid technological developments that challenged existing defense concepts and aggravated the services' struggle for funding and responsibilities. Critics charged that the organization of military affairs under three departments headed by a fourth was expensive and cumbersome. Shortly after Eisenhower assumed the presidency he ordered another commission led by former President Hoover to study the entire executive branch. The study was published in June 1955. It found that the National Security Council was not providing a "clear and integrated national policy."[11]

In late 1957 and early 1958 the rising cost of weapon systems and public shock over Soviet scientific advances, particularly Sputnik, sparked intense criticism of the Department of Defense. In addition, a national defense study published in January 1958 called for further reorganization within the department because of continuing duplication of effort and interservice rivalry. President Eisenhower concurred with the panel. Appearing before Congress on April 3, 1958, he pointed to thermo-nuclear weapons, missiles, and aircraft capable of tremendous speed and range as the results of a "revolution . . . in the techniques of war . . . We cannot," he emphasized, "allow different service viewpoints to determine the character of our defenses—either as to operational planning and control, or as to the development, production, and use of newer weapons . . . The country's security requirements should not be subordinated to outmoded or single service concepts of war."[11]

Thus, backed by the public and the President, Congress passed the Department of Defense Reorganization Act of 1958 on August 6. The act placed the unified and specified commands* directly under the control of the Secretary of Defense and the President. It removed the service secretaries from the operational (combat) chain of command and placed them over operational support activities such as training and logistics. It retained the service secretaries' right to present their recommendations before Congress on the approval of the Secretary of Defense. With this allowance Congress, always desirous of access to information, was favoring itself, not the service secretaries.[12] To quell inter-

---

* According to Air Force Manual 1–1, Basic Aerospace Doctrine of the United States Air Force, "Specified commands have a broad continuing mission and are normally composed of forces from one Service. In unified commands . . . forces from two or more Services are commanded by a single commander with operational command and control of assigned forces normally exercised through subordinate component commanders . . . This relationship demands that the Services develop mutual confidence, common understanding of primary and supporting missions, and a common doctrine for unified action."

service disputes, the act granted the Secretary of Defense the authority to decide which services would assume leadership roles in the development of weapon systems. It further stipulated that the military departments would no longer be separately administered; each would be organized under its individual secretary who answered to the Secretary of Defense.[13]

The increased power of the Office of the Secretary of Defense was gained at the expense of the service secretaries to whom any of the assistant secretaries of defense could now issue orders. The service secretaries and their offices were expected to cooperate fully with the Office of the Secretary of Defense. In addition, all research and engineering activities were to be placed under the new Director of Defense Research and Engineering who answered to the Secretary of Defense.

The Department of Defense Reorganization Act of 1958 left no doubt that the Secretary of Defense was in charge. Robert S. McNamara, appointed by President John F. Kennedy, took full advantage of the powers it granted. He instituted a program of centralized control without having to initiate further legislative changes to the National Security Act. When he became Secretary of the Air Force in January 1961, Eugene M. Zuckert, who had worked for eight years in the Office of the Secretary of the Air Force and its predecessor, was shocked by the decline in the authority of his office.

The Secretaries of the Air Force had to adjust, each in his own fashion, to many challenges and major legislative changes between 1947 and 1965. This book discusses how they did so.

Acknowledgments

This book reflects the generous assistance of many people. I am most grateful to Herman S. Wolk, Senior Historian of the Center for Air Force History, who read, reread, insightfully reviewed, and monitored the book to its completion.

Fellow historians in the Histories Branch of the Center for Air Force History—Marcelle S. Knaack, Dr. Rebecca H. Welch, Dr. Robert P. Smith, Dr. Daniel R. Mortensen, and Dr. Walton S. Moody—were panelists in the final manuscript evaluation and thoughtfully commented on each chapter. To them I express my warmest thanks. Dan Mortensen, running and weight-lifting partner, encouraged me to push on, and Walt Moody consistently suggested improvements. To them I owe my deepest appreciation. Also from the Histories Branch of the Center for Air Force History, Bernard C. Nalty offered editorial advice that shaped the book's early chapters, and Lt. Col. Vance O. Mitchell, USAF (Ret.), supplied welcome companionship as we shared research problems during numerous treks to the Federal Records Center in Suitland, Maryland.

For also serving on the final manuscript review panel I am indebted to Dr. Benjamin F. Cooling, former Chief of the Special Histories Branch of the Office of Air Force History; Jacob Neufeld, Director of the Center for Air Force History; Dr. Alfred M. Beck, Chief of the Histories Division of the Center for Air Force History; Col. John F. Shiner, former Deputy Chief of the Office of Air Force History; Dr. Richard H. Kohn, former Chief of the Office of Air Force History; Prof. John Morrow of the University of Georgia; Prof. Ira Gruber of Rice University; and General Ross T. Milton, USAF (Ret.). Dr. Kohn made particularly helpful recommendations concerning theme and consistency.

William C. Heimdahl, Chief of the Historical Support Division of the Center for Air Force History, and former branch assistants SMSgt. Al Hargatt and MSgt. Roger Jernigan cheerfully devoted many hours to helping me locate information.

Most of my sources were located at the Manuscript Division of the Library of Congress, the National Archives, and the Federal Records Center at Suitland, Maryland. There are many people who helped me obtain thousands of documents. Dr. Gibson Smith of the National Archives' Military Reference Branch (formerly the Modern Military Branch) was essential to my successful search through the files on the Office of the Secretary of the Air Force (Record Group 340). Both of us spent hours carting Hollinger boxes from the stacks for review. Also of great assistance were archivists Wil Mahoney, Edward Reese, Robin Cookson, and LeRoy Jackson, as well as technicians Terri Hammett and Angie

Fernandez who copied so much of the material that I needed.

I wish to thank Gary J. Kohn, formerly an archivist at the Manuscript Division of the Library of Congress, and William Gaston, Records Manager for the Office of the Secretary of the Air Force, both of whom kindly allowed me access to their files. Grace Rowe at the Pentagon cleared the way for me as I sought classified materials on the Office of the Secretary of the Air Force at Suitland. Ms. Rowe and Mr. Gaston also granted me permission to transfer secret materials from the Federal Record Center to my own office. At Suitland I received substantial help from David Foster, Myra Freeman, and other staff members who found hundreds of archives boxes for me to peruse in the classified reading room.

Charles Warren Ohrvall, an archivist at the Harry S. Truman Library in Independence, Missouri, gave generously of his time with the Symington Papers and expressed repeated concern for my welfare.

Senator W. Stuart Symington, first Secretary of the Air Force, kindly submitted to several interviews and showed a keen interest in the book. One of our meetings, which I will always remember, took place at his family's summer home in Camden, Maine. He extended true hospitality, combining extraordinary charm and a commanding presence. Mr. Stephen F. Leo was also present and revealed a profound reverence for his former chief, having served as his adviser and Director of Public Relations in the Office of the Secretary of the Air Force. Mr. Leo was generous with his time and maintained contact with me until his death. Senator Symington's administrative assistant, Toby Godfrey, was unfailingly courteous and efficient.

Mr. Eugene M. Zuckert, seventh Secretary of the Air Force, freely granted three interviews, two of which covered his experiences as Assistant Secretary of the Air Force under Secretaries Symington and Thomas K. Finletter. Mr. Zuckert was kept from acting as a final manuscript review panelist because of illness; however, he gave me fascinating and perceptive written comments which provided unique insights into personalities and events that no other documentation could convey.

General William F. McKee, USAF (Ret.), Assistant Vice Chief of Staff under General Hoyt S. Vandenberg and Vice Chief of Staff under General Curtis E. LeMay, who knew first-hand the workings between the Office of the Secretary of the Air Force and the Air Staff, furnished essential information on Air Force Secretary Harold A. Talbot's tenure. Former Under Secretary of the Air Force Malcolm A. McIntyre provided valuable information about James H. Douglas's service as Secretary of the Air Force. Brig. Gen. William G. Hipps, USAF (Ret.), former executive officer to Secretary Thomas K. Finletter, interrupted a trip to be interviewed at Bolling Air Force Base. He also took the time to answer in writing the many questions I sent him.

Brig. Gen. Brian S. Gunderson, USAF (Ret.), former executive officer to Secretary Zuckert, contributed some humerous anecdotes about Zuckert's staff relations that helped to humanize the manuscript. Brig. Gen. Turner A. Sims, USAF (Ret.), supplied very helpful observations about his term as Symington's executive, as did Lt. Gen. Glen W. Martin, USAF (Ret.), who wrote of his experiences in the same capacity for Symington, Finletter, and Zuckert.

I am indebted to David R. Chenoweth, Airman Terry R. Nance, and Sgt. James R. Branham of the Center for Air Force History for helping me with the difficult task of transferring my manuscript from one computer system to another. Kim East transcribed my interviews in timely fashion and the Office of the Air Force Surgeon General allowed me to use its time-saving, state-of-the-art copier.

I am also indebted to members of the Headquarters Air Force Graphics staff, particularly Evelyn Buhl and Kathy Jones, who lent their lent their talents to produce the book's cover and organizational charts.

Finally, I thank the editor of this work, Mary Lee Jefferson, who streamlined the text into its final form, gathered photographs, designed the volume, and shepherded it through the final stages of publication. Her professionalism and enthusiasm made the editorial process a pleasure.

I dedicate this book to my wife, Nancy, who patiently listened to my many progress reports, and to our children, Leah, Tyler, and Devon.

Contents

Tables and Charts

Photographs

The Office of the
Secretary of the Air Force
1947–1965

Chapter 1

Precedent for an Air Secretary

Although not well known to the public, Robert A. Lovett, Assistant Secretary of War for Air during World War II and confidant of General Henry H. Arnold, Commander of the U.S. Army Air Forces (AAF), was one of the most influential officials in the War Department. Lovett's influence rested not on statutory authority, but on his close and friendly relationship with General Arnold and on his ability to combine toughness and informality when dealing with leading government officials.

Lovett was involved in solving many war-related problems with General Arnold, but his formidable abilities and expertise were concentrated on aircraft procurement. He kept factories functioning seven days a week, helped negotiate the settlement of strikes, and saw to it that the necessary technical labor force remained exempt from military service. Lovett strongly supported the "Europe First" concept of Allied strategy. He recommended the placement of various forces early in the war and later proposed the creation of a force—apart from the established, numbered air units—to strike at Germany's communications network and dispersed industry.

Robert Lovett made a direct and lasting impact on the Office of the Secretary of the Air Force (OSAF), influencing its establishment, its authority, and the nature and scope of its responsibilities. The activities that occupied him during World War II can be traced to the late 1920s when F. Trubee Davison became the first Assistant Secretary of War for Air.

The Roots of the Office

Army airmen had long worked to establish an air arm separate from the ground forces. In 1925 they made their views known when the Secretaries of War and the Navy convinced President Calvin Coolidge of the necessity for a study on air power and national defense.* He appointed the Morrow Board, headed by Morgan Bank partner Dwight W. Morrow, to conduct it. The board

---

* The Army Air Service had been recognized as a separate combat arm since June 1920.

produced a report that persuaded Congress to undertake an extensive review of America's air defense. Resultant legislation—the Army Air Corps Act of 1926—established the Army Air Corps, granting it more personnel, aircraft and, in effect, more prestige than its predecessor, the Air Service. The act also called for the inclusion of Air Corps representatives on the Army General Staff and reestablished a second Assistant Secretary of War—the Assistant Secretary of War for Air.

The office had existed briefly during World War I. Two coequal agencies had managed aviation—the Division of Military Aeronautics (DMA) under a military head who assumed responsibility for personnel, training, and requirements; and the Bureau of Aircraft Production (BAP) under a civilian head who dealt with production problems. President Woodrow Wilson wished to avoid potential clashes between these agencies. Thus, in April 1918, Secretary of War Newton D. Baker reorganized his office, and Congress authorized two additional Assistant Secretaries of War—the Second and the Third Assistant Secretaries of War. In August 1918, John D. Ryan became the Second Assistant Secretary of War and Director of the Air Service. Ryan had been president of the Anaconda Copper Company and also chairman of the Civilian Aircraft Board. President Wilson had appointed him director of Aircraft Production in April 1918. Ryan held the position for only three months until the war ended. After his resignation, the office was disestablished.[1]

Between 1920 and 1926, attempts to legislate needed changes in the nation's air defense were blocked by jurisdictional conflict between the Air Service on one hand and the War Department and the Navy on the other. The Air Service was dominated by a small group of men bound together by their passion for and practical knowledge of military aviation. They firmly believed that the Air Corps should support the advancement of aeronautical science. However, they doubted that it could while subject to the direction of those whose views on aviation differed from their own. Lined up against the Air Service were powerful administrators of both the War and Navy Departments who perceived in the airmen a threat to their own authority.[2]

The Army Air Corps Act did not grant the air arm either full independence or autonomy within the War Department; even the new Assistant Secretary of War for Air, who was appointed by the President, had to answer to the Secretary of War. The act stipulated that the Assistant Secretary of War for Air aid the Secretary of War in fostering military aeronautics and, in the name of the Secretary of War, promote the efficiency of the Army Air Corps. The act further specified that the new assistant secretary deal with all Air Corps reports related to procurement—from domestic manufacturers, other services, and foreign sources—and to the budget and refer them to the Secretary of War.[3]

The first Assistant Secretary of War for Air was F. Trubee Davison, a graduate of Yale University and Columbia University Law School, who became a member of the New York bar in 1922 and later spent several terms in the New

York state legislature. He had served overseas during World War I and had been instrumental in organizing the "First Yale Unit," which formed the nucleus of the first Naval Reserve Flying Corps.* Among the many activities in which Davison involved himself as Assistant Secretary of War for Air were fund raising for Air Service programs and procurement. Procurement was important to Davison and would become the natural focus for Robert A. Lovett during World War II.

In the autumn of 1932 Davison resigned his office to run for lieutenant governor of New York. President Herbert Hoover did not name his replacement. The next President, Franklin D. Roosevelt, also kept the position vacant, ostensibly because Secretary of War George H. Dern believed that the air forces, like all other branches of the Army, should report directly to the Chief of Staff (the Air Corps did not report directly to Davison).

Roosevelt was not encouraged to fill the post by the Army because its General Staff in particular had never really believed that the Air Corps warranted a special representative to the Secretary of War. Davison himself was convinced that the position remained unfilled because of "the jealousy of the older services."[4] During the 1930s the Air Service, without an Assistant Secretary of War for Air, had great difficulty obtaining the funding it desired. There were no civilians within the War Department to argue for its programs before Congress.

F. Trubee Davison, first Assistant Secretary of War for Air.

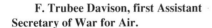

* During the summer of 1917, Davison broke his back in an airplane crash and was prevented from taking an active part with his unit during World War I.

In addition, the Depression, which reached its depth in 1933, had brought cuts in most military spending programs.

The Office of the Assistant Secretary of War for Air remained vacant until April 1941, when the special assistant to the Secretary of War, Robert A. Lovett, was appointed to it. Prior to his redesignation, Lovett had served, since December 27, 1940, as a representative of the Under Secretary of War on Air Corps procurement.[5]

Robert Lovett was no stranger to the first Assistant Secretary of War for Air. He had learned to fly during the summer of 1916 while staying at the Davison home in New York.* Like Davison, Lovett had served in the Naval Air Service during World War I and, having retained a keen interest in aviation throughout the interwar years, brought to his job a high degree of knowledge and experience. After the war, from 1919 to 1921, he studied both law and business administration at Harvard University. In 1921 he joined the National Bank of Commerce in New York. Five years later he assumed a partnership in the investment firm of Brown Brothers Harriman and Company. He resigned that partnership in December 1940 to become special assistant to the Secretary of War.[6]

During the 1920s and 1930s, Lovett was obliged to travel frequently throughout the United States and abroad on business and had taken every opportunity to study advances in aeronautical science and military aviation being applied wherever he was sent. He was especially interested in developments overseas. On a trip to Milan, Italy, during the spring of 1940, in casual conversation with two German airmen at his hotel, he learned something of the scope and intensity of their country's air rearmament effort. What he heard disturbed him greatly and caused him to wonder about America's military preparedness. He was determined to personally assess the state of American aircraft manufacturing when he returned to the United States and was able to do so—tour factories and renew friendships with important industrialists—while performing his responsibilities for Brown Brothers Harriman.

He discovered an alarming lack of direction and coordination from Washington regarding aircraft production and concluded that American industry, on the whole, was not up to the demands that full-scale warfare might entail. Many aircraft executives urged Lovett to make industry problems known to the Roosevelt administration. He confided his concerns to fellow Wall Street operative and new Under Secretary of the Navy James V. Forrestal. Forrestal suggested that Lovett present a report on his ideas to Assistant Secretary of War Robert

---

* In 1916 Mrs. Henry P. Davison, wife of the partner in J. P. Morgan and Company and mother of F. Trubee Davison, turned her New York summer home at Locust Valley on Long Island into a camp for her son and his friends from Yale so they could attend a nearby flying school.

P. Patterson,* who was responsible for the Army's total procurement requirements.[7]

No problem had proved more formidable in 1940 for Secretary of War Henry L. Stimson, Army Chief of Staff General George C. Marshall, and Assistant Secretary of War Patterson than aircraft procurement. Patterson saw its solution in Lovett's report and the wealth of information it contained. Highly impressed, the Secretary of War decided to hire Lovett immediately as a special assistant for air matters.[8]

In December 1940, Congress created a new position, the Under Secretary of War, which absorbed all procurement functions formerly assigned to the Assistant Secretary of War. The incumbent assistant secretary, Robert Patterson, became the first under secretary. In April 1941, the President appointed Robert Lovett to fill the reestablished post of Assistant Secretary of War for Air.[9]

As Assistant Secretary of War for Air, Lovett joined a hand-picked four-man civilian team, part of the so-called "eastern establishment." Its members were investment bankers who gravitated to government during World War II. Stimson would describe them as the best staff he ever assembled. The others were Patterson, Assistant Secretary of War John J. McCloy, and Harvey H. Bundy, a special assistant to the Secretary of War. All four made a considerable financial sacrifice to enter government service. None had political ambitions. All were attached to Stimson's office, but their talents enabled them to exert influence throughout the War Department.[10]

Although not actually granted statutory power to direct procurement, Lovett was encouraged by Secretary Stimson to devote his energy to the promotion of aircraft production. While advising Stimson, Lovett worked closely with military leaders and was free to offer opinions on a variety of questions outside the formal chain of command.

From April 1940 until the end of World War II, Lovett was vitally concerned that nothing threaten industry's adherence to realistic aircraft production schedules. He attempted to settle labor disputes and at times intervened when the Office of Production Management (OPM) and, subsequently, the War Production Board were at odds with AAF contractors, subcontractors and suppliers. He openly objected to President Roosevelt's production goals in 1942 and 1943 as excessively optimistic and tried to help strengthen the management of inefficient aircraft manufacturing companies. During the war, Lovett acted as a sounding board for industry's complaints and requests. Stimson had a clearer

---

* Patterson graduated from Harvard Law School in 1915. In 1930 he was appointed a judge of the U.S. District Court for Southern New York. In 1939 he was appointed a judge of the U.S. Circuit Court of Appeals. He resigned to become Assistant Secretary of War in July 1940. Six months later, he became Under Secretary of War, a post he held throughout World War II. In September 1945, he became Secretary of War.

Organization of the Army (The Marshall Reorganization)
March 1942

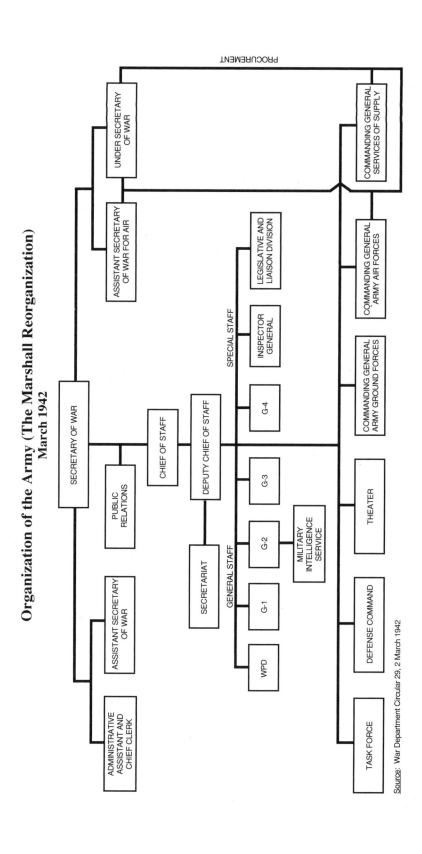

Source: War Department Circular 29, 2 March 1942

Under Secretary of War Robert P. Patterson (*left*) **and General George C. Marshall, Chief of Staff, U.S. Army.**

conception of Lovett's role and told him, "Whatever authority the Secretary of War has, you have."[11]

However, even four years after Lovett assumed office, his duties remained undefined. According to Brig. Gen. George A. Brownell, his executive officer, at one time or another the specific activities of the Assistant Secretary of War for Air touched upon every phase of AAF activity and obliged him to deal with problems of "technical development, production, organization, finance, legislation, public relations, both foreign and domestic civil aviation, and to coordinate these and like matters with other governmental agencies concerned."[12]

Lovett issued orders to no one. It was from his authority over procurement granted by Stimson that his influence flowed; his closeness to Stimson gave him a great deal of leverage. He created a direct and personal line of communication between the Secretary of War and the air arm. General Arnold credited Lovett with reducing the number of decisionmakers involved in air production from nine to two—Patterson and Lovett himself.[13]

Lovett's ability to work harmoniously with key members of the air arm and the War Department was one of his most important attributes. Stimson's biographer, Elting Morison, described Lovett as "full of brief sophisticated witticisms, rueful humor and a perception of incongruity that expanded in bureaucratic circumstances where such perceptions ordinarily wither away."[14] During the war, he corresponded warmly with such prominent AAF commanders as General Carl A. Spaatz, General George C. Kenney, and Lt. Gen. Ira C. Eaker. His intimate friendship with General Arnold enabled him to communicate smoothly with Army Chief of Staff General George C. Marshall, who prized the judgment, calm appraisal, and intellectual balance that Lovett brought to policy meetings.[15]

Because their offices adjoined, Arnold and Lovett saw each other daily, working easily and informally together. Thus many of their discussions were not recorded. A year after Lovett's appointment, Arnold revealed that his early anxieties about the new Assistant Secretary of War for Air had been quickly dispelled. He had hoped that the Air Corps would have a friend at court. Lovett as that friend exceeded the general's highest hopes. Arnold and his staff considered Lovett not only a sympathetic listener who shared their problems but also a "fellow airman whose extensive knowledge of aviation, its characteristics and capabilities, equaled and often surpassed their own."[16] In fact, Arnold thought so highly of the Air Secretary that he considered securing him a wartime commission in the AAF should he decide to resign his post. Lovett, according to General Arnold, "was better acquainted with the various phases of War Department and AAF programs as they affect one another than any other individual."[17]

The organization of Lovett's office was as undefined as his duties and, although no charts have survived that describe its structure, he always operated with a very small staff.*[18] Col. George A. Brownell served as Lovett's legal adviser from March 2, 1942, to August 1, 1943, whereupon he became his executive officer. Brownell was Lovett's most valued aide who had dealt with organizational and legislative questions confronting the AAF early in the war. As executive officer he administered the Office of the Assistant Secretary of War for Air (OASWA). Brownell also represented Lovett or other members of Stimson's team on many highly important projects.[19]

Many questions that confronted Lovett shortly after he assumed office concerned the independence of the air arm, whose status had been debated periodically since before World War I. He favored its independence, but not in June 1941. Believing, with others, that America's entry into the war in Europe was inevitable, he viewed any attempt at major realignment as confusing and possibly dangerous at a time when the Air Corps was expanding at an unprecedented rate. He argued that an independent air force could not operate without a "Unified General Staff and a Supreme War Plans Council" to coordinate army, navy and air efforts. Also, many Air Corps functions were handled by other branches—ordnance, for example, by the quartermaster. After advising against the immediate creation of an independent air force, he suggested that the reorganization of the Air Corps into the Army Air Forces, then being studied in the

---

* Elting E. Morison, in his biography of Stimson, sustains the view that the Office of the Assistant Secretary of War for Air was closely connected with the Office of the Secretary of War. Morison maintains that Stimson could easily ring his secretaries and assistants and expect their immediate presence. Stimson and Lovett apparently formed a tightly knit organization. This was also the view of Col. Thetus C. Odom, who succeeded George A. Brownell as executive officer in January 1946. Odom maintained that Lovett's staff was very small and predicted that the next Assistant Secretary of War for Air would want to expand it.

Two new Assistant Secretaries of War are sworn in by Secretary of War Henry L. Stimson (*left*). Robert A. Lovett (*right*) has just become Assistant Secretary of War for Air. Assistant Secretary of War John H. McCloy looks on, April 23, 1941.

War Department,* would be a more workable method of "developing air power in this stage of the existing emergency."[20]

The War Department endorsed Lovett's views. In September 1941, Under Secretary of War Patterson declared that such reorganization would permit unrestricted development of the air arm under full control of qualified air officers as well as unity of command within the Army. General Marshall agreed with Patterson. Although the War Department favored delaying action on the subject of an independent air force until after the end of the war, Marshall, in early 1943, initiated sustained postwar planning.[21]

Lovett, like Marshall, realized that such planning was not premature but was vitally important, and he suggested that it incorporate the ideas of America's key businessmen and economists. He suspected that the independence of the air arm would not be actively discussed again for some time. Nonetheless, he began to prepare for any questions that could arise on the subject from Congress.[22] He did not favor entrusting national defense to two independent departments—War and Navy—which were "not designed to translate the tremendous effort of the nation into maximum effectiveness and efficiency in waging modern war." He believed that a single department of armed forces embracing the Army, the Navy,

---

* On June 20, 1941, the War Department created the Army Air Forces, which gave the air arm a degree of autonomy and provided unity of command over the Air Corps and the Air Force Combat Command, the former General Headquarters Air Force (GHQ Air Force).

and the Air Force provided the best means of ensuring progress in aviation, unity in planning and operations, and the most economical use of human, material, and monetary resources.[23]

The Air Arm Expands

When Robert Lovett took office, Adolf Hitler's forces had overrun Holland, Belgium, and France in six weeks, and Western Europe was under Axis control. During the summer of 1940 England endured a pounding by the Luftwaffe, but the heroic performance of the Royal Air Force (RAF) had warded off the immediate threat of a cross-channel invasion. Although professing neutrality, the United States consistently found ways to support Britain and seemed resigned to eventually joining the battle to free Europe from Nazi domination.

Years later, Lovett would reveal that at the heart of his role in wartime procurement and production was the exercise of judgment—determining which requests were reasonable and politically acceptable, which could be filled despite shortages of equipment and machinery, and which were desirable in his view, despite conflicting military recommendations.[24] When the Lend-Lease Act under which the United States provided arms to nations fighting German aggression was passed in the spring of 1941, competition among American aircraft producers intensified. Lovett's task was to improve the delivery of aircraft overseas. The United States retained control over the distribution of arms, but the plight of Britain was desperate enough that the requirements of the RAF appeared to outweigh those of the AAF. When the AAF resisted surrendering aircraft, President Roosevelt sided with the embattled ally, as he had early in 1940, and cautioned General Arnold, Chief of the Army Air Corps, that "there were places to which officers who did not play ball might be sent, such as Guam."[25]

Lovett immediately sought to determine the effects of growing British demands on U.S. aircraft production. The Lend-Lease endeavor, he felt, lacked a "definition of goal" to guide domestic manufacturers as they tried to adjust to requirements which were never satisfactorily projected. Lovett predicted that the United States would require 5,000 airplanes per month and urged the construction of new facilities for their production. He further maintained that the war would not be won solely with defensive weapons. Bombers were essential to victory, and plants being devoted to heavy bombers should be used "solely for quantity production" of standard types. The engineering and research staffs of established companies, he believed, should be separated from production facilities to concentrate on experimental models.[26]

General Arnold agreed with Lovett. In January 1941, he emphasized that President Roosevelt's announced manufacturing goal of 36,000 planes per year should be met and, if possible, exceeded to total 50,000. However, he did not share Lovett's opinion that engineering and research staffs should be completely removed from production areas. He felt that rivalry within the aircraft industry was healthy, pointing to the race between the Boeing and Consolidated aircraft companies to complete new bombers with projected speeds of 380 to 390 miles per hour and a 5,300-mile range.[27]

On January 22, 1941, Under Secretary Patterson approved Assistant Secretary Lovett's request to review a host of procurement-related issues: production capacity, training, the heavy bomber program, aid for Britain, labor needs in the aircraft industry, aircraft engines, and research and experimentation. He further recommended that Lovett consult with General Arnold.[28] Lovett discovered that engines and airframes from new factories would require at least twelve to eighteen months' construction and preparation time before they could be released to the Army. To compensate for the delay, he insisted on expanded facilities and increased production rates for 1942. He also recommended that the proper authority, the OPM, issue clear directives specifying monthly production goals. Eventually, directives were issued and production rose. Presenting his case to Harry L. Hopkins, President Roosevelt's trusted aide and Lend-Lease specialist, Lovett stressed that while air power alone could not win the war, the war would not be won without it.[29]

In March 1941, Lovett warned General Marshall that one of the most serious obstacles to the Air Corp's production goal of 5,000 advanced aircraft per month was industry's reluctance to gear up despite its anticipation of government contracts. Industry insisted that only on the basis of fully executed, not merely pending, contracts could its labor force be assured of steady employment

Robert A. Lovett, Assistant Secretary of War for Air from 1941 to 1945.

and prevented from being laid off and dispersed to other plants eager for its special training and skills. Lovett therefore recommended that where the necessary labor force was in place maximum production capacity be maintained; to expedite the manufacture of tactical aircraft, he recommended that all new orders be attached to existing contracts.[30] By the autumn of 1941 Lovett no longer tolerated business as usual with its forty-hour work week. He wanted plants to operate around the clock, if necessary, and he received permission from Under Secretary Patterson to sanction overtime payments. He also succeeded in establishing a twenty-four-hour, seven-day work week for all principal machine tool producers.

Although these producers were indispensable to America's rearmament, Lovett urged that OPM, under William S. Knudsen,* be strengthened with new executives who were "hard boiled enough to deal with the rugged individuals in industry."[31] The machine tool industry was reluctant to start production without signed orders. Lovett argued that the shortages of both machine tools and new plants were proof enough of a market for their products. He even asserted in a letter to Clayton Burt, president of the National Machine Tool Builder's Association, that the industry's insistence on signed orders was "unpatriotic" and added that he assumed its members would, in time of emergency, make every effort to produce those elements essential to the national defense.[32]

Lovett knew instinctively just how far industry could be pushed. Thus when Donald Nelson, soon-to-be head of the War Production Board, recommended to President Roosevelt in late 1941 that 1942 aircraft production rates be raised from 36,000 to 50,000, Lovett warned Harry Hopkins that such an increase was far too ambitious. Roosevelt, perhaps influenced at the ARCADIA Conference,† acceded to Winston Churchill's wishes for more aircraft and on January 3, 1942, conveyed his decision to Stimson, calling for a goal of 60,000 aircraft for 1942. Lovett wrote of his disappointment with typical good humor to Harry Hopkins: "When you advised me not to fall out of my chair when I saw the target figures for plane production it was a friendly act, for I might have broken my neck instead of something minor like my heart." He warned that the President's unrealistic goal resembled "the trap of the old numbers racket," tempting them to "build the easy types and forget about spares."[33]

---

* Knudsen, who had emigrated from Denmark to the United States, worked in various capacities for the shipbuilding and railroad industries until settling on the automobile business. After working for Ford and Chevrolet, he joined General Motors and became its president in 1937. President Roosevelt asked him to serve as General Director of the Office of Production Management in 1940.

† The ARCADIA Conference between President Roosevelt and Prime Minister Churchill was held in Washington, D.C., from December 24, 1941, to January 14, 1942. It was the occasion of the first wartime meeting of U.S. and British Chiefs of Staff.

British Prime Minister Winston S. Churchill and President Franklin D. Roosevelt at a White House press briefing on the eve of the ARCADIA Conference in Washington, D.C., December 23, 1941.

Britain's pleas for additional aircraft constituted a daunting obstacle to Lovett in his efforts to expand the U.S. Army air arm and keep it adequately supplied. The Director General of the British Air Commission, A. H. Self, had asked Secretary Stimson in May 1941 for as many aircraft as the United States could supply, particularly heavy bombers. He also wanted more B-26s to substitute, if necessary, for B-25s.[34] Self used tables to show that monthly aircraft deliveries to the Air Corps would rise steadily until its needs were met, while deliveries to the United Kingdom would be comparatively few, showing little change until March 1942, when they would rise sharply with a sudden influx of new releases.

In May 1941, Lovett reminded Arnold, after evaluating Self's request, that the Army had already deferred the delivery of thirty-five B-24s and had transferred twenty B-17s from its own tactical units to Britain, and that the United States had pledged more than 50 percent of all B-24s to be built between May and December 1941. He concurred with the War Plans Division of the Army General Staff that any more transfers to Britain would undermine his all-important goal of building up the Air Corps to fifty-four groups. Lovett cautioned Arnold that until that goal was reached, the United States would never have an Air Corps, "except on paper."[35] He also noted that many new planes, once released by the Army, were not being put directly to use. Of twenty B-17s relinquished in January 1941, sixteen remained in the United States, despite Britian's urgent need and the struggle by both industry and the Air Corps to accommodate it. Lovett, therefore, questioned the desirability of further delays on the heavy-bomber program and Britain's ability to deploy rapidly and effectively enough those aircraft already given them.* [36]

Despite his anxiety about the draining of U.S. aircraft inventories, Lovett's dealings with the British were essentially congenial. The Air Secretary communicated with them on a number of subjects and highly valued the combat information they provided through American observers in London.† In the autumn of 1941 he wrote to Air Marshal Arthur T. Harris, a member of the RAF delegation in Washington, D.C. (soon to take over RAF Bomber Command in February 1942), inviting British air crews to the United States so that they could acquaint their American counterparts with the realities of the war in Europe. Lovett also requested samples of training equipment, such as flight simulators, to duplicate them for the Air Corps. The Air Secretary had always tried to establish a cordial quid-pro-quo relationship with the British, maintaining that the supplies, equipment, and technical knowhow they provided were "worth more than the ninety-nine-year leases on western hemisphere bases that America had received for fifty old destroyers." [37]

Releasing airplanes to Britain was one problem; getting them there was another. Lend-Lease could work only if transatlantic ferry routes from New England through Newfoundland, Iceland, and Greenland were protected against possible attack by the Luftwaffe and German U-boats. In March 1941, Lovett recommended that a civilian organization be created to recruit and train pilots and to establish the bases necessary through which to deliver multi-engine aircraft to the United Kingdom. Lovett proposed that a man of Eddie Rickenbacker's stature be chosen to head such an operation.‡ [38] In May 1941, the Air Corps Ferrying Command was established, but did not include civilian pilots.

The defense of Iceland§ involved consultation between the President and the island's Prime Minister on the replacement of British defense forces whose

---

* This was a critical time for the British. German U-Boat attacks were taking a tremendous toll on their shipping. Between June and December 1940, over 3 million tons of British, Allied, and neutral merchant shipping were lost—an average of 450,000 tons each month. Denis Richards, *Royal Air Force, 1939–1945*, vol 1, *Fight At Odds* (London: Her Majesty's Stationery Office, 1953), p 221.

† Special American observers stationed in England reported to Arnold on developments in the air war over Europe. Maj. Gen. James E. Chaney commanded the Special Observers Group from May 1941 to January 1942.

‡ Edward V. Rickenbacker was a pilot, industrialist, and the most celebrated American air ace of World War I. He became president of Eastern Air Lines in 1938 and served during World War II as a special representative for Secretary of War Stimson. He was offered, but did not accept, the job Lovett proposed.

§ Although Iceland had attained independence from Denmark in 1918, it retained the Danish sovereign until it proclaimed itself a republic on June 17, 1944.

arrival there had occurred after the German conquest of Denmark. The President guaranteed Iceland's postwar sovereignty and assumed responsibility for its wartime defense with a squadron of P-40s. Lovett felt that the promised release was insufficient and expressed his concern in July 1941 to Secretary Stimson, reminding him that the AAF had recommended sending at least one squadron of B-17s and one squadron of pursuit interceptors. The bombers would provide offshore striking power and long-range patrol and reconnaissance capability while the interceptors defended the island against German bombers. In Lovett's opinion, one P-40 squadron could intercept enemy aircraft but could not defend a territory the size of Iceland.

Lovett's misgivings were resolved at a White House meeting during July 1941. Conferees included General Marshall and representatives of the Army, the Navy, and the AAF. They retained the option of sending bombers should they be necessary and released the P-40s. Apparently on his own, Lovett recommended that General Arnold enlarge the single squadron to 125 percent of authorized aircraft. He further recommended that the unit be provided a base and enough equipment and support personnel to maintain it for several months.[39]

It was at this point that Lovett had to compete not only with the British but also the U.S. Navy for aircraft. In July 1941, he was compelled to defend the AAF's order for aircraft against the Navy's. He accused the Navy not only of attempting to replace obsolete aircraft on existing carriers but of ordering "aircraft for carriers not now in existence" as well. He complained that approval of the Navy's request would delay completion of the aircraft schedule ordered by the President. It would nullify the priorities set for the Army's heavy-bomber program and dilute the purpose of newly constructed mines and smelters designated for it. In effect, Lovett warned, all Army production other than heavy bombers would be subordinate to the production of a large variety of naval aircraft. Whereas some of the Army's 4,554 heavy bombers were slated for the British, all of the Navy's 4,692 were designated for itself. In Lovett's view, accord between the AAF and the Navy was unlikely, and he suggested that the matter be settled by the President himself. Eventually, Secretary of the Navy Frank Knox, Secretary of War Stimson, General Arnold, and Lovett met with Navy officials and worked out a compromise. At the AAF's suggestion, a list of combat plane allocations was accepted by the services and approved by the President on January 14, 1942. (See Table 1.)

Thus, early in his tenure, Lovett proved willing to work hard obtaining support for issues about which he felt strongly and, in the interests of the AAF, to take his arguments directly to the President. Even though he had been given a free hand in aviation matters by Secretary Stimson, Lovett understood the value of sharing his ideas with the military chiefs and revealed himself as a steadfast defender of the aims and needs of the Army air arm.[40]

Table 1

Schedule of Combat Plane Allocations for 1942 and 1943

Aircraft types	1942			1943		
	Army	Navy	Total	Army	Navy	Total
Long-range, heavy & medium bombers	9,780	1,520	11,300	26,190	3,810	30,000
Light, dive, torpedo, & scout bombers	7,270	3,730	11,000	9,160	7,840	17,000
Pursuits	14,350	1,650	16,000	30,600	7,400	38,000
Observation & transports	3,430	3,320	6,750	12,260	2,740	15,000
TOTAL	34,830	10,220	45,050	78,210	21,790	100,000

Source: James Lea Cate, "Establishments of the Fundamental Bases of Strategy," *The Army Air Forces in World War II*, vol 1, *Plans and Early Operations, January 1939 to August 1942*, Wesley Frank Craven and James Lea Cate, eds (Chicago: University of Chicago Press, 1948), p 247.

The Air War Ensues

The Japanese attack on Pearl Harbor on December 7, 1941, plunged the United States into a war in which Germany and Italy promptly sided with Japan. The entry of the United States into the conflict gave Secretary Lovett the opportunity to influence air procurement as well as strategy and plans at the highest level of the War Department. With war in both the Atlantic and Pacific, Lovett's greatest fear became real—Lend-Lease had left the United States short of aircraft and equipment.

In 1941, alarm spread about the possible appearance in Atlantic waters off the United States of the *Bearn,* a French aircraft carrier supposedly loyal to the Vichy regime.* The Air Secretary quickly reacted to the situation. On December 8, he requested authority from Secretary of War Stimson to uncrate 150 P-40s awaiting shipment to the Soviet Union† from Boston, as well as several A-20s in New York. They were to be used in defense of New York and Connecticut, areas that Lovett believed were vulnerable.[41] The threat did not materialize, however, because of an agreement between the State Department and the Vichy regime under which the French fleet remained neutral. Some appropriated aircraft were retained for a time while others were sent to the Soviet Union early in 1942. The *Bearn* remained at anchor in Martinique until 1944, when it sailed to the United States for new antiaircraft guns. It was later used as an aircraft transport.

Secretary Lovett particularly relished the kind of planning that went on in the early days of the war. In December 1941, he worked closely with the War Plans Division of the Army General Staff and the Air Staff on strategies to reinforce the Philippines and Malaya and to attack Tokyo from airfields in areas of China not controlled by Japan.[42] He also studied the possibility of protecting the commercial airfields located along the western bulge of Africa. He considered them as important as those around the northeastern shoulder of South America to the ferrying of aircraft to Russia, the Middle East, and the Far East. Anticipating German designs on Spanish Morocco and French Algeria, he suggested to Secretary Stimson that the Cape Verde Islands and points south of the French colony of Dakar be immediately secured, believing that the presence of Allied air forces might prevent German penetration into these areas.[43]

Lovett contributed significantly to the development of Air War Plans Division Plan 1 (AWPD-1) which became the foundation for U.S. air participation in the war. General Arnold had ordered Lt. Col. Harold George, a former

---

* The Pro-Nazi state was established at Vichy in France by the victorious Germans who placed the pro-fascist Marshal Henri Philippe Petain at its head.

† The Soviet Union was also receiving Lend-Lease assistance.

instructor at the Air Corps Tactical School, to Washington in July 1941 to head the Air War Plans Division. When President Roosevelt requested that the War Department prepare a report on what would be required to win the war, both Arnold and Lovett decided that air priorities should be detailed in a separate section of the report. All recommendations were to be incorporated into the national war plan then in force, Rainbow 5.* Working tirelessly, George and his staff completed AWPD-1 in two weeks. Lovett gave them valuable counsel on the political implications of their efforts and made sure that their recommendations emphasized the importance of concentrating U.S. war power on the European theater first.[44]

Three months later Lovett incorporated his ideas on fighting with limited resources into a plan he called the "strategy of scarcity." The Allies, he explained to Brig. Gen. Dwight D. Eisenhower, Chief of the War Plans Division of the Army General Staff, should take the war directly to the enemy, making his working conditions intolerable, destroying his factories, and disrupting his sources of electricity and communications. Such actions would "thereby soften [him] up for the inevitable engagement between [hostile] ground troops and [amphibious] naval forces."[45] Lovett's plan isolated three jumpoff points: one in England to attack Germany, a second in North Africa to attack Italy, and a third in China to attack Japan. Essential aircraft, equipment, and personnel should be concentrated in these critical areas, he emphasized, not scattered throughout the world. His approach helped shape the British-American "Europe First" plan developed during the winter of 1941–1942 by Roosevelt, Churchill, and the Combined Chiefs of Staff (CCS) at the ARCADIA Conference in Washington, D.C. Their objective was to win the war in Europe while containing Japanese aggression with the fewest aircraft possible. Japan's turn would come once Germany had been defeated.[46]

Lovett did not support the Allied plan for the invasion of North Africa (Operation TORCH) which he believed would siphon critical resources from the major European front. Secretary Stimson recorded in his diary that its approval had put Lovett "in deep blues because the new plans have cut into . . . prepara-

---

* Rainbow 5 was developed by the Joint Board which, until 1942 with the creation of the Joint Chiefs of Staff, was the coordinating body for the Army and the Navy. The last in a series of war plans, it outlined U.S. intentions against more than one enemy in more than one theater at a time. It went into effect on October 14, 1939. Rainbows 1–4 basically enabled the United States to counter violations of the Monroe Doctrine, to sustain democratic powers in Pacific Zones, to secure control of the western Pacific, and to send defensive task forces to South America and the eastern Atlantic. Rainbow 5 incorporated the goals of 1–4 and enabled the United States to send forces to Africa or Europe for the decisive defeat of Germany and Italy. Rainbows 1–4 were rendered obsolete and cancelled. Rainbow 5 was the "grand composite" in effect when the United States entered World War II in December 1941. Mark Skinner Watson, *Chief of Staff: Prewar Plans and Preparations, The United States Army in World War II* (Washington: U.S. Army Historical Division, 1950), pp 103–9.

tions terrifically and our Air Force . . . has been split up into fragments, and the prospect of a powerful mass is farther off than ever."[47]

Lovett, however, remained willing to experiment. When Californians and Floridians became panicked by reports of enemy submarines, he recommended that volunteer pilots from the Office of Civil Defense be detailed to coastal patrol. He argued that their planes need not carry bombs or armament, but could be painted with AAF insignia to intimidate intruders.[48] Lovett argued that his solution would expose the inadequacies of America's shoreline defense until the Army and the Navy were equipped to take it over.[49] General Arnold agreed but wanted to arm sea-going motor boats with either .50 caliber or 37mm guns, or depth charges, if available.[50] As it turned out, volunteer yachtsmen, enrolled in a Coast Guard auxiliary, for a time patrolled the coasts using these weapons.

Despite General Arnold's direct access to the President through the Joint Chiefs of Staff (JCS), he often deferred to Lovett on procurement and non-strategic questions. However, lines of authority often blurred.[51] Lovett was usually attentive to the factual analysis of production capability; he adhered to realistic production goals coordinated with strategic considerations; he pursued widespread consultation through both formal and informal channels; and, when faced with what he regarded as unwise decisions, was capable of resisting pressure from above to accept them.[52]

Consequently, when his views happened to clash with General Arnold's, he was not afraid to take a stand. In October 1942, for example, he challenged Arnold's acceptance of a projected 1943 production schedule of 131,000 aircraft (100,000 tactical and 31,000 training). To Lovett this fantastic figure, advocated by the President on September 9, 1942, was one which no authority within the Materiel Command, the Bureau of Aeronautics, or the War Production Board would attempt to justify. In endorsing what he viewed as an unattainable goal, the Air Secretary warned, the AAF was deluding itself, the public, and the President. "It is a little bit like asking a hen to lay an ostrich egg," Lovett emphasized, "It is unlikely that you will get the egg, and the hen will never look the same."[53] He estimated the likely production of 88,000 aircraft, but no more than 90,000 to 100,000. He insisted that any great expansion of 1943 output, especially to the level desired by General Arnold, was out of the question, and he cited the failure of the government to assign the aircraft program the overriding priority it had deserved in January 1942.[54] Finally, he pointed out that, in any case, a shortage of materials would delay by at least twelve months the opening of any new production facilities. Under Secretary of War Robert P. Patterson advised General Arnold that he agreed with Lovett.[55]

On October 20, 1942, Arnold responded in a blistering memorandum to the Air Secretary. He acknowledged that the goal was ambitious, much "like requiring a peacetime hen to lay a wartime egg of ostrich proportions, but if we can induce her to lay it, I, for one, feel that we must accept the wear and tear on the hen."[56] Certain that the President's plan would encourage manufacturers to

Industry Goes All Out.
Boeing Aircraft Company B-17s
on the factory floor *(above)* and
on the airfield *(center)*. It was
through the ceaseless efforts of
Assistant Secretary of War for
Air Robert A. Lovett to create a
smoothly running military-
manufacturing partnership that
Allied aircraft needs were met
during World War II. He is
shown *(right)* accepting a gift to
the U.S. Army Air Forces of a
P-47 built on the free time of
the employees of the Republic
Aircraft Corporation in 1942.

redouble their efforts, Arnold declared that self-imposed obstacles and rigid planning had hampered the growth of air power. He warned that "the negative assumption that requirements cannot be met, supported by facts as they are and not as we are capable of making them, too often has characterized thinking on this subject."[57] He vowed not to compromise on the figure of 131,000 except where the "clearest showing of fact" demanded it.[58]

In March 1943, Lovett advised Harry Hopkins that competition for raw materials, machine tools, alloy steels, and manpower would restrict production to no more than 90,000 aircraft. He further noted that factories would need time to retool before replacing combat aircraft types which, having proved unsatisfactory, were to be discontinued.

Lovett was correct in the end, as factory acceptances of all military airplanes in 1943 totaled 84,433. It seems clear that Arnold wished to use the President's goal to increase the momentum of the war effort. In any event, he had demanded data from an acknowledged expert, then had rejected it. Characteristically, Arnold believed that he could achieve his aims through the sheer force of will. This incident illustrates clearly the nature of Lovett's position and his administrative style. In this instance, he was able to persuade Patterson to reconsider production figures. But Arnold remained adamant.

Lovett suggested to Harry Hopkins that the President revise his September 9, 1942, directive and announce to the public that he was lowering aircraft production to balance it with other programs. This would more easily permit the phase-out of obsolete types and facilitate the introduction of several promising combat models such as the P-47, the P-51, and the B-29.[59]

A Multitude of Concerns

As the war progressed, industry experienced an alarming loss of skilled workers to the armed services. When queried on the subject by Edsel Ford of the Ford Motor Company in the autumn of 1942, Lovett explained that the Secretaries of War and Navy had signed a memorandum urging all essential workers at key industries to stay on the job until they were drafted or could be spared to volunteer. The Army and the Navy had agreed that they would exempt workers employed in aircraft and ship building as well as any who had left those activities within sixty days of applying for enlistment. Industry foremen were thus given time to train replacements for workers scheduled to leave for military duty.[60] Lovett had contributed the policy statement relating to the aircraft industry. The following spring, the Civil Aeronautics Administration experienced a similar manpower problem—the loss of workers to the draft and voluntary enlistments. Lovett saw to it that a policy statement similar to the one he had drafted for the aircraft industry was approved and signed by both Secretary of War Stimson and Secretary of the Navy Knox.[61]

Whether the aircraft industry's problems involved the Wright Field installation in Ohio,* the War Production Board, the War Manpower Commission, the Department of Justice, or any other federal agency, Lovett's office served as an informal court of appeals. He dealt candidly yet compassionately with industry executives, most of whom he knew on a first-name basis, and assisted them readily in dealing with such issues as scheduling and contract negotiating. He nonetheless felt that "it was a pity . . . to spend so much time on things not directly productive of aircraft and engines." [62]

Constantly on the lookout for new sources of information to benefit the Allies in the air war, Lovett turned his attention to the interrogation of German prisoners of war as soon as the first groups were captured in North Africa. He requested that those who had worked in German manufacturing plants be singled out for any facts they might divulge which would aid in target selection. As a result of his inquiries, the intelligence office of Headquarters, AAF, conducted a thorough study to establish uniform procedures for questioning prisoners and processing target information.[63]

In 1943 the Air Secretary became concerned about the classification of AAF officers and enlistees, noting that for the most part they were not being assigned to the jobs which best suited them. He discovered that AAF personnel officers were not fully acquainted with relevant Army regulations and directives. He stressed the importance of recasting the occupational descriptions of individuals with divergent skills and encouraged frequent command visits by field representatives of A-1—the Air Staff section dealing with Lovett's concern—or the Military Personnel Division to insure that regulations were being properly interpreted. Although dissatisfied because the AAF was unable to better exploit unique talents, he realized that the influx of over one million people throughout its ranks in only two years had imposed an almost unimaginable administrative burden. It would have been "the miracle of the war," Lovett declared, had all of the members of the AAF been placed where they could have served to the greatest advantage.[64]

War Issues

By mid-1943 the Air Secretary had become uneasy about the growing tension between Maj. Gen. Ira C. Eaker, Commander of the Eighth Air Force, and General Arnold. Arnold was displeased that Eaker had not launched more heavy

---

* Wright Field, which in 1948 merged with Patterson Field to form Wright-Patterson Air Force Base, was the locus of the Air Corps Engineering School (successor of the Air Service Engineering School and predecessor of today's Air Force Institute of Technology) and the major facility for military aviation research, development, testing, and evaluation.

strategic bombing raids against Germany, even though the force's mission had been impeded by bad weather, the diversion of planes to North Africa, and the lack of long-range fighter escort.

Lovett pointed to operational time lost because of aircraft modification, combat crew training, and the repair of bombers grounded by battle damage. But he attributed the fundamental reason for any misunderstandings between Arnold and Eaker to the Eighth's inadequate methods of reporting and of accounting for the aircraft it received. He also detected an attitude at AAF Headquarters in Washington toward the Eighth Air Force similar to that of a father irritated with his grown son, "frequently to the intense irritation of the son but equally frequently to his ultimate benefit."[65]

In an effort to mediate, Lovett discussed the situation with Arnold. He then informed Eaker that Arnold was aware of his difficulties and had agreed to exert pressure on the sources of spare aircraft, replacement crews, and better instructors of gunners and pilots for high-altitude and formation flying.[66] Like Arnold, Lovett had possessed a personal commitment to the strategy of sustained bombing since his days as a pilot during World War I, when, as Acting Wing Commander of the Northern Bombing Group, he led assaults against heavily defended German submarine bases. As a lieutenant, Lovett believed that penetration of the German air defense system could only be achieved by unremitting night attacks against one base at a time. Random bombing, he had observed, did not dampen enemy morale.[67]

In August 1943, the Eighth Air Force suffered heavy losses over Germany while attacking Schweinfurt and Regensburg and had ceased deep penetration raids. Lovett, sympathizing with Eaker, continued to defend his leadership, and in a letter to him, expressed great concern for the Eighth Air Force's morale. He also tried to comfort him with some mathematics on the Eighth's operations. Lovett maintained that the loss of fifteen percent of the force at Schweinfurt was the equivalent of three days' operations with losses of five percent each. Instead of operating Monday, Tuesday and Wednesday and losing five percent on less important targets, it was more profitable, he reasoned, to rest on Monday and Tuesday, and take the fifteen percent loss on Wednesday bombing a vital target.[68] Lovett calculated that the loss would average much less than fifteen percent over a month's time. Heavy losses on one raid would be offset by other factors. Thus, average monthly losses would remain relatively constant.

Acknowledging the lack of adequate fighter escort, he promised Eaker that the problem would be rectified with the introduction of longer range P-51Bs and P-38s. Lovett realized, however, that the Eighth's crews would prefer the reality of fighter protection to the consolation of statistics—"a little bit like . . . the heroine in *Gentlemen Prefer Blondes* who knows that a kiss on the hand is all very well, but a diamond bracelet lasts forever."[69]

It was a difficult time for Eaker, who felt daily pressure from Washington to keep launching strikes. He insisted to Arnold that he wanted the Eighth Air

Force to fulfill its mission as a growing, not a diminishing force. Eaker's bitterness reached a climax in January 1944, when General Arnold sent him to command the Mediterranean Allied Air Forces after replacing him with Lt. Gen. Carl A. Spaatz. Lovett could not persuade Arnold to reconsider his decision. Eaker was appreciative of Lovett's concern and wrote in a letter to him, "Your friendship and your kindly interest never meant more to me than during this changeover period."[70] Command assignments rested solely with military leaders, and Lovett was sensitive to that fact.

By the winter of 1943, Lovett worried that continued exaggeration by the press of the Eighth Air Force's activities might create the impression that the Allies had already launched an air offensive capable of destroying the German war machine. They had not, but Lovett feared that if Germany continued to stand firm at year's end, a demoralized American public might conclude that the all-out offensive had failed.[71] Both Lovett and Arnold wanted the AAF's accomplishments highlighted, but not with glorified phrases, generalities, and graphic embellishments. In June 1943, they had directed the AAF to limit releases to concise statements of fact.

To prevent any misapprehension about the Eighth Air Force and the Allied offensive, Lovett embarked on a campaign to educate the press, stressing that current bombing runs were only a preview of things to come and that the true air offensive had not yet begun. As he had called on his friends from Wall Street and industry when he needed help with aircraft production problems, he called on his friends in journalism to help publicize this critical fact. They included Cass Canfield of *Harpers;* Charles Merz, editor of the *New York Times;* Merrill Meigs of the Hearst chain; columnists Arthur Krock and Walter Lippmann; Henry Luce of *Time;* Edward Harriman of *Newsweek;* and Eugene Meyer, publisher of the *Washington Post* (he and other members of his family had been Lovett's clients at Brown Brothers Harriman for many years).[72] Throughout the war, Lovett acted as a trouble-shooter, squelching public relations difficulties whenever they threatened to erupt.

In July 1944, the advance of the Allied armies in Normandy ground to an abrupt halt. That fact, as well as many questions, were carried by the press. To foster the appearance of progress, General Marshall proposed moving General Eisenhower's headquarters—Supreme Headquarters, Allied Expeditionary Force (SHAEF)—from Britain to France. To Lovett, the proposed move afforded a chance to simplify the command structure governing tactical aviation in Europe. AAF leaders had never accepted the Allied Expeditionary Air Force (AEAF) or the British tendency to dominate it. The AEAF was made up of the RAF 2nd Tactical Air Force and the U.S. Ninth Air Force, which was responsible for softening enemy defenses prior to D-Day and for providing tactical support to the Allied invasion forces. When Air Chief Marshal Trafford Leigh-Mallory, Air Officer Commanding, RAF Fighter Command, was appointed to head the AEAF, he assumed that he would issue orders to General Spaatz and Air Chief Marshal

General Henry H. Arnold, Commanding General, U.S. Army Air Forces *(left)* **and Maj. Gen. Ira C. Eaker, Commanding General, U.S. Eighth Air Force.**

Arthur Harris, Air Officer Commanding, RAF Bomber Command. During earlier POINTBLANK activities (Operation POINTBLANK was the U.S. portion of the Combined Bombing Offensive), both Spaatz and Harris had taken their orders from Air Chief Marshal Charles Portal, who had been empowered by the CCS to direct the operations of both strategic air forces. But there were no direct lines of authority from Leigh-Mallory's headquarters to Spaatz's U.S. Strategic Air Forces (USSTAF) or Harris's RAF Bomber Command. Lovett had already concluded that the AEAF was unnecessary and unworkable. Lovett believed that with Eisenhower's transfer to France the AEAF would be "chucked out the window." The air arm, in his view, should take advantage of the growing concern over the invasion and free itself from the "stuffiness of classical thinking as well as from the impediment of cumbersome, face-saving machinery." * [73]

From time to time, the War Department allowed Lovett, himself, along with the other assistant secretaries, to appear for press conferences. He used them all as occasions to praise the AAF. In July 1944, he stressed the importance of strategic bombing during the D-Day invasion in June and its contribution to a successful outcome. The proof of its effectiveness, he asserted, lay in the Luftwaffe's failure to intervene. He credited USSTAF with reducing the German air force to sec-

---

* Apparently Lovett thought very little of the way the AEAF was organized. Under its chain of command, the Ninth Air Force had to serve two masters—the AEAF in operational matters and USSTAF in administrative matters. The AEAF was eventually disbanded on October 15, l944. David G. Rempel, "Check at the Rhine," *Europe: Argument to V-E Day, January 1944 to May 1945, The Army Air Forces in World War II,* vol 3, Craven and Cate, eds (Chicago: University of Chicago Press, 1951), pp 620–22.

ond-class status—unable to mount a sustained offensive but capable of the aerial equivalent of guerrilla war, fighting furiously at a single point on a given day.[74]

Late that year, Lovett complained that only a few senior air officers seemed acceptable to the Combined Chiefs of Staff as theater commanders. Lovett valued theater command highly as an important symbol to the public. He charged that the AAF was not receiving its fair share of the credit for Allied victory, even though it had carried the brunt of the Combined Bombing Offensive for several years (as opposed to several months for the ground forces). This perception of aviation as auxiliary to the Army troubled Lovett, who had worked assiduously to secure the AAF recognition as an equal to the ground and service forces.* He was especially anxious "lest the wangling for power and the maneuvering for national prestige . . . result in the top air command always being used as a trading point which this country gives up in order to get ground command." [75]

In November 1944, Lovett also complained that too much time was being spent on certain aspects of postwar planning. He maintained that in almost half of all decisions on operations the problem of industrial reconversion and redeployment in peacetime was injected. Such speculating, when the end of the war was not yet in sight, seemed to him highly inappropriate and even harmful to Allied efforts. He criticized those who appeared to believe it was possible "to fight a cashier's campaign in which the last American bullet kills the last German soldier on the day before pay day."[76] He firmly opposed halting the production of P-47s, for example, and the theory that if war ended by January 15, the AAF would have more aircraft than it could possibly shift to the Pacific. Not wanting to lose the opportunity to test the role of U.S. air power against Japan, he said, "We ought to be shot if we don't have more than we can deploy in the Pacific," and he cautioned against trying "to balance the thing out to the last penny." He did not see how "we can make a bear rug unless we have killed the bear."[77]

Lovett got along well with his peers in the War Department and corresponded freely with air commanders in the field. Nonetheless, his executive officer, Brig. Gen. George A. Brownell, in December 1944, identified a lack of coordination between the War Department and other headquarters organizations whose staffs, as the war progressed, had tended to operate more and more independently. He charged that the Air Staff and the OASWA often responded to War Department inquiries without first consulting each other. Brownell maintained that while personal contacts among the four War Department secretaries (Stimson, Patterson, McCloy, and Lovett) and corresponding contacts between the executives of various offices were frequent enough, contacts at staff and administrative levels were not.

---

* The Army Air Forces was made an equal organizationally to the Army Ground Forces and the Army Services of Supply, subsequently the Army Service Forces in March 1942.

He recommended that the four secretaries first refer all AAF matters to the OASWA. That office would then direct them to the General Staff or the Air Staff. Brownell believed that his staff would be more efficient if it could communicate with the Air Staff regularly and if General Arnold and the Air Staff cultivated closer ties. Brownell also maintained that communications problems were exacerbated by the lack of clearly indicated lines of authority and function within the OASWA itself. Lovett's habit of operating rather casually on the basis of friendships left Brownell often wondering how best to meet administrative responsibilities.[78]

The War Ends

In early 1945, the United States was engaged in war on several fronts. In Europe, German resistance had toughened during the counteroffensive leading to the Battle of the Bulge. Certain types of German weapons had outperformed those of the Allies. The recuperative power of German industry had exceeded U.S. expectations with the buildup of a fighter force from 500 operational first-line aircraft to 2,000 in only five months. And rockets as well as jet-propelled aircraft had entered German inventories. Reacting to this flare-up of enemy activity, the Air Secretary offered General Arnold a proposal for forcing Germany into submission. At the core of his plan was the exploitation of Allied superiority in the air. Despite German resilience, the Allies controlled the skies. The Air Secretary suggested that a special European Theater of Operations strike force of 500 fighters and bombers with a 100 percent reserve be established to function independently while serviced and maintained by the Ninth Air Force. Lovett called his force the "Jeb" Stuart Unit, after the hero of the Confederacy. Its primary mission would be to destroy Germany's dispersed industry by systematically disrupting its communications and destroying the small factories and power plants scattered deep inside its territory. Heavy bombers, he maintained, had been unable to achieve the wholesale destruction of German industry. Because decentralization had placed a greater burden on transportation systems, Lovett viewed roads, canals, and rail lines as critical targets. He believed that a raiding force flexible enough to attack troops massed on the battlefield, while it flew the best fighter-bombers available and enjoyed freedom of action under competent leadership, could bring victory in 1945.*[79]

---

* Lovett's "Jeb" Stuart operation, for the most part the idea of Maj. Gen. Elwood Quesada, Commander, Ninth Air Force, was agreed to by General Arnold and eventually carried out under Operation CLARION, a plan that involved the large-scale employment of strategic bombers as well as fighters. John E. Fagg, "The Climax of Strategic Operations," *Europe: Argument to V-E Day, January, 1944 to May 1945, The Army Air Forces in World War II,* vol 3, Craven and Cate, pp 715–16, 732–33.

With victory, Lovett would attempt to influence the design and role of America's triumphant postwar air arm. He doubted the effectiveness of an international police force, citing the Soviet Union's reluctance when American airmen wished to establish wartime air bases there. "Her back to the wall at Stalingrad and in the Caucasus," he recalled, "she declined to allow American squadrons to come in, stating that she would prefer to have the equipment."* He seemed convinced that the American people tended to be "international suckers." In his view, the United States had financed the entire war for the United Nations, receiving in return little but envy, resentment, and, in some cases, actual hatred. He suggested that the United States, to achieve a stable postwar environment, obtain through agreement or purchase such outposts as were needed to protect the nation and to keep the peace. He believed, as did General Arnold, that the United States should have the most powerful air force in the world, but it would have to junk much of the equipment left at the end of the war and devote its funds to research, development, and production of new designs. A victorious nation with 10,000 planes built in 1943 could, he argued, end up "playing second fiddle" to a vanquished foe forced to acquire new planes that incorporated the latest engineering and battle experience.[80]

As World War II drew to a close, Lovett and other civilian and military leaders advocated continued support for U.S. aircraft industries through new development programs designed to keep their experimental and key production organizations intact. Lovett believed that these programs would prove successful if the Army and the Navy were more closely coordinated.[81] With the production of such weapons as the B-24 and B-17 soon ending, he wanted to limit the purchase of additional spares to critically short items. He preferred cannibalizing spare planes to stockpiling parts that would never be needed. His concern about excess equipment would involve him in planning for surplus stock disposal once the war had ended.[82]

Lovett foresaw the need with the coming peace for a federal policy toward aviation coordinated by the several departments and agencies with interest in and authority over it. He therefore proposed to Harry Hopkins in January 1945 that a committee be formed within the Office of War Mobilization and Reconversion to deal broadly with the subject. At first the Departments of State and Commerce rejected Lovett's plan, suspicious of possible military dominance.[83] Lovett and Artemus Gates, Assistant Secretary of the Navy, who endorsed his idea, were able to persuade the other agencies to form a more representative body, the Air Coordinating Committee (ACC)†, which was estab-

---

* Stalin would later allow the basing of American planes at Poltava for shuttle bombing missions during Operation FRANTIC.
† The activities of the committee and its industrial, economic, and technical divisions were diverse. Indeed, Air Navigation Facilities and Systems (FAS), Communications (COM), Air Space—Rules of the Air and Air Traffic Control, Search and Rescue (SAR) Facilitation, and International Civil Aviation—as well as matters relating to cus-

Lt. Gen. Henry H. Arnold, Commanding General, U.S. Army Air Forces, and Assistant Secretary of War for Air Robert A. Lovett in 1942. The pair worked closely and successfully together on all air matters throughout World War II.

lished by interdepartmental memoranda on March 17, 1945. The committee was originally established to smooth aviation's transition from war to peace and confined itself to developing a unified federal policy "that would be followed up by the member Departments."[84]

Lovett's Legacy

Robert A. Lovett made lasting contributions to the Army Air Forces and to the office which in September 1947 became the Office of the Secretary of the Air Force. His conduct in public service and his vision of the Office of the Assistant Secretary of War for Air set the pattern in 1946 and 1947 for his successor, W. Stuart Symington. In a real sense, Secretary Lovett can be seen as an important bridge between Trubee Davison and Symington, and in his exercise of responsibility and authority, he established continuity between the old and the new.

Lovett solidified his authority over many air matters such as strategy and

---

toms, public health regulations, travel documents and monetary and tax questions were some of the areas that the ACC considered. Robert A. Lovett, as Assistant Secretary of War for Air, held the seat designated for the War Department (other members represented the State, Post Office, Navy, and Commerce Departments and the Civil Aeronautics Board). When he was absent, his executive officer attended as his alternate. Walter H. Wager, "The Air Coordinating Committee," *Air University Quarterly Review,* vol 2, no. 4 (Spring 1949), pp 17–32.

organization and, like Davison, made procurement his primary responsibility. He played a role in the AAF reorganization of March 1942, and his ideas influenced the character of the postwar Air Force. The manner in which Lovett and General Arnold divided authority and responsibility set the pattern for civilian and military interactions at the top echelon of the AAF and throughout the War Department. Lovett's authority was not defined by statute but by his superiors, who placed their utmost faith in his talents.

He was a man who could maneuver adroitly within the sometimes tortuous channels of the War Department and form friendships with and earn the respect of most of those with whom he dealt in the armed forces, in government, or in business. Perhaps the best assessment of the Air Secretary was provided by General Arnold, who fully appreciated his character, ability, and patience. He called Lovett "a partner and teammate of tremendous sympathy, and of calm and hidden force" and treasured the experience of having worked with him throughout the war.[85] Their close relationship would easily serve as a model for succeeding Air Secretaries and Chiefs of Staff to follow. When Lovett retired from office on December 8, 1945, General Arnold credited him with having recognized ahead of many others the potential of strategic bombing and the importance of long-range fighter escort, and he praised him for his astute awareness of technical innovations and their application to AAF needs. He acknowledged Lovett's contributions in organization, management and procurement, and congressional and public relations. Arnold predicted that Lovett would be best remembered "by the Air Force officers in these headquarters and throughout the combat zones for . . . wise counsel . . . ready and modest advice, and . . . thoughtful encouragement when the going was hard."[86]

Lovett helped the AAF gain equality with the Army Ground Forces and the Army Service Forces and, ultimately, to win its independence in 1947. Had he served in a less tumultuous period or betrayed an interest in bureaucratic empire-building, he might have been induced to provide a clearer definition of the role and function of his office.*

Secretary of War Stimson expected Lovett to be able to handle all aviation issues and Stimson's successor, Robert Patterson, would expect the same from Lovett's successor. Lovett had enjoyed the freedom to choose the problems to which he devoted his skills. His expertise in aviation and business had led him to military procurement. Military procurement had led him to myriad tangential areas. His successor might easily conclude that he, too, could select those areas that best suited his own expertise as long as they coincided with the needs of the Air Force.

---

* Lovett apparently impressed President Truman because he served as Under Secretary of State from 1947 to 1949, as Deputy Secretary of Defense under George Marshall from 1950 to 1951, and, finally, as Secretary of Defense from 1951 to 1953.

Whether his views actually swayed military leaders is difficult to determine. In one instance involving the Europe First strategy, his views mirrored, but did not inspire, the policy those leaders actually adopted. Certainly they would expect a new Assistant Secretary of War for Air to express his views as freely as Lovett had. Lovett's most important contribution in their eyes, however, was helping industry to equip the world's largest air force to defeat Italy, Germany, and Japan. At the end of the war, the United States owed its possession of the strongest air force in the world in very large measure to Robert Lovett.

Lovett's nearly carte blanche authority did not exist on paper but was firmly planted in the minds of Secretary Stimson, Under Secretary Patterson, and Generals Marshall and Arnold. This authority was no doubt enhanced by his vast network of contacts within business and the press. His congenial wit endeared him to his many friends and helped make him highly influential within the War Department. He was an enormous asset to the Army Air Forces and set the standard for his successors for years to come.

Chapter 2

The Interlude (1946–1947)

As 1945 drew to a close, the United States was enjoying its first peaceful Christmas in five years, secure in its newly earned status as the world's most powerful nation. Pro-Communist satellite governments had been established in Eastern Europe, inspiring Winston Churchill to warn of the Soviet Union's world-wide ambitions. Nonetheless, a sense of optimism prevailed. The Axis powers had been decisively defeated and no new military threat immediately loomed. This period of relative quiescence, from 1946 through 1947, eased the reorganization of the nation's armed forces and the disposition of obsolete military equipment.

It also saw the Assistant Secretary of War for Air negotiate a successful transition from war to peace. Cost control, independence, and parity with the other services became crucial to the Army Air Forces (AAF). Robert A. Lovett had paved the way for a cost control program by instituting a comptrollership within the Office of the Assistant Secretary of War for Air (OASWA). He could not press the cause of separation during the war, but W. Stuart Symington took it up with enthusiasm. He used his office as a fulcrum for civilian control under the President as Commander in Chief of the armed services.

With the changing of the guard after the end of the war, Secretary of War Henry L. Stimson was succeeded in September 1945 by his Under Secretary of War, Robert P. Patterson. Patterson expected the new Assistant Secretary of War for Air, Stuart Symington, to function generally as Robert Lovett had, handling aviation in general and procurement in particular. He also wanted Symington to lead the drive for an independent air force. Consequently, during 1946 and 1947 the OASWA expanded in authority and responsibility. Symington's relationship with Patterson was as congenial as Lovett's had been with Stimson. His relation-ship with General Carl A. Spaatz, who followed General Henry H. Arnold as Commanding General of the AAF in February 1946, differed from Lovett's with Arnold. Whereas Lovett had delved into varied activities with Stimson's and Arnold's blessings, Symington and Spaatz established a more rigorous division of labor. Spaatz handled daily operational matters and Symington, for the most part, concentrated on promoting the independent air force to Congress.

An independent air force had been agreed upon in principle during the war by General Marshall, General Arnold, and Assistant Secretary of War for Air Lovett. Congress, about to begin the process of reorganizing the military ser-vices, had indicated support for it.[1] There were, however, advocates in the AAF who favored the status quo and zealots in the Navy who feared the loss of their air mission, resisted change, and waged a vigorous campaign against air force autonomy. Marshall, Arnold, and Lovett fully realized that Congress would have to treat the Navy very carefully, exercising patience and diplomacy before it instituted any reforms.

In 1946 and 1947, the OASWA and its extremely small staff continued to provide expert responses to the War Department on all air matters. The Assistant Secretary of War for Air during this period was dealt more responsibility but no more power or prestige. Despite a dearth of administrative assistance and a growing workload, Secretary Symington imprinted his style and character on his office, defended the goals of the AAF, and gained the attention and support of both the White House and Congress.[2]

The Office of the Assistant Secretary of War for Air

After the war, the OASWA, like many government offices, witnessed the return of its leadership to private enterprise. With Robert A. Lovett's departure in December 1945, and the subsequent resignation in January 1946 of his executive officer, Brig. Gen. George A. Brownell, the position of the Assistant Secretary of War for Air remained vacant until February 1946. During this time the office continued to function under the management of Col. Thetus C. Odom. For this brief period, Odom operated more or less on his own initiative.[3]

Almost immediately he did what Lovett had avoided doing; he prepared an organization chart,* based on the duties set forth in the legislation which established the OASWA on July 2, 1926. (See Appendix 1, p. 258.) The Air Secretary was to advise or represent the Secretary of War on aviation, supervising "matters pertaining to the Army Air Forces (a change in wording that reflected the current status of the air arm) and contacts with other agencies, governmental and private, on policy matters of interest to the War Department."[4]

---

* In September 1945, Brig. Gen. George A. Brownell, executive officer of the OASWA, admitted that his office had no official organization chart. There were four commissioned officers on duty: an executive officer (brig. gen.), two assistant executive officers (lt. cols.) and one pilot and staff officer (lt. col.). The duties of the assistant executives and the staff officer were interrelated and were assigned "from time to time by the Assistant Secretary of War for Air" and the executive officer. At this time, the OASWA also included four civilian secretaries (one each for Lovett, Brownell, and the two assistant executive officers), two civilian file clerks, and two enlisted chauffeurs. Undated memo signed by George A. Brownell; memo, George A. Brownell to Air Adjutant General, subj: Handling of Telephone Calls to the Office of the Assistant Secretary of War for Air by the AAF Duty Officer, Oct 1, 1945; both sources, George A. Brownell Collection, Chronological File Sep–Dec 1945, AFHRC, Maxwell AFB, Ala.

Odom pointed out that the Air Secretary's duties included working closely with the Air Staff and the Commanding General of the AAF on personnel, intelligence, requirements, plans, experimentation and development, and maintenance and supply. The Air Secretary also represented the War Department on air issues of concern to other government agencies including the State, Navy, and Commerce Departments and the Civil Aeronautics Board. The OASWA also represented the War Department on the Air Coordinating Committee (ACC). Further, it was the agency through which U.S. commercial airlines, aircraft manufacturers, and civilian agencies dealt with the War Department.[5]

According to Odom's chart, the executive officer followed the Air Secretary in line of authority and relieved him of day-to-day business by "approving, processing, and deciding on matters of routine and minor policy and procedure." Such matters included corresponding with individuals and contractors on base closings and contracts; expediting the work of various office components; assuming additional responsibilities and activities for the Air Secretary during his absence; and providing general supervision of internal office service activities (procedures, personnel, equipment, and special assignments).

A special assistant to the Secretary of War and three assistant executives were next in authority. Eugene M. Zuckert became special assistant in February 1946. In that capacity he monitored all AAF budgetary activities and supervised information services. Three assistant executives, all colonels, performed various duties. Col. John K. Hester monitored all activities involving with the Assistant Chiefs of the Air Staff for personnel, training and program planning and the Deputy Chief of Staff for Research and Development. Col. Harold Ohlke worked on intelligence and program planning; and the third assistant, Col. William Mitchell, handled proposed legislation, modification of existing laws, AAF contracts, and the drafting and interpretation of directives, policies, and other control documents. All three assistant executives as well as the special assistant were subject to special assignments as designated by the Air Secretary or his executive officer.[6]

Colonel Odom established office policy for ten civilian and four military staff members (as of March 6, 1946) and a normal work schedule, 8:30 A.M. to 5:00 P.M., Monday through Friday. Each day, either the executive officer or one of the assistant executives remained until 6:00 P.M. when late-working sections of the War Department required assistance. In addition, a skeleton force reported to the office on Saturday mornings to manage high priority projects and to assist other sections working that day. The Saturday contingent usually consisted of the executive officer or the special assistant, one secretary, and one member of the Records Section.

Anticipating the needs of a new Assistant Secretary of War for Air, Colonel Odom prepared a list of major concerns under two principal categories: "air matters within the War Department" and "air matters of War Department interest which concerned other agencies in both government and the private sector."[7]

Odom realized that as the AAF massively reduced its strength in the transition from war to peace,* it would be obliged to continue maintaining its world-wide weather and communications network, providing supplies and services for U.S. civil aircraft operating overseas, disposing of surplus aircraft and aeronautical equipment, continuing essential research and development projects, assisting in the demobilization of the American aircraft industry, and furnishing personnel and aircraft to the occupation forces in Europe and Asia.[8] Other matters important to Odom included War Department organization—especially the relationship of the OASWA to the Air Staff and the General Staff—and the manning and training of the peacetime AAF. As for air matters and other agencies, Odom believed that ongoing support for the Air Coordinating Committee would be necessary to protect the interests of the War Department.[9]

Symington Takes Over

In February 1946, President Harry S. Truman selected another successful businessman, W. Stuart Symington, to become Assistant Secretary of War for Air. Symington had earned a reputation for saving companies from bankruptcy and transforming them into profitable enterprises. After he had exercised these skills with the Emerson Electric Company of St. Louis, Missouri, where he had served as president and chairman of the board, the Office of Production Management requested in 1941 that he accompany a group of aeronautical engineers to England to study new British power-driven gun turrets. Upon returning to the United States, he made the Emerson Electric Company the world's largest manufacturer of aircraft armament. He resigned from the company in July 1945 to become chairman of the Surplus Property Board, and in October of that year, became administrator of the Surplus Property Administration. President Truman, as a senator from Missouri and chairman of a special committee investigating the national defense program, had become aware of Symington and had been impressed by his efficient management of Emerson Electric.[10]

As head of the Surplus Property Administration, according to one observer, Symington's "keen insight and aggressive approach won him the admiration and support of the business community" and convinced Congress that he was "one man who could develop a successful disposal policy."[11] He had planned to stay in government for only six months, but President Truman wanted him to remain and offered him the choice of three positions: Assistant Secretary of the Navy for Air, Assistant Secretary of State, or Assistant Secretary of War for Air.

---

* The AAF's highest group strength during World War II was 232 in early 1945. By September 1945 the group total had dropped to 201; by October to 178; by November to 128; by December to 109. In January 1946, AAF total groups stood at 89; in August they stood at 52.

Symington felt that his business background would be of greater service to the Army Air Forces than to the Navy. He had, after all, dealt with the AAF during the war. The air arm, on the verge of independence, would require the development, almost from scratch, of a systematic, yet adaptable, logistics network. He believed that the AAF offered the greater challenge, one that his creativity as much as his managerial and organizational talents could overcome.[12] Symington would later point out that his general business experience, rather than his handling of surplus property, had induced President Truman to urge him to continue in government service.

Although confident of his business skills, Symington, unlike Lovett, was a novice regarding operations. As a result, he left the day-to-day running of the air arm to professional airmen and did so even as Secretary of the Air Force. He did not have the opportunity to establish the kind of rapport with field commanders that Lovett had enjoyed during the war. He felt he could accomplish his management goals by persuading Congress of the importance of air power, by selling, in effect, the operational programs devised by General Spaatz and other uniformed leaders. Thus Symington's conception of his responsibilities differed from Lovett's. As Assistant Secretary of War for Air and later as Secretary of the Air Force, he was undaunted by confrontations with Congress when advocating air power. Perhaps such daring could be attributed to his secure financial status—he had become wealthy in his own right after selling his shares in Emerson Electric and, had he chosen to, he could have returned to the presidency of that corporation.[13] On the other hand, he was a true believer in air power and his advocacy came naturally to him.

W. Stuart Symington, Assistant Secretary of War for Air from 1946 to 1947 and Secretary of the Air Force from 1947 to 1950

Symington proved especially fortunate in his choice of assistants, one of whom was Eugene M. Zuckert. From 1940 to 1944 Zuckert had been assistant dean of the Harvard Graduate School of Business Administration, at times serving as a special consultant to the Commanding General of the AAF while developing statistics on supplies. He was also an instructor at the Army Air Forces Statistical Control School,* which had trained more than 3,000 officers. He worked under Symington at Emerson Electric on the recommendation of Eliot Janeway, the economist, but his tenure there was cut short in 1944, when, with Symington's endorsement, he received a commission as a lieutenant (junior grade) to work on the Navy's new inventory control program. When Symington became involved with the Surplus Property Board, he obtained Zuckert's release from the Navy. After a six-month tour as executive assistant to the administrator of the Surplus Property Administration, Zuckert followed Symington from that agency to the AAF and remained with him for four years, initially as a special assistant, and then as Assistant Secretary of the Air Force.[14]

After assuming office as the Assistant Secretary of War for Air, Symington remained interested in the disposition of surplus property throughout the military services. He was pleased that as of November 30, 1946, property worth only $34 million in AAF custody awaited action after having been determined excess. He had earlier complained to Under Secretary of War Kenneth C. Royall that the discretionary power of the War Assets Administration (WAA) had stifled the AAF's attempts to improve surplus property disposal. WAA regulations, according to Symington, did not permit the normal laws of supply and demand to function. While the AAF had a relatively unlimited supply and the public had "an apparently unlimited demand," the WAA's methods limited the flow of transactions to a trickle. Symington pointed out that over a year had passed since V-J Day, but surplus was "still hanging over us," worth millions of dollars, and costing additional millions of dollars monthly to safeguard and maintain.[15]

After considering Symington's complaints, Under Secretary Royall ordered an investigation at Warner Robins Field in Georgia, which prompted a meeting between local AAF officials, WAA personnel, and representatives of the War Department's General Staff. They finally agreed to a disposition process which Royall hoped would establish a precedent.[16]

Symington believed that the swift disposal of surplus property would demonstrate to Congress "that the Air Forces were doing an excellent job." He therefore recommended that the AAF exert continued pressure on the WAA to do its job, especially at the depot level, and he felt that the AAF should keep its

---

* This school helped prepare officers to collect, process, and analyze statistical data regarding the AAF's vast resources. Zuckert's job included teaching the statistical tracking of aircraft, aircraft equipment, unit equipment, recruitment, training, and assignment of personnel.

Survivors of War. Thousands of aircraft of every type, such as these B-29s (*above*) and P-40s (*below*), were stored at various military installations throughout the United States. Many remained overseas. The disposition of vast amounts of AAF surplus property became the responsibility of the Assistant Secretary of War for Air.

"own skirts clean" by promptly designating any excess stock, by cooperating fully to expedite paperwork, and by resorting only in necessity to freezes, withdrawals and other practices which might hamper the disposal agency's operations. Finally, he urged that the AAF keep up-to-date, easily available performance records on its "part of the disposal job."[17]

As important to the AAF as the disposal of surplus property was readiness in the event of national emergency. Equipment and facilities had to be marshalled to enable rapid mobilization. Symington was as familiar with mobilization as he was with surplus property management through first-hand experience at Emerson Electric, and he firmly believed that the aircraft industry should be ready to act under a specific emergency plan in the event of future conflict. He believed that a policy statement from the Army-Navy Munitions Board would be necessary before the AAF developed a comprehensive strategy for the rapid expansion of aircraft production; and he felt, based on his professional background, that he could contribute to that strategy's design. In light of such innovations as pilotless aircraft (the guided missiles of that era) and the achievement of supersonic speeds, he suggested that air industrial planning be geared to recovery from sudden attack. However, he argued against government subsidy of essential industries, recommending that they establish themselves and prosper according to sound business practices.

Symington further maintained that no industry should be forced to relocate solely for reasons of national defense. Factories should move from admittedly vulnerable industrial areas only "when economic conditions and the extent of the business of the manufacturers make such a move feasible."*[18] He held that the national economy would be best served if government-owned installations and equipment were placed in civilian hands. Plants essential to future industrial mobilization could be declared surplus and sold or leased as soon as possible; their new owners or operators would be prohibited from instituting any structural changes which might impede mass production. He stressed the importance of accelerated production in the early stages of rearmament and advocated a program to maintain the latest models of air weapons and equipment as prototypes for volume manufacture. Finally, he believed that physical security should be enhanced throughout the aircraft industry. He studied the feasibility of underground sites, which he believed could be easily camouflaged to resist damage from high explosive bombs, although not necessarily from nuclear weapons.†[19]

---

* Congress endeavored to distribute defense contracts and jobs nationwide.

† Some of Symington's ideas on industrial mobilization, which had been supported by others, were eventually instituted, but not during his brief tenure as Assistant Secretary of War for Air.

Manpower

One of the most troubling issues facing the OASWA involved achieving and maintaining a "real 70-combat-group program" in the face of crippling personnel reductions.* Symington emphasized to Secretary of War Patterson that the AAF had agreed to accept 400,000 military positions instead of 550,000 on the assumption that it would be furnished additional troops to support the National Guard, the organized Reserve, the Reserve Officers' Training Corps (ROTC) and the Universal Military Training (UMT)† programs.

During the war, the AAF and the War Department had anticipated a significant void in the postwar national defense structure because of demobilization and pressure from Congress and its austerity-minded constituents. The War Department hoped that UMT along with a strong reserve program would be sufficient to field an M-Day (Mobilization Day) force and argued that the cost of maintaining a regular standing army would be unacceptable to the American public. Unlike the War Department, however, the AAF in 1945 expressed doubt about whether UMT would provide the skills necessary to a 70-group Air Force, charging that the program depended solely on available aircrews and aircraft to absorb most of the military trainees intended for a proposed 400,000-strong AAF. Because Congress was no closer to passing UMT legislation by early 1946, Symington complained that the AAF was at that point having great difficulty absorbing these training components and taking over jobs formerly performed by the Army Service Forces.

Complicating matters was a reduction of civilian AAF jobs from 200,000 to 131,000, necessitating the filling of key positions by uniformed personnel. As a result, Symington concluded that "any further semblance of a 70-Group Program cannot be maintained without kidding the War Department, the administration, the Congress, and the people . . . These cuts in personnel," he added, "have in turn cut to pieces the planned program of the Air Force."[20]

Symington's colleagues helped him prepare the transition of the AAF to the United States Air Force (USAF) and solve other, less basic problems as well. In charge of routine operation of the OASWA was a new executive officer, Brig. Gen. Turner A. Sims, Jr., who had replaced Colonel Odom in May 1946. Sims had been working across the hall from Symington's office as executive officer

---

* The 70-Group Program was deemed by the AAF as necessary to the defense of U.S. interests at home and abroad. Attaining that strength became a problem which continued to plague the AAF after it achieved independence. Symington and the OSAF would become deeply enmeshed in this issue in 1948. For a detailed account of the evolution of the 70-Group Program see Herman S. Wolk, *Planning and Organizing the Postwar Air Force, 1943–1947* (Washington: Office of Air Force History, 1984).

† UMT provided for the drafting of all men in the United States of a prescribed age They would be subject to physical and mental examinations as well as to training and service for a definite period determined by law.

for Lt. Gen. Ira C. Eaker, Deputy Commander of the AAF. Symington hoped, in a time of rapid technological change, to draw upon Sims's experience at the Air Materiel Command at Wright Field in Ohio, where he had provided technical advice to the commanding general and at various times had headed the propeller laboratory, the wind tunnel, and an experimental aircraft projects section.

General Sims directed the OASWA during Symington's three-month recuperation from an operation during the spring of 1947. He felt that his most pressing task was organizing and staffing the soon-to-be-independent Air Force, even though the nation's workforce was responding more to the attractions of private rather than public employment with the new peace. Sims shared Symington's determination to control costs at all echelons of the AAF, but, unlike his superior, he believed in government support of the aircraft industry. While Symington wanted the industry to pay its way, Sims held that only with adequate federal support would it be capable of outfitting an air force in the event of emergency. He cited the delays in rearmament that occurred between 1939 and 1941 to illustrate his point and argued that an "industrial mobilization plan is not worth the paper it is written on unless industry can produce equipment . . . at the time it is required." He added that the AAF must do more to stabilize the industry at some agreed-upon level of production and research. Finally, he called for sufficient transport aircraft to hold and supply advance bases as well as a strong "national reserve."[21] Symington directed that a workable organization chart for the new Department of the Air Force be drawn up, incorporating such AAF reserve components as the Air Guard and the Air Reserve to "eliminate the friction between them and the Regular Air Force establishment and to make them a more effective part of the air power team."*[22]

Cost Control

Robert Lovett had foreseen the need for the adaptation of successful AAF wartime principles and procedures to a peacetime economy. He had likened the AAF to a large business which required corporate support systems, particularly a comptroller's office.[23] Stuart Symington realized in 1946 that gaining authority and responsibility over AAF spending and accounting would prove difficult. He took issue with the Secretary of War, who advocated the existing practice whereby the military services obtained their supplies from other agencies of the War Department. Under such a scheme, the AAF's chemicals would be provided by the Army Chemical Warfare Service; its cannon would be developed by

---

* In fairness, it should be noted that Sims's statements were made nearly a year later than Symington's. The realities of an inert aircraft industry as well as of foreign events more than likely abetted Symington's decision to support Sims's position. Sims, when giving his advice, might have been parroting Symington's views.

the Ordnance Corps; and its uniforms would be bought by the Quartermaster Corps. Symington strenuously objected to the air arm's operating from so dependent a position, citing the Army Technical Service's past attempts to dictate to the AAF the type and quantity of equipment it should acquire. To Symington, the larger issue was the need by the AAF to control its own support network. The authority "to specify the type and quantity of equipment necessary to carry out its missions" rested, he believed, with the using agency. He argued that the AAF should not be penalized for inaccuracies within the budgetary estimates prepared by the War Department's supply agencies, and he questioned the ability of agencies providing services to infantry, armor, and artillery to defend the budget for the air arm. Nothing, Symington declared, should prevent "our instituting normal standards of control."[24] General Spaatz agreed with Symington and urged him to make their view known as forcefully as possible before Congress. Their position, seconded by Maj. Gen. Hugh J. Knerr, Secretary General of the Air Board, a policy recommending group, became integral to the AAF's drive for independence.

Symington envisioned an air arm with the same authority as the Army and the Navy, with a civilian head equal in power and status to the Secretaries of the Navy and War, and with full responsibility for its own research, development, and procurement. It would establish standards for personnel, materiel, and services, would apportion the funds appropriated to it by Congress, and would reimburse the War Department's Technical Services for any support rendered. Finally, the air arm would operate a network of bases and develop its own system of maintenance and supply after independence.[25]

In controlling costs, Symington drew directly upon his business experience, deciding that as Emerson Electric rewarded efficiency and punished waste, so should the AAF.[26] It was critical that the AAF conquer its entrenched inefficiency and "lack of knowledge of the importance of . . . figures to the operations of a business." He wished to demonstrate to both Congress and the public that the AAF could keep its own house in order and set a standard of cost control and efficiency throughout the armed forces.

But could a military organization operate as successfully as a business? Symington saw this as an absolute requirement, the inevitable adjustment to peacetime. In wartime the air arm had been able to spend whatever was necessary, developing a B-32, for example, should the B-29 fail. Symington wanted the AAF to account for every dollar. Those responsible for pilot training, for example, now had to weigh the cost of gasoline against the skills another hour in the air might develop. Planners had to decide which bases could be most productive for the least investment. New economies meant determining the size of the fighting force according to the number of airplanes, people, and runways that could be purchased with appropriated funds.

Symington wanted cost control to show the AAF how to live within its means and adjust to the austerity of peacetime.[27] He soon discovered, however, that he could not even obtain statistics when he required them. "Why," he asked, "do I have to send out a search party every time I want a number in the Air Force?"[28] Building on Lovett's concepts and working with Eugene Zuckert, Symington asked Generals Spaatz and Eaker to establish the Office of the Comptroller in June 1946. Brig. Gen. Grandison Gardner became the first Air Comptroller* and five months later was replaced by Lt. Gen. E. W. Rawlings.†[29]

Begun in 1946 during the campaign for an independent Air Force, the cost control program would significantly improve the management of the new service. Critics within the War Department predicted that inexperienced AAF officers would be unable to cope with cost-cutting measures. Symington responded that they would likely prove more adept at it than long-time bureaucrats in the other services whose own ability rested on doubtful methods. He promptly arranged that modern business management training courses be offered for their benefit.[30] The AAF, Symington emphasized, "had an unusual opportunity to look toward efficiency, no past heritages, no barnacled procedures to first overcome."[31] He did not, however, insist that it turn its back on the older services. "Our policy is to seek integration with the other services wherever possible, and whenever we can utilize, within the framework of the policies of the Defense Establishment, common services for the fulfillment of our requirements, we intend to do so." Symington wanted the air arm to profit from eventual unification of the services.[32] By early 1949 he was able to report that cost consciousness throughout the Air Force was being emphasized in the "Management Control through Cost Control" program.[33]

Independence

Much of the ground work for an independent Air Force had been completed by the time Secretary Symington took office. President Truman, Secretary Lovett, as well as Generals Arnold and Spaatz and other AAF leaders had testified in support of an independent air force before Congress in 1945. President Truman, addressing a joint session, had called for "air parity." He had also pressured both Secretary of War Robert Patterson and Secretary of the Navy James

---

* General Gardner had been one of the AAF's observers in England in 1940. During World War II he held several positions as an armament expert before heading the AAF Proving Ground Command from 1942 to 1945. He had also served as deputy to the chairman of the U.S. Strategic Bombing Survey before becoming the Air Comptroller.

† General Rawlings had earned an MBA from Harvard University in 1939. He was considered one of the AAF's outstanding production and procurement authorities. Besides Symington, General Rawlings, in his *Report on the Comptrollership within the Air Force, 1946–1951*, credited Robert Lovett, Generals Arnold, Spaatz, Eaker and Vandenberg along with Eugene Zuckert and Edmund Learned for their help in establishing a service comptroller.

Forrestal to help speed the passage of legislation for a National Military Establishment which included a separate air force. By May 1946, even though in profound disagreement over the issue of roles and missions, they agreed to postpone further arguments, cooperate, and support the establishment of a Department of National Defense as outlined in pending Senate legislation (S 2044). Complicating the settlement of roles and missions was the Navy's and the AAF's dispute over larger strategic questions such as which service would deliver the atomic bomb and control guided missiles. General Eisenhower maintained that the President might have to intervene and decide himself. In any case, Symington kept a watchful eye on the issue for the Air Force as he helped to push the National Security Act through Congress.[34]

As noted, many of the specific activities in which Symington engaged were part of his larger vision for eventual air independence. He undertook efforts to deal with industrial mobilization, force levels, and cost control to make the AAF master of its own house. To this end, he carefully orchestrated his subordinates' activities. He sent Col. John B. Montgomery to Britain to confer with high ranking Royal Air Force (RAF) officers about gaining air autonomy and assigned Brig. Gen. James D. McIntyre to handle congressional relations.

Symington firmly believed that unification under a National Military Establishment and a Department of National Defense would save the government money and, in early 1947, he pressed the point spiritedly before Congress. The services had measured success in terms of relative appropriations. They had viewed acquiring funds as most critical; they had viewed deciding how they should be spent as less so. Whether under the "New National Defense" system cost consciousness would "permeate all levels of service management"[35] remained to be seen; funds would eventually be apportioned throughout three services rather than two.

Symington did not hesitate to admonish commanders who seemed unwilling to help in the drive toward independence. In May 1947, during debate over the unification bill, he warned General George C. Kenney, Commander of the Strategic Air Command (SAC), not to emphasize the primacy of strategic air forces in the nation's defense phalanx. Symington feared that opponents of the bill in the services and in Congress would mistakenly assume "that the Air Force is out to prove that the main way to win a war is through strategic bombing," and he urged circumspection.[36] He reminded Kenney that the AAF was in the final round of the unification fight and if "we don't win it, and the war [unification battle] is officially declared over, the Air Force reverts to its previous impossible position as a minor addendum to the War Department."[37]

The AAF and the War Department believed that there should be three coordinate service branches, each having a civilian head and a military commander. Each civilian head should function as autonomously as possible and have access to the President. The Navy, on the other hand, demanded that the integrity of the Department of the Navy, headed by a civilian of cabinet rank, be maintained. The

**General George C. Kenney, Commander, Strategic Air Command,
testifies before Congress during its 1947 hearings on service unification
and the independence of the air forces.**

Navy argued that it had integrated aviation as soundly within its structure as it
had other components, both surface and subsurface. The Army, it believed,
could do likewise.[38]

The AAF and the War Department believed that the independent air force
should assume responsibility for the development, procurement, maintenance,
and operation of military aviation. They nonetheless acknowledged that the
Navy had certain responsibilities requiring land-based aircraft. These responsibilities—essential internal administration, transport over routes of sole interest
to naval forces, and training—should remain vested with the Navy or the
Marines. Secretary of War Robert P. Patterson and Army Chief of Chief
General Dwight D. Eisenhower believed that several completely self-sufficient
services were luxuries the nation could ill afford. They argued that with respect
to land-based aircraft there were no "purely naval functions which justify
uneconomical duplication of equipment and installations."[39] Eisenhower supported an Air Force coordinate with the Army and the Navy, arguing that "such
parity was mandatory for the nation's postwar security."[40]

The Navy asserted that it was perfectly capable of assessing and administering its own aviation. It wanted complete control over the design, procurement, and operation of the land-based aircraft it used in reconnaissance, anti-
submarine warfare, and the protection of shipping. It also wanted complete
control over the special training required of all personnel engaged in these
activities. It believed firmly that any efforts by the AAF to limit naval aviation
would, if successful, impair sea power and jeopardize national security.[41]

With the struggle for independence, the authority of the OASWA grew.
Symington's advocacy of a separate service took him to the halls of Congress

and to almost every corner of the country. While General Spaatz attended to the daily operations of the AAF, Air Secretary Symington was very much out front and visible.

Stuart Symington's vision of the postwar Air Force grew from the concept of civilian control developed in Henry Stimson's War Department and bequeathed to him by Robert Lovett. The military departments would function under the President's leadership and the strategic guidance of the Joint Chiefs of Staff (JCS). Upcoming legislation would guarantee this and provide a formal structure for the new national defense program.

Symington looked to Lovett's relationship with Generals Arnold and Marshall. The close interaction and single purpose of the secretary and the chief of the military component had been essential in war and would be in peace.

On the eve of air independence the Assistant Secretary of War for Air was, because of his experience with industry during the war and with the AAF in 1946 and 1947, exceptionally well prepared for the extraordinary challenges that lay ahead.

Chapter 3

Separate and Equal: The First Secretariat

The National Security Act of 1947 (Public Law 253), passed on July 26, established the Department of the Air Force and the United States Air Force (USAF), fulfilling the dreams and aspirations held for many years by U.S. Army air leaders. The act created a National Military Establishment (NME) which included three military departments, Army, Navy, and Air Force. Although it made the Air Force equal to the Army and the Navy, the act was at best a compromise that left many issues unresolved. Its supporters understood that it would have to be revised. On September 18, 1947, W. Stuart Symington took the oath of office as Secretary of the Air Force upon activation of the Office of the Secretary of the Air Force (OSAF). He became head of the Department of the Air Force and was assisted by an under secretary and two assistant secretaries.[1]

With his new status, Symington held more authority over the Air Force and within the Department of Defense (DOD) than he did as Assistant Secretary of War for Air when he functioned chiefly as an advisor to the Army Air Forces (AAF) on procurement and aviation. In 1947 he became equal to the Secretaries of the Army and the Navy.

The service secretaries were obliged to some extent to answer to Secretary of Defense James V. Forrestal, who acted more as a coordinator than an administrator, however, and did not exercise the same authority over them as Henry Stimson and Robert Patterson had. As Secretary of the Air Force, Symington sat on the National Security Council (NSC), and, because he was friendly with President Harry Truman, could go directly to him whenever he wished to circumvent the Office of the Secretary of Defense (OSD). He maneuvered much more independently in his new position, and although he had to consult with Forrestal and Bureau of the Budget Director James Webb on financial matters, he operated quite freely, focusing on issues that interested him personally and brought him before Congress.

Symington announced that he would pursue four primary objectives. He wanted, first of all, a modern and efficient 70-group Air Force; second, a trained Air National Guard and Air Force Reserve; third, an adequate commercial air transport industry to support Air Force needs; and fourth, a healthy aircraft and component production industry.

Symington believed that by emphasizing economy through the application of modern business techniques to Air Force management he could best achieve

Stuart Symington, former Assistant Secretary of War for Air, is sworn in as the first Secretary of the Air Force by Chief Justice Fred Vinson, September 18, 1947. Looking on are (*left to right*) Secretary of the Army Kenneth Royall, Secretary of Defense James Forrestal, and Secretary of the Navy John Sullivan.

his aims at a time when Congress, the President, and the American people were eager to return to peacetime spending. Realizing that promoting economy would not necessarily preclude a struggle for funds, he introduced what he called "Management Control through Cost Control." An outgrowth of the AAF's wartime management and statistical control, it would be the backbone of his economy drive and set "procedures for detection and reward" to foster "logistic (business) efficiency . . . and operational (flying) efficiency." [2]

Symington worked as hard to achieve a cooperative spirit between the services as he did to acquire funds for Air Force programs. He achieved a model cooperative association with the military leaders of the Air Force but at times vigorously disputed the policies of President Truman, Secretary of Defense Forrestal, Bureau of the Budget Director Webb, and the other service secretaries. Any struggles that occurred were primarily over funding and pitted the administration, represented by Forrestal and Webb, against the service secretaries and their military chiefs. No struggles occurred between the civilian and military elements of the Air Force.

The Air Force's formative first year was a time of experimentation and learning. Some of the many problems which arose were settled during Symington's tenure; others defied solution until later. Both the transfer of functions from the Army to the Air Force—scheduled to take two years—and the planning for new Air Force organizations such as the Air Force Engineering Development Center (later Arnold Engineering Development Center) were begun immediately.

Decisions on the location and design of the Air Force Academy, however, were deferred until such local environmental factors as weather and its effect on flying could be studied.

Symington himself had to endure a period of adjustment before establishing a sense of order and routine. He was responsible for assigning duties; and if his authority was challenged, as it was when he sought to establish Air Force responsibility for procurement, administration, and personnel, he was not averse to imposing his will on dissenters. Under the National Security Act of 1947 the new Air Secretary had, besides additional authority, a high degree of flexibility in organizing his office. He was not forced into a mandatory organizational mold but could shape the Air Force according to its needs. With his business background, previous government experience, contact with the AAF, and understanding of military requirements, he set out to establish the most efficient organization possible. Symington organized the OSAF to facilitate direct contact by the Air Staff with its civilian and military counterparts on his team. Thus he and Air Force Chief of Staff General Carl A. Spaatz were able to maintain close supervision over the handful of operators to whom they delegated authority and to concentrate their own "individual and collaborative efforts on problems of the first magnitude."[3] Symington's role as chief spokesman for the Air Force before Congress had been established during his tenure as Assistant Secretary of War for Air. He and General Spaatz worked out a *modus operandi* whereby Spaatz provided information on military needs and Symington conveyed that information to Capitol Hill. They also agreed that Symington would not directly involve himself in operational matters.

Seven days after the passage of the National Security Act, Arthur S. Barrows became Under Secretary of the Air Force. Cornelius V. Whitney and Eugene M. Zuckert took their oaths of office as Assistant Secretaries of the Air Force. Barrows's long business career had culminated in the presidency and later vice chairmanship of the board of Sears, Roebuck and Company. After retiring, he was induced by Symington, a long-time friend, to share his vast management expertise with the fledgling Department of the Air Force. Whitney was related to Symington's wife, had served on General Eisenhower's staff during World War II, and possessed a wealth of business experience. Symington believed that the Whitney name, famous since the late 19th century in American finance and politics, would lend the Air Force prestige. Zuckert had worked for Symington, who regarded him highly, since 1946. All appointments including Symington's, were confirmed by the Senate on December 8, 1947, and approved by the President the next day.[4]

Initially, the under secretary and assistant secretaries undertook whatever duties Symington assigned to them, but after a brief period, they functioned according to a formally adopted division of labor. (See Appendix 1, OSAF Organization Charts, p. 261.) Barrows concentrated on procurement, production, research and development, liaison with the Atomic Energy Commission, and planning for industrial mobilization. He was a shrewd, no-nonsense negotiator who expected contractors to honor their agreements. When some of them complained that their companies were the subjects of unfavorable Air Force rumors, Barrows retorted, "We haven't said anything bad about you, we've just let it be known that we think you're a bunch of cheap, chiseling thieves."[5]

Cornelius Whitney became Assistant Secretary of the Air Force (Civil Affairs). He worked with other government agencies on military-diplomatic air matters, negotiated land purchases for air bases, and developed agreements for the protection and defense of U.S. bases on foreign soil. He also coordinated with the State Department and other agencies on international security. Whitney was a liaison with the Air Staff on planning and intelligence and represented the Department of the Air Force on the Air Coordinating Committee and other boards designated by the Air Secretary.

As Assistant Secretary of the Air Force (Management), Eugene Zuckert was responsible for programming, cost control, and organizational and budgetary planning, having overseen the same functions as special assistant to the Secretary of War.[6] Breathing life into the concept of Management Control through Cost Control to attain "the best defense per tax dollar expended," he instituted such accepted industrial and business techniques as comprehensive statistical reporting whereby a comptroller insured the proper distribution of centrally collected information to Air Force managers worldwide. Zuckert maintained that no one ever knew exactly what the slogan Management Control through Cost Control meant, but by repeating it, the Air Force seemed, at least to Congress, the most cost-conscious of the military branches. Zuckert also informed Symington of budgetary developments within the OSD and represented the Air Force's position on monetary policy taken up by the OSD, the Bureau of the Budget, and the House and Senate Appropriations Committees.

The Office of the Secretary of the Air Force

Anticipating the need for a clearly defined "pecking order," especially during his absences from Washington, Secretary Symington established a chain of authority. His hierarchy placed the Secretary of the Air Force at the top, followed by the Under Secretary of the Air Force, then the Assistant Secretary of the Air Force (Civil Affairs) and the Assistant Secretary of the Air Force (Management).* In early 1948, the Secretary of the Air Force found it necessary to expand his office because of an increasing workload. The Under Secretary of

---

* The order of assistant secretaries was reversed on Dec 15, 1949, per OSAF Memo 20-2, Jan 9, 1950. *History of the Office of the Secretary of the Air Force, September 18, 1947, to June 30, 1950,* vol 1, section on the OSAF, CAFH file.

Leading Air Force aides take their oaths of office September 26, 1947. U.S. Air Force Chief of Staff General Carl A. Spaatz looks on as newly appointed Under Secretary of the Air Force Arthur S. Barrows is administered the oath of office by Supreme Court Associate Justice Stanley Reed. Waiting their turns are Assistant Secretaries Eugene M. Zuckert (*left*) and Cornelius V. Whitney.

the Air Force and two assistant secretaries shared five special assistants "to provide better means for establishment of policy, review, and advice, and for assistance in the planning and development of functions which were the operating responsibility of the Chief of Staff."[7] These special assistants performed a variety of tasks but specialized in manpower, personnel, procurement, and installations. Under Symington, the five special assistants and their four appointed supervisors constituted a nine-man team whose members worked closely with each other and the Air Staff. Symington recognized that his personal selection of assistant secretaries and special assistants would not necessarily insure harmony within the OSAF. Various activities had to be defined, specific jobs identified, and an internal structure established. Because Zuckert had become an organizational specialist, he devised a personnel requirements plan and prepared an appropriate manning table for both military and civilian personnel.[8]

With the activation of the Department of the Air Force, 11 positions from the old Office of the Assistant Secretary of War for Air (OSWA) and 44 positions from the former Directorate of Information, AAF Headquarters, were transferred to the OSAF. By October 31, 1947, 29 positions were added, increasing the number of civilian and military personnel to 84 and raising combined annual salaries to $300,000. The following month, Zuckert proposed a nearly four-fold expansion for 1949, projecting a need for 317 positions at a cost of $1.3 million. He explained that these figures compared favorably with the $4 million estimate of both the Navy and the Army.[9] When the National Security Act was passed, the Secretary of the Air Force's salary was $14,500. The Under Secretary of the Air Force and the Assistant Secretaries of the Air Force each received $10,000 per year. (See Table 2 for Zuckert's personnel projections.)

In keeping with Symington's desire to maintain an efficient organization, Zuckert estimated that the OSAF would require 235 positions at a cost of $900,000.[10] He soon revised his estimate to 329 positions (119 officer, 27 enlisted, and 183 civilian) with Symington's approval.*[11]

Although the Air Force was founded on the premise of civilian control, most functions and offices of the OSAF were closely allied with and complemented those of the Air Staff (HQ USAF). Thus the Air Adjutant General served the Air Staff as the Administrative Assistant served the OSAF, and the Air Judge Advocate resolved air force legal problems in coordination with the OSAF's General Counsel. The Air Staff and the OSAF alike hired consultants, and the Air Staff's Deputy Chief of Staff for Personnel handled awards and other employment-related matters for both civilian and military employees.

Three new OSAF positions which proved especially helpful to the Air Secretary, his under secretary, and two assistant secretaries were a General Counsel, a Public Affairs Directorate, and a Legislative and Liaison Directorate, all of which communicated closely with the Air Staff and major command information offices.

The new General Counsel, Brackley Shaw, a former special assistant to the Assistant Secretary of War for Air, assumed office on September 25, 1947. He reported directly to the Secretary of the Air Force as the final authority on all legal questions for the Department of the Air Force. A General Counsel's authority was essential, particularly to the proper administration of the Air Force's procurement program, which was expanding rapidly as various contracts were shifted to it from the Army. Contracting advisors to the Assistant Secretary of War for Air had not been granted final authority on legal questions because they had functioned outside the procurement chain of command.

The Directorate of Public Relations was established on September 20, 1947, replacing a military staff agency. Stephen F. Leo and Maj. Gen. Emmett O'Donnell assumed respectively the posts of Deputy Director of Public Relations and Chief of the Office of Air Information. Symington rated O'Donnell highly and considered Leo the best young newspaperman he knew. Later, to resolve conflicts between the services and to cut costs, Secretary of Defense Forrestal on March 17, 1949, ordered the consolidation of many of the Army's, the Navy's, and the Air Force's public relations organizations. To prevent "quadruplification" of effort, he ordered the establishment of an Office of Public Information within the OSD. It would have sole charge of disseminating infor-

---

* The 329 positons were effective as of June 1948.

Table 2
Office of the Secretary of the Air Force
Civilian Personnel Requirements

	Number	Salary
Secretariat	4	$ 45,000
Office of the Secretary	23	69,660
Office of the Under Secretary	43	160,517
Assistant Secretary (Civil Affairs)	19	85,216
Assistant Secretary (Management)	21	95,574
Administrative Assistant	58	158,989
General Counsel	26	128,623
Office of the Director of Public Relations	13	48,301
Air Information Division	47	164,832
Legislative & Liaison Division	33	98,007
Air Force Personnel Board	27	71,768
Air Force Awards Board	3	7,433
Special Consultants	—	150,000
Estimated Overtime	—	15,000
TOTAL	317	$ 1,298,920

Source: Office of the Administrative Assistant, Correspondence and Control Division Budget Estimates and Justifications 1948–1954, RG 340, Office of the Secretary of the Air Force, NARA.

Former journalist Stephen F. Leo, Director of Public Relations in the new Office of the Secretary of the Air Force, receives the Exceptional Civilian Service Award from Chief of Staff General Hoyt S. Vandenberg.

mation about the NME. To comply with Forrestal's order, Symington limited his public relations staff to 110.

On December 27, 1947, the responsibility for all congressional correspondence regarding the Air Force was transferred from the Army's Legislative and Liaison Department to the Air Force's Legislative and Liaison Division. The Legislative and Liaison Division had been organized within the Directorate of Public Relations until it was elevated to directorate status in August 1948. The original staff of three officers and five civilians, all Army transferees, increased to a total of sixty-three by September 1948 (thirty-four officers and twenty-nine civilians). This directorate, after consultation with the Air Staff, helped draft legislative proposals and analyzed and prepared recommendations concerning proposed or pending legislation. It also monitored all Air Force congressional testimony and correspondence.[12]

Controversies

The Air Force had scarcely achieved independence and established the new OSAF when it was faced with two embarrassing incidents. Perhaps the more publicized was the case of Maj. Gen. Bennett E. Meyers. During the war, General Meyers, who had served on the Air Staff as Deputy Chief, Logistics, profited from the ownership of a company established specifically to channel public funds to him through false contracts. Investigating his illegal activities, a committee headed by Senator Homer Ferguson of Michigan wanted to know whether Meyers retired in June 1945 on the basis of a nonexistent disability; whether a cover-up designed to ease him out of the AAF without acknowledgment of his wartime fraud was conducted with the approval of General Arnold; and, finally, whether his crime should have been detected earlier and a court martial promptly scheduled.

The Ferguson Committee accused the Air Force of failing to move as early as 1945 against Meyers after an anonymous letter incriminating him arrived at AAF Headquarters. Symington responded that the AAF could not delve into Meyers's financial affairs because it had no legal authority to subpoena his bank accounts and business records. He did not address whether the AAF had too willingly accepted Meyers's denials of wrongdoing. Once the investigation, which started in October 1947, turned up evidence of guilt, the Air Force approached the Justice Department.[13] Symington maintained that the service had no choice but to defer any consideration of a court martial until the Ferguson Committee completed its hearings and released its records to prosecutors in the Justice Department. He credited Senator Ferguson with performing a valuable public service by exposing "this officer who has so flagrantly broken his oath to his flag."[14]

Because the Justice Department planned to charge Meyers with subornation of perjury, Symington proposed that the Air Force, in the event of a court martial, charge him with conduct unbecoming an officer, "unless Justice specifically states in writing, that they do not want us to . . ."[15] Meyers, however, demanded in General Spaatz's presence that Symington order a court martial in lieu of a civilian trial, and when Symington refused, threatened to implicate key Air Force officials, including General Arnold. Symington told Meyers, "Any chance you ever had of a court martial just went out the window."*[16]

Meyers was tried in civilian court. On March 15, 1948, he was convicted in U.S. District Court for the District of Columbia on three counts of subornation of perjury and sentenced to prison for twenty months to five years. On July 16, 1948, President Truman signed an order dismissing him from service.[17] He lost all government benefits, which had been suspended, at Symington's insistence, when he was accused of inducing Bleriot H. La Marre, dummy president of one of the false companies, to lie in court. The former general spent almost three years behind bars.

However distressing the Meyers case might have been to Symington, it showed him clearly that the Air Force needed a procurement system to prevent what he termed so "disgraceful" a fraud from occurring again.[18] He assigned the

---

* Symington recalled General Spaatz's penchant for calm under pressure as well as his sense of humor. When Maj. Gen. Bennet E. Meyers left Symington's office, angered because he had been refused a court-martial (instead of a civil trial) and had threatened to implicate some very important Air Force people, Symington turned to Spaatz and asked: "Tooey, what do you think?" Spaatz answered: " I think that I never won in a poker game with him in thirty years." Intvw, W. Stuart Symington by author, Oct 21, 1981.

task of formulating such a system to Under Secretary Barrows, an expert on procurement, planning, and administration. Barrows began studying all aspects of the procurement process "incident to standardizing, streamlining, and allocating of straight line operating authority along with responsibility."[19] He was able to reform it and monitored it closely not only at his own office, but at Wright Field as well.

As a result of the Meyers case, Congress concluded that the Air Force should have primary responsibility for detecting and preventing fraud and impropriety within its own ranks, both uniformed and civilian. Secretary Symington, thereupon, directed a study which revealed that the service's investigative methods were "confused" and "haphazard." He urged that J. Edgar Hoover, Director of the Federal Bureau of Investigation (FBI), assign Col. Joseph F. Carroll,* a successful criminal investigator for the Surplus Property Office, to the Air Force. Hoover did so and Carroll became the first director of the new Office of Special Investigations (OSI). The Meyers incident, according to Symington, more than any other, was directly responsible for that office's creation.†[20]

Less serious than the Meyers case was the Air Force's dispute with the nationally known journal, *Aviation Week*. According to its publisher, Robert F. Boyer, Air Force public relations officers had tried to persuade certain military aviation equipment suppliers to curtail or cease advertising in the magazine. The Air Force looked into his charge and declared it groundless.[21] Meanwhile, Stephen F. Leo, Director of Public Relations, had discovered classified information in the magazine on the Bell XS-1, the first in a series of rocket-powered research planes, and he alerted Symington. Symington then complained to James H. McGraw, Jr., president of *Aviation Week*'s owner, McGraw-Hill Publishing Company, pointing out that the magazine had, in its exclusive stories and coverage of new technological developments, violated a pledge to withhold certain facts about the plane.[22] Later, *Aviation Week*'s chief editor, Eugene Duffield, admitted that Symington was correct and promised to exercise greater caution in future. As a result of this incident, Symington proposed that Secretary of Defense Forrestal direct service representatives to develop a uniform policy on the release of technical information.‡[23]

No sooner had Symington laid the Meyers and *Aviation Week* controversies to rest than he was called before Congress and questioned about the recommendations of the O'Brian Board. He testified vociferously against two in particu-

---

* Carroll later became head of the Defense Intelligence Agency (DIA). General Carroll maintained that W. Stuart Symington more than any other person was responsible for the establishment of the Office of Special Investigations (OSI). Intvw, Maj. Gen. Joseph F. Carroll by Edward Mishler, Feb 22, 1982.

† This office still existed in 1988 as a special operating agency and was known as the Air Force Office of Special Investigations (AFOSI).

‡ Present day DOD classification codes do not owe their beginnings to Symington, but he might have influenced their ranking.

lar—that flying and submarine duty pay be discontinued and that death benefits be increased. The board was established in early 1947 by the Secretaries of War and Navy and headed by John Lord O'Brian, a Washington attorney. After reviewing the board's findings at Forrestal's request, Symington declared them "ludicrous" and not "practicable or in the best interests of national security."[24] He complained that they reflected the board's ignorance of military aviation and cautioned that the elimination of flying pay "would soon render [the Air Force] incapable of fulfilling its responsibilities to the nation."[25] Flying pay, he maintained, attracted competent Air Force personnel to a hazardous but necessary career activity. Later in the year he attacked another committee's objection to flying pay in time of war, declaring again that the Air Force could not approve or support any pay plan that failed to provide adequate compensation for flying.[26] Because of Symington's spirited attempts to persuade Congress that it should be protected, flying pay was retained and threats of its termination were thwarted.

By early 1948, the OSAF was forced to refute charges of waste by Senator Henry Cabot Lodge of Massachusetts who questioned Symington about the Greek government's use of American tax dollars to purchase British Spitfires, even though surplus Air Force fighters were available in Germany. The Air Secretary acknowledged the Greek government's receipt of U.S. funds to purchase aircraft for use against Communist-led insurrectionists. He explained that the Greek Air Force was familiar with Spitfires, but not with American aircraft, and that the transfer of American aircraft to Greece would create problems of supply, maintenance, and training. In addition, the United Kingdom was supplying spare parts at a fraction of their original cost. Symington conceded that at the end of the war a large number of U.S. planes remained in Germany. They were, however, obsolete; Congress would have been obliged to divert money from research and development of new models to pay for their storage. Moreover, the cost of their return to the United States for sale as salvage would have been prohibitive.[27]

Symington Exerts His Charm

Symington's greatest strength was dealing with Congress, perfected when he spoke before its delegations during World War II and served as Assistant Secretary of War for Air. He thus felt qualified to inform General Spaatz that he was dissatisfied with Air Force briefings, particularly those he had witnessed before such powerful groups, individuals, and agencies as the Finletter Commission,* the Secretary of Defense, and the Bureau of the Budget. In September

---

* The Finletter Commission, headed by Thomas K. Finletter, prepared a report, published in January 1948, on national aviation policy at President Truman's request in July 1947.

1947 he set out to improve Air Force performances and quicken their too leisurely pace by imposing new requirements—professionally orchestrated presentations supported with written reports and eye-catching instructional charts. These extensive preparations, he insisted, would enable a listener to "follow with his eyes as well as his ears," save time, and insure acceptance of Air Force points of view by more receptive audiences.* "I don't think," Symington commented, "that Mr. Forrestal [would] appreciate hearing briefings . . . from a bunch of notes . . . On the contrary," he continued, "I think he would much prefer to hear and read at the same time . . . a carefully prepared package in order, if he so desires, that he can take the facts away with him for further study . . ."[28] Symington developed, according to Zuckert, a defensive strategy to protect the new Air Force and enhance its position. He skillfully used public relations and legislative and liaison specialists to prevent or minimize damage to the Air Force's image.

According to Eugene Zuckert, Symington was able to keep in touch personally with almost every facet of his operation without becoming mired in detail. He was concerned about enlisted personnel throughout the Air Force, questioned them personally whenever he could, and pushed, often abrasively, the bureaucracy to better serve their needs. He was deeply involved in the development and general organization of his entire office.

Under his guidance the Air Force pioneered in adapting for government the techniques of American business such as cost surveys and budget controls. He allowed his statutory appointees a free hand in performing their specific duties and backed them fully, provided they achieved what he wanted.[29]

Symington had the greatest respect for his Chiefs of Staff General Carl A. Spaatz and General Hoyt S. Vandenberg, and their relationships with him and with each other solidified during his tenure. Zuckert maintained that although the differences between military and civilian elements were less distinct during Spaatz's and Symington's amicable association, one thing was clear: Symington was the boss. Col. Glen W. Martin, Symington's executive officer from October 1948 to April 1950, maintained that the civilian side of the OSAF "wielded a branding iron, not a rubber stamp," and neither ignored nor suppressed any voice or recommendation. He further asserted that decisions were "made at the top level of responsibility" by Symington.[30]

Symington enthusiastically supported and credited innovators. Robert Lovett, for example, during his tenure as Assistant Secretary of War for Air, had often insisted that a comptroller would greatly increase the efficiency of AAF operations. Symington agreed and adapted much of Lovett's thinking on the

---

* It is not known whether Symington influenced the way Air Force congressional presentations are planned today, but the problem of clarity still exists because of increasingly sophisticated Air Force weapon systems. Symington most likely realized the difficulty of trying to sell Congress something it could not comprehend.

Secretary of the Air Force W. Stuart Symington with General Carl A. Spaatz *(left)*, first Chief of Staff of the Air Force, and his successor, General Hoyt S. Vandenberg, during retirement ceremonies for General Spaatz on July 1, 1948. Secretary Symington worked amicably and effectively with both chiefs in the early days of the Air Force's independence.

benefits of a comptrollership to his Management Control through Cost Control program for fiscal responsibility. Symington was exactly what the Air Force needed at the time: an intelligent, energetic, forthright, and strong-willed leader with the ability to analyze problems thoroughly and lure competent experts to work in a challenging, yet enjoyable, environment.[31]

Symington thus saw the wisdom in Defense Secretary Forrestal's recommendation that the Air Force and the Navy employ a standard method by which to determine their aircraft needs. Complaining that the divergent methods used by the services "gave rise to confusion and cast doubt on the validity of each," the Defense Secretary maintained that a single method of calculating numbers of replacement aircraft would instill greater confidence in the accuracy and soundness of annual military requests.[32]

Symington designated Maj. Gen. Frederic H. Smith, Jr.,* to discuss the matter for the Air Force at a series of conferences with Navy representatives.[33]

---

* During the war, General Smith served as Deputy Chief of the Air Staff, Headquarters, AAF, and Commanding General, Fighter Command, in the Philippines and Okinawa. After the war, he returned to Headquarters, AAF, to head the Office of

After deliberating for more than a month, the conferees were unable to come to terms by Forrestal's deadline—his 1950 military budget justification to Congress. General Smith reported to Symington that necessary changes would be too far-reaching for immediate implementation, and he expressed hope that a formula would be accepted in time for the 1951 budget justification.[34] The issue would be raised again, but both services retained their own methods.

Building the New Air Force

In 1947 other important activities engaging the OSAF included determining the rate at which the B-29 could be taken out of storage; increasing runway length to accommodate jet aircraft and provide greater take-off distance; establishing an in-flight refueling program for bombardment aircraft; purchasing turbo jet and turbo prop engines; leasing 115 C-46F aircraft to responsible operators at a monthly rental of $300; comparing the jet and the long-range propeller fighter; and selling military aircraft to other American republics.

With Symington's support, the Air Force looked to aerial refueling to extend the range of its strategic bombers and fighter escorts. General Spaatz and a special committee he headed studied the merits of aerial refueling and endorsed it fully to enhance the 1,500 nautical-mile combat radius limitation of the Air Force's new medium bomber, the B-47 (due to enter the Air Force's inventory in late 1951). In June 1948, the Strategic Air Command (SAC) activated its first air refueling squadrons, the 43d and 509th, at Davis-Monthan and Roswell Air Force Bases.

Because new engines were needed to power jet aircraft, the Air Force continued its jet and turbojet experimental program begun during World War II. After disappointing tests with the P-59A, the Air Force had turned to the J33 turbojet engine and designated it for the P-80 fighter. Later, the more powerful and more fuel efficient J35 was used in the Shooting Star. On February 28, 1946, this engine powered the XF-84's first flight and in August 1947 propelled the Douglas Skystreak (D-558) to a world speed record. The Air Force also contracted with the Pratt and Whitney Corporation to conduct experiments with its version of the turbojet engine, the XJ57. The engine, which had a 9,000 pound thrust and was capable of operating at 55,000 feet, was later used for the B-52 intercontinental bomber, Century series fighters, the KC-135, and the B-57D.[35]

Under Secretary Barrows suggested that the Air Force purchase a promising new British-made turbojet to analyze its design features and conduct exten-

---

Special Organizational Plans. Later, he served as Chief of Staff, Strategic Air Command (SAC), at Bolling Air Force Base, Washington, D.C.

The Air Force Modernizes. New aircraft such as the B-47 medium bomber (*above*) could be aerially refueled for extended range. The jet engine was a spectacular leap in aviation technology. Two models, the centrifugal-flow J33 and the more advanced axial-flow J35, successfully powered the P-80 (*center*) and the F-84 (*below*) respectively.

sive performance tests. He reasoned that Britain could repay much of the aid it expected from the proposed European Recovery Program by waiving its patent rights and license fees, thus allowing the construction of its engines in the United States. He recommended that the British government be asked to supply three turbojets, one turboprop engine, and spare parts. Symington agreed with Barrows and convinced Defense Secretary Forrestal that a technically qualified Air Force representative accompany General Spaatz to discuss the exchange with the British.[36] During the next few years, several joint engine-development projects between U.S. and British manufacturers were undertaken.

When Congress questioned the Air Force's choice of turbojet rather than piston-engine fighters, Symington and Spaatz maintained that the necessity for additional speed, even at the expense of range, determined their decision. They emphasized that any potential enemy would be employing jet-propelled aircraft. No propeller fighter could outdistance a jet fighter which flew almost a hundred knots faster. While Symington realized that the jet fighter of that day could not provide long-range escort for bombers, he was confident that as "our armed forces gain strength . . . we will be able to inaugurate mass bombing attacks under fighter cover." He did not predict when or how this would happen.[37]

The sale to other American republics of aircraft that were not vitally needed at home or likely to become instruments of a recipient nation's aggression posed no difficulty. To "preclude approval of purchases which interfere with Air Force procurement or which are inimical to hemisphere solidarity from the military point of view,"[38] Symington urged that the Department of State coordinate the approval of export licenses with each transaction. Former Assistant Secretary of War for Air, Robert Lovett, who by 1947 was acting Secretary of State, heeded the Air Force's caution and agreed that his department would consult with the OSAF regarding any further requests for export licenses.[39]

During Symington's term, the ground work for two Air Force institutions began—the Air Force Engineering Development Center and the Air Force Academy. During World War II, Air Force research and development planners at Wright Field in Ohio, had recognized that they would need a new wind tunnel to evaluate the latest AAF engines and air frames. Symington had long supported the establishment of the Air Engineering Development Center, of which a new wind tunnel would be a part. He would face, however, over several years, two major tasks: convincing Congress of the center's necessity and pacifying the members who insisted on its location in their districts. Symington dealt with the latter task through the exercise of tact and with the former through the power of argument. He emphasized that while the Air Force's wind tunnel and tools for developing and testing military aircraft were still useful, they were designed only for subsonic speeds. He contended that a new center could bridge the gap between "our present limited capabilities and our requirements for coping with the problems incident to supersonic speeds." Mere numbers of aircraft, he contended, were not enough. The Air Force had to "maintain technical superiority and . . . assume a place of predominant importance in our peacetime military planning." The Air Force's ultimate effective fighting strength depended on research and development.*[40] Symington consulted with several engineers who surveyed possible sites and concluded that an adequate electrical energy source would be necessary to reduce the adverse impact of the "power-load . . . upon the economic development of the area" being considered. The Air Force finally selected a suitable location but only after mandatory and extremely time-consuming coordination with the Research and Development Board† and interested government agencies. It then requested and was granted by Congress legislation enabling the center's establishment.[41]

Air Secretary Symington and the OSAF appointed an advisory board responsible for selecting the Air Force Academy's location. Symington acted chiefly as a buffer for the Air Force against politicians and civic leaders who attempted to influence the board's decision. Symington related that one Congressman even threatened not to vote monies for the Air Force ever again if his state were not chosen as the academy's home.‡[42]

Unification

Meanwhile, it had become apparent to Symington, Spaatz, Forrestal, and others that the National Military Establishment needed substantial reorganizing. A bill to revise the National Security Act of 1947 expressed the desire by the administration and the OSD to provide more authority to Forrestal's office.[43] In

---

* It should be noted that by March 1949 the Tennessee-Cumberland valley was recommended by Sverdrup & Parcel, Inc., the firm contracted to select the most suitable location for the Air Engineering Development Center. On November 7, 1949, that firm selected Camp Forrest, Tennessee, as the site, largely because its facilities provided a convenient staging area within which to begin construction activites almost immediately. The firm's decision was approved by the President and the Secretary of Defense on November 9. Ltr, W. Stuart Symington to Senator Pat McCarran, Dec 21, 1947, Vandenberg Papers, Oct 1949–Dec 1949, LC Manuscript Division. On December 30, 1949, the Secretary of the Air Force established the Air Engineering Development Division effective January 1, 1950. Ltr, Maj Gen E. M. Powers, Asst Dep Chief of Staff, Materiel to Chief of Staff, subj: Status of Huntsville Arsenal with Respect to Air Engineering Development Center, Mar 10, 1949, RG 340, Special Interest Files, Special File 29A, Air Engineering Development Center, 1948, NARA.

† The Research and Development Board was established by the National Security Act of 1947 to advise the Secretary of Defense on the status of scientific research and development relating to national security. The board was composed of a civilian chairman appointed by the President and two representatives each from the Departments of the Army, Navy, and Air Force. The Research and Development Board was abolished in 1953 by Reorganization Plan No. 6. Its functions were absorbed by the Assistant Secretary of Defense for Research and Development.

‡ The academy was authorized by Congress on April 1, 1954. Its first graduating class started at Lowry Air Force Base, Denver, Colorado, in July 1955.

February 1948, the Commission on the Organization of the Executive Branch of the Government, headed by former President Herbert Hoover, established a task force under Ferdinand Eberstadt* to study a more economical restructuring of the nation's defense. Throughout 1948 Symington and key members of his staff, Eugene Zuckert, representatives of the Air Staff, and two Chiefs of Staff— General Spaatz and his successor, General Vandenberg—testified frequently before the Eberstadt Committee. The testimony of more than 245 leading civilian and military witnesses was included in the final report completed in November 1948.[44]

In preparing its position for the Eberstadt Committee, the Air Secretary consulted W. Barton Leach, a wartime officer who had resumed a teaching career at Harvard Law School, on the subject of defense reorganization. In June 1948, Leach advised Symington that in the national interest both political parties should promote the greater unification of the military services. According to Leach, the National Security Act of 1947 at best represented only a compromise between parties who disagreed fundamentally on matters of principle. Its inherent weakness could be eliminated, he argued, if the Secretary of Defense had more author-

James V. Forrestal, first Secretary of Defense.

---

* Eberstadt was a long-time friend of Defense Secretary Forrestal. The pair had been partners in the investment banking firm of Dillon and Read. Eberstadt served as Forrestal's closest advisor and had a hand in many of the policies Forrestal endorsed as Under Secretary of the Navy, Secretary of the Navy, and Secretary of Defense. Arnold A. Rogow, *James Forrestal: A Study of Personality, Politics and Policy* (New York and London: The Macmillan Company, 1963), p 95.

ity than the service secretaries and the OSD were enlarged.[45] Leach further urged that the service chiefs surrender some of their independence to a military chief of staff who would out-rank them and break any deadlock within the Joint Chiefs of Staff (JCS) and would be responsible to the Secretary of Defense. Leach considered this "super chief" the key to reform. Even though such a chief might advocate his own service, any possible lack of evenhandedness or detachment would have to be tolerated.[46]

Later that summer, on Leach's recommendations, Symington expressed similar views. He believed that the effectiveness of the OSD could be increased if the Secretary of Defense were provided with an under secretary who could act as his assistant. He favored creating a single Chief of Staff of the Armed Forces who answered only to the Secretary of Defense and exercised authority and power of decision over purely military matters.[47] Symington reiterated that "it has always been our position that such a chief of staff from one of the three services is essential not only for economic administration of the Department of Defense, but also for maximum security of the country."[48]

Roles and Missions

In January 1948, Symington urged that the roles and missions of the three services be clarified and conflicting points resolved before the modification of the National Security Act occurred. At issue were strategic bombing, submarine reconnaissance, anti-submarine warfare, and the place of aircraft carriers in U.S. strategy. He had emphasized to the Eberstadt Committee in October that the strategic bombing mission had essentially been settled. It belonged to the Air Force. The anti-submarine mission, which the Air Force desired, had not been assigned but seemed appropriate to the Navy.

The Joint Chiefs of Staff had discussed these questions in Key West, Florida, March 11–14, 1948, and at the Newport Conference in Rhode Island in August 1948, but did not resolve them. In Key West Secretary Forrestal had summoned the JCS—Admiral William D. Leahy, Chief of Staff to the President; General Omar N. Bradley, Chief of Staff of the Army; Vice Admiral Louis E. Denfeld, Chief of Naval Operations; and General Carl A. Spaatz, Chief of Staff of the Air Force, to correct paralyzing service differences and to fashion a more cooperative team. The service chiefs selected primary functions that established clear responsibilities and collateral functions by which one service supported another. The Air Force received primary responsibility for strategic air warfare and the Navy received primary responsibility for air support operations necessary to a successful campaign. The Navy was not prohibited from attacking any targets, inland or otherwise, to accomplish its mission. In addition, it received primary responsibility for anti-submarine warfare, which the Air Force supported collaterally.

Attempting to resolve disagreements over service roles and missions, Secretary of Defense James V. Forrestal meets with the Joint Chiefs of Staff and their advisers at the Naval War College, site of the Newport Conference in Rhode Island, August 1948. *Left to right*: **Lt. Gen. Lauris Norstad, USAF; Gen. Hoyt S. Vandenberg, USAF; Lt. Gen. Albert C. Wedemeyer, USA; Gen. Omar N. Bradley, USA; Forrestal; Adm. Louis E. Denfeld, USN; Vice Adm. Arthur W. Radford, USN; and Maj. Gen. Alfred M. Gruenther, USA.**

By allowing each service the opportunity to contribute to the war efforts of another, the JCS was able to reduce only slightly interservice squabbling over roles and missions.[49] The Secretary of Defense was forced to summon the JCS again. At Newport, once more, the Air Force received the primary mission of strategic air warfare and the option of calling on naval air for assistance. The Navy was assigned the exclusive role in anti-submarine warfare. All participants realized that only through a concerted effort by the services could any agreements work.[50] Forrestal and the JCS reconciled other basic questions regarding the control and use of atomic weapons, the formation of a weapons evaluation group, and the structure of a unified command for Western Europe. However, the Secretary of Defense came away "under no illusions" that the conference had "solved the manifold problems of a unified military policy."[51] Symington persisted in believing that ninety percent of all service problems could be "licked, if someone would simply make a decision."[52]

As the roles and missions debate continued, Navy partisans used the press to accuse the Air Force of coveting the Navy's air function. An article printed in the May 10, 1948, issue of the *Buffalo Evening News* under the pseudonym Richard Essex, indicted the Air Force for muzzling the Navy and for conducting a three-year propaganda campaign to "identify itself as the exclusive proprietor of American air power." The Air Force believed, the author implied, that victory in the Pacific during World War II could have been gained without naval air support. Symington, who brought the article to Secretary of Defense Forrestal's attention, considered it the bitterest attack yet against the Army and the Air Force.

Another article, appearing in the *Armed Forces Journal*, caused further controversy by accusing the Army and the Air Force of conspiring to vote against naval aviation interests. Its author advised that Congress needed to determine the role of naval aviation and to find out who had "tied a gag on the Navy—in flagrant violation of the spirit of the unification program." Symington assured Forrestal that although the Air Force respected the Navy, it regretted the tactics of the present regime which "has condoned these continuous attacks on its sister services."[53]

Highly exasperated by the articles, Symington wrote Forrestal complaining of the Navy's contention that the security of the country depended on an integrated Navy team of land, sea, and air defenses, with "any cooperation from the Army and the Air Force . . . welcome but incidental." The Navy had implied, he added, that any decision by the "Executive Department of government, including your office, which is contrary to the Navy's interpretation of the law is a violation . . . making compliance with that decision impracticable if not impossible."[54]

Symington had taken exception to much of the Navy's testimony before the Eberstadt Committee. He maintained that the Navy had attempted to rationalize its requests for large numbers of attack carriers and aircraft by pointing to its obligation under law to perform all air functions. Symington denied the validity of the Navy's challenge and questioned the propriety of such assertions which cast doubt on the Air Force's competence before a committee whose investigative purview, he felt, should not include the assignment of roles and missions. He did "not consider it in the public interest to become party to a public brawl" but added that if the Navy's presentation had any influence on the findings of the committee, the Air Force would reconsider its position.[55]

Symington regarded the October 18, 1948, Navy presentation before the committee as a repudiation of the Newport Conference's joint agreements, which, the press and the public had been informed, had resolved the assignment of roles and missions. The Navy had again denigrated the effectiveness of strategic bombing. In fact, Symington had sought to allay the Navy's fear of losing its air power on many occasions by explicitly stating to Secretary Forrestal that the Air Force objected to the consolidation of all military aviation into one service. Symington warned that "unless these attacks from regular officers, in direct violation of the instructions of the Secretary of Defense, were stopped, efficient functioning of the military establishment was impossible;

and therefore the security of the country [would be] seriously jeopardized."[56]

In a memorandum to Forrestal, Symington wrote "It is our understanding . . . from newspaper people that Admiral Arthur W. Radford,* who was one of the Navy respondents at the 18 October presentation, was back at his old stand . . . attacking the long-range bombers in favor of the carriers and is consistently critical of me." Symington questioned the right of anyone in uniform to "attack a civilian secretary of another service." Radford apparently believed that he could help determine the Navy's future through "these attacks against the Air Force." † Symington admitted that he had approached Secretary of the Navy John L. Sullivan about Radford's statements but had encountered only indifference.[57]

By November 1948, the Eberstadt Committee had concluded its national defense study with a report and recommendations that were generally acceptable to Symington and other Air Force leaders. Changes proposed by the committee included the addition of an Under Secretary of Defense and elimination of the service under secretaries, the strengthening of the authority of the Secretary of Defense, the elimination of the wartime Chief of Staff to the President, the designation of a Chairman of the Joint Chiefs of Staff, the dropping of the service secretaries from the National Security Council, and the granting of membership on it to the Secretary of Defense as sole representative of the military services.‡[58]

The Eberstadt report recommendations, the Hoover Commission findings of February 1949, and the President's March 5, 1949, message to Congress all approved changes to the National Security Act of 1947. After much deliberation, both houses passed the National Security Act amendments. Signed by the President in August 1949, they replaced a coordinated federation with a centralized administration under a strong Secretary of Defense with a larger support staff, a deputy secretary, and two assistant secretaries. The status of the three executive departments, each with direct access to the President, was thus altered, the new law having "changed the synonym of unification from 'coordination' of the armed forces to 'centralization' under the Secretary of Defense."[59] This change had long been desired by the Air Force and the Army.

The National Security Act amendments of 1949 were not finalized without

---

* Admiral Radford, who was then serving as Vice Chief of Naval Operations, had formerly been Deputy Chief of Naval Operations for Air. During the October 18, 1948, presentation he said, "The Air Force long has tried to submerge naval aviation within its own organization. However large and powerful the Air Force may become, the Russians have an Air Force to oppose it. The weld of air and surface power in the Navy today is our unmatched advantage. Crippling the Navy could assure the Russians a choice of weapons, as well as their choice of time and strategy for attack."

† It appears that Symington was attempting to gain Forrestal's support for the Air Force by bringing Radford's attacks to his attention.

‡ Under the National Security Act of 1947, all three service secretaries and the Secretary of Defense sat on the National Security Council.

acrimony. On several occasions Defense Secretary Forrestal contemplated demanding Symington's resignation, their views were so at odds.* Forrestal supported President Truman's wish that the services subordinate their own objectives to the broader interests of the national defense program by presenting a "solid front" on American foreign policy, particularly before Congress.[60] Forrestal's lack of authority, however, had rendered him more of an equal than a leader to the service secretaries and had complicated his efforts to compel their cooperation. Symington and the other secretaries, perceiving the advantage of a power vacuum, took their arguments to Congress, which weighed them against the administration's point of view.

Supporting the administration, Forrestal had wanted as little public evidence as possible of friction between the services as well as between the NME and other departments and agencies of the federal government. He had specifically designated "general policies" and "budget making" as subjects about which no information should be released unless cleared by the OSD. He stipulated that no article touching on a controversial subject should be "delivered by any of the Secretaries, Chiefs of Staff, or Vice Chief of Naval Operations without prior submission to an authority approved by the Secretary of Defense."[61] While Forrestal felt it unnecessary to enumerate every "controversial subject," he did single out the topic of appropriations "where all of us, as part of the administration, have the job of supporting the budget which the President submitted to Congress."[62] Any departures by the NME from the 1949 budget would be made only on the basis of an order received "by me from the President."[63]

Although Symington endorsed the Eberstadt report's approval of more authority for Forrestal and less for the service secretaries, he was aware of the prerogatives of his office and took issue with even minimal infringements on them. For example, the Committee of Four Secretaries,† which met regularly for a year and a half, discussed on May 26, 1948, the need for mutual clearance of press or other statements about military installations in which more than one ser-

---

* Symington and Forrestal had an almost adversarial relationship according to Clark Clifford in his book *Counsel to the President* (New York: Random House, 1991). Clifford, who had known Symington since 1934, maintains that in 1946 a good deal of friction between the two had developed as they defended the interests of their respective services, the AAF and the Navy; Forrestal was Secretary of the Navy at that time. They carried this friction through unification and beyond.

† This group consisted of the Secretary of Defense and the three service secretaries and was responsible for policy direction on inter-service matters. Since much of the preparatory work was done at a lower level, Assistant Secretary of the Air Force (Civil Affairs) Cornelius Whitney would brief Secretary of the Air Force Symington on the agenda and items requiring particular attention. The committee first met on October 26, 1947, and was abolished on April 6, 1949, by direction of the Secretary of Defense. *History of the Office of the Secretary of the Air Force, September 18, 1947, to June 30, 1950,* vol 1, section on the Assistant Secretary of the Air Force (Civil Affairs).

vice was interested. On this occasion, Symington objected that such a rule was not "necessary or justified by reason of any particular circumstance or on any general principle."[64] It would, he believed, unduly restrict the freedom and independence of each secretary to express his own views and answer correspondence. He maintained that he was unable to find anything in the National Security Act which was compatible with such a restriction. The act clearly and specifically "contemplated the preservation of the status of each department as an individual executive department with each secretary exercising all powers and duties relating to the administration of his department, except those powers specifically conferred on the Secretary of Defense."[65]

In short, he believed that there was no basis in the act for authorizing "one head of an executive department to encroach on the prerogatives of the head of another department within the National Military Establishment."[66] Each Secretary had the discretion to determine the controversial aspects of any issue and, in lieu of the proposed rule, he suggested the adoption of a procedure in such instances by which one secretary should furnish copies of correspondence* to the other two secretaries and other agencies within the NME.†[67]

On the very issue that Forrestal's demand for solidarity rested, Symington rebelled. On the budget, he took the offensive for the Air Force when Defense Secretary Forrestal gave the impression before Bureau of the Budget Director Webb that the Air Force was "mixed up" regarding a $400 million difference in figures between fiscal years 1948 and 1949 indirect appropriations for the Army.‡[68] Later, Forrestal in a letter to Senator Owen Brewster of Maine, Chairman of the Congressional Aviation Policy Board, included figures that implied a difference of opinion between the Air Force and the Bureau of the Budget on indirect appropriations. Symington considered Forrestal's action a mistake; in his view, a difference of opinion between the Bureau of the Budget and the Air Force was not the concern of the Brewster Committee. He suggested to Forrestal that all letters of this scope having to do with Air Force problems be coordinated with the Air Force Secretary before being furnished to Congress "otherwise we will be testifying against each other because we will be working

---

* It appeared that what Symington wanted was the opportunity to comment on such correspondence before it was released. He never got the opportunity to review the Richard Essex article when the Navy sent copies to the Air Force.

† When discussing the distinction between the powers of the Secretary of the Air Force and the Secretary of Defense, Symington found no contradiction. He was perfectly willing to report to a Secretary of Defense, but he did not want to subordinate himself to any of the other service secretaries. He was protective of the Office of the Secretary of the Air Force. Intvw, W. Stuart Symington by author, Oct 21, 1981.

‡ The Air Force was not completely separated from the Army financially in 1948 and 1949. Air Force appropriations for various technical services such as finance, quartermaster, and engineering were handled through the Army. It was not until 1950 that the Air Force submitted its first independent budget.

with different figures."[69] Symington explained that the seeming discrepancy in the $400 million for fiscal year 1949 represented part of the Department of the Army's budget, prepared and submitted as was customary prior to the passage of the National Security Act of 1947. It would have been impossible, Symington explained, for the Air Force to have yet developed its own budget structure.[70]

Symington's views again diverged from Forrestal's over the question of the 70-group program. Forrestal supported a 55-group program and insisted that a strong Air Force by itself "could not ensure peace or gain victory in war." Even though Forrestal wanted the services to support President Truman's military budget, they would not commit themselves to it, and Symington was its most consistent critic.[71] Indeed, Symington told Bureau of the Budget Director Webb that the Air Force had continually maintained that it needed seventy groups to carry out its mission in the postwar world* and pointed to studies completed by the JCS that categorized fifty-five groups as a minimum force. Symington added that an interim goal of fifty-five groups had been established for January 1, 1948, and that the Bureau of the Budget had extended it for another year.†

Symington attacked the Bureau's proposal and its underlying misconception that the Air Force's budget requirements were directly proportional to the number of groups in operation. In addition to operating units, there was "an equally essential requirement" for maintaining a minimum organizational structure, Symington added, on which "we must depend for an orderly expansion to the required seventy groups, and in case of emergency, to meet the needs of war."[72]

When speaking before the Senate Armed Services Committee in March 1948, Symington provided a view of fiscal year 1949's budget that was anything but harmonious with the administration's. He cautioned that regardless of the international situation, "unless there is world agreement between now and then, our position will be far more critical when the Russians have the bomb . . . We will not have an adequate modern Air Force on either of these two dates unless we start building that Air Force now."[73] This rather alarmist view did not seem to coincide with Forrestal's plea for solidarity and moderation in support of the

---

* See Wolk, *Planning and Organizing the Post War Air Force, 1943–1947*. The 70-group Air Force had evolved into more of a symbol of air power than a specific program. See also Paul Y. Hammond, "The First Clash Over Aircraft Roles and Missions: Military Judgments and the Fiscal 1949 Budget" cited in *American Civil-Military Decisions: A Book of Case Studies*, edited by Harold Stein (University of Alabama Press, 1963), p 47.

† President Truman's January 12, 1948, budget submission to Congress for fiscal year 1949 called for $11 billion to be divided evenly between the three services. That budget included fifty-five full-strength air groups for the Air Force. Paul Y. Hammond, "The First Clash Over Aircraft Roles and Missions: Military Judgments and the Fiscal 1949 Budget" cited in *American Civil-Military Decisions: A Book of Case Studies,* edited by Harold Stein (University of Alabama Press, 1963), p 471.

President's budget. A 70-group program, Symington believed, was a peace time program and would provide a mere means of survival against an initial enemy onslaught. It would not provide the United States with the means to win a war.[74]

The 70-group issue reached its apex with the supplemental 1949 budget. Although gaining supplemental appropriations to support its basic request—despite a cut of $100 million—appeared to be a victory for Symington and the Air Force, it should be noted that Congress was encouraged to support the outlay because of evolving international tensions. Supported by the Soviet Union, a communist government was established in Czechoslovakia in February 1948; Chinese communists had gained victories over the nationalist Chinese in North China; and on March 5, 1948, General Lucius D. Clay, U.S. Military Governor in Germany and Commander in Chief of U.S. Army Forces in Europe, sent a top secret telegram to the Chief of Army Intelligence indicating that war with the Soviet Union might be imminent. Participants in the March 1948 Key West conference also emphasized to Congress the need for a supplemental appropriation "to bring total armed strength more nearly in proportion to the realities of the world situation."[75] The Air Force estimated that it needed $922 million, in addition to the 1949 budget submission, to finance aircraft procurement in a first step toward seventy groups. Congress cut this by $100 million, and on April 15, 1948, the House of Representatives authorized $822 million for aircraft procurement and Air Force modernization (H.R. 6226). On May 11 the Senate approved the bill. Ten days later the President signed it into law.[76]

These events induced the military departments to pursue a kind of budget free-for-all to get everything they could while they could. Director of the Bureau of the Budget James Webb subsequently recalled that Symington and General George C. Kenney were the most extreme of the service proponents, employing pressure "to scare the country into believing that anyone who wouldn't go along with these plans would be responsible for a catastrophe."[77]

Symington took full advantage of all the budget jockeying to benefit the Air Force. His firm stand before Congress for additional monies gained him the support of Senator Chan Gurney, Chairman of the Senate Armed Services Committee, who asserted during the hearings that he and his committee had compelled Symington to speak. With such powerful support, the Air Secretary was able to ward off the "spanking" from Forrestal and Truman that the *New York Times* predicted he would receive.* [78]

Symington's and Forrestal's relationship suffered further strain with dis-

---

* The *Washington Post* reported on April 14: "For the first time at the recent Senate hearings Forrestal gave Symington free rein to speak out, and Symington took full advantage of it." Forrestal had earlier directed Symington to follow the party line, but, later, did not want Symington to perjure himself before Congress.

putes over extending selective service and initiating Universal Military Training (UMT)* In April 1948 reports were circulating throughout Washington† that the Air Force was opposed to both these measures and that Symington had been critical of the President. On April 13, 1948, Symington told a House committee that although he had previously supported selective service legislation, the Air Force did not require the draft to increase its strength.[79] Forrestal confided to friends and associates that he considered Symington's testimony before Congress insubordinate and disloyal. In his view, Symington had deliberately tried to disrupt the balance between the services and to discredit the judgment of the Secretary of Defense and that of his military advisers. It was then that Forrestal considered asking for Symington's resignation.‡[80]

Symington wanted the issue resolved. He informed Forrestal that he objected to the way Air Force programs were being presented to Congress in conjunction with UMT and a larger Army and Navy. He felt that Congress, facing a choice among them, would choose to sacrifice air power to get UMT established. An Air Force tied to UMT would, Symington believed, be limited to only about 25 percent of all military funds, and thus fail to achieve seventy groups. Fueling his argument, he held that any obstacles to the Air Force's 70-group goal would directly contravene the recommendations of both the President's Air Policy Commission (the Finletter Commission) and the congressional Aviation Policy Board (the Brewster-Hinshaw Board).§ By linking his defense of Air Force programs to these two studies, Symington had placed himself in an impossible situation because he would have to repeat his December 1947 testimony to the Finletter Commission in which he expressed his support for UMT. Symington decried the fact that neither he nor General Spaatz had received the

---

* Symington did not state their source specifically, only that they were acknowledged by Forrestal.

† Under Selective Service, draftees served for two to three years. Under UMT, all men would have to serve a short active duty period (usually for training) and then be assigned to the ready reserves. The Air Force believed that UMT would not provide an adequate supply of the highly trained individuals it needed. The Air Force favored longer enlistments to satisfy and properly manage its growing technological needs. Because UMT funds would be drawn from those already appropriated to the services, Air Force support for it soured.

‡ Symington maintained that during this period—the spring of 1948—General Spaatz and Assistant Air Secretary Zuckert told him that the Air Force's portion of the budget had been cut from $5 billion to $3.6 billion. Symington could not believe it since he was not informed by Forrestal. He called the Secretary of Defense to tell him that he would not support the budget, whereupon Forrestal said, "If you won't support it, then why don't you quit?" Symington retorted that he would neither resign nor support the budget cut. Intvw, W. Stuart Symington by author, Oct 21, 1981.

§ Reports by both groups favor the Air Force, which used them consistently to justify the 70-group program. The Air Policy Commission, known as the Finletter Commission, was created by President Harry S. Truman in July 1947 to inquire into national aviation problems as well as to assist the administration in formulating an inte-

opportunity to present their positions to Defense Secretary Forrestal or even his staff. The Air Secretary was especially irritated because Forrestal's staff included no one "who ever served a day in the Air Force."[81]

Thus Symington reminded the Senate Appropriations Committee on April 27, 1948, that in answering its question in previous testimony about whether a minimum peacetime Air Force was of greater value to the security of the United States than UMT,* he had replied that "the minimum peacetime force in being is the first requirement . . . " He was quick to add, however, that "this in no way changed our previously expressed support of UMT."[82] Later that year, Symington clarified for Forrestal the Air Force's position on UMT. While he supported it as a long range plan, he held that "adequate forces in being, properly supported, trained, equipped, and manned are absolutely essential and must be of first priority."[83] He believed that because of the "present world situation," selective service was the most effective means of building up and maintaining adequate military forces. He emphasized that before UMT legislation was passed, every consideration should be given to the political effect on selective service and the current programs of the armed forces. He predicted that funds, personnel, and facilities for UMT would come from the military services and that this diversion would reduce their effectiveness. The UMT program should be activated only after "the present tense world situation" had improved and after selective service was no longer required as a means of maintaining strength.[84]

Conflict between Symington and Forrestal erupted again in July 1948, this time over a speech allegedly given by Symington before the Institute of Aeronautical Sciences in Los Angeles, California, on July 16, 1948. Forrestal was under the impression that Symington had rejected a prepared speech to extemporize and to attack as "ax-grinders dedicated to obsolete methods of warfare"

---

grated national aviation policy. The Air Policy Commission presented its report in January 1948. The Aviation Policy Board, known as the Brewster-Hinshaw Board, which presented its report in March 1948, was the congressional response to the Finletter Commission. Both commissions drew their names from their chairmen, Thomas K. Finletter, Senator Owen Brewster, and Congressman Carl Hinshaw. Memo, W. Stuart Symington to James V. Forrestal, Mar 16, 1948, RG 340, Special Interest Files, Special File 14, Correspondence Oct 47–Sep 48, NARA; remarks by W. Stuart Symington, Secretary of the Air Force, at the Institute of Aeronautical Science, Jul 16, 1948, CAFH; *Survival in the Air Age: A Report by the President's Air Policy Commission* (Washington: GPO, 1948), p 5

* The *Washington Post* maintained that Symington reversed his stand on UMT before the Senate Armed Services Committee in April that year. Symington was quoted as having stated, "It is true that we testified for universal military training. We did that before we knew the Air Force was going to be cut. We felt it would be a 70-group program." When Virginia's Senator Harry Byrd asked Symington whether that meant he considered a 70-group Air Force more important than UMT, Symington replied, "Yes Sir, and I can go farther than that. I think it is the most important thing that has been presented to this committee from the standpoint of military preparedness." "Symington Speaks His Mind" (Washington Merry-Go-Round), The *Washington Post,* Apr 14, 1948, p 27.

those who objected to large appropriations for the Air Force because they feared that the balance between the three services might be disturbed. Symington apparently had asserted that air power should be compared not with the power of the Army or the Navy, but with the power of potential enemies. Further denigrating the approved budget, he supposedly had added that "no department store could obtain financing for a line of merchandise with such a disjointed program."[85] The speech, reported in the *New York Times*, so infuriated Forrestal that he orderd Symington to resign unless he could provide an explanation for his action.[86] The Air Secretary's words constituted, in his view, an "act of official disobedience and personal disloyalty."[87]

Symington encountered the angry Secretary of Defense at home in his garden on Prospect Street in Washington, D.C., and told him that he had not delivered the speech printed in the *New York Times*. Symington explained that a speech prepared and sent to him by Stephen F. Leo, Air Force Director of Public Relations, had seemed excessively critical, so he decided not to use it and wrote one himself instead. The *New York Times* had obtained a copy of the original, however, as the speech the Air Secretary had given. Symington, unable to blame Forrestal for feeling the way he did about the published version, succeeded in calming him. The Secretary of Defense never mentioned the speech or the resignation again.[88]

The Berlin Airlift

The event that received the most extensive press coverage during Stuart Symington's term as Secretary of the Air Force was not the Los Angeles speech or the Bennett Meyers case or the B-36 dispute* but the Berlin Airlift. It dominated the news for over a year. Carried out from June 1948 to September 1949, the airlift occupied almost all Air Force transport aircraft. Even so, it did not have any special impact on the day-to-day workings of the OSAF, although the Air Secretary made several flights to Berlin during the crisis. The real job was done by the Air Force's Military Air Transport Service (MATS) and United States Air Forces Europe (USAFE).†

Symington, by his own admission and according to both his Chiefs of Staff, Spaatz and Vandenberg, kept out of operational matters for the most part and left them to the experts. There were peripheral aspects of the airlift, however, that affected the OSAF and commanded his attention. Among them were the

---

* See Chapter 4.

† The Berlin Airlift was a huge air supply operation undertaken by the United States, Britain, and France in 1948 and 1949 to counter a Soviet blockade of the western sectors of Berlin. The city was inside the Russian zone of occupied Germany. The Soviets had completely shut off access to roads, rails, and waterways leading there.

The Berlin Airlift. U.S. Air Force C-47s *(above)* from all over the United States await takeoff from Rhein-Main Air Base in Frankfurt, Germany, to transport thousands of tons of food, coal, and other supplies to the western sectors of the Soviet-blockaded city of Berlin. Planes flew round-the-clock and were unloaded in assembly-line fashion. C-82 Packets were large enough to accommodate bulky equipment such as the tractor *(below)*, which would have required dismantling and reassembly if carried aboard any other type of aircraft.

budgetary adjustments needed to pay for the airlift and occasional strikes at contractors' plants that, had they remained unsettled, might have interrupted scheduled deliveries of goods to Berlin. Once the airlift was under way, the Air Secretary and his office did not monitor or control it. He and his staff did not become involved in such details as determining amounts and kinds of foodstuffs and supplies to be sent. He did, however, involve himself with the needs of his airmen in Berlin. On one of his trips there during Christmas 1948, Symington, according to Maj. Gen. William H. Tunner, in charge of airlift operations, made an intensive study of problems at Rhine-Main Air Base. He listened to the complaints of the men stationed there and learned first hand of unpleasant housing conditions and the lack of proper tools and supplies. On the same trip, he stopped in England to learn about living conditions at the base in Burtonwood. Noticing that the men seemed reluctant to talk in front of high ranking officers, he asked "the brass to disappear." Symington took Lt. Gen. James H. Doolittle, who was dressed in civilian clothes, on a tour of the facility and asked their driver to point out some of the worst quarters. The Air Secretary was appalled by what he encountered. He found

> something like twenty men in one hut with mud over the floor, only two dim lights in the barracks, a stove which was red hot on all sides—an old coal stove—they could not put anything on it—terrible lockers, bedding which they said was full of bedbugs. One of the boys volunteered that they had tried to get DDT but had not been able to. As soon as they saw we were really sympathetic they opened up and gave us the story of all of it. One boy had no teeth and said he had tried for months to get them, without results. He could not digest his food, and he hated to go downtown because he did not smile and [people] thought he was homesick. They showed us showers which were bad. They said there was little warm water. Dirt and mud [were] on the floors and the latrines [were] unspeakably filthy—worse than any I have ever seen on any base housing American soldiers and even worse than any of my experience in World War I.[89]

Symington completed his tour, got down to business, demanding facts and figures from General Tunner. Tunner and his staff worked for two days and provided Symington with his requested data. The general soon got results—orders to requisition better housing were forthcoming; construction began on emergency barracks; and long-needed supplies began flowing in. Tunner credited Symington with initiating action. "Symington must have gone straight to his office after arriving home from Berlin and started pushing buttons right away, [because] staff officers from the Pentagon began arriving almost immediately."[90] The real burden of the Berlin Airlift fell on Air Force administrators, including the Assistant Secretary of the Air Force (Management) and the Air Staff, rather than on the Air Secretary himself. The airlift consumed resources that had been earmarked for other purposes. Throughout 1948 and 1949 administrators involved in the transition from the 70-group to a smaller Air Force faced the additional task of revising earlier established figures. Consequently, procurement programs were cancelled, units deactivated and activities concentrated on fewer stations. General Tunner credited Symington with supporting a larger transport, the C-124 Globemaster. They had spoken about larger load-carrying transport during Symington's Christmas trip. Symington listened intently and carried the idea back to Washington where he encouraged numerous aircraft refinements and improvements.[91]

During his first year as Secretary of the Air Force, Symington clearly established himself as the service's most powerful civilian voice—a staunch proponent of air power rather than a director of operations. Even an article in *Time* magazine, which featured Symington on its January 19, 1948, cover, described General Spaatz as the "real Air Force boss," stating that on all matters of strategy, Symington turned "reverently" to Spaatz and to Lt. Gen. Lauris Norstad, "but in matters of management, procurement and costs 'Stu' Symington was the man."[92]

There was clearly no Air Force civilian and military power struggle during this time. If a conflict existed it was between civilians; between Forrestal, who represented the administration's desire for moderate increases in the defense budget, and Symington, who sought to attain the Air Force's goals by spending more than the administration wanted. The problem of the lack of centralized control of the services deprived the Secretary of Defense of the authority to dominate the service secretaries. In accordance with the National Security Act of 1947, Forrestal was little more than a coordinator between the President and the services. Symington took advantage of this organizational weakness and argued in Congress for additional monies to help the Air Force gain its 70-group program. He acknowledged the Air Force's capacity for running its own operations. Recognizing his own inexperience in such matters, he sought as best he could to serve the Air Force by representing its needs in Congress. This marriage of convenience survived Symington's tenure. However, the 1949 amendments to the National Security Act began to shift power in favor of the Secretary of Defense.

Chapter 4

The Battle over the B-36

In January 1949, General Dwight D. Eisenhower warned of trouble if the military services did not stop seeking headlines to gain additional funds:

> Someday we're going to have a blowup . . . God help us if ever we go before a congressional committee to argue our professional fights as each service struggles to get the lion's share . . . Public airing of grievances . . . some day . . . will go far beyond the bounds of decency and reason and someone will say, "Who's the boss? The civilians or the military?"[1]

Eisenhower's warning went unheeded as the Air Force and the Navy fought for money and strategic missions.

Their differences were publicized in congressional hearings on the B-36, a massive, six-engine bomber designed to hit targets 5,000 miles away and return to base. The B-36 was the subject of a debate that shook the new Air Force to its roots, dominating both the final year of Symington's tenure and the time and effort of the Office of the Secretary of the Air Force (OSAF). The controversy surrounding the aircraft's procurement gained national exposure and seemed to threaten the very survival of the Air Force as an institution. The integrity and careers of the Secretary of the Air Force and a number of prominent Air Force officials and the future of the service's roles and missions were called into serious question. Symington in a real sense defined his office during congressional hearings on the B-36. He took control, marshalled his forces, orchestrated the Air Force's case, and presenting compelling testimony, carried the day. He performed brilliantly, demonstrating the authority of his position and settling the issue of civilian control of the military services.

In August 1949, Congressman James E. Van Zandt of Pennsylvania, member of the House Armed Services Committee, released an anonymous document containing damaging charges against the Air Force and the contractors engaged to produce the B-36. The document prompted a congressional investigation not only into the B-36, but into larger issues such as overall defense strategy and service competition over roles and missions. So heated was the conflict between the Air Force and the Navy that observers on both sides urged revisions to the National Security Act of 1947. Congress had taken a back seat to the military services as they fought and won World War II but, confronted with a new postwar world, it had to struggle forcefully to reclaim and reassert its authority over them by steering the hearings to a general discussion of strategy and unification.

The Navy feared the loss of its aviation and position as the nation's first line of defense and its reduction to little more than a convoy escort force. The Navy felt excluded from atomic weapons delivery, a strategic mission to which it believed its future was tied. The mission had been given to the Air Force, however, and the Navy used the opportunity of the hearings to challenge the Air Force's ability to manage it. To survive, the Air Force was forced to defend its procurement record, prove the viability of the B-36, disprove insinuations of irregular practices involved in acquiring the aircraft, and define the mission of a strategic nuclear delivery force.

Planning for the B-36 began in 1941, after Robert A. Lovett, Assistant Secretary of War for Air, and Maj. Gen. George A. Brett, Acting Chief of the Army Air Forces (AAF),* decided in conference on August 19 that the possible loss of bases in England necessitated the development of an aircraft with a 10,000 mile range, capable of leaving the United States, bombing Europe, and returning home. Boeing Aircraft Company, Consolidated Aircraft Corporation, Northrop Aircraft Corporation, and Douglas Aircraft Company presented competitive design proposals. Consolidated Aircraft Corporation's was the winner. On October 16, General H. Henry Arnold, Chief of the AAF, directed that a contract be written for the research, development, and mock-up of two experimental models. On November 15, a contract with Consolidated Aircraft Corporation was approved, and work on the B-36 began.

No aircraft had ever attained a range even close to that required of the B-36; its many innovations in aerodynamics, equipment, materials, structure, and manufacturing processes required nearly two years to complete. By July 23, 1943, General Arnold directed that the AAF procure 100 B-36 aircraft from Consolidated. By 1944 and 1945 the Allies had managed to change the course of the war in their favor partly because of the production and use of tremendous numbers of B-17, B-24, and B-29 bombers. All-out production of these models had consumed enormous resources, leaving little for a full B-36 production program. In addition, Consolidated-Vultee (Convair) Aircraft Corporation (Consolidated had merged with Vultee Aircraft, Inc. in March 1943) had to interrupt and reduce its B-36 effort to resolve engineering and production problems on the B-32, an aircraft built to complement the B-29 in the war against Japan.

After the end of World War II, the AAF justified continuing the B-36 program by emphasizing that the Soviet Union could overrun Europe, dominate the Mediterranean, and deny the United States access to overseas bases. In addition, the atomic bomb had elevated the strategic bomber to an unparalleled position as a means of inflicting mortal wounds to an enemy. Thus the plane could serve as a

---

* General Brett became Acting Chief of the AAF when General Marshall appointed General Arnold Acting Deputy Chief of Staff for Air in October 1940.

The B-36. The massive, six-engine bomber *(above)* was the subject of controversy and competition that pitted the Air Force against the Navy and its proposed super-carrier, the USS *United States,* shown in an artist's sketch *(right).* The chart *(below)* compares the B-36 with its contemporaries.

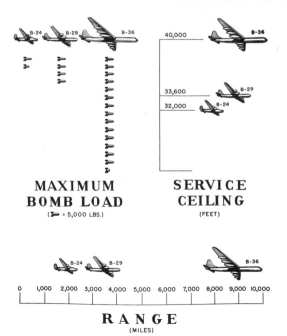

B-24   B-29   B-36

40,000   B-36

33,600   B-29
32,000   B-24

MAXIMUM BOMB LOAD
(✈ = 5,000 LBS.)

SERVICE CEILING
(FEET)

B-24   B-29   B-36

0   1,000   2,000   3,000   4,000   5,000   6,000   7,000   8,000   9,000   10,000

RANGE
(MILES)

deterrent to another world war with its ability to deliver atomic weapons and provide the AAF with the desired quantity of heavy bombers of sufficiently advanced design to warrant new tactics, techniques, and doctrine. There were no more technical innovations on the aircraft until December 1947, when General Carl A. Spaatz, Chief of Staff of the Air Force, directed that the last thirty-four B-36s be modified with more powerful variable discharge turbine (VDT) engines. This move also reduced the total number of aircraft on order to ninety-five.[2]

The B-36 first came to the attention of the OSAF as a source of controversy in late 1947 and early 1948 when letters critical of the bomber were published in several newspapers and journals. Some attacks were the work of Hugh L. Hanson, a Navy employee with the Bureau of Aeronautics. He had also made his views known to Congress and Secretary of Defense James V. Forrestal. Hanson's interest in the development of shorter-range bombers, such as the B-50C (B-54) and the B-49,* convinced Air Force leaders that he and others were trying to turn the Secretary of Defense against long-range strategic bombing.[3] Secretary of the Air Force Symington complained to Secretary of the Navy John L. Sullivan that such actions did not foster a spirit of unity among the services. Nevertheless, as testing of the B-36 continued, so did criticism.

Senior Air Force officers also questioned the utility of the B-36. General George C. Kenney, Commanding General, Strategic Air Command (SAC) from 1946 to 1948, doubted its predicted 10,000 mile range, believing it vulnerable to fighters because it lacked self sealing fuel tanks, had insufficient armament, and was slow. He favored the B-50 and urged the Air Force to conduct further studies before approving full B-36 production. However, General Nathan F. Twining, Commanding General, Air Materiel Command (AMC), did not want to scrap the B-36 simply because a better plane such as the B-52 would be available in four years. He deemed it unwise, if not detrimental to the Air Force's long-range capabilities, to wait for a new bomber. General Spaatz took Twining's side, with some reservations about the B-36's range, but believed that the addition of 3,500-horsepower engines would solve any problems.

During the early months of 1948, disappointing test results on the VDT engine and relatively slow speeds induced some planners to consider limiting the Air Force's procurement contract with Convair for the production of 61 planes. The B-36 was sixty knots slower than the B-50 at maximum over-the-target speed. However, when its greater load-carrying capacity and range were compared with those of other bombers, speed differentials became less important. The Air Force discovered that if the full contract, which had been amended for the production of 95 instead of 100 aircraft, were continued and not terminat-

---

* The B-49 was a variant of the Northrop B-35 Flying Wing. Its production was also cancelled.

ed at the production of 61, the cost of 34 remaining aircraft would be $1.5 million per unit against $5.5 million per unit. The Air Force also realized that cutting the B-36 program would sooner disperse a valuable group of technical experts. While aerial refueling promised to extend the inadequate range of a faster plane like the B-50, the B-36 would be the only means over the next few years of delivering the atomic bomb to any overseas target from bases in the United States.

Discussing the future of the B-36, in May 1948 Air Secretary Symington met with Under Secretary Barrows; Air Force Chief of Staff General Hoyt S. Vandenberg; Air Force Vice Chief of Staff General Muir S. Fairchild; and General Joseph T. McNarney, new AMC commander. They decided to approve at least sixty-one of the ninety-five aircraft on order, to postpone accepting or rejecting the thirty-four in question, and to cancel the VDT engine. Five days later, after visiting Convair's plant in Forth Worth, Texas, to examine new test results, Secretary Symington expressed renewed confidence in the B-36's performance. He scheduled a meeting for June 24, 1948, at which the final decision on the B-36 program would be announced.

In the meantime, the Soviet Union had blockaded the western zones of Berlin, and the Allies had responded with an over-the-city airlift. The possibility of war seemed real. Generals George Kenney and Lauris Norstad reversed their earlier positions, and a planning group* under Secretary Symington voted unanimously to continue the full contract for ninety-five B-36s with standard engines. The disruption of the aircraft industry from the cancellation of production orders was unthinkable, even though the plane might not attain the maximum speed predicted from development of the new experimental engine.[4]

During the latter half of 1948, a major budget revision brought the B-36 again into focus. At the time, the Air Force had fifty-nine total groups, but the President's fiscal year 1950 budget called for a reduction to forty-eight. The Air Force had hoped for an increase to seventy. Its problem was no longer procuring additional airplanes but canceling, with minimum loss to the government, airplanes already on order. Lt. Gen. Curtis E. LeMay, new SAC commander recommended to the Air Force Board of Senior Officers† in late 1948 the creation

---

* The group also included General Fairchild, Brig. Gen. Donald L. Putt, and Maj. Gen. Kenneth B. Wolfe, who represented the Commanding General, Air Materiel Command.

† The Board of Senior Officers was appointed by Secretary Symington to reassess the Air Force's entire aircraft program. Its members included General Muir S. Fairchild, Vice Chief of Staff, and board chairman; General Joseph T. McNarney, Commanding General, Air Materiel Command; Lt. Gen. Howard A. Craig, Deputy Chief of Staff for Materiel, Headquarters USAF; Lt. Gen. Lauris Norstad, Deputy Chief of Staff for Operations, Headquarters USAF; and Maj. Gen. Edward M. Powers, Assistant to the Deputy Chief of Staff, Materiel, Headquarters USAF, recorder without vote.

of two additional B-36 bomber groups and one strategic reconnaissance group equipped with RB-36s. The board granted LeMay's request by agreeing to the cancellation of thirty Northrop RB-49s and the procurement of thirty-two additional B-36s and seven RB-36s.[5]

In February 1949, General LeMay recommended to General Vandenberg that the Board of Senior Officers review the B-54 program* to determine the feasibility of curtailing or canceling it, because the B-36, installed with jet pods, was testing impressively. LeMay had previously favored the B-54 because it was already procured and represented a considerable advancement over the B-50D.[6] He felt that the B-54's margin of superiority over the B-29 and B-50 no longer justified its high cost in view of the markedly improved jet bombers coming into production—the B-47 and B-52. He added that the B-36 could best accomplish SAC's heavy bomber mission until B-52s were manufactured in quantity. The board carefully reviewed the comparative performances of the B-36, B-50, B-47 (production version) and the B-54. The B-36 with jet pods was faster, operated at a higher altitude, and had greater range and bomb-carrying capacity than the B-54. The board unanimously recommended to the Chief of Staff and the Secretary of the Air Force that B-54 production be cancelled, that B-47 production be stepped-up, and that additional B-36s be purchased to augment the scheduled four heavy bomb groups' and one heavy reconnaissance group's allotment of aircraft from eighteen to thirty.[7]

In April 1949, to comply with presidential budget restraints, the Air Force concentrated its procurement program on as few models as possible to obtain the lower unit prices resulting from quantity production.† Because the performance of B-36 and B-47 bombers had improved steadily, the Air Force, on the Board of Senior Air Force Officer's recommendation, ordered thirty-two B-36Bs with jet pods, seven RB-36Bs with jet pods, and five more B-47s. On April 9, the President approved the purchases.[8]

The Air Force was certain that the B-36 could perform its strategic mission until the B-52 became available. Air Secretary Symington emphasized to Defense Secretary Forrestal that the B-36 was now a true intercontinental bomber that could take off from the United States and, "because of its speed and altitude, penetrate enemy country without fighter escort, destroy the strategic target, and return non-stop to its base on this continent."[9]

The Air Force was not the only service feeling presidential budget restric-

---

* The B-54 program was an outgrowth of the B-29 design which had been ordered when Soviet activities in Eastern Europe first indicated an unsettled postwar world.

† It was Maj. Gen. Muir S. Fairchild's recollection during the House Armed Services Committee's hearings on the B-36 that the schedule according to which an aircraft could be produced heavily influenced the board's decisions.

tions. On April 23, 1949, the new Secretary of Defense, Louis A. Johnson* cancelled the Navy's long sought-after USS *United States*, a large flush deck (no superstructure on the starboard side) 65,000 ton supercarrier, larger than any naval ship afloat, capable of carrying up to 100,000 pounds of aircraft. Three days later Secretary of the Navy Sullivan resigned, charging that Johnson had acted without consultating the Navy. He declared himself deeply disturbed by what seemed to be the first attempt by the government to prevent the "development of a power weapon."[10] Sullivan added that this "renewed effort to abolish the Marine Corps and to transfer all naval and marine aviation elsewhere adds to my anxiety."[11] What fueled the Navy's apprehension was the press's focus on interservice rivalry in such headlines as, "The Bomber has Sunk the Supercarrier." *Newsweek* magazine even predicted that the "nation would hear arguments about the supercarrier versus the B-36 for many months to come."[12]

The Air Force had kept a close watch on the rising development costs of the supercarrier. Lt. Gen. Edwin W. Rawlings, Air Comptroller, detected that the Navy had failed to clearly represent an authorized hidden cost allowance in its fiscal year 1950 budget of $4.347 billion. $279 million, designated primarily for the supercarrier, had increased the actual budget to $4.626 billion. Rawlings also discovered that only the Bureau of the Budget seemed aware of the discrepancy, which he suggested that Symington mention when pleading the Air Force's case for construction funding.[13]

Thus the B-36 and its complicated history became the object of Navy criticism which reached its most dramatic intensity on May 26, 1949, when, on the House floor, Congressman Van Zandt† made public a series of disturbing questions. He admitted that, although their source was an anonymous document rife with implications of wrongdoing by the Air Force, they warranted congressional inquiry nonetheless. He wanted to know why the Air Force had found the B-36 unacceptable in the first half of 1948 but acceptable by September and October; why contracts for other types of aircraft had been cut repeatedly to release funds for more B-36s; and whether Stuart Symington was involved in establishing a giant aircraft business organization which he would operate "under the thumb" of Floyd Odlum, president of Convair and manufacturer of the B-36.[14]

Subsequent charges against Symington and Secretary of Defense Johnson alleged that they had ordered the B-36 because Johnson had once worked for

---

* Louis A. Johnson had served as Assistant Secretary of War from June 28, 1937, to July 25, 1940. Before becoming Secretary of Defense on March 28, 1949, he had served as Harry Truman's fund raiser during the 1948 presidential campaign. Johnson remained as Secretary of Defense until September 19, 1950. James V. Forrestal, Johnson's predecessor, suffered from severe depression and was admitted to the Naval hospital at Bethesda, Maryland, shortly after he resigned his office. He committed suicide on the evening of March 21–22, 1949, by jumping from a window on the sixteenth floor.

† Van Zandt, who had served in the Navy during World War I, was considered the spokesman for the Navy in the House.

Floyd Odlum, while Symington knew him socially. It was further alleged that the Emerson Electric Company, which Symington once directed, had profited unethically at the taxpayer's expense manufacturing gun turrets for the B-29.[15] The originators of these charges were unknown, but, by July, the press had become aware of an anonymous smear sheet first circulated by Glenn L. Martin of the Glenn L. Martin Company of Baltimore, well known manufacturer of Navy planes.[16] The author of the document used by Congressman Van Zandt also remained unknown.

Symington's reputation within the Air Force was impeccable. However, Hanson Baldwin, columnist, military editor of the *New York Times,* and Naval Academy graduate, best represented the extreme element of the secretary's detractors. Baldwin denounced Symington as one of the "nastiest" politicians in Washington, a man who had "ganged up on Forrestal" because he wanted to become Secretary of Defense himself. Baldwin maintained that Symington's "methods were dirty pool and dirty politics" and called him a "two-faced goad, who was not respected by most of the people in the Air Force."[17] He even alleged that Symington was the only service secretary not asked to be a pall-bearer at the funeral of James Forrestal because certain family members believed that he had contributed to the late Defense Secretary's death. While most of Symington's critics were not as harsh as Baldwin, they felt that he was no friend of the Navy. Stephen F. Leo, Director of Public Relations under Symington, when differentiating between Navy and Air Force "capers" at the time, characterized the Navy as "out of control."* He held that certain Navy zealots acted not as part of a consoli-

Louis A. Johnson, Secretary of Defense from March 28, 1949 to September 19, 1950.

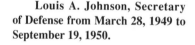

* Years later Symington would confirm Leo's recollection.

dated Navy position, but as individuals who, acting to further the principles and policies of their service, were actually hurting them.[18]

Nevertheless, the seriousness of Baldwin's and others' complaints was not lost on Symington. Congress, acceding to Van Zandt's request, had begun formal hearings by the House Armed Services Committee on the procurement of the B-36. In early June 1949 Symington appointed Barton Leach, professor of law at Harvard University, to manage the preparation of the Air Force's testimony. Colonel Leach held a reserve commission in the Air Force at the time and had been chief of the Operations Analysis Division in Headquarters, AAF, during the war. Symington authorized Leach to issue directives in the name of the Secretary of the Air Force to the Office of the Under Secretary of the Air Force and agencies of the Air Staff. He then ordered the Under Secretary of the Air Force, the General Counsel, the Director of Public Relations, and the Air Staff to conduct, under Leach's supervision, their own investigation. He also asked Leach to outline the Air Force's defense against Van Zandt in a concise chronology of events and accusations.[19] Leach quickly got to the heart of the matter. He saw that an explanation of the Air Force's change of mind about the B-36 between the springs of 1948 and 1949 and its subsequent change of policy on the aircraft's procurement would require the complete perusal of all correspondence files for material on any dealings with Convair, Boeing, Martin, and Northrop.[20]

Symington then wrote to the Chairman of the House Armed Services Committee, Congressman Carl Vinson of Georgia, denying that B-36 procurement had been riddled with politics, influence, and disregard for the country's military security. "At no time since I have been Secretary," Symington declared, "has any higher authority attempted to recommend in any way the purchase of any airplane, but, rather, every aircraft that was purchased by the Air Force during my tenure was recommended to me by the Chief of Staff of the Air Force and his staff." He emphasized that he approved every major change in the B-36 program only after he had heard recommendations from Generals McNarney, Norstad, and Vandenberg and from Air Force Under Secretary Barrows.[21]

Symington called the alleged Odlum connection a lie, citing only two visits in two years to the Odlum residence, once when bad weather grounded his official party after an inspection trip, and again when he had to discuss a number of important matters, including B-36 production. Symington asserted that he had severed all ties with Emerson Electric when he began working for the government in 1945.*[22] He denied unequivocally that he had discussed, directly or indirectly with Odlum, his associates, or any other aircraft manufacturer, creating a huge aircraft combine. "To have done so," he wrote, would have been "highly improper and probably a violation of my oath of office." Symington

---

* Emerson Electric held Symington's job for him until 1952, when he ran for the U.S. Senate. Intvw, W. Stuart Symington by author, Oct 21, 1981.

concluded by calling for Congress to trace and expose all sources of accusations relating to the B-36.[23]

At stake was more than an investigation into the merits of the plane. Air Force missions and strategic doctrine were under fire, as well as Air Force leaders. For two months, a storm gathered around the B-36 hearings. The national press, sensing a showdown at hand, speculated on its outcome. On August 9, 1949, former Assistant Secretary of War for Air, Robert A. Lovett, appearing before the Van Zandt Committee, testified that he could not recall any protests from competing aircraft companies when the award of contract to Consolidated for 100 B-36s was announced. Nor could he think of any connection that his former employer, Brown Brothers Harriman, had with any aircraft manufacturing company.[24]

Many prominent Air Force general officers also testified, chiefly on their rationale for proceeding with the B-36 over the B-54 and the YB-49, among others. They were all asked if Secretary Symington had in any way pressured them. General Kenney, Commander of the Air University and former Commander, SAC, had to explain why he reversed himself in June 1948 and elected to support a continuation of the full B-36 contract. He referred to technical changes and improvements that led him to reconsider—the achievement by the airplane of effortless flight at 40,000 feet in 1948 and the development of considerably increased over-the-target speed. Kenney recalled that by June 1949 the airplane that had once performed no better than those "we already had, suddenly changed." The Air Force now possessed in the B-36 "the fastest, longest-range, best altitude-performing, and heaviest load-carrying bomber in the world."[25] When asked if his views were changed under political pressure, Kenney declared that nothing could "sell" him a bomber "except the bomber . . . If the bomber had the performance and would do the job that I was charged with carrying out, I would buy it."[26]

General LeMay, current Commander of SAC, testified that because his Requirements Committee had recommended of the B-36 as the best possible airplane for the Air Force's mission, he advocated that the Air Force acquire thirty-six additional B-36Bs* in January 1949. "I agreed with them, and I made that recommendation to the Senior Officers Board, and it was approved."[27] LeMay denied that his decision had been influenced by anyone inside or outside the Air Force. He added that he would assume responsibility for advocating the B-36 and declared, "If I am called upon to fight, I will order my crews out in those airplanes, and I expect to be in the first one myself."[28]

---

* The B-36, by 1949 known as the B-36B, had been improved by a fuel-injected engine, new bombing and navigating radar, and an additional 14,000-pound bomb-carrying capacity. It could also accommodate an atomic bomb. The evolution of the B-36 is covered fully in Marcelle Size Knaack's *Encyclopedia of U.S. Air Force Aircraft and Missile Systems,* vol. 2, *Post World War II Bombers, 1945–1973* (Washington, Office of Air Force History, 1988).

General Vandenberg testified that he followed the recommendation of his staff in March 1949 and cancelled the B-54 contract in favor of increased B-47 and B-36 procurement. As a result, according to Vandenberg, Secretary Symington requested recertification of funds on March 31, 1949. His request was approved by the Secretary of Defense on April 14, 1949, and by the President on May 4, 1949. Vandenberg explained that approval of the B-36 represented a balance of relative performance against tasks to be completed. Like Kenney and LeMay, he asserted that no political factors influenced his decisions to procure the B-36 and cancel the other planes.[29]

On August 12, 1949, Secretary Symington presented his views. He maintained that if the B-36 had been abandoned there would have been no intercontinental bomber without in-flight refueling. The Air Secretary declared that "no other bomber has ever been built with the range—the legs—to go from bases on this continent to the targets in question and return."[30] Attempting to prove the legality of the B-36 decision-making process, he repeated the chronology cited by General Vandenberg; certification for release of funds to procure thirty-nine new B-36s was approved "by my office January 28, 1949; by Forrestal March 2, 1949; and by the President April 8, 1949." Certification for the release of funds to add jet pods to twenty-one B-36As and two RB-36Bs already in Air Force hands and to purchase seventy-three new B-36s outfitted with jet pods was approved "by my office February 4, 1949, by Forrestal March 2, 1949, and by the President May 4, 1949. In March 1949, it was decided to cancel the B-54 contract and increase the procurement of B-47s and B-36s."[31]

The Air Secretary added that he had not, "directly or indirectly, gone counter in the procurement of any aircraft to the recommendations made . . . by the Chief of Staff and his staff, the Under Secretary of the Air Force and the special boards set up for recommending particular aircraft purchases." Symington charged that the attacks on the service "caught us at the period of absolute maximum workload on our top people" and could not have been more ingeniously timed if there had been a deliberate plot to undermine the Air Force's position in the competition for fiscal years 1950 and 1951 funding.[32] He reproached Congress for basing its probe on mere hearsay and an insinuating, unsigned letter as it attempted to regain proper oversight of the armed services. He acknowledged that possibly the purchase of the B-36 was an error; it was not a collective criminal act; he would not tolerate anyone's assailing the motives of the Air Force's high command, saying:

> That means a mass conspiracy or nothing—I take very bitter exception to that, and when the justification for such charges is articles in the newspaper . . . and anonymous letters, it is my opinion that that is a rather disgraceful way of utilizing congressional immunity. If Mr. Van Zandt believes the things he has said, I think the least we can do as long as he has so severely smeared the entire Air Force, is to repeat these charges over the radio, so we can have the proper recourse in replying to them.[33]

As a witness for industry, John K. Northrop of Northrop Aircraft Corporation and the manufacturer of the B-49, was asked if he thought General LeMay's recommendation to cancel the plane was made honestly, without political implications. Northrop stated that the recommendation, in his view, was made honestly, and he added that he did not fear reprisals by the Air Force. He recalled having first heard of the proposed merger of his company and Convair from General Joseph McNarney, AMC commander, who told him that the Air Force at that time doubted that Northrop's facilities in Hawthorne, California, could produce sufficient quantities of aircraft in which the service was interested—the B-49 or the RB-49, for example. McNarney then asked Northrop to consider a method whereby facilities operated by Convair at Fort Worth, Texas, might be used for the B-49 program. Northrop related that he attended a meeting on July 16, 1948, in Los Angeles, California, with Floyd Odlum and LaMotte Cohu, leading executives of Convair, and General McNarney at which they decided to build a major portion of the B-49 at Convair's Fort Worth facility.*

When asked whether the Air Force pressured him or his company to merge with Convair, Northrop stated that any pressure exerted was not improper. He viewed the decision as a logical solution to a difficult problem. Northrop had assumed that B-49 production was to "merge with and to continue the operation of the Fort Worth plant as the B-36 program terminated."[34] He denied that Symington had ever intimidated him or threatened his business interests to compel his company's merger with Convair. Northrop added that he had never heard of the formation of a huge corporation to be headed by Stuart Symington.[35]

J. H. Kindelberger of North American Aviation Company, defending the Air Secretary, argued that if he were in Symington's position, he would consider himself duty bound to provide for the country's security by guaranteeing a healthy aircraft industry. He added that an aircraft company required technical skills, engineering knowledge, and teamwork. These took years to acquire. It was thus essential that such groups be kept together "if we are going to have any safety in the country at all."[36]

Each contractor refuted Van Zandt's allegations regarding the Air Force's decision to approve production of the B-36 in the spring of 1948. No evidence was ever presented of Symington's and Odlum's plans for an aircraft conglomerate or of pressure by the Air Force on contractors to merge under the threat of losing business. Individual contractors felt that keeping abreast of the difficulties encountered by the aircraft industry was very properly the business of the Air Force.

The committee had not uncovered the source of the anonymous document. Symington had earlier indicated that he was fairly sure of its author's identity,

---

* The Air Force favored using the Fort Worth plant primarily because it was government owned. Congress would have resisted funding new facilities for Northrop when others were available.

but he did not reveal it in testimony. He and General Vandenberg had requested the help of Maj. Gen. Joseph F. Carroll, Director of the Office of Special Investigations (OSI) when the Van Zandt letter became known. Using a photostatic copy of an unsigned original, an OSI team—through Carroll's connections—secretly obtained typing specimens from the Office of the Assistant Secretary of the Navy and arranged for the FBI to check a number of suspect documents. After many negative returns, the FBI identified a typewriter from the office of Cedric Worth, a special assistant to the Assistant Secretary of the Navy. General Carroll prepared a report that was subsequently approved by Symington and Vandenberg and presented to House Armed Services Committee Chairman Vinson. Finally, Vinson called Worth, a World War II Navy commander, to testify. Under interrogation, he quickly admitted full authorship of the document.[37]

Even more surprising than the Worth revelation, was the testimony of Dan A. Kimball, Under Secretary of the Navy, who professed unawareness of his employee's activities. Kimball admitted not having pressed the issue of the anonymous letter even after Worth mentioned that he might be questioned about it. He had assumed that any connection Worth had to the letter would be brought out in the hearings. His argument impressed neither Congress nor the Air Force.[38] Following Worth's testimony, the House Armed Services Committee agreed to recess. In the meantime, events moved swiftly. The Navy decided to convene a court to examine the background of the Worth document as well as the activities of OP-23, a Navy organization established to gather information regarding the B-36. OP-23 was part of the Organizational Policy and Research Division of the Office of the Chief of Naval Operations. During the summer of 1949, OP-23 functioned much the way the organization run by Barton Leach did for the Air Force. Capt. Arleigh A. Burke, who would become Chief of Naval Operations in 1955, headed OP-23. Some of his staff were personally involved in public relations activities not approved by the Secretary of the Navy.[39]

By September, Navy leaders had become increasingly worried by recent disclosures before the House Armed Services Committee. While the Air Force had defended itself, the Navy became fearful that the Army, the Air Force, and the Secretary of Defense together were determined to reduce its size. This feeling was sustained by a September 8, 1949, cut of $353 million from its budget.[40] Then, Capt. John G. Crommelin, a distinguished naval aviator during the war, who had been called as a witness by a Navy board investigating Worth, vehemently attacked unification and claimed that the Joint Chiefs of Staff (JCS) and the Secretary of Defense were set on a course to eliminate the Navy.[41]

Thus on October 5, 1949, when hearings resumed, tension was high. The House Armed Services Committee had decided that the bulk of Worth's letter was comprised of statements from press clippings, official documents to which he had access, figments of his own imagination, rumors, and hearsay. Without demonstrable factual support, he had to withdraw his charges. As a result of the committee's findings, he was discharged from the Navy Department.[42]

The next day, October 5, 1949, the House Armed Services Committee began hearings to study the general topics of unification and strategy. In reality, however, the committee wished to examine the performance of the B-36 and the soundness of the decision to cancel construction of the Navy's supercarrier, the USS *United States*. It wished also to determine the effectiveness of strategic bombing and whether the Air Force was concentrating on it at the expense of tactical aviation. The committee, finally, sought to consider the JCS's procedures associated with the development of weapon systems.[43]

From October 7 to 13, following remarks by Secretary of the Navy Francis P. Mathews, the Navy brought out most of its leaders, civilian and military— including Admiral Arthur W. Radford, Commander in Chief of the Pacific Fleet; Fleet Admiral William F. Halsey; Admiral William H. P. Blandy, Commander in Chief of the Atlantic Command and United States Atlantic Fleet; and a host of other key witnesses. Radford called the B-36 "a billion dollar blunder" and "unacceptably vulnerable" when unescorted, citing its inability to hit precision targets from very high altitudes under battle conditions. He repeated the argument brought up in the August hearings—that the Air Force throughout all of 1948 was dissatisfied with the B-36. He claimed that Secretary of Defense Forrestal seemed very surprised when he read in a newspaper of the Air Force's intention to build additional B-36s. While Admiral Radford believed that strategic bombing was the primary role of the Air Force, he did not believe that the threat of "atomic blitz" was an effective deterrent to war. If strategic nuclear deterrence were to become the policy of the United States, Radford continued, then a much better weapon than the B-36 would be necessary.[44]

Symington took the offensive, also using arguments from the August hearings. He disputed the Navy's accusations that the Air Force had gone over Forrestal's head to procure additional B-36s and was "putting all its eggs in one basket" by overemphasizing strategic bombing. The Air Secretary pointed out that the costs of those B-36s purchased since the original contract for 100 equaled only 1.25 percent of the National Military Establishment's budget for fiscal years 1949, 1950, and 1951. Symington maintained that such a small percentage proved how little had been spent on "the surest way to deliver the atomic bomb or any other type of bomb against any aggressors, and from our own shores."[45]

Symington was well aware that with the B-36 and its 10,000-mile range the Air Force could compete with the Navy in intercontinental operations. He stressed that this cutting across the lines of roles and missions was what the Navy's critics of the B-36 feared most. To his knowledge, no one had ever debunked the development of an aircraft because of speed, altitude, or weight-carrying capacity. He charged that every time an Air Corps plane exceeded the 100-mile sea limit (the off-shore line beyond which Air Corps planes were not permitted to fly under a 1938 agreement with the Navy) "the storm broke." Distance had become "the sore point."[46]

Symington cautioned again and again that a minimum peacetime Air Force of seventy groups was required "as soon as possible," even though he realized that he would ultimately have to support the administration's contention that the country could not afford one.[47] He feared that the hearings and the attacks against the NME had "more than anything damaged the security of the United States," and had more than likely exposed to any aggressor vital technical information on the nation's latest equipment as well as detailed descriptions of U.S. military doctrine. In addition, he believed that the preservation of constitutional government itself had been endangered as Congress's focus shifted from investigating the attacks on the B-36 to questioning civilian control of the military establishment.[48]

General Vandenberg also refuted Admiral Radford's "all its eggs in one basket" argument. He disclosed that SAC had only 29 percent of all combat and combat support aircraft, and that only 5 percent of that total were B-36s. He stated that with the strategic bomber force "as it exists and as its development is planned, the American people have an instrument which can do the job assigned to it."[49] The hearings had hurt the military establishment, he asserted, and "serious problems of official and personal relationships have been added to the serious military problems with which we were already faced."[50] He denied that the Air Force was attempting to absorb naval aviation, saying, "We are not attempting in any way to organize any type of movement that would get naval aviation into the U.S. Air Force. Sufficiently satisfied with Vandenberg's point, Chairman Vinson stated that "if these hearings don't do anything else they have at least cleared up that point for the American public."[51]

In January 1950, the House Armed Services Committee concluded its investigation. It had found the procurement record on the B-36 clean and declared that not "a scintilla of evidence" existed to support charges brought against the Air Force. The committee wanted it made known that Secretary of the Air Force Symington, the leaders of the Air Force, and Secretary of Defense Louis Johnson had survived the inquiry with "unblemished, impeccable reputations."[52]

As a result of the hearings, the House Armed Services Committee's report on defense unification and strategy found none of the services without fault. Intercontinental strategic bombing was not the sole realm of air power; in fact, military air power consisted of "Air Force, Navy, and Marine Corps air power," and strategic bombing was only one part. This was essentially the position of the Air Force. It had never intended to control all military aircraft. To resolve the Navy's irritation because its aviation personnel had been barred from SAC activities, the committee recommended interservice war games to evaluate weapon systems and help reduce tensions between the services. While the committee supported civilian control of the armed forces, it did not want to prevent military personnel from freely testifying before Congress or to relegate the Congress to a "bystander role in issues pertaining to national defense."[53]

The report pointed out that the evaluation of the B-36 was properly within the jurisdiction of the Joint Weapon Systems Evaluation Board and recommended that the board should be consulted and its views fully considered, except during time of national emergency, in future "mass procurement of weapons." However, the board should not dictate to the services the types of weapons they could or could not develop. The committee, in a gesture of compromise, emphasized that it had no choice but to rely on the judgment of experts with respect to the development of any weapon systems. In the case of the B-36, it looked to the Air Force; in the case of the supercarrier, it looked to the Navy. Although deploring the manner in which the supercarrier was cancelled, Congress ruled that its construction would have to be postponed indefinitely because of high costs.

The B-36 controversy was a struggle between the Navy and the Air Force over the roles and missions of the services. Congress served as the natural arbitrator as controller of the budget. No longer did the free-spending wartime attitude prevail; the services had to compete for funds. It was the funding scramble and the subsequent cancellation of the supercarrier by Secretary of Defense Johnson that forced the B-36 issue to a head and brought it to the attention of Congress. Had the Navy obtained its supercarrier and a means to deliver the atomic bomb, it perhaps would not have challenged the Air Force and the B-36. The hearings thus brought certain conflicts into the open and allowed Congress to reestablish itself in its oversight role.

The Air Force attained the vindication of its civilian and military leaders by remaining steadfast on its primary responsibility for conducting strategic bombing with the B-36, the best means available for the mission. However, investigators realized that their rulings would not resolve future difficulties between the Air Force and the Navy. They believed that divergences would continue because of "fundamental professional disagreements on the art of air warfare" that eventually would have to be resolved by the two services themselves.[54]

The B-36 issue occupied the attention of the Air Force for most of a year. At stake were its basic roles and missions, the integrity of its leaders, and more specifically, the credibility of the Secretary of the Air Force. Symington admitted being pessimistic at the prospect of the hearings, and it was not until Cedric Worth revealed himself as the source of the anonymous document that the Air Secretary felt safe. He wrote to Barton Leach, recalling his apprehension just before entering Chairman Vinson's office after Leach had warned him of rough going . . . "I tried hard to whistle in the dark," Symington wrote, "and hope I deceived you and went in [to the Hearings] with a bucket of false assurances and could have embraced Worth when he pulled me out . . ."[55]

Meanwhile, Symington emphasized a consistent theme in the final months of his tenure—the increasing strength of the Soviet Union. He acknowledged that both the President and Secretary of Defense had repeatedly stated that security must come before economy. However, he cautioned that what he and others perceived as a rising Soviet menace must be recognized by those who clamored for a balanced budget. "Even in these prosperous times, how can the budget be balanced if we are to face honestly the implication of what is going on behind the Iron Curtain."[56] In February 1950, he emphasized that the Soviets possessed a ground army greater in number than the combined armies of the United States and its allies, the largest and fastest growing Air Force, and the world's largest submarine fleet. He wanted the American people to understand that the Soviet Union was capable of delivering a surprise atomic attack against any part of the United States, which had no certain defense against it.* He argued that its mistakes of the 1930s should have taught the United States to be militarily prepared at all times. Despite the merits of a balanced budget, Symington believed that the defense establishment could not sustain further spending cuts.[57] Thus he became the embodiment of the crusade for "defense first, economy second," and as Barton Leach saw it, Symington could not turn back. He told Symington, "You have raised the fiery cross, the clans are falling in here behind you, and you can't throw the cross away now or ever lower it."[58]

The 70-Group Program

The Air Secretary also took issue in October 1949 with Senator Leverett Saltonstall of Massachusetts, who stated before Congress that President Truman's fiscal year 1950 budget called for a greater amount of strategic bomber and reconnaissance strength than was recommended in the Finletter Report for a 70-group program. Symington wrote to Senator Saltonstall, "In no case did the aircraft program of the President's 48-group budget for fiscal year 1950 satisfy the requirements as shown in the Finletter Report of the 70-Group Air Force."[59] The Finletter Report's 70-group program called for an operating strength of 988 heavy- and medium-bomber and reconnaissance aircraft, whereas the President's 48-group program recommended 733. As for Saltonstall's statement that Air Force aircraft inventories exceeded a 70-group force, the Air Secretary pointed out that the majority of the aircraft in these inventories were World War II types which had to be replaced with technically superior varieties.[60]

As he had with Defense Secretary Forrestal, Symington in March 1950 made his views known to Defense Secretary Johnson. Calling Johnson's attention to recent budget cuts, he asked to be consulted before more were imposed in future. He told Johnson that while the Air Force could publicly support the cuts, the Chief of Staff and the Air Staff actually believed that "the present air strength of this country was not sufficient to protect it against an attack from

---

* The Soviet Union had exploded an atomic bomb in August 1949, and the event was announced in the United States the following month.

Russia." They strongly believed that the modernization of the 48-group Air Force should proceed without delay.[61]

Symington seriously doubted that the Air Force could adequately perform its training and war-waging missions without seventy groups. He also found it increasingly difficult to accept the fact that the Air Force was continually compelled to do more with less.* So, after having struggled for three years to cement the Air Force's status as an independent service and having failed to attain the 70-group program, he resigned his office effective April 24, 1950. At the same time, he told the President he was willing to accept another position within the administration. Symington was confident that he had built a sound organization within the OSAF. He believed that he had moved air power in the proper direction by "stressing modernity over tradition."[62] He had personally selected his under secretary, assistant secretaries and others and had attempted to balance his staff with experts from the business and academic worlds to provide innovative management techniques.

As the first Secretary of the Air Force, Symington established the important precedent of strong civilian leadership. He respected military leaders and knew he could not match them in military matters. Symington believed that his time had been best spent obtaining for the Air Force what it needed from Congress and acting as the civilian buffer between the service and the administration. Symington had demonstrated that the newly independent Air Force could function successfully under extraordinarily strong, dynamic civilian leadership. In fact, it could be argued that he left the Air Force with certain expectations of its future civilian leaders, becoming the model against which those leaders would be measured.

Symington chose his tasks as Air Secretary carefully. For example, he had not hesitated to promote air-to-air refueling before Congress, but had declined to quibble with the Chief of Staff over the kinds of resources earmarked for the Berlin Airlift. Although no legislative measure forced him to, he had stayed clear of operational decisions, acknowledging his lack of operational expertise. His role as he saw it was to learn what the Air Force required, to be accessible to Air Force leaders, to offer them his views, and to gain Congress's support. The vital difference between Symington and his predecessor, Robert A. Lovett, was that Symington had the authority of the Department of the Air Force behind him. Like Lovett, Symington was immersed in procurement matters, but, unlike Lovett, he had to work with the funding restraints of peacetime. By the end of his tenure, Lovett was concerned with discarding obsolete aircraft and with terminating production schedules. Symington was concerned with modernizing an Air Force that had been greatly reduced through demobilization.

---

* Nearly two years after leaving office as Secretary of the Air Force, Symington still felt that not having achieved the 70-group Air Force was the deepest disappointment of his career. *New York Herald Tribune,* Oct 29, 1951.

The Air Force had been skillfully steered by Stuart Symington through many crises in four years. It had, through his leadership, achieved autonomy as an equal member of the national defense team. It had recovered substantially from the effects of post-war demobilization and had made a good start toward building the kind of service that was "essential to our security in this air-atomic age."[63]

He stayed with the Truman administration as chairman of the National Security Resources Board and administrator of the Reconstruction Finance Corporation. In 1952 he won election as Senator from Missouri and subsequently distinguished himself through four terms. Perhaps the best assessment of his accomplishments as Assistant Secretary of War for Air and as Secretary of the Air Force was provided by W. Barton Leach. Writing to Symington, after hearing of his intention to step down, Leach concluded:[64]

> A democratic form of government, the realities of party politics, and the ingrained anti-militarism and isolationism of the American people form a combination which is diabolically contrived to prevent the development of adequate peacetime military forces in this country. Your accomplishment has been that you have taken these unlikely instrumentalities and operated them with such skill, patience, and persistence that, by damn, you have succeeded in making them do the job. And I think it is the first time in the history of the United States that this has ever been done.

No doubt Symington was an excellent leader. However, he had the distinct advantage over all of the Secretaries of the Air Force who followed him. He had authority. The National Security Act of 1947 had provided the Air Force Secretary, as well as the other service secretaries, a seat on the National Security Council. Because the President and the Secretary of Defense sat on the council, the Air Force, Army, and Navy Secretaries were able to speak for their respective services before the highest levels of the administration. This avenue was essential to the service secretaries since they did not enjoy the status of cabinet members. It was frequently said that Stuart Symington was the third most powerful man in the government after Truman and Forrestal. That would never be said of future service secretaries. The 1949 amendments to the National Security Act began a process that steadily eroded their authority while it enhanced the authority of the Secretary of Defense.

Symington endured an administration whose frugalities dampened his hope of securing a 70-group Air Force. However, with the beginning of the Korean War, the federal coffers were again opened and produced a "how much do you need" attitude from a previously austerity-minded administration and Congress. Despite a paucity of funds, the Air Secretary had managed to distribute sufficient Air Force contracts to keep the aviation industry afloat. He built a modern force as well as the research and development facilities to keep it going—all credible achievements. W. Stuart Symington was the kind of leader that the Air Force needed during its imperiled infancy.

Chapter 5

The Finletter Era (1950–1953)

The Air Force's principal task after Secretary Symington's departure was build-ing an atomic retaliatory force in spite of the budgetary restraints imposed by President Truman. In the postwar period, the American people were not about to spend lavishly for defense. Following World War II, demobilization and funding limitations had directly affected the size of the Air Force. From a wartime peak of 243 groups, 1,933 installations, and 2,411,000 troops, the Air Force had dwindled by June 30, 1950, to 48 groups, 210 installations and 411,000 troops.[1]

Thomas K. Finletter assumed office on April 24, 1950, as the second Secretary of the Air Force. His personality differed completely from Symington's. People who had worked for both men recalled that Finletter operated far more secretively than his gregarious predecessor and tended to keep tightest control over those issues which interested him most. He brought in John McCone as Under Secretary of the Air Force, but used him more as a deputy. The two carved out areas of influence, virtually shutting long-time Assistant Secretaries Eugene M. Zuckert and Harold Stuart out of policy matters. The nearly unhindered access to the Secretary of the Air Force granted by Symington was soon denied by Finletter and McCone.

The change in atmosphere within the Office of the Secretary of the Air Force (OSAF) quickly penetrated the military ranks of the Air Staff. The friendliness that had characterized Symington's interaction with uniformed personnel was nonexistent during the next regime. Finletter did little to foster the free exchange of military and civilian points of view. Certainly he and Air Force Chief of Staff General Hoyt Vandenberg did not get along as well as Symington and General Carl Spaatz had.

While Finletter concentrated on the larger issues of nuclear strategy and U.S. relations with the countries of the North Atlantic Treaty Organization (NATO), the power vacuum within the National Military Establishment (NME) that had existed when James Forrestal was Secretary of Defense began to diminish as authority became centralized within the Office of the Secretary of Defense (OSD). The National Security Act's 1949 amendments, which had begun to take effect, placed the Secretary of Defense over the service secretaries and furnished him an under secretary, three assistant secretaries, and additional staff. The NME was convert-ed into an "Executive Department" and renamed the Department of Defense (DOD). The services lost their executive branch status and were redesignated as military departments within the DOD. In addition, the service secretaries lost their membership on the National Security Council where they had previously sat as equals to the Secretary of Defense

After several months in office, Finletter and McCone, in consultation with the Air Staff, drew up a new set of Air Force objectives largely in response to the Korean War. These objectives were to provide first, the primary air defense of the United States; second, a strategic retaliatory force; third, tactical air support; and fourth, air transport. Symington's long-sought goal, a larger, 70-group Air Force, could now be realized. It was Finletter's task to evaluate the Air Force's needs and to present them before a Congress now willing to spend. The Korean War, which began in June 1950, forced significant changes in fiscal policy by President Truman and Congress from which the Air Force benefitted almost immediately. The 48-wing force of June 1950 swiftly grew, at least on paper, over the next two years, from 68, to 95, to 120, to 137, to 143, to 168 wings.* The increase in planes, equipment, and personnel proved difficult to manage for both the OSAF and the Air Staff. Adjusting budgets to comply with these varying figures and, afterwards, attempting to explain them to Congress required the efforts of both organizations. As expansion proceeded, a congressional subcommittee, evaluating the services' supply functions, pointed to duplication and called for a single separate establishment to equip all the services—Army, Navy, and Air Force. Because of the war, Finletter had to deal with the nagging problem of improving and expanding facilities for an increasing flow of personnel. Difficult training conditions and the lack of permanent barracks at some bases brought the Air Force unwanted publicity. He also had to acquiesce to Congress and solidify the Air Force's internal organization. After much effort, the Air Force Organization Act of 1951 became law and gave the service statutory authority over its own structuring.

The new Air Secretary came from a prominent Philadelphia family and had been a successful partner in the New York law firm of Coudert Brothers. His government career began in 1941 with a three-year assignment as a special assistant to Secretary of State Cordell Hull. Finletter was responsible for planning economic activities in areas liberated by the Allies during World War II, controlling foreign exchange, and overseeing the operations of the Alien Property Custodian. In May 1945, he became a consultant to the U.S. delegation to the United Nations Conference on International Organization held in San Francisco, California. He

---

* Gradually, the term wing became synonymous with the term group. Because of a Strategic Air Command (SAC) 1947 reorganization (Hobson Plan), the larger headquarters wing began to assume the same numerical designation as the bombardment or fighter group. By 1951 SAC wings had absorbed group headquarters functions, allowing a wing commander to serve as a group commander. The wing eventually replaced the group throughout the Air Force. The 95-group Air Force became the 95-wing Air Force. J. C. Hopkins, *The Development of Strategic Air Command, 1946–1981: A Chronological History* (Office of the Historian, Headquarters, Strategic Air Command, Jul 1, 1982), pp 7, 29.

accomplished his most notable public service between 1947 and 1948 as Chairman of the President's Air Policy Commission. The commission's findings, entitled *Survival in the Air Age*—but commonly called the *Finletter Report*—cautioned that an understrength Air Force would be unable to defend the United States against atomic attack. It urged that service capability be restored as soon as possible with the help of a viable aircraft industry, and it endorsed a 70-group Air Force of 6,869 first-line aircraft backed by a 27-group Air National Guard and an "adequately equipped" 34-group Air Reserve. After the commission disbanded, Finletter headed the Economic Cooperation Administration's special mission to the United Kingdom until 1949. President Truman selected him to succeed Stuart Symington as Secretary of the Air Force in April 1950 primarily because of his recognized excellent work on the Air Policy Commission.[2] Finletter believed that he had favorably impressed Symington during their frequent meetings on commission business and that he had been appointed as the second Air Secretary largely on Symington's recommendation.[3]

Finletter's background,* viewed by some people as too "eastern establishment," proved no impediment to Truman or to the U.S. Senate, which unanimously approved his appointment as Secretary of the Air Force. The *New York Times* called Truman's appointment of Finletter, "admirable . . . totally nonpolitical . . . eminently logical." There was some criticism from Secretary of Defense Louis Johnson, who was not as impressed with Finletter's background. He may have felt uncomfortable about an acknowledged expert in air power whose endorsement of more aircraft and forces directly contravened his own retrenchment policies. Johnson let the White House know of his displeasure with Truman's choice and hinted that he would resign if it were upheld by Congress. The President called Johnson's bluff and stood by Finletter. The following month, Clyde A. Lewis, Commander in Chief of the Veterans of Foreign Wars, wrote to Truman attacking Finletter for his association with the United World Federalists, an organization favoring peace through international unity.[4] Lewis declared Finletter an "avowed disciple of world government" whose patriotism was therefore suspect and demanded that he terminate his relationship with the group or be refused office. President Truman did not regard Finletter's membership as a threat to national security. Defending his appointee, he maintained that there was no more able a public servant than Finletter, and, because of his work on the Air Policy Commission, no better equipped man in the country to be Secretary of the Air Force.[5]

---

* His wife's family was as socially prominent as his own. Helen Gill Damrosch was the daughter of the famous New York Symphony Orchestra conductor, Walter J. Damrosch, who later became an adviser to the National Broadcasting Company. Her mother, Margaret J. Blaine, was the daughter of former Secretary of State and Republican presidential candidate, James G. Blaine.

Finletter's Team

Replacing Arthur S. Barrows as Under Secretary of the Air Force was another successful businessman, John A. McCone. It was McCone who had recommended that Symington soften his July 1948 Los Angeles speech, and it was Symington who recommended McCone to Truman and Johnson as under secretary. McCone, a Republican, had worked closely with Finletter on the President's Air Policy Commission. He was primarily responsible for coverage of military subjects in the *Finletter Report* and was credited with the specific recommendations that emphasized the increasing importance of air power. After publication of the report, he worked as a deputy for Secretary of Defense James Forrestal, advising him on air policy and the preparation of military budgets for fiscal years 1949 and 1950. In 1937 McCone had helped found the Bechtel-McCone Corporation and served as its president and director. His firm engaged in the design, engineering, and construction of factories, refineries, and power plants. One of its major wartime projects was the Birmingham Modification Center in Birmingham, Alabama, built to update B-24s and B-29s. It was one of the largest plants of its type ever operated by the Army Air Forces (AAF). Finletter wanted his good working relationship with McCone, established on the Air Policy Commission, to continue. In June 1950, when McCone assumed office, Finletter made it clear that they would act as partners and that the under secretary's jurisdiction would be as wide as his own. McCone would share with him "the responsibility for the general supervision and operation of the Department of the

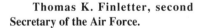
Thomas K. Finletter, second Secretary of the Air Force.

106

President Harry S. Truman and the Air Policy Commission. *Left to right*: **Palmer Hoyt, George Baker, John McCone, Truman, S. Paul Johnston, Thomas K. Finletter, and Arthur Whiteside, January 1948.**

Air Force, including procurement and related matters, previously the major responsibility of the under secretary's office."[6]

Another member of Finletter's team, Harold C. Stuart, was a Symington-appointed replacement for Cornelius V. Whitney, who resigned as Assistant Secretary of the Air Force (Civil/Military/Diplomatic) in April 1949. When Stuart took over the position in October 1949, it was redesignated Assistant Secretary of the Air Force (Civil Affairs). Stuart had been a lawyer and, later, a judge but resigned from the bench in 1942 to join the AAF, entering as a first lieutenant and advancing to colonel in 1946. Stuart retained a reserve commission in the Air Force and in 1949 became a highly valued special consultant to Stuart Symington, who admired his work and suggested to Louis Johnson that he be appointed Assistant Secretary of the Air Force.[7]

An addition to this cast of new characters was Eugene M. Zuckert, the old hand among civilians at the OSAF. The Assistant Secretary of the Air Force (Management) had been with the office since it was the fourteen-man Office of the Assistant Secretary of War for Air. Although only thirty-eight years old in 1950 when Finletter took office, Zuckert had already spent over four years with the Air Secretary's office and its predecessor. He was a recognized expert on the workings of the Air Force and the OSAF and had been instrumental in implementing Symington's ideas on fiscal management throughout the service. He knew who within the Air Staff and the OSAF could help him "get things done." Zuckert and Assistant Vice Chief of Staff Maj. Gen. William F. "Bozo" McKee had established the daily momentum which governed Air Force operations, while Symington and Chiefs of Staff Spaatz and Vandenberg attended to broader concerns such as the B-36 debate. Zuckert had been involved in many problem areas including racial integration, security, and the budget. The possibility that Finletter and McCone, both of whom knew little about how the OSAF and the Air Staff functioned internally, might clash with a subordinate, Zuckert, who knew practically everything, was very real.

Perhaps to avoid friction, Finletter, shortly after taking office, asked President Truman for permission to fire both Zuckert and Stuart. The President at first agreed that Finletter should be able to hire his own people. Meanwhile, Zuckert's friends in the White House adamantly opposed his removal, arguing that he be retained not only because of his expertise, but because of his affiliation with the Democratic party. He was, they reminded Truman, the only "real" Democrat among the OSAF's appointees.* Their protests persuaded the President to forbid Finletter from dismissing the pair.† The cordial working relationships that had existed within the civilian staff during Stuart Symington's tenure as Air Secretary were thus disrupted, if not finished.

Disappointed by what he regarded as interference by Under Secretary McCone, Harold Stuart chose to resign on May 25, 1951, and return to private law practice. Finletter recommended Roswell L. Gilpatric as Stuart's replacement. Gilpatric was another lawyer and a member of Cravath, Swaine & Moore, a leading New York law firm which served large corporate clients with which Finletter had previously been associated. In marshalling support for his nomination, Gilpatric contacted Frances Perkins, his mother's college roommate and President Roosevelt's former Secretary of Labor, and Jim Farley, Roosevelt's Postmaster General from 1933 to 1940, who had also served as chairman of the Democratic National Committee. On May 25, 1951, Gilpatric was sworn into office, but with a new title, Assistant Secretary of the Air Force (Materiel). Civil Affairs was split between him and Assistant Secretary of the Air Force (Management) Zuckert.[8]

Finletter's Relationship With The Air Staff

The solid relationship between the OSAF and the Air Staff that had flourished under Secretary Symington remained severely strained under Secretary Finletter. Specifically, a conceptual conflict emerged over the interpretation by

---

* McCone was a Republican, but apparently Zuckert's friends considered Finletter too "eastern establishment" to be a true Democrat.

† Zuckert professed that only after twenty-five years did he learn of Finletter's action and come to understand more clearly much of what had happened to him when he worked under the second Air Secretary. Intvw, Eugene M. Zuckert by author, Jan. 24, 1984.

the Chief of Staff and the Air Staff of the law defining the Air Secretary's role as head of the Department of the Air Force. The Korean War provided Finletter with many opportunities to inject his views on various aspects of planning and operations, and questions soon arose about his participation in determining force structure and the location of foreign bases. How much secretarial activity in Air Force policy intruded on a right held by the Air Staff? Was the Air Secretary merely a figurehead and, if he was, should he remain one? His personal involvement in the establishment of Thule Air Force Base in Greenland broke down the accepted arrangement under which the OSAF handled policy, the Air Staff handled operations, and both interacted as a team.

Secretary Symington's purposeful avoidance of operational decisions may have led the Air Staff to presume that it would continue to manage its areas of responsibility more or less separately from the OSAF.[9] His accessibility may have led his own staff to presume that any question requiring immediate attention by the Air Secretary would receive it. Eugene Zuckert recalled that he could approach Symington with a problem and be invited to suggest its solution, which would more than likely be supported. However, the more withdrawn Finletter was like "a Buddha." He would "mumble something" about a solution to a problem, then state that he did not "know if we are quite ready to . . . go ahead with it right now."

Comparing the two secretaries, Zuckert recalled that Symington telephoned the OSAF from Alaska one New Year's eve and ordered that the delivery of pay to enlisted personnel stationed there be expedited. Members of his staff and the Air Staff gladly worked until nearly midnight to accommodate him. Finletter

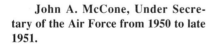

John A. McCone, Under Secretary of the Air Force from 1950 to late 1951.

Harold C. Stuart *(left)*, **Assistant Secretary of the Air Force (Civil Affairs) from 1949 to 1951, and Roswell L. Gilpatric, Assistant Secretary of the Air Force (Materiel) in 1951 and Under Secretary of the Air Force from 1952 to 1953.**

would never have directly acted in behalf of the lower echelons.[10] Whereas Symington kept track of even minor issues and made people feel that he was genuinely concerned about them, Finletter seemed disinterested in day-to-day Air Force routine. He was not generally viewed as "a warm person" or a skillful politician according to his executive officer, Col. William G. Hipps.[11]

Roswell Gilpatric felt that many of Finletter's critics were unfair, such as an officer who complained that the Air Secretary did not go up "on the Hill and fight, bleed, and die for the Air Force the way Mr. Symington did." Gilpatric believed that, although Finletter was a controlled, somewhat introverted, dispassionate man, he achieved in his way as much for the service as his predecessor.[12] At appropriations and armed services hearings in Congress, he went "all out within his capabilities to present the Air Force's case."[13] His style contrasted sharply with Symington's, which, in Gilpatric's view, was more flamboyant and indicative of a very keen sense of politics and publicity.

Under Secretary McCone's failure to get along with the Air Staff almost from the day he assumed office only worsened the tension between the OSAF and the Air Staff. According to Assistant Secretary Gilpatric, McCone was overstepping his role and "throwing his weight around" to such an extent that he created a serious rift between himself and his boss. General McKee, Assistant Vice Chief of Staff, regarded McCone as a "know-it-all" who showed little interest in dealing with the OSAF and treated the Air Staff with contempt.

McKee held McCone partly responsible for inhibited communications between the Air Staff and the OSAF.[14] Perhaps when McCone ran his own company he had not been obliged to answer to a corporate board or advisory group as, for example, Arthur Barrows had at Sears Roebuck. At any rate, in the fall of

1951, McCone resigned "for personal reasons,"[15] adding that he had stayed in office six months beyond his initial commitment of one year.

Although Eugene Zuckert appeared to be McCone's logical successor, he was not Finletter's choice. The Air Secretary selected the less experienced Roswell Gilpatric rather than someone from outside the OSAF because only a year remained before the next presidential election and Truman had chosen not to run. Gilpatric maintained that it was generally believed within the Air Staff and the OSAF that Zuckert was disappointed by having been passed over. Zuckert recalled, however, that in light of his less than cordial relationship with Finletter, he had no more chance of becoming under secretary than he had of "taking St. Peter's place." Zuckert was not surprised by Gilpatric's appointment and left office four months later to take a post with the Atomic Energy Commission.*[16]

The Air Staff and particularly the Chief of Staff, already sensitive to what they perceived as Finletter's isolation and McCone's disdain, became increasingly irritated by the actions and influence of Col. William G. Hipps, the Air Secretary's executive officer. Finletter relied heavily on Hipps's diligence and tact and valued what he termed his "wise and imaginative counsel." However, according to General McKee, Hipps overrode custom when he offered the Air Secretary opinions that countered those of the Chief of Staff and other senior members of the Air Staff. McKee argued that this was not the executive officer's job. Hipps's approach to serving the Air Secretary may eventually have cost him promotion beyond the rank of brigadier general. In fairness, he was probably trying to fill what he perceived as a void created by Finletter, who tended to withdraw even from the OSAF. Hipps had daily access to Finletter and may have felt free to submit his personal views despite their divergence from the Chief of Staff's. Hipps had been placed in a very difficult position when he was called aside by Finletter on their first meeting and emphatically told, "You work for me." He had most likely received no briefing on office politics. His predecessor, Col. William S. Steele, had already left the executive assistantship for his next assignment.[17] Hipps's conduct as man in the middle, while no cause of permanent damage, further soured the relationship between the Air Staff and the OSAF.[18]

During this period, more unpleasantness developed as Mrs. Vandenberg and Mrs. Finletter vied to be "first lady" of the Air Force. They often confronted each other over such matters as seating arrangements at social functions. Naturally, Secretary Finletter and General Vandenberg must have been embarrassed by their wives' growing antagonism and most likely expressed their dis-

---

* Both Gilpatric and Zuckert respected each other's talents. In fact, it was Gilpatric who later as Under Secretary of Defense advised Secretary of Defense McNamara that Zuckert was the best candidate for Secretary of the Air Force, which he became in January 1961.

comfort to each other and perhaps to their staffs.[19] Finletter would later declare that if the Air Secretary and the Chief of Staff did not work well together, the Air Secretary should replace the Chief of Staff. Apparently Finletter and Vandenberg worked well enough together. Their professional relationship remained intact.[20]

The Press and Public Relations

Before Stephen F. Leo resigned from the OSAF to work for Stuart Symington at the National Security Resources Board, he recommended that public relations, which he had directed, be transferred to the Air Staff. He was concerned about further cuts in Air Force personnel such as those that occurred when Secretary of Defense James Forrestal consolidated public relations within his own office. The Air Force had been more vulnerable than the other two services because its public relations had been conducted within a directorate of the OSAF. The Army's and the Navy's had been dispersed among combat arms, support agencies, and bureaus.[21] On May 9, 1950, the Air Staff accepted responsibility for public relations.

The services soon realized that Forrestal's purpose behind consolidation, to "eliminate competition for headlines and the airing of service controversy in the public press," had not worked.[22] The Office of the Secretary of Defense's (OSD) Office of Public Information (OPI), in fact, enjoyed no legal basis whatsoever for assuming the individual services' public information responsibilities. When OSD-OPI ordered the services to reduce their public information offices to small liaison groups, it never relieved them of their obligation to report the news in as timely and professional a manner as they always had. Forrestal may have eliminated some contention among the services by reducing the number of public relations offices, but he still had a public relations job to perform. OSD-OPI with its liaison groups represented less than 15 percent of the services' former public relations function. It was unable to track the progress of the Korean War accurately or efficiently.

In August 1950, General George E. Stratemeyer, Commander, Far East Air Forces (FEAF) expressed his displeasure with what he viewed as uncomplimentary and inadequate press reports of the close air support being carried out by the Fifth Air Force. He was extremely upset that after fifty-eight "consecutive days in direct and intimate support" of nearly 100,000 American and Korean soldiers, his forces had received less favorable coverage than a Marine air group that had supported fewer than 5,000 Marines for two weeks.[23] The Army, the Navy, and the Air Force all declared such a lapse intolerable. The individual services eventually regained their autonomy over public information and subsequently increased their staffs. The Air Force's public information functions were returned to the OSAF from the Air Staff on February 8, 1952.[24]

The Deputy System

As the Air Force expanded during the Korean War, the Air Staff and the OSAF hired consultants to help with crises in specific areas, such as manning and transportation. At times their work overlapped with that of the special assistants who had been part of the OSAF since the Unification Act. It became necessary for the Air Force to determine not only exactly where its special assistants and their areas of interest belonged—within the OSAF or the Air Staff—but also their organizational status and the basis of their authority. Thus special assistants became deputy assistant secretaries with specific areas of responsibility, such as the Deputy Assistant Secretary of Materiel for Installations, and the Deputy Assistant Secretary of Management for Personnel Management. (See Appendix 1, p. 262.) They became distinguished from short-term consultants and served as a communications bridge between the Air Staff and the OSAF. Some, like the Deputy for Manpower and Organization, were completely occupied within their own functional areas. Others were involved in outside but related responsibilities. The Deputy for Family Housing, for example, facilitated the acquisition and disposal of real estate. The deputies were able to prove to the Air Staff that they could complete many projects at considerable savings. They could also make it possible for statutory appointees to leave their offices for extended periods of time by screening much of the correspondance which normally would have been reviewed and signed at the highest levels of the OSAF.[25]

The designation of deputy assistant secretaries and their functions clarified where specific duties lay and lessened the Air Force's dependence on the individual skills and interests of a particular deputy or former consultant. But under Finletter more and more management responsibility slipped away from the OSAF to the Air Staff. Since Finletter stayed strictly removed from daily procedures at the OSAF and the Air Staff, the latter came to depend on the former for broad guidance rather than specific direction. Whereas Secretary Symington had showed great interest in nearly everything the OSAF and the Air Staff were doing, Secretary Finletter did not. Under Finletter the OSAF seems to have had little or no active role in the formulation of Air Force plans, policies, or programs.* It might not actually have had that much of a role under Symington. But because of his openness, curiosity, and political astuteness, he, and therefore the OSAF, seemed to have a hand in everything.[26]

The B-36 controversy, the ill-defined status of the OSAF under Symington, Symington's willingness to defer decisions on operational matters, and his natural effervescence might have obscured the OSAF's real detachment from policy

---

* Finletter would soon participate in developing strategies with the Air Staff to take advantage of Congress's positive new attitude toward the Air Force as the lead deterrent service.

formulation. Symington had made his job what he wanted it to be, and his methods pleased the Air Staff, but the Korean War exposed some of the shortcomings of their arrangement. It became evident to both the Air Staff and the OSAF that one man could never shoulder sole responsibility for an organization as large and complex as the Air Force.

While the Air Secretary and civilian appointees could generally inquire about policy, much of the preparation of answers to congressional and executive agency questions and requests for action would necessarily be accomplished at the operating levels of the Air Staff. Since the 1949 amendments to the National Security Act of 1947, the service secretaries had had to contend with an additional layer of policy direction from the Under Secretary of Defense, further squeezing their authority. The Air Staff could work with the OSAF to deal with the OSD, or it could on occasion shorten the route by dealing with the OSD directly, where policymaking was becoming increasingly centralized.

Procurement Difficulties

Within only six months of the beginning of the Korean War, Eugene Zuckert, Assistant Secretary of the Air Force (Management), concluded that his additional responsibilities for procurement were too burdensome. He was so busy with budget and personnel matters, as well as membership on various boards, that he had no time even to read many of the papers he signed. Fearful that this practice would cause him trouble, Zuckert sought relief from Under Secretary of the Air Force John McCone, believing him eminently suited to provide it because of his business experience, his knowledge of production, and his frequent interactions with such high-ranking military experts as Lt. Gen. Kenneth B. Wolfe, General Benjamin W. Chidlaw, and Lt. Gen. Orval R. Cook.* Zuckert argued that the Air Staff was reluctant to support his procurement decisions without concurring with McCone anyway, and he voiced frustration over "trying to exercise some indeterminate responsibility without any clear charter of authority." McCone hesitated to undertake any specially designated duties, believing that they would interfere with what he viewed as his primary task—to function as Finletter's overall general manager. To Zuckert, however, the time had come for a reappraisal of McCone's role and management philosophy in light of wartime demands on procurement.[27]

----

* All three had held various positions at Wright Field. Lt Gen. Kenneth B. Wolfe had been Director of Procurement and Industrial Planning for the Air Materiel Command (AMC) before becoming Deputy Chief of Staff for Materiel at HQ USAF in 1949. General Benjamin W. Chidlaw was commander of AMC before taking over Air Defense Command in July 1951 and Lt. Gen. Orval R. Cook was Director of Procurement and Industrial Planning for AMC from September 1949 to July 1951.

Because the Air Force had not instituted the same civilian checks as the other services on procurement, McCone regarded it as virtually impossible to manage. The Navy relied on a review process undertaken within the Office of Naval Materiel by an assistant secretary specifically dedicated to procurement.* The Army's procurement, carried out through technical services, was coordinated with civilians attached to the Office of the Assistant Secretary of the Army (Materiel). All Air Force procurement was handled at the Air Materiel Command (AMC) and coordinated with McCone. The under secretary had failed to see the need for further civilian control over it during peacetime. However, as the war created more and more demands on procurement, McCone became uncertain of his ability to stay abreast of rapid developments. He preferred to maintain his distance from the complexities of Air Force operations but remained fearful of congressional questioning if another crisis, such as the B-36 probe, arose. He thus suggested that a chartered civilian review committee answerable to him be established at Wright Field. He was eventually assigned a Deputy for Procurement and Material Programs within his office.[28] It seems clear that statutory appointees to the OSAF were compelled by the sheer enormity of their wartime responsibilities to leave Air Force procurement to the military specialists.† Civilian appointees were generally prevented by the brevity of their terms from fully mastering an increasingly complicated Air Force procurement system or comprehending the sophisticated weapons on which it focused.

The Effects of the Korean War

While the Korean War brought to light certain aspects of the relationship between the Air Staff and the OSAF, it also convinced the American people of the need for a ready Air Force. When war broke out on June 24, 1950, Secretary Finletter was visiting his summer retreat on Mt. Desert Island, off Bar Harbor, Maine. He departed for Washington early the following morning.‡ The President raced back from his weekend sojourn in Independence, Missouri, and that evening he and Finletter were among twenty participants discussing the emergency in a meeting at Blair House.[29] Besides the three service secretaries, Secretary of State Dean Acheson, Secretary of Defense Louis Johnson, and members of the Joint Chiefs of Staff (JCS) were also present. At subsequent

---

* Assistant Secretary of the Navy John T. Koehler handled procurement. The Navy also had a special assistant for procurement, and within the executive office of the Secretary of the Navy there was a procurement division.
† This was most likely the case with the other services as well.
‡ Secretary Finletter would make many trips between his Pentagon office and his Bar Harbor home that summer, causing some concern to at least one taxpayer who complained to his senator about the cost of the Military Air Transport Service's placing a

Blair House meetings over the next few days, President Truman consistently emphasized that any U.S. participation on the side of the South Koreans should be part of a United Nations (UN) effort to restore peace and security in the area. Even though the North Koreans were not members of the UN, they had flagrantly violated its charter. Consequently, the United States would be answering the call of the UN Security Council to effect a cessation of hostilities through a North Korean withdrawal to the thirty-eighth parallel.[30]

North Korea's aggression proved catalytic and roused the American public and the administration to spend whatever was necessary on the means for waging limited as well as total war. In Korea, Finletter contended, the United States had to prove to the communists that it would intervene against hostile acts in distant areas of the world. He espoused a policy of "peace through strength" that would allow progress in other areas (economic, political, social, moral, and spiritual) and would some day aid in the creation of a "world without war."[31]

Postwar demobilization, he believed, had hampered that policy. Finletter and McCone lamented this fact as they praised former Air Secretary Symington for continually demanding a larger and more modern Air Force. They took every opportunity throughout the Korean War to expand the service and, coordinating with the Air Staff, tenaciously pressed Congress for the means to fulfill what they had determined were the Air Force's four most important objectives: first, to provide for the nation's air defense; second, to provide a strategic counterattack; third, to provide tactical air support; and fourth, to provide air transport.

By September 1950, Finletter and the Air Staff had outlined their vision of an Air Force supported by a balance of radar, interceptor planes, anti-aircraft artillery, Navy picket ships, and guided missiles. The Secretary recognized the need for more and better radar stations in both the United States and Canada, as well as more interceptor planes to thwart any polar attack from the Soviet Union. He predicted that guided missiles would someday prove superior to piloted aircraft in penetrating enemy defenses and advocated scientific research to perfect them. Both he and McCone became deeply involved in an attempt to centralize missile control authority within the DOD.

Turning to his second task, to build a strategic counterattack, the Air Secretary argued before the Senate's hearings on defense appropriations for fiscal year 1952, that although the "strategic air weapon was the greatest asset the

---

four-engine Constellation and its crew at the disposal of one man. Answering the critic, Finletter acknowledged his several flights. He pointed out that many key officials had little opportunity to leave their desks during that critical period of the Korean War, and so the Secretary of Defense encouraged departmental secretaries and chiefs of staff to leave Washington for several days whenever they could. He authorized their use of military aircraft, knowing that at a moment's notice they could be called back to the capital. Ltr, Henry P. Becton to Senator Robert C. Hendrickson, Dec 28, 1951; Ltr, Thomas K. Finletter to Senator Robert C. Hendrickson, Jan 12, 1952, RG 340, File 020, Box 1060, NARA.

United States possessed,"* it required nearly continuous improvement to stay ahead of immediate technical responses by the Soviet Union. He believed that, in the event of war, strategic air would be the country's most powerful weapon against a possible enemy attack. He also recommended reevaluating the usefulness of tactical air, which had been largely ignored by the Air Force in the immediate post-World War II years. Tactical air could not of itself win ground battles but could create favorable conditions for ground forces by knocking out enemy aircraft. He revealed that the Air Force had been unable to acquire enough of the various types of aircraft needed for tactical air interdiction and close-in support.

He also revealed that the Air Force's troop carrier mission was at risk. In the event of war, the United States would not have enough planes at its disposal, either military or civilan, for air drops or for the transport and rapid deployment of troops. He expressed hopes about the recently approved expansion program to relieve air transport deficiencies.[32] The Korean War prompted a series of decisions between July 1950 and January 1951 that allowed the Air Force to expand, as of June 30, 1952, from 48 regular wings and a personnel limit of 416,000 to a total of 95 wings and a personnel limit of 1,061,000. Both new and stored aircraft would fill out the service's inventories. Secretary Finletter believed that the 95-wing goal would serve to keep the nation's industrial base functioning until a force could be built up to support future all-out mobilization. "We believe that we cannot afford now to build up a standing military establishment which will be able to fight a future war," the Air Secretary emphasized to Congress, "without placing too severe a drain on the economy."[33] He realized that achieving 95 wings would take time.

The quest for experienced personnel to fill the ranks of a swiftly growing wartime force was proving so difficult that Finletter found it necessary in 1950 to order to active duty the Air National Guard and elements of the Air Force Reserve as quickly as facilities and equipment would permit.[34] Some bases were not prepared for the rapid influx of recruits and reservists called to active duty. Overcrowding occurred at several locations, was tolerated for a time and soon overcome, but not before it was publicized in the press. At Lackland Air Force Base's training center in San Antonio, Texas, for example, accounts surfaced of sickness and hardship. Senator Lyndon B. Johnson of Texas quickly formed a committee to verify them. In response, Finletter directed Eugene Zuckert, who was vacationing on the west coast, to form a commission and with it to survey conditions at Lackland himself. Named to Zuckert's investigative team were Merrill Meigs, a Chicago newspaper executive; Arthur Fleming, president of Ohio Wesleyan University and former head of the Civil Service

---

* Finletter argued that the strategic air weapon's great offensive potential prevented the Soviet Union from attacking the United States.

Commission; and General Courtney H. Hodges, U.S. Army, (Ret.). For four days the commission shadowed the Johnson committee at Lackland, randomly selecting recruits to interview, even waking some in the middle of the night to ask them if they were warm enough. Zuckert's team proceeded to squelch rumors that people were "dying like flies" and reported to Finletter that, despite the extensive use of tents, housing facilities at the base were adequate. The incidence of disease was below that expected in such a large concentration of troops, pneumonia was not a problem, and respiratory infections were few. Recruits had to endure some privation, but soon adjusted to their spartan surroundings. Zuckert, however, had angered Johnson by conducting a competitive investigation.*[35]

Problems with reservists occurred as soon as expansion began. During the early months of the war, the majority of Air Force personnel in Korea were members of air reserve components who had volunteered or had been recalled to active duty. By April 1951, 72 percent of the officers in the Far East Air Forces (FEAF), the major air command directly involved in the war, were reservists. A Fifth Air Force study revealed that soon after the war started, approximately 80 percent of personnel were recalled air guardsman and Air Force reservists.[36] Some of them soon developed a "fear of flying" syndrome. They were World War II veterans who had fought overseas and were reluctant to fight again so soon. They deeply resented the disruption of their newly begun or resumed careers, civilian and military. General LeMay, head of Strategic Air Command (SAC), according to Finletter's executive officer, General Hipps, sought to make examples of all who refused to fly and ordered that they be court-martialed. The Air Secretary, fearful that such stern punishment might create negative publicity, interceded by summarily separating from the Air Force those who had pled "fear of flying." He then denied them all benefits. Finletter's actions infuriated LeMay, who blamed Hipps for them.[37]

The confusion in many service programs as a result of the Korean War—particularly in those for personnel, materiel, and the reserves—exposed the need for a different approach to projecting future requirements. In August 1950, the Air Staff suggested that longer-range programming be tied to specific goals rather than fiscal years. In March 1951, an Air Staff study group, estimating the size of the service for 1954, investigated four main activities: personnel, aircraft procurement and industrial mobilization, base utilization, and mutual defense assistance. In May 1951, after considering many factors such as force requirements, deployments, and concepts of operations, and after collective review and comment, the Air Staff presented its findings entitled "The 140-Wing Air Force Program."[38]

---

* Zuckert recalled that "he called me up and really chewed [me] out."

Finletter placed his faith in SAC as the core of the deterrent force. In a speech before the Commercial Club of Cincinnati, Ohio, in January 1952 he said, "The Air Defense Command will strike at the birds, the Strategic Air Command will strike at the nest, their bases, and other installations."[39] Holding to his theory of deterrence, Finletter calculated that a 126-combat wing force would enable the United States to play an indispensable role in preventing war anywhere and would provide enough time for the United Nations to become the primary enforcer of world peace. The Air Secretary often testified that he hoped "our sword [would] never be used first. But if the blow comes upon our shield [it] will be used." The 126-combat wing force would constitute an armada so strong that "no enemy would think it safe to attack."[40]

When Finletter spoke of the importance of modernizing air defense, he emphasized the strategic bomber force and often noted Soviet technological capabilities and capacity for weapons production. Addressing a National Industrial Conference Board in San Francisco, California, in March 1952, he stated: "It came as quite a surprise to those who believed the Russians were not much good at engineering that they were able to build . . . the MiG-15. It would be well for us to recognize that the Soviets have exploded an atomic bomb, that they have produced the MiG-15, and that they are capable of very high manufacturing, and scientific performance."[41] He added that the United States, in the midst of the greatest arms revolution in history, should pay the closest attention to achieving high quality production. His message was clear: to stay ahead, the United States had to modernize its forces.

Finletter and General Vandenberg were protective of SAC and made every effort to prevent the diversion of its funding to a strengthened air defense system and a tactical atomic force. During the summer of 1951, the three services established Project Vista with a group of scientists at the California Institute of Technology to discuss and report on adapting atomic weapons to limited warfare. Lee DuBridge, who headed the project, had invited Robert Oppenheimer, the prominent scientist of Manhattan Project (Atomic Bomb) fame, to participate. Oppenheimer reorganized chapter five of the Vista report and called for a three-way distribution of fissionable materials, part to SAC, part for smaller tactical weapons development, and the remainder to a contingent reserve. This proposal alarmed Finletter, Vandenberg, and David Griggs, Chief Scientist of the Air Force, who all wanted SAC to continue receiving the largest share of nuclear materials. Oppenheimer's revision significantly restricted SAC's importance and made him suspect to Air Force leaders.

Because the Vista report dealt largely with Western Europe, the project's scientists felt obliged to present their conclusions to General Eisenhower, the European Commander. James Perkins, aide to Secretary of Defense Robert A. Lovett, promised DOD support of such a presentation to circumvent the jurisdiction and control of any one military service. Finletter was outraged and accused Perkins of "stabbing him in the back." Finletter called home General Lauris

The MiG-15 jet fighter, the equivalent of North American Aviation's F-86 Sabre.

Norstad, the highest ranking Air Force officer in Europe, to counter the Vista group's recommendations. Returning to Europe, Norstad lectured the visiting scientists on the importance of strategic warfare. Discerning his displeasure, they submitted recommendations that he was able to approve.

Despite Norstad's conversion of the group, Oppenheimer did not win any Air Force friends in Washington. He further alienated service leaders when he involved himself in the 1952 "summer study" which deemed air defense as important, if not more important, than strategic deterrence. The Air Force had consistently supported air defense, but was concerned that an enhanced air defense system with a newer and advanced early warning line would be bought at the expense of SAC. Oppenheimer's air defense stand—and his subsequent non-support of a second weapons laboratory to speed work on the development of a hydrogen bomb, a crucial Air Force priority—disturbed Finletter, Vandenberg, and the Air Staff.

Finletter tried to dispel the impression among scientists that he was a war-monger for supporting the hydrogen bomb. He also tried to reach an accord with Oppenheimer. The Air Secretary and two of his assistants, William Burden and Garrison Norton, invited Oppenheimer to a luncheon attended by David Griggs. Oppenheimer was uncommunicative and did not endear himself to Finletter. The renowned scientist would later be called before the Atomic Energy Commission (AEC), for which he had acted as a consultant, to answer for his affiliations with former members of the Communist party and to explain his resistance to U.S. development of the hydrogen bomb. His security clearance was subsequently withdrawn.[42]

Force Structure

The buildup of the U.S. Air Force was a response to more than the Korean conflict. The war merely pointed to the need for constant preparedness and emphasized the importance of NATO should the Soviets attempt to encroach on Western Europe. The threat of atomic war loomed more menacingly as the Soviets improved their ability to deliver weapons. In addition to the atomic bomb, the Soviets possessed the Tu-4 bomber and were perfecting an advanced bomber.

As the Korean War progressed, pressures from both the administration and Congress for balanced budgets compelled all three services to delay their expansion programs and severely disrupted Air Force planning. It appeared that new figures regarding the size of the Air Force were being revised monthly, "stretching out" or delaying the hoped-for attainment of 143 wings until 1957.[43]

In February 1952, Air Secretary Finletter summarized his mid-year budget report for Defense Secretary Robert A. Lovett, pointing to three primary areas of Air Force activity. First, the Korean operation; second, the ongoing build-up toward 80 combat wings plus 15 airlift wings (the 95-wing force) as authorized by Congress and scheduled for achievement by June 30, 1952; and third, the further deployment of air strength into other strategic areas in accordance with U.S. international commitments, principally to NATO. The Air Force Secretary boldly stated that the Korean War "has inescapably affected our capacity to fulfill our plans and schedules in the other two primary areas."[44] He noted that approval of 126 combat wings by the Joint Chiefs of Staff (JCS) and Secretary of Defense proved that those most responsible for planning the total military requirements of the nation were shrewd enough to realize the crucial role of air power in the immediate future.

Before settling on a 126-combat wing force plus a 17-airlift wing force (a 143-wing force), the Air Staff had examined various numbers. A subsequent combined Air Staff and Air Force Council* (AFC) review determined that a 140-wing Air Force could be far more easily activated by the end of 1955 than by the end of 1954. After reconsidering proposed programs and consulting with the Air Staff, Secretary Finletter and General Vandenberg directed the Air Force to build a 138-combat wing force by 1954 (plus 25-airlift wings for a total of 163 wings) constituted and phased somewhat differently from the force originally

---

* The Air Force Council was established by General Vandenberg on April 26, 1951, to formulate Air Force objectives and policies; to review, approve, and implement programs; and to disseminate program and policy guidance to the Air Staff. Its membership consisted of the Vice Chief of Staff, Assistant Vice Chief of Staff, Deputy Chiefs of Staff, Comptroller, and the Inspector General. Directorate of the Air Force Board Structure Office, "Study of the Air Force Board Structure" (HQ USAF, Washington, 1973), pp 6–7.

described to the AFC. A final revision was published as "Air Force Objectives through FY 54" on July 30, l951. This statement of strategic guidance and program objectives for attaining the 138-wing force by the end of 1954 became the foundation for the subsequent development of the 1953 Air Force Budget Program.[45]

After the 138-combat wing program was approved by the Chief of Staff and the AFC, it was presented to the JCS, which sanctioned only a 126-combat wing program on October 1, 1951, to be developed at the same rate as the 95-wing program. This requirement was supported by a logical analysis of the nature of the threat seen at the time. (See Table 3 for a breakdown of the 80-and 138-wing programs.)

Of course, the change from a 138- to a 126-combat wing program required the Air Force to alter its budget drastically. For 1951 alone, four supplemental appropriations were enacted by Congress. However, an October 29, 1951, budget ceiling for 1953 imposed on each of the services by the Secretary of Defense complicated financial preparations. The purse strings loosened by the war were being tightened. Of a $45 billion budget, the Air Force's portion was $17 billion, including construction funds, with a suballocation of $5.1 billion for aircraft procurement. This directive completely upset the budgets being devised by the Air Staff and Air Force field components. An Air Staff review disclosed that the new ceiling completely ruled out the possibility of a modernized service with 126 modern combat wings and supporting forces by 1954.

The Air Force had to find avenues to additional monies. Secretary Finletter suggested that scheduled slippages be allowed, that future progress payments (payments for work accomplished before final product completion) be held to a minimum and, if these actions were not successful, that modernization of the 126-combat wings be delayed. He cautioned, however, that the Air Force should not lose sight of its ultimate goal: the attainment of the wings and the modernization of SAC. During the last weeks of 1951, the Air Staff worked late hours to arrive at a new total budget request of $20.9 billion which was approved by Secretary Finletter and General Vandenberg on December 31, 1951.[46] The President eventually approved a budget estimate of $20.7 billion. The Air Secretary and the Chief of Staff agreed to "stretch out" the 126-wing program and complete it by the end of 1955.

With 17 additional troop carrier wings, the goal grew to a 143-wing Air Force that included 1,210,000 military and 410,000 civilian personnel. Publicly, Secretary Finletter defended 126-combat wings as adequate. Privately, he was cautious about what the Air Force could really accomplish with 143 wings. He believed that the Air Force was just powerful enough to handle three main tasks—the air defense of the country, tactical operations (mainly in NATO), and strategic nuclear deterrence—with nothing left for local wars.[47] This view would appear to confirm former Secretary Symington's view that no fewer than seventy groups should constitute a peacetime Air Force. This was a different

Table 3

Unit Aircraft Assigned the 80- and 138-Combat Wing Program

Wings	Program		Aircraft	
	80 Wings	138 Wings	80 Wings	138 Wings
Heavy Bomber	6	12	180	360
Medium Bomber	20	40	900	1,800
Strategic Recon (Heavy)	4	6	120	1,800
Strategic Recon (Medium)	4	8	180	360
Fighter Escort	7	10	525	750
Fighter Interceptor	20	31	1,500	2,325
Light Bomber	4	5	122	240
Fighter Bomber	11	5	825	1,125
Fighter Day	0	6	0	450
Tactical Recon	4	5	264	330
Total Combat Wings	80	138	4,686	7,920
Total Airlift Wings	15	25		
TOTAL WINGS	95	163		

Source: Vandenberg Collection, Library of Congress.

time. Spurred on by the Korean War and increasing U.S. obligations to NATO, the American public was ready to spend; 126 wings were not enough.

Finletter himself became involved in establishing service policy to take advantage of the era of positive feeling toward air power. At his summer home in Bar Harbor, Maine, during the summer of 1952, he met with Lt. Gen. Laurence Kuter, Deputy Chief of Staff for Personnel and Acting Vice Chief of Staff; General Nathan F. Twining, Vice Chief of Staff and Acting Chief of Staff for General Vandenberg, who was hospitalized; and Under Secretary of the Air Force Roswell Gilpatric. They produced a document called the Bar Harbor Memorandum that, in effect, outlined a political strategy for the Air Force. Because the premise that land-based air power was at last recognized by Congress as the keystone of American military power, the conferees felt free to press for 143 wings. They believed that the service now had to bear the responsibilities of power: "No longer can the Air Force accept the proposition that it is not ready to assume any kind of command over mixed forces of the United States or over allied forces."[48] The strategy expressed in the memorandum, which they entitled the "new phase," was based on the faith of the Congress and the public in the efficiency of air power as a deterrent force. The memorandum stressed several specific goals such as the constant maintenance of strategic bombing forces on a wartime footing against the Soviets and the achievement of the means to fight local wars.

Air Force Under Secretary John McCone had been surprised in February 1951 when the Air Staff, reacting to the new attitude toward military spending, presented him with a $5.5 billion "bill" to sign for bases and research and development facilities. He sought the advice of Stuart Symington, noting that now the Air Force seemed to have everything that the former Air Secretary had turned down over the previous five years. Symington responded that he had been forced to say no to the Air Force when funds were unavailable. McCone stressed that he wanted the Air Force to have what what it needed to function properly but also stated, "I don't want to gild the lily just because the public purse seems open."[49]

Finletter held that the Korean War finally broke the budgetary log jam maintained by the administration's fiscal experts. However, increased appropriations covered far more than the immediate needs of the war; they countered the anticipated threat of expanded Soviet atomic capability as well.[50]

In spite of Congress's generosity, Under Secretary McCone ordered a review of the rationale by which the Air Force prepared its public works budget. In April 1951, he soundly rejected the Air Staff's decision to support 100 percent of the estimated cost of facilities appropriated for 1952. McCone wanted more information from the Air Staff justifying its decision because he knew that Congress (specifically Chairmen Russell, Vinson, and Mahon) wanted to phase construction over a period of several years and to include in the fiscal year 1952 budget only funding of minimum facilities necessary to operations. He thus asked Harold Stuart, Assistant Secretary of the Air Force (Civil Affairs), to provide rigorously defined construction needs with cost break-downs and comparisons at four typical bases: a medium bomber base, a troop carrier base, a fighter-interceptor base, and a Military Air Transport Service (MATS) base. McCone further stipulated that Stuart focus on facilities being reactivated, not on those already in operation. He directed him to consult command representatives, the Air Staff, and expert civilian advisors from distinguished engineering firms and to present his findings to the OSD and the Bureau of the Budget in only four days. It is not known if Stuart ever completed his task, but he regarded it as an intrusion by McCone into matters that he used to handle personally for Stuart Symington. Exasperated, he resigned his office one month later on May 25, 1952, and returned to his family's oil business in Tulsa, Oklahoma.[51]

The seemingly continual play with the numbers relating to allotted funds and service size projections was taking its toll on the OSAF. In April 1951, McCone complained to the Secretary of Defense that revised fiscal year 1952 budget estimates caused the deferment of important procurement and construction decisions, and that a mutual understanding as to the implications of reductions was essential.* He noted that in compliance with 1952 budget estimates, the Air Force had planned to build the productive capacity of the aircraft industry from 200 units to 1,100 units per month by December 1952. After attaining 95 wings, the Air Force would taper off its requests to around 300 units per month. McCone warned that if follow-on orders were not placed by January 1, 1952, a "precipitous drop in production would occur early in 1953." He called for immediate supplemental funding to ensure the 1,100-unit production schedule. Should such funding be withheld, he recommended that a smaller level of production, around 700 units per month, be authorized. He urged a quick decision because a substantial number of alternate sources for aircraft engines and components, most of which were non-aircraft companies, would have to be established to serve the larger program. McCone's expertise in the procurement field had proved to be an asset to the Air Force and would be difficult to replace.[52]

Other Issues

Secretary Finletter felt that matters associated with air bases deserved more attention from the Air Staff and should be handled by a Deputy Chief of Staff (DCS), a general officer, rather than a colonel. In his view the three pillars of Air Force operations were men, machines, and air bases. He failed at every attempt to secure a DCS for bases, but succeeded, ultimately, in acquiring a major general and a series of special assistants. Finally, Edwin V. Huggins, who

---

* Finletter, regarding McCone as his partner, had from the beginning allowed him great authority. However, he did step in and assert his own authority if he disagreed with McCone's views or activities.

replaced Roswell Gilpatric in January 1952 as Assistant Secretary (Materiel)* was given primary civilian responsibility for bases.[53]

Finletter possessed a clear understanding of the Soviet threat and the necessity of expending huge sums to help contain it. He was dismayed that while the Soviet Union had devoted a great deal of its post World War II energy to developing military air power, the United States had dismantled its Air Force and brought airplane production to a virtual standstill. At the outset of the Korean conflict, the Air Secretary acknowledged that the Soviet Union enjoyed a huge lead in aircraft production over the United States but held that U.S. planes were better. In a letter to Congressman John F. Kennedy of Massachusetts in September 1952, he warned that the country should not become complacent about its technological superiority. "We are well behind the Soviet Union," he admitted, and "have not yet reached the level of strength that is necessary for our security."[54]

The Air Staff supported Finletter's view. General Nathan F. Twining, Air Force Vice Chief of Staff, felt that the United States focused too much attention on the Soviets Union's massive land army and not enough on its "highly versatile complex of air forces." He noted that since World War II, the Soviet Union had produced more than twice as many tactical aircraft as the United States and had also "outproduced the United States in strategic bombers" despite a cooperative effort of the Air Force, JCS, and National Security Council to support the continuous development of SAC. General Vandenberg confirmed that the Soviet Union had outdistanced the United States in aircraft production through prodigious industrial expansion and had, in fact, built a larger air force. He also cautioned that they were fast approaching the U.S. Air Force qualitatively, converting rapidly to modern jets. Finletter, however, believed that "our long-range bomber force combined with our national advantage in atomic weapons" tilted the balance of military power in favor of the United States.[55]

Of particular interest to Under Secretary McCone was the effect on missile technology of congressional anxiety over projected Soviet growth. In August 1950, he concluded that the future of U.S. air defense and offense lay in supersonic ground-to-air guided missiles. He advocated the intensive research and development of the entire missile family—ground-to-air, air-to-ground, and air-to-air—and the complete reorganization of missile development programs in all three services. He compared what he felt were meager expenditures by the United States on such weapons as the Army's ground-to-air Nike missile ($20 million) and the Navy's Bumble Bee missile ($60 million) with $1.5 billion the Germans had reportedly devoted to the V-2 rocket. "Obviously," McCone stated, "our shots have been spread and our effort thus far on any missile project is

---

* This was the same office that would be redesignated the Office of the Assistant Secretary of the Air Force (Installations and Logistics) on February 28, 1964.

insignificant when contrasted with the German V-2 effort."[56]

McCone looked to the Manhattan Project as the management model for his missile development effort. He recommended the appointment of a virtually all-powerful managing director whose communication with the DOD, the Congress, and the White House, would be facilitated by a "board of directors" composed of the Secretaries of the Army, the Navy, and the Air Force, or their under secretaries, and the chairman of the Research and Development Board. He also recommended an appropriation of $2 to $3 billion.[57]

Finletter supported McCone's idea, but the two men were disappointed when President Truman decided that such an undertaking be directed by the Secretary of Defense. Truman had worked very hard for passage of the National Security Act of 1947 and had upheld its 1949 amendments in an attempt to strengthen the Secretary's power. He would not tolerate the dispersal of authority from the OSD.

Finletter and McCone had been naive to imagine that the President would support the Air Force's plan. Further, it appears that they had paid insufficient attention to the clash between the services over roles and missions since World War II. Whether the Army or the Air Force gained control of air defense had not been settled and would not be until the late 1950s. At that time none of the services was willing to concede it to another. Even when the Air Force gained control of ballistic missiles, both the Navy and the Army continued to develop their own.[58] The idea of a "missile czar" with full oversight was a good one, but almost impossible to implement given the intensity of interservice competition.

General Hoyt S. Vandenberg, USAF Chief of Staff from April 1948 through June 1953.

Frustrated in his effort to establish a centralized authority for missile development, Finletter continued to press the issue of research. In September 1950, Finletter created the position of Special Assistant for Research and Development and appointed William A. M. Burden to fill it. Burden built the organization which, five years later was redesignated the Office of the Assistant Secretary of the Air Force (Research and Development).[59] In July 1952, a Senate subcommittee report on the decline of U.S. air power since World War II denounced the Korean War air buildup as "a saga of bad programming; neglected warnings; unbelievable lack of coordination; abuse, misuse, and disuse of power; bad advice to the Executive;"[60] and overall lack of cooperation between many government agencies. The subcommittee found no excuse for the DOD's failure to set realistic production schedules, but exonerated the aircraft industry for any slippages, pointing to the "bureaucratic inattention" with which it met every time it required such necessities as tools, facilities, materials, and manpower. The DOD had furnished neither promised equipment and components nor urgent lists for equipment until eighteen months after the war had started. "Blow hot, blow cold" production timetables caused by the "stretch-out" of various programs produced a nearly crippling effect on industry. In addition, the report stated that the DOD lacked procurement and production expertise and had wasted money by placing contracts with incapable producers.[61]

In light of such findings, the Senate advised the DOD to reassess the country's "mobilization philosophy" and to develop fiscal and industrial strategies suitable to a limited conflict. It urged the Secretary of Defense to appoint a full-time "production czar" with the power to determine priorities, establish schedules, and order

General Nathan F. Twining, USAF Chief of Staff from June 1953 through June 1957.

quantity production. Further, it requested that the Aircraft Advisory Committee of the Munitions Board present Congress with recommendations to guarantee an aircraft industry healthy enough in peace to quickly mobilize in war.[62]

The sudden onset of the Korean War emphasized the ill-defined duties of the Munitions Board* and allowed its decisions to be regularly challenged by the services. In the fall of 1952, Secretary of Defense Lovett recommended to President Truman that the Munitions Board be eliminated and replaced by an Assistant Secretary of Defense. In June 1953, a new position, the Assistant Secretary of Defense for Supply and Logistics was created. This action placed yet another layer of authority between the OSD and the service secretaries.[63]

The Air Force Organization Act of 1951

The Air Force Organization bill was introduced by Congressman Carl Vinson of Georgia, Chairman of the House Armed Services Committee. It became law September 19, 1951, and granted the Air Force statutory authority over its internal organization. The National Security Act of 1947 had established a Department of the Air Force and a United States Air Force independent of the U.S. Army and allowed the Secretary of the Air Force broad discretion in establishing and staffing his office. Public Law 150, the Air Force Organization Act of 1951, supplemented the 1947 act and set down a brief codification of the system under which the Air Force had been operating.†[64]

Secretary Finletter was reluctant to support the measure before the House Armed Services Committee in January 1951, arguing that the Air Force had not existed long enough as an independent service to competently formalize its structure and was totally preoccupied with the Korean War and the burdens of rapid expansion. He preferred that legislative action be postponed and acceded to Congress's wish to discuss the bill at that time but only if he were assured that it would incorporate certain changes before being passed.[65] In the strongest terms he urged that the bill clearly specify the status of the Air Force's civilian and military leadership. The authority exercised by the Chief of Staff over the Air Force, which, he noted would not interfere with the authority exercised by the Secretary,

---

* Zuckert, McCone, and Gilpatric were members.
† The National Security Act of 1947, which described the Air Force only broadly, was flexible and allowed the Air Secretary to shape the service's organization as needed. The Air Force realized that eventually it would have to adopt a formal structure codifiable in law. It did so, and the Air Force Organization Act was passed in 1951. According to the National Security Act and its 1949 amendments, the Chief of Staff of the Air Force, under the direction of the Secretary of the Air Force, exercised command over the United States Air Force and was charged with the duty of executing all lawful orders and directions which might be transmitted to him. At least on paper the Secretary of the Air Force was in charge of the Air Force.

should be expressed as "command" rather than "supervision," the word command more aptly defining the military function. General Vandenberg expressed his belief that command of the Air Force's combat elements should reside directly with the Chief of Staff. He added that he did not anticipate the Chief of Staff's fully exercising this complete control except in times of emergency.[66]

Against congressional pressure to combine certain service elements, Finletter insisted that the Air Force would be incomplete without its own Quartermaster General, Surgeon General and Chaplain.* He testified that the Air Force could only support a unified medical organization within which all three services were represented. If the Army or the Navy were to have their own, so should the Air Force. Finletter supported Congress's wish to specify the Air Defense Command (ADC), the Strategic Air Command (SAC), and the Tactical Air Command (TAC) by statute and grant their leaders four stars. However, he wanted to avoid creating an organization so "terrifically rigid" that it could not be changed or granted a new command "without a new bill."[67]

After much debate over House and Senate versions, Congress passed legislation granting the major changes desired by Finletter and Vandenberg. The Chief of Staff, under the direction of the Secretary of the Air Force, was granted authority over ADC, SAC, TAC, and such other major commands as might be established by the Secretary of the Air Force during war or national emergency.[68] The Air Force would consist of these three major combat commands and other such commands and organizations established by the Secretary of the Air Force in the interests of economy and efficiency of operation.[69] Essentially, passage of the bill legalized the Air Force's structure and reaffirmed the authority of the Secretary of the Air Force by firmly establishing the principle of civilian control.

Logistical Control

Another issue in which Secretary Finletter and particularly Under Secretary Gilpatric became involved, was supply management. When the Air Force gained independence in 1947, it agreed to divide responsibility for supply management with the Army. The Air Force took over budgeting for use of items purchased by the Army, such as clothing and equipment, while the Army continued to store, distribute, and maintain them. In compliance with a November 1949 policy statement from the Secretary of Defense, the Air Force, beginning in 1950, would gradually assume responsibility for storage and maintenance of some

---

* The Air Force at the time had its own Surgeon General, Chaplain, and logistics functions, which had been formerly provided by the Army before unification and for a time afterwards.

clothing and small arms "for which a counterpart already existed in the Air Force depot system."[70] The Air Force hoped by June 1954 to absorb all supply and maintenance performed for it by the Army. On February 23, 1951, the Army and the Air Force agreed that the latter would be responsible for the supply and maintenance of all items handled for it by the Quartermaster Corps. The following April, Assistant Secretary Zuckert further clarified Air Force supply policy, stating that except for ammunition (bullets), subsistence (food or provisions), medical supplies, and certain other categories included in interdepartmental agreements, the Air Force would begin on July 1, 1951, to assume, gradually, responsibility for all its supplies.[71]

In the meantime, as part of a larger congressional effort to assess the country's industrial mobilization program, the Inter-Governmental Relations Subcommittee of the House Committee on Government Relations headed by Congressman Herbert C. Bonner of North Carolina began investigating federal supply management, particularly within the military services. On June 27, 1951, Bonner's subcommittee issued its first report challenging the Air Force's assumption that it required its own separate supply system to best prepare itself for war. The subcommittee was convinced that field commanders cared little about where their supplies came from, where they were stored, or who exercised control over them, as long as they had them when they needed them. Terming an autonomous Air Force supply system "wasteful triplification," the subcommittee recommended that the Army, through its Quartermaster, buy and distribute for both itself and the Air Force.

Perhaps motivated by the subcommittee's findings, Secretary of Defense Lovett announced a new Department of Defense supply service policy directive on July 17, 1951. It stipulated that the Secretary of Defense approve any future agreement by two or more services to expand the supply system under which common items were procured and distributed. Lovett would permit an expansion only if it increased combat effectiveness. The Air Force now had to deal with the Army to find out which agreements would and would not require approval by the Secretary of Defense. In the fall of 1951, the subcommittee charged that the Air Force was continuing to build its own separate supply system for common items. The Air Staff responded that each service should exercise complete control of the resources allocated to it and opposed both the subcommittee's and the Munitions Board's notion that a fourth service of supply be formed to outfit all combat forces.[72]

In the spring of 1952 both Finletter and Gilpatric defended the Air Force's supply policy before various congressional committees including the Senate Committee on Appropriations. Gilpatric denied that the Air Force was creating a completely new, duplicate supply system as the Bonner Subcommittee had suggested. He pointed out that the Air Force, in comparison with the other services, carried out its activities and operations on a vast scale—in England, Germany, North Africa, Greenland, the Philippines, and the Middle East. Common sense dictated, therefore, that it procure and distribute its own supplies and that any DOD system be flexible enough to accommodate various arrangements at various levels in various parts of the world. He added that the Air Force, under a system in place for almost thirty-five years, was, in any case, handling 80 percent of all its supplies. Its absorbing of the remaining 20 percent would not fundamentally change that system. Like many other civilian officials, Under Secretary Gilpatric felt that the creation of a single DOD supply system for all three services would pose an insurmountable management problem. He urged that Congress not disregard a long-accepted practice of American business—assigning subordinate units the management of supply when an institution reached a certain size.[73]

On June 9, 1952, Congressman Bonner introduced H.R. 8130, a bill to promote military economy and efficiency by combining military supply and service activities and creating an additional Under Secretary of Defense. In effect, the Bonner Bill proposed a form of centralized DOD control over logistics. It also included a proposal to abolish the Munitions Board and transfer its logistical functions, along with those of the JCS, to the new Under Secretary. The Air Staff opposed the bill, citing Gilpatric's point that a single logistics organization would be huge, inflexible, and unwieldy.[74]

Secretary of Defense Lovett would not support the bill and it was not passed. He objected specifically to provisions requiring the Secretary of Defense to delegate logistical power exclusively to the new Under Secretary. He was not ready to recommend specific changes without further study and in September he instituted DOD Directive 4000.8, entitled "Basic Regulations for the Military Supply System."[75] This directive, revised on November 17, 1952, addressed Congress's concerns and ordered the practice of cross-servicing, the use by the services of each other's supplies and facilities whenever possible. Cross-servicing could be by-passed, however, in the event it proved detrimental to military operations or disadvantageous to the DOD.[76]

Secretary of Defense Lovett realized that the directive was not the ultimate solution to separatist tendencies among the services. He perceived a contradiction in the National Security Act which called for three "separately administered" military departments on the one hand and for "direction authority, and control" over the entire Defense Department by the Secretary of Defense on the other. Lovett maintained that it was supply which became most problematical because of this "straddle" and it was supply about which ardent separatists complained most vociferously. Satisfied that the law allowed the Secretary of Defense to involve himself in supply when necessary, Lovett realized that the struggle to gain authority over it for the Air Force and the other services would continue.[77]

In December 1952, Under Secretary Gilpatric reviewed for the Inter-Governmental Relations Subcommittee all that the Air Force had done to comply with Secretary of Defense Lovett's Directive 4000.8. Recalling the Air Force's record over the previous two years, Gilpatric pointed to the efforts that had been made in "improving the organization, techniques, and management of our logistical support system." He stated that it was not surprising that many of the principles enunciated in the directive had already been put into effect.[78]

He also stressed that the Air Force had followed the directive's stipulations for procurement, distribution, cataloging, standardization, and production, and had engaged in cross-servicing whenever possible. He noted that the Air Force used only one agency for procuring, warehousing, distributing, and controlling inventories, which prevented duplication and allowed stock levels to be held to a minimum. The Air Force was fully cooperating with the DOD on the use of standard language for identifying items common to all services. The under secretary claimed that a great deal of his own time was spent scheduling Air Force production around such limiting factors as funding, materials, manpower, and facilities.[79]

While supply would remain an unsettled problem for several years, one trend was becoming clearer: the OSD was acquiring more responsibility at the expense of the service secretaries. With the passage of Reorganization Plan No. 6 in June 1953, the Munitions Board, which oversaw supply, procurement, and industrial mobilization was abolished and its function replaced by a single executive, the Assistant Secretary of Defense for Supply and Logistics. Under the new Republican administration, the Bonner Subcommittee became the Pullman Committee and soon reported that the services were still too slow in improving their management of supply.[80]

Summary

By the end of Secretary Finletter's term, the Air Force had grown considerably. The Truman administration had been forced to rescind its budget-conscious defense spending policies of the immediate post-World War II years. The Korean War prompted not only a change in direction but also a closer look at the nation's air power. For nearly two years Finletter had the sympathetic ear of Congress as he built up the Air Force and tried to explain the complicated formula by which it would be enlarged from forty-eight groups in the spring of 1950, to ninety-five wings in the fall of 1951, to 143 wings by the end of 1955 (later 1957). The acquisition of more planes and personnel required by the Korean conflict as well as the expansion of necessary logistics and maintenance systems had to be carried out within reasonable budgets, however, since Congress' generosity was not as unrestrained as it had been during total war.

The Air Force was still adjusting to its status as a separate service. In Korea it fought for the first time without its logistics, supplies, and budgets handled by the Army. It was inevitable that an investigative body such as the Bonner subcommittee would uncover duplication within the services' supply systems. The Air Force's internal organization, after extensive discussion, was finalized in the

Air Force Organization Act of 1951. The act did not resolve such problems as those associated with supply but did clarify the roles and responsibilities of the Air Secretary and the Chief of Staff. Finletter himself believed that the Chief of Staff should command the three major combat commands, SAC, TAC, and ADC. He argued that the direction of operations was a military rather than a civilian function. Under the Air Force Organization Act of 1951 the Secretary was still the nominal head of the Air Force. Civilian control remained—at least on paper. Just what did the Air Force expect of its civilian head? Did it really want a show of strength? The Korean War had demonstrated plainly that military leaders could properly manage operations without the constant oversight of a civilian authority. Stuart Symington had left operational decisions to uniformed experts, creating the expectation among them that future civilian leaders would do the same. Thus Finletter did not really feel as free as Symington did to impose his will on an Air Staff that regarded him as essentially a non-operational executive.

Secretary Finletter had little effect on the Air Force's arrangements for securing the supplies and equipment to wage the Korean War. Like Symington, he supported the Air Force's case before Congress and argued along with its leaders for increasing its size. He was, at the same time, concerned about service budgets and was closely involved with the selection of the final figures that determined the force's structure. Much of an individual Air Secretary's influence stemmed from his personal qualities. Lacking Symington's charisma, the more pensive and reticent Finletter did not project the same forceful image or sharpen the Air Force's awareness of the importance of civilian control.

The OSAF under Finletter reflected the changes occurring within the power structure of the DOD. Although the 1949 amendments to the National Security Act were passed during Symington's tenure, their effect was not readily apparent until Finletter's. Authority was gradually shifting and becoming centralized by law to the OSD. Symington had been the equal of James Forrestal on the National Security Council; Finletter was not the equal of Secretaries of Defense George C. Marshall or Robert A. Lovett. Easy access to Marshall and Lovett had become blocked by a growing OSD. Assistant Secretaries of the Air Force, for example, were required to deal with two assistant Secretaries of Defense and the Deputy Secretary of Defense, whose positions had not existed under Forrestal.

Secretary Finletter consistently advocated the creation of an Air Force strong enough to deter the growing Soviet threat and adaptable enough to react to sudden or limited hostilities. For more reasons than the Korean War Finletter must be credited with furthering the modernization and growth of the Air Force which, by the end of his tenure, was nearly three times the size it had been under Secretary Symington. He accomplished this feat at a time when the OSD was expanding its jurisdiction. By September 1953, seven new Assistant Secretaries of Defense had been added to the civilian hierarchy over the military departments and the service secretaries.

Chapter 6

Talbott and Quarles (1953–1957)

Soon after taking office, President Eisenhower directed the Department of Defense (DOD) to take a "new look" at the nation's military programs. He had consistently sought to achieve adequate military strength without overstraining the economy and soon struck a keynote, "maximum security at minimum cost," which his Secretary of Defense, Charles E. Wilson, translated into "a bigger bang for the buck."[1] For the Air Force, this "new look" meant a three-year concentrated effort to obtain a 137-wing force.

The Air Force's immediate goals, which Congress had come to accept, were to maintain the numerical strength it had gained during the Korean War and to retain a significant margin of technical superiority over its Soviet counterpart. Thus the new Secretary of the Air Force, Harold E. Talbott, was free to concentrate on other matters, such as improving the living conditions and increasing the pay of everyone in the Air Force to solve the service's number one problem—its inability to attract and retain enough competent personnel. Talbott undoubtedly would have solved other service problems as successfully as he did that one had he not been forced to resign his office because of a misuse of influence.

The gradual diminishment of the service secretaries' autonomy and the simultaneous enhancement of the Secretary of Defense's influence was, during President Eisenhower's administration, acknowledged as fact in Reorganization Plan No. 6 of 1953. Plan No. 6 eliminated various boards and agencies on which the service secretaries could serve and added another tier of authority to the Office of the Secretary of Defense (OSD) with additional assistant secretaries. The responsibilities of the Secretary of the Air Force became explicitly circumscribed. The regimes of both Talbott and his successor, Donald A. Quarles, were affected by this diminution of authority. (See Appendix 1, OSAF Organization Charts, pp. 264, 266.)

In August 1955, Quarles was the first Air Force Secretary with a respected scientific background. He was also the first Air Force Secretary whose views on important issues diverged from those of such prominent airmen as Chief of Staff General Nathan F. Twining and Commander of the Strategic Air Command (SAC) General Curtis E. LeMay. Secretary Quarles, in support of the administration's economy drive, urged that research and development funds be cut and that both the long-pursued 137-wing program and newly emphasized missile program be "stretched out." His recommendations caused him difficulty, not only with his own military leaders, but also with a Democratically controlled Senate subcommittee investigating America's air power, headed by former Secretary of the Air Force Stuart Symington.

New People under the New Look

The change from a Democratic to a Republican administration in 1953 brought new statutory appointees to leading positions within the federal government, including the Department of Defense (DOD). Most of them were highly successful conservative businessmen. Charles E. Wilson, former president of General Motors, gave up an annual salary of $600,000 to become Secretary of Defense. His Under Secretary of Defense, Roger M. Kyes, had been vice president at General Motors in charge of procurement and schedules. Robert T. Stevens, the new Secretary of the Army, had been affiliated with his family's textile company which provided uniforms to the military services. Robert B. Anderson, Secretary of the Navy, had managed the King Ranch and its associated oil refineries in Texas.[2]

The new Air Secretary, Harold E. Talbott, was typical of the businessman entering government in all respects but one—at age sixty-five, he was nearly twenty years older than his peers. Talbott was no stranger to the problems of aircraft production. He had served as president of the Dayton Wright Airplane Company from 1916 to 1920 and as chairman of the board of the North American Aviation Company from 1931 to 1932. His Dayton Wright Company had produced more DH-4s and DH-9s than any other U.S. aircraft manufacturer during World War I. In 1918 he had found time to serve as a major in the Air Service in charge of maintenance and repair of aircraft in France. His duty was curtailed, however, by the armistice on November 11, 1918.

After the war, the Dayton Wright Company merged with General Motors, and Talbott continued as president of Dayton-Wright and the Inland Manufacturing Company. In 1925 he moved to New York and became a director of the Chrysler Corporation. Over the next several decades he acquired a wealth of experience as chairman of the board of the Standard Packaging Corporation and North American Aviation Company; vice president of the Talbott Company; director and chairman of the finance committee of the Mead Corporation and the Electric Auto-Lite Company; and as a limited partner in the firm of Paul B. Mulligan and Company. He was briefly, from 1942 to 1943, head of aircraft production for the War Production Board. While heading his own New York financial firm, he sat on the boards of directors of several corporations, and in 1947 New York Governor Thomas E. Dewey named him to a three-year term on the State Banking Board. Before World War II, he was eastern chairman of the Republican Finance Committee and in 1948 and 1949, its national chairman. Of all his accomplishments, Talbott was proudest of persuading General Dwight D.

Eisenhower—the man who appointed him as Air Force Secretary—to run for President.[3]

Other presidential appointees to the Office of the Secretary of the Air Force (OSAF) were not quite in Talbott's mold. Although some had business backgrounds, they had neither attained six-digit salaries nor headed large corporations. Some, such as the new Under Secretary of the Air Force, James H. Douglas, Jr., were successful lawyers and had served in the Army Air Forces (AAF) during World War II.

Douglas had no close connection with either the President or Secretary Talbott and, in fact, attributed his selection as Under Secretary of the Air Force largely to chance. Although he had known many important Republicans and had taken part in Wendell Wilkie's campaign for the presidency in 1940, he had met Talbott only in passing during the nominating convention in Philadelphia, Pennsylvania. Douglas's World War II experience as Deputy Chief of Staff, and later as Chief of Staff of the Air Transport Command (ATC) from 1942 to 1945, helped gain him a position with a National Security Resources Board (NSRB) study group in 1951. Formed by the board's chairman and former Secretary of the Air Force, Stuart Symington, the study group was assigned to evaluate the adaptability of civil air transport facilities to military uses in time of war or emergency.

It was Douglas's connection with the NSRB that had brought him to the attention of Air Secretary Talbott. When asked to serve by Talbott, Douglas hesitated, pleading professional and personal obligations. He had planned to build his own law firm. However, his oldest son, about to enter Northwestern Univer-

Charles E. Wilson, Secretary of Defense from 1953 to 1957.

sity, convinced him to reconsider, reminding him that he had frequently referred to his experiences in the Air Force as some of the best in his life. "Now somebody asks you to help run it, and you say you can't."[4] When asked again by Talbott, Douglas promised to work in Washington for eighteen months. He stayed for eight years—four as Under Secretary of the Air Force, two as Secretary of the Air Force, and two as Deputy Secretary of Defense.

Douglas had received a bachelor's degree from Princeton University in 1920, attended Corpus Christi College at Cambridge University in England and, in 1924, was graduated from Harvard Law School. Admitted to the Illinois bar in 1925, he entered the Chicago law firm of Winston, Strawn and Shaw and in 1929 joined Field, Glore and Company, investment bankers. From March 1932 to June 1933, he served as Assistant Secretary of the Treasury and in 1934 started his own firm—Gardner, Carton, and Douglas. Prior to his appointment as Air Force Under Secretary, he was a director of the Metropolitan Life Insurance Company, the Chicago Title and Trust Company, American Airlines, and the Chicago Corporation. He had also been a member of the Washington, D.C., law firm of Proctor, MacIntyre and Gates.

Roger Lewis, who became the new Assistant Secretary of the Air Force (Materiel), had long been associated with the aircraft industry. He had served as director of materiel and assistant sales manager for Lockheed Aircraft Corporation from 1934 to 1947, vice president of Canadair in Montreal from 1947 to 1950, and vice president of the Curtiss-Wright Corporation from 1950 to 1953.

H. Lee White was a partner with the New York law firm of Cadwalader, Wickersham, and Taft before becoming Assistant Secretary of the Air Force

Harold E. Talbot, third Secretary of the Air Force.

Clockwise from above: **Roger Lewis, Assistant Secretary of the Air Force (Materiel) from 1953 to 1955; Lyle Garlock, Assistant Secretary of the Air Force (Financial Management) from 1954 to 1961; and David Smith, Assistant Secretary of the Air Force (Manpower, Personnel, and Reserve Forces) from 1954 to 1959.**

(Management). During little more than a year as assistant secretary, he supported Secretary Talbott's view that the government would be exercising "good business" sense if it raised service morale by constructing better military housing, granting more allowances for medical care, and increasing reenlistment bonuses to meet the manpower crisis. White left office in July 1954 and returned to practicing law.

Following his departure, White's post was split and filled by two assistant secretaries. Public Law 562, passed on August 3, 1953, increased the number of assistant secretaries within the military departments from two to four. Lyle S. Garlock became the Air Force's Assistant Secretary (Financial Management) in August 1954 and David S. Smith became Assistant Secretary (Manpower, Personnel and Reserve Forces) in October 1954.

Garlock joined the U.S. Employment Service in 1934 and in 1942 served as a member of the War Production Board's Labor Supply Division. In 1942 he joined the Navy as a reserve lieutenant on the staff of Dr. Joseph W. Barker, who dealt with manpower problems while serving as an assistant to the Secretary of the Navy. After the war, Garlock became a special consultant to the War Department, studying labor problems and policies in Japan. He next became Assistant Director for Business Management with the U.S. Employment Service and

139

remained there until 1948. He then went to work for the Department of Defense as Chief of the Budget Division from 1948 to 1951 and as Deputy Comptroller for the Budget from 1951 to 1954.

After graduation from the Columbia University Law School, David Smith spent four years in the Navy during World War II, first as a communications officer and then as a deck officer. Serving with the USS *Mercury*, he participated in numerous amphibious landings in the Pacific and won the Purple Heart for wounds he received during action on the island of Saipan. After his release from the Navy Reserve in 1946, he worked for various law firms and the legal department of the American Broadcasting Company from 1948 to 1950, becoming a member of the bars of New York, Connecticut, and the District of Columbia. Politically active, he volunteered for the New York Republican campaigns and the Republican national conventions of 1948 and 1952. He also aided in the organization of Citizens for Eisenhower during the New Jersey and Pennsylvania primaries. Prior to becoming Assistant Secretary of the Air Force, he worked in Washington as a special assistant in the State Department.[5]

Talbott's Turn

The Eisenhower administration's belief that it could achieve leaner defense budgets without compromising military power markedly affected the Air Force's wing structure. When Harold Talbott became Secretary of the Air Force in January 1953 the schedule governing wing formations had been virtually settled by the previous administration. But by January 1953 attainment of the 143-wing Air Force, which had been proposed for 1953, was delayed until 1956. That same month, President Eisenhower asked the Defense Department to take a new look at the entire defense program. In response to several memoranda from Secretary of Defense Wilson on wing requirements, the Air Force was able to adjust to an "interim" goal of 120 wings by the end of 1956, and 17 more by the end of 1957. On December 10, 1953, the Joint Chiefs of Staff (JCS) approved the Air Force's revised wing program. Six days later, the National Security Council did the same.[6]

By 1953 the Air Force had grown to nearly three times the size it had been in early 1950, thanks largely to the efforts of Secretary Talbott, who adeptly presented the service's point of view to Congress. In fact, former Secretary of the Air Force Stuart Symington credited Talbott with almost single-handedly gaining Congress's commitment to an expanded force.[7]

Talbott believed that in 1953 adequate U.S. air power was the greatest single deterrent to war and that one of the Eisenhower administration's greatest problems would be to achieve a balance between military requirements and the nation's economic health. He and Air Force Chief of Staff General Hoyt S. Vandenberg, who shared that view, testified during hearings before the Senate's

Appropriations Committee in June 1953 on the necessity of a minimum force (then 143 wings) able to deter an all-out Soviet attack.[8]

Once the schedule for the 137-wing Air Force was determined and left to the Air Staff's planners early in his tenure, Talbott was free to deal with other priorities. He thus sought the advice of knowledgeable service leaders, such as Lt. Gen. William F. McKee, Vice Commander, Air Materiel Command (ATC). Talbott chose to devote his attention to a particularly nettlesome problem—the maintenance of the morale and welfare of Air Force families. This problem bore directly, he insisted, on the service's ability to attract and retain competent personnel. Most of the rank and file had become resigned to what they believed was a miserable housing situation; nonetheless, McKee encouraged Talbott to do all he could to improve it.[9]

His first task was to improve the reenlistment rate. To become familiar with the Air Force and the needs of its members, Talbott undertook an arduous tour of the field. After only seven months in office, he had traveled over 70,000 miles to see for himself the many difficulties that beset the service day to day. His duty as he saw it was to increase the Air Force's strength and effectiveness by applying common sense economy to bettering conditions within its ranks. He realized that as people acquired special training and experience their value to the Air Force rose with each year of service. He also realized that the Air Force and the other services were unable to keep enough highly qualified specialists. The Air Secretary felt that "the tendency by some people who were antagonistic toward the military" to downgrade servicemen publicly was unfair. "Applying the faults of a few to many,"[10] in effect, undermined military morale and America's trust in the integrity and ability of its "citizens in uniform."

When speaking before the Air Force Association (AFA) in August 1953, Secretary Talbott justified his frequent recommendations to Congress for a pay increase by pointing out that since 1937 military pay and allowances had fallen far behind the 315 percent increase achieved by the private sector. He explained that medical care for servicemen and their dependents, long a standard fringe benefit, was now being questioned. In addition, housing for families and for single officers and airmen which, for the most part, consisted of tarpaper shacks constructed hurriedly during World War II, was simply inadequate. Built to last five years, it had, after twelve, deteriorated to a shocking state. Talbott knew from various studies that the Air Force might lose up to 180,000 airmen who would decline to reenlist in 1954 alone; that it was spending about $14,000 to admit and train each one for a particular skill; and that it would have to spend around $2.6 billion to replace them. Talbott suggested that by dedicating a portion of this $2.6 billion to the improvement of pay and fringe benefits, the Air Force might well induce many of these men to remain within its ranks and build careers.[11]

Talbott succeeded in obtaining more housing for airmen and their families than any other Air Secretary.* At the end of his tenure in August 1955, housing, although still seriously short at bases worldwide, was being increased. Between June 1954 and June 1955, 1,171 family housing units overseas were under construction, and 720 units were completed. In addition, contracts for 1,730 units in France and 700 units in French Morocco were being negotiated. As an interim measure, the Air Force had awarded $7.4 million toward the purchase of 2,689 trailers for use by troops in North Africa and in Europe.[12]

Talbott's efforts to stem the Air Force's declining retention rate by linking its improvement to enhanced military benefits were unflagging. In early 1954, he informed the Secretary of Defense that in the previous six months, from July to December 1953, approximately 19,500 officers and 121,800 enlisted members, all trained for special skills at considerable cost to the taxpayer, had been separated from the Air Force. This flood of departures could be reduced, he insisted, if, in addition to increased pay and more comfortable housing, other benefits to enhance the quality of military life were extended, specifically, medical care of dependents, extension of officer tours, home loan guarantees, commissaries, and base exchanges.[13]

To encourage reenlistment, Talbott even asked the aircraft industry to donate some of its radio and television advertising time to the Air Force. Each week, leading programs would turn over their commercial time to the service for special commercials. The Air Force could not reimburse such sponsors for their commercial time. Nonetheless, Talbott was certain that they would, on the whole, derive great satisfaction from the results achieved through such a cooperative venture.[14] Talbott carried his plea for curing the reenlistment problem to the Air Force itself. Speaking during commencement exercises at the Air University in June 1954, he urged nearly 1,000 graduates of the Air War College and Air Command and Staff College to do their utmost to reverse the falling reenlistment rate. Lt. Gen. Laurence S. Kuter, Commander of the Air University, introduced the Air Secretary as "the gentlemen who leads our great crusade," whose support was critical to the Air University's achievement of a $5 million building program.[15]

In August 1954, Secretary Talbott at the AFA's annual convention announced what came to be called a "Bill of Rights" for members of the armed services and their families. He gave a solemn promise that he would work for an across-the-board pay raise, a sixty-day notice prior to change of station, special dislocation allowances of up to one month's pay, a raise in the weight allowance for a permanent change of station, and a general improvement in housing and medical care. "We spend millions for equipment," he complained, "and nickels for the manpower which has to operate it."[16]

---

* According to General William F. McKee, many Air Force barracks and family quarters all over the world exist because of the efforts of Harold Talbott. Intvw, General William F. McKee by author, Mar 20, 1984.

New Year's Eve, 1954. Concerned with service morale, Secretary of the
Air Force Harold E. Talbott *(fourth from left)* personally carries the
President's greetings to officers and airmen at Thule Air Base in Greenland,
where he is accompanied by the base commander, Col. B.F. Hanson, enter-
tainer Arthur Godfrey and a member of his troupe, Janette Davis, and
General Curtis E. LeMay, Commander, Strategic Air Command.

As to commissaries and base exchanges, he noted that they were under constant attack by paid Washington lobbies bent on closing them. They were viewed
by the public as unnecessary because of the utterly false impression that Air
Force families could live cheaply, purchasing nearly everything they needed at
cut-rate prices. The facts, he revealed, were that at post exchanges and commissaries stocks had been cut, prices raised, and surcharges imposed on sales.

For defending the Air Force against such organized attempts which tried to
deprive military personnel of any opportunities to expand their meager purchasing power, Talbott was commended by Congress. Senator Margaret Chase Smith of
Maine called him a "very humane person," and Senator John Stennis of Mississippi
congratulated him for doing a "splendid job" as Secretary of the Air Force.[17]

Talbott occasionally corresponded with former Air Secretary Thomas
Finletter. Privately, Talbott took issue with Finletter's view that the 1955 defense
budget had failed to grant top priority to air-atomic striking power.* Talbott
wanted very much to consult with Finletter from time to time but felt that their

---

* In his book *Power and Policy: U.S. Foreign Policy and Military Power in the
Hydrogen Age* (New York: Harcourt, Brace and Company, 1954), former Air Secretary
Finletter expressed his fear that by 1957 the Russians would be able to destroy U.S. cities
and industries in a single surprise attack. He thus supported the Air Force's recommended
budget of $18 billion rather than the administration's budget of $12 billion for the next
three years. He wanted the highest priority placed on an "air-atomic striking force" with
its strategic and tactical missions combined under one command and a greatly improved

correspondence and exchanges of views should be kept confidential.[18] The Air Secretary wanted to avoid a public debate between himself and Finletter.

In only a few months, the Eisenhower administration's new austerity policies had created severe apprehensions within the aircraft industry. Twenty years had passed since a Republican had held the presidency. During that time the industry and the Air Force had grown enormously. Talbott thus undertook a tour of the west coast, where the industry was concentrated, to calm the fears of those manufacturers who were on "pins and needles" because of the government's "long hard look at everything that requires an outlay of large sums of money." The Air Secretary attempted to assure them that the new administration intended to give industry every possible consideration while attempting "to lay out an adequate defense program for the future."[19] Talbott tried his best to be receptive to industry's concerns and and to further its interests by advising it when he could. In May 1953, for example, after a visit to Convair Aircraft Corporation's San Diego, California, plant, he wrote to Thomas G. Lanphier, Jr., company vice president, suggesting that new planes whose noise levels were diminished would be more acceptable to military purchasers.[20]

Talbott's attempts to aid industry,[21] however, were overshadowed by his recommendation during House appropriations hearings in 1955 that, in the interest of national security, expansion of the aircraft industry along the west coast be curtailed. Talbott argued that the aircraft industry centralized as it was had become a highly vulnerable target to even a single enemy attack and had created a dangerous dependency on military contracts throughout one-quarter of southern California. Aircraft producers and labor unions in that area protested vehemently. The chairman of the Los Angeles Chamber of Commerce cynically suggested that Secretary Talbott not authorize the purchase of trucks or cars in Detroit because 46 percent of the city's industrial work force was employed in the automotive industry. Talbott clarified his remarks by distinguishing between contracts and facilities. The DOD, he emphasized, did not support the reduction of aircraft production contracts in the west coast area. It supported only the dispersal of new facilities away from locations where the defense industry had already become entrenched. However, he was adamant about the placement of some guided missile production plants well inland.[22]

Assistant Secretary of the Air Force (Materiel) Roger Lewis testified that because the days of the Korean War crash program were over, the Air Force intended to buy only products whose performance had not been just promised but rigorously tested and proved superior in demonstrations. He cautioned industry that the service would enforce tighter contracting procedures and nego-

---

base organization. He also called for heightened protection of bases, more and better aircraft capable of saturation bombing, and more research and development. Robert H. Wood, "Arming for Keeps," *Aviation Week*, Oct 11, 1954, vol 61, no 15, p 114.

tiate firmer, more detailed agreements whose obligations were clearly understood and accepted by all parties.

Lewis enumerated for the subcommittee three principal tasks facing the Air Force as it shifted from building its inventory to maintaining its premier position in the world: first, keeping combat units in a high degree of readiness for an indefinite period of time; second, developing a technically and financially sound equipment replenishment program to minimize obsolescence; and third, reorienting industrial mobilization plans to meet the threat of atomic war. Lewis further explained that although the Air Force was sensitive to the administration's economy policy goals, it could not ignore the rapidly advancing technology being assiduously applied by the Soviet Union. He warned Congress that the United States had to maintain its international political leverage since the Atlantic and Pacific Oceans afforded no safety against atomic attack. He warned industry that tougher competition lay ahead. The Air Force would in future base its selection of aircraft on technical competence and cost. The OSAF supported the administration's insistence on industry's sustaining reasonable time limits for production as new contracts were let. In 1953 Secretary Talbott informed Donald W. Douglas of Douglas Aircraft Company that the administration was highly displeased with industry's overall record on cost, production, and delivery schedules. He had promised that the Air Force would remain as reliable and protective a customer as possible, but it expected better performance in return.[23] Lewis felt that the Air Force was not obliged to keep an aircraft manufacturer alive; the service did not owe anyone a living.[24]

President Eisenhower's review of national military strategy and subsequent imposition of budgetary limits following the Korean War compelled the Air Force to work more efficiently. The service would reach 137 wings by June 30, 1957, with less than one million uniformed specialists available to serve them. Talbott contended that the balance between a prosperous economy and a powerful military force, the twin pillars of national security, could be seriously upset by excessive military spending.[25] In March 1954, he listed for the Secretary of Defense measures by which the Air Force could save hundreds of millions of dollars. It would replace military overseas personnel with local civilians, reduce manning for support functions, approve earlier separation from the service of some airmen in non-technical skills, tighten materiel procurement programs, improve maintenance and supply procedures, and standardize equipment. All this, Talbott assured the Secretary of Defense, would be achieved without any loss of combat effectiveness.[26]

No sooner had he established the Air Force's cost-cutting agenda than the Air Secretary met with a very serious professional disappointment. Talbott, who had listed his occupation in *Who's Who* as "capitalist," became involved in a conflict of interest that eventually forced his resignation, following a congressional investigation of his business activities. Talbott had retained his partnership in the New York investment group, Paul B. Mulligan and Company. He had received over $132,000 from them, but, he held, not for work he had done while he was Secretary of the Air Force. Nonetheless, several months after taking office, he began working for the benefit of a member of his old concern—using Air Force stationery and telephones to contact various businesses, some of which were Air Force contractors. Talbott freely admitted that he had continued to help his former associate. He also conceded that he had erred in using Air Force stationery, telephones, and offices.[27]

He felt strongly that he should not resign and resolved not to do so. Hopeful that his prompt resignation from the company would lay the controversy to rest, Talbott reminded congressional investigators that the Senate had allowed him to retain his business interests before confirming him as Air Secretary. He asserted that the connection had neither influenced him nor prevented him from fulfilling his official responsibilities. He doubted that he had devoted "two and a half days to Mulligan out of two and a half years" as Air Secretary.[28]

Talbott's activities became a major political issue in 1955. Three leading newspapers, the *New York Times*, the *Washington Post and Times Herald*, and the *Los Angeles Times* called for his resignation. The administration wished to appear supportive of the highest standards of behavior for public office holders. The President worried that Talbott's conduct, while not illegal, could be construed as unethical and would doubtless be a subject of debate during the 1956 presidential campaign.[29]

Under pressure, Secretary Talbott relinquished his position in August 1955, maintaining that he wished to spare the President further embarrassment.[30] Opinions of him diverged largely along political lines. Not everyone felt that he had been treated fairly. His executive officer, Brig. Gen. William G. Hipps, was convinced that what Talbott did was being duplicated by other political appointees in government without repercussions and that what he became, because of bad timing, was a convenient example for the administration as an election year approached. In accepting Talbott's resignation, the President commended him for his "tireless energy and unexcelled performance" in administering the Air Force. Talbott's Assistant Secretary of the Air Force (Materiel), Roger Lewis, applauded his boss as "honest and forthright," as one who "acted always as he thought entirely proper." Lewis lauded Talbott as an outstanding Secretary of the Air Force, saying, "He was courageous and earnest; he devoted his very great energy and his time without reserve to the interest of our national security."[31] According to Hipps, Talbott left government feeling deeply hurt. The absence of Eisenhower's support did not help his case, nor did his often "abrasive, hot tempered nature" and "damn the torpedoes" attitude elicit Air Staff sympathy.[32]

Senator Wayne Morse of Oregon and member of the Senate's Banking and Currency Committee which was investigating the outside activities of many administration appointees, charged that Talbott, Secretary of Defense Charles Wilson, and former Deputy Secretary of Defense Roger Kyes had failed to anticipate and appreciate the problem of conflicting interests when accepting public office. They all had initially resisted divesting themselves of substantial holdings in corporations with which the DOD dealt, and finally surrendered them with great reluctance. Morse felt that all of them had "demonstrated a callous lack of understanding."[33]

Under Secretary of the Air Force James H. Douglas, Jr., would later praise Talbott highly for speaking out to improve the well-being of service members, particularly those stationed overseas, and for trying to meet their needs for decent housing, adequate medical care, and recreation. For taking an active interest in the establishment of the Air Force Academy and for aggressively pushing the Air Force's programs despite a lack of cooperation from Secretary of Defense Charles Wilson, he became popular with Congress.[34]

Less than eighteen months after resigning, Talbott died of a heart attack in Palm Beach, Florida, on March 2, 1957. How he would have fared with the major issues that followed him—the research and development and missile debates that plagued his successor—must remain a matter of conjecture. While the OSAF neither gained nor lost prestige from his unfortunate departure, it and the Air Staff might have better confronted the increasing centralization of authority within the OSD through the continuity of a longer tenured civilian leader.

The Air Force during Talbott's brief term, January 1953 to August 1955, made great advances in a number of weapon systems. The Martin B-57, the North American supersonic F-100 fighter, and what Talbott considered the best bomber in the world to increase the operational readiness of SAC, the Boeing eight-jet B-52, were activated. The F-100 day fighter and the B-57 light bomber were coming off production lines, and the F-101 strategic fighter and the F-102 all-weather interceptor were undergoing extensive testing before quantity production. The F-104 lightweight day fighter, the KC-135 jet tanker, and the T-37 jet trainer were under development as was the intercontinental ballistic missile (ICBM), of critical importance to Talbott.[35] The TM-61 Matador, the first operational guided missile, was entering the service's inventory and had been assigned to two units stationed in Europe; the SM-62 Snark, was undergoing extensive testing. The Air Force was also substantially expanding its new continental air defense radar system. The Pinetree Line, the first of three radar warning components, was already operating; a second line of stations was under construction and would be operated by Canada; and sites had been selected on a third network of stations, the Distant Early Warning (DEW) Line.

Talbott did not have a direct hand in all of these or other programs, since many were initiated before his term began, but he played a significant, if not highly conspicuous, role in their furtherance and completion. The Air Force Academy, for example, was approved by Congress during his tenure and opened temporary quarters at Lowry Air Force Base in Denver, Colorado, on July 11, 1955, to 300 students.

Secretary of the Air Force Harold E. Talbott thanks President Dwight D. Eisenhower for signing the Air Force Academy Act on April 1, 1954. Looking on are Rep. Carl Vinson, ranking minority member, House Armed Services Committee; Gen. Nathan F. Twining, USAF Chief of Staff; Rep. Dewey Short, Chairman, House Armed Services Committee; Under Secretary of the Air Force James H. Douglas; and Lt. Gen. Hubert Harmon, special assistant for Air Force Academy matters.

Talbott had needed no defenders within the Air Force. He was greatly esteemed throughout the service for his enthusiastic drive in endeavoring to raise living conditions and compensation. He cautioned the Secretary of Defense that although the Air Force was obtaining the planes, supplies, and bases it needed and was able to offer more "fringe benefits," base housing remained insufficient for nearly 300,000 families.[36] He subsequently won approval for new family housing and a reenlistment bonus bill. He can be credited with having done much to turn around the Air Force's manpower problem. The service, in Talbott's last year in office, had been manning 121 wings with 10,000 fewer people than at the end of 1953 when it manned 106.*[37] By the end of the fiscal year in June 1955, the total number of reenlistments and enlistments had nearly doubled over that of the previous year, from 144,954 to 267,827. Increases continued for the next several years, but did not exceed the 1955 rate. Statistics for 1956 and 1957 were 247,501 and 204,811 respectively.[38] Had his term been longer, Talbott might well have left a more visible imprint on other Air Force activities.

---

* In 1953, personnel serving the 106-wing Air Force numbered 1,282,000 (908,000 military and 302,000 civilian).

The Scientist Secretary

On August 14, 1955, Donald A. Quarles replaced Harold E. Talbott as Secretary of the Air Force. Since September 1953 he had been Assistant Secretary of Defense (Research and Development). Like Talbott, Quarles, who was sixty-one years of age, had seen service with the U.S. Army during World War I. After graduation from Yale University in 1916, he enlisted and served for two years in France and Germany, attaining the rank of captain in the field artillery. As an engineer for the Western Electric Company during the early 1920s, he studied theoretical physics at Columbia University. Quarles stayed with the inspection engineering department of Western Electric, which later became the Bell Telephone Laboratories. He was director of the transmission development department and director of apparatus development until becoming the company's vice president in 1948. He also was a member and, in 1949, chairman of the Committee on Electronics of the Joint Research and Development Board of the DOD. In 1952 he was made president of Sandia Corporation, a Western Electric subsidiary that operated the Sandia Laboratory in Albuquerque, New Mexico, for the Atomic Energy Commission (AEC). The following September, President Eisenhower appointed him Assistant Secretary of Defense (Research and Development), and he was subsequently selected by both the Secretary of Defense and the Secretary of Commerce to become the first chairman of the reorganized Air Navigation Development Board. In March 1954, the President appointed Quarles to the National Advisory Committee for Aeronautics.

The Air Force was generally pleased that the DOD's top research and development expert was named Secretary of the Air Force and relieved that he preferred to avoid controversy. The service was still smarting from the unfavorable headlines brought by his predecessor's departure. To some observers Quarles's appointment proved that the technological race with the Soviet Union was of critical importance. They speculated that because of his military connections and Talbott's problems, the Senate would be expected to question Quarles closely regarding a possible conflict of interest. Since Congress was not in session, he was given an interim appointment and sworn into office on August 15, 1955.[39]

Dudley C. Sharp, Assistant Secretary of the Air Force (Materiel), who would himself become Secretary of the Air Force, had the utmost respect for Secretary Quarles, citing his tremendous intellect, astuteness, and dedication to work. He was a man who was needed by the Air Force at a very difficult time when, according to Sharp, it had decided to go "full blast" in developing the ICBM and satellites.[40] Sharp would blame Quarles's death in 1959 on too heavy a professional burden.

Trevor Gardner had been selected by Secretary Talbott in 1953 as Special Assistant for Research and Development where he remained until his promotion to the newly created position, Assistant Secretary of the Air Force (Research and

Air Force Acquisitions under Talbott. *Clockwise from above*: the B-57, the F-100, the B-52, and the TM-61 Matador cruise missile entered service inventories between 1953 and 1955.

Development). Born in Cardiff, Wales, in 1915, Gardner became a naturalized U.S. citizen in 1937, the same year he was graduated from the University of Southern California where he studied engineering. Two years after earning a masters degree in business administration from the same school, he stayed on to teach industrial management. He also taught the subject at the California Institute of Technology. During World War II, Gardner was in charge of developmental engineering there and worked on rocket and atomic bomb projects for the Office of Scientific Research and Development. He was subsequently awarded the Presidential Certificate of Merit and the Naval Ordnance Award for his work. Following the war, he became an executive vice president of General Tire and Rubber Company of California. In 1948 he formed the Hycon Manufacturing Company, where he remained as president until joining Secretary Talbott's staff in 1953. At the time Quarles became Secretary of the Air Force, Gardner was rumored to be a strong candidate for Quarles's former job as Assistant Secretary of Defense for Research and Development. Gardner stayed on working for Quarles in that position, playing a pivotal role in the ICBM program. He resigned his position in February 1956, however, in disagreement with the administration over its conservative research and development funding policies.[41]

Dudley C. Sharp, designated to replace the departing Roger Lewis as Assistant Secretary of the Air Force (Materiel), was graduated from Princeton University in 1927 and joined the Mission Manufacturing Company in Houston, Texas, as vice president. He held that position until 1935, when he became executive vice president. After serving in the Navy from 1942 to 1945, he returned to

Donald A. Quarles, fourth Secretary of the Air Force.

the Mission Manufacturing Company as its president. Sharp also became president and director of Texas Fund, Inc., based in Houston, Texas; director of Bradschamp & Company and Fund Management Association, Inc., both of Houston; and director of Houston, McConway and Troley Corporation of Pittsburgh, Pennsylvania. It was widely believed that Sharp had been recommended by fellow Texan, Robert Anderson, who had recently resigned as Deputy Secretary of Defense. Sharp assumed his duties as Assistant Secretary of the Air Force (Materiel) in October 1955, more than a month after Secretary Talbott had resigned.[42]

Shortly after taking office, Secretary Quarles commended Talbott for his success in correcting the Air Force's retention problem and in raising morale so that the Air Force would "grow stronger and more skillful, as our personnel become more stable and better trained."[43] He later noted that because of the reenlistment incentives and pay raise pushed by Talbott and passed by Congress, 11,000 more airmen had, during the first four months of 1956, chosen to stay in the service upon completion of their initial tours of duty than had done so during the same period in 1955. He pointed out that the Air Force, by spending less than $50 million on pay raises, had been able, between June 1955 and June 1956, to retain skills which had cost $160 million and thus gain 300 percent on its investment. Secretary Quarles would argue, as had his predecessor, that reenlistment solved only part of the service's personnel problem. Adequate housing, medical care for military families, and proper survivor benefits were among the improvements that would help close the gap between Air Force and private sector compensations.[44]

Trevor Gardner, Assistant Secretary of the Air Force (Research and Development) from 1955 to 1956.

Secretary Quarles also stressed the importance of the United States' maintaining qualitative superiority in the face of the Soviet Union's rapid technological advances. He urged that the Air Force devote adequate attention to research and development. Pilots and ground crews had to "have at their disposal the best possible equipment."[45] Besides a strong and sustained research and development program, Quarles supported the ongoing strengthening of the service and recommended that B-52, F-101, and F-104 production proceed without a slowdown.

It was over the amount of money to be spent on research and development that Secretary Quarles and Assistant Secretary Gardner clashed. Quarles generally supported the administration's attempts to keep across-the-board defense spending down and defended certain cuts. In August 1955, Gardner, before Congress, accused Air Secretary Quarles and Defense Secretary Wilson of dismissing Air Force research and development programs as ineptly managed and, consequently, wasteful. Gardner countered that injecting into such programs "the necessary degree of imaginativeness and risk without . . . some waste and duplication" was impossible.[46] He warned that the Soviet Union was quickly closing the qualitative gap. Recent intelligence had revealed startling improvements in missiles, aircraft, and nuclear weapons that the United States could not ignore in spite of the Bureau of the Budget's demands for fiscal restraint. Gardner argued that sufficient funds for research and development were as important as those for production.[47]

The issue of research expenditures festered within the DOD in late 1955 and into 1956, as did the question of which weapon systems should receive priority. Air Secretary Quarles believed that U.S. atomic weapons and delivery systems, while fewer in quantity than the Soviet Union's, were better and more varied.[48] He had generally supported Trevor Gardner's argument for additional research and development funding. In late January, however, because of duplication between the Army's, Navy's, and Air Force's competing missile programs, he shifted his position in favor of the administration's smaller research and development budget. In February 1956, Gardner, disgruntled, informed Quarles that he intended to resign his office. Even a last minute meeting with Defense Secretary Wilson failed to change his mind. His specific complaint was not solely with Wilson, but also with Quarles, who had rejected proposed fiscal years 1956 and 1957 research and development increases. Gardner was concerned that U.S. technical progress in relation to the Soviet Union's was slowing.

It was speculated that Gardner resigned in disappointment because he had not been appointed the DOD's "missile czar,"* and was about to be questioned by Congress over a possible conflict of interest. He returned to private life as pres-

---

* The position of Special Assistant (later Director) to the Secretary of Defense for Guided Missiles, was created in March 1956. The first incumbent was Eger V. Murphree, an Esso Oil Company executive.

ident of the Hycon Manufacturing Company in California. He wrote several articles on the growing successes of Soviet technology in the missile field and on the necessity for the United States to accelerate its missile programs.[49] He later admitted that his battles with Secretaries Wilson and Quarles, commonly believed to be focused solely on the funding of missile research, were actually wider in scope and dealt with the funding of a variety of fields related to all weapon systems.[50]

As insistent as Gardner's articles were both a February 1956 speech by the Air Force Vice Chief of Staff, General Thomas D. White, and a presentation before the Senate Armed Services Committee that same month by the Air Force Chief of Staff, General Nathan F. Twining. General White's sharp warning of the Soviet Union's persistence in seeking superior air power came only days after the Air Secretary had assured a Texas audience that any recent Soviet technological developments were of minimal importance. White claimed that the Soviet Union was not only "making scientific and technological advances at a faster rate" than the United States, but was also "beating us at our own game—production."[51] He noted that the Soviet Union's ability to complete several projects on a crash basis reflected the extent of their dedication to research and development. White conceded that the nature of research and development generally, "in which failure is routine and success extraordinary," rendered large-scale funding difficult to justify to the public. White called on American industry to shoulder more responsibility for research and development and not leave it entirely to government, lest, the Vice Chief argued, the United States, like the Soviet Union, stifle private initiative.[52]

In testimony before the Senate Armed Services Committee, General Twining admitted that the Soviet Air Force was already larger by thousands of aircraft than the U.S. Air Force, was closing the quality gap precisely because of intensified research and development, and was also putting more "men and money into the battle of the laboratories than we."[53] He predicted that the Soviet Air Force would be able to make good on its threat to deploy an ICBM in the near future and would continue to "outpace our estimates of [its] capability."[54]

At the same hearings, Secretary Quarles, like General Twining, acknowledged before the committee all of the speculative reports on the status of U.S. and Soviet air-atomic power. He admitted that the Soviet Union was already flight-testing a ballistic missile with a range of 1,500 miles, while no comparable weapon had yet left the drawing boards in the United States. He further confirmed that he had cut the Air Staff's fiscal year 1957 minimum budget request from $20 billion to $18.5 billion. However, Secretary of Defense Wilson had subtracted an additional $2 billion, lowering the total to $16.5 billion, a level Quarles considered austere.* Quarles testified that this "bare bones" budget was loaded with many "one-shot savings" which could not be maintained and would significantly

---

* Actually, in late February 1956, Trevor Gardner had exposed the administration's

reduce overall Air Force strength. Quarles's and Twining's presentations shocked some senators who had, like many of their constituents, complacently accepted the superiority of U.S. military and technological might as fact.[55]

As a result of these revelations, the Senate established a special investigative committee headed by former Secretary of the Air Force Senator Stuart Symington to study the reasons for the nation's lagging air power. The hearings brought together many military leaders who applied their expertise to discussions on the arms race. The Symington Committee would confirm that, in fact, the Soviet Union was outpacing the United States in overall air power, had improved the quality of its aircraft, and had taken the lead in a number of research areas.[56]

Quarles and Missiles

Secretary Quarles quickly became known as a competent administrator who seemed, because of his professional and educational background, eminently suited to his new post. According to Assistant Secretary of the Air Force (Materiel) Dudley Sharp, Quarles's strong points were his closeness to many of the nation's foremost scientists and his special knowledge of the technical issues he would face as Secretary of the Air Force. Sharp, however, downplayed the importance of administrative skills in a Secretary of the Air Force, arguing that if a sound organization already existed, "the leader [should] just be able to make decisions on knotty problems."[57]

Immediately after taking office, Quarles instituted weekly meetings to enable the Air Staff and the OSAF to concentrate on specific issues and to exchange ideas freely. Held each Tuesday throughout most of Quarles's tenure, these meetings were based on "fully staffed" proposals, that is, proposals properly coordinated with the OSD, in suitable form for executive action.[58] Such coordination had become a reality, not just a formality, and reflected the steady encroachment of the OSD into the service secretaries' spheres of activity.

---

position when he testified before the House Appropriations Committee in executive session and provided a complete picture of the evolution of the fiscal year 1957 budget. The former assistant secretary stated that the President, the Secretary of Defense, the Secretary of the Air Force, and the Director of the Bureau of the Budget had failed to support the Air Force's original program of $20 billion. Gardner complained to the committee that the budget ceiling imposed on the Air Force by the DOD had hampered research and development progress for three years despite scientific breakthroughs that, if pursued, would have assured U.S. superiority over the Soviet Union in aerial weapon systems development. "Gardner Says Budget Guarantees Nation Second Best Air Force," *Aviation Week*, vol 64, no 9, Feb 27, 1956, p 30.

In November 1955, Quarles recommended that projects for the development of the ICBM and the intermediate range ballistic missile (IRBM) be managed under a single authority within his office. The OSD subsequently approved the creation of the Air Force Ballistic Missile Committee (AFBMC) and formed a special Ballistic Missile Committee (OSDBMC) of its own to which the AFBMC reported on a quarterly basis.* The AFBMC reviewed and approved annual development plans prepared by the Western Development Division† and the Air Research and Development Command. It also reviewed and approved modifications to annual programs and provided assistance, technical advice, and recommendations to the OSDBMC.[59]

The AFBMC's membership included the Secretary of the Air Force who served as chairman, the Assistant Secretary (Research and Development) who served as vice chairman, the Assistant Secretaries (Materiel) and (Financial Management), and the Assistant Chief of Staff (Guided Missiles). The latter kept the Chief of Staff and other interested parties within the Air Staff informed on ICBM and IRBM‡[60] programs and provided administrative support. Secretary Quarles was fully committed to achieving 137 wings and to maintaining the recently emphasized ICBM and IRBM programs as well as other research and development initiatives. Because his budget had been cut by nearly $3.5 billion, however, he was forced to economize and suggested in July 1956 that certain ICBM program activities be stretched out. He criticized the dual development of missile subsystems as "over insurance" and ordered that the building of new missile facilities be kept to a minimum. As head of the AFBMC he scrutinized all aspects of ballistic missile development according to his "poor man's" approach, delaying what he could to save funds.[61]

---

* For complete coverage of the ICBM and IRBM program approvals, see Jacob Neufeld's discussion of the Gillette procedures in his book, *Ballistic Missiles in the United States Air Force, 1945–1960* (Washington: Office of Air Force History, 1990).

† The Western Development Division (WDD) was a division of the Air Research and Development Command (ARDC) established on July 1, 1954, under the command of Brig. Gen. Bernard Schriever at Inglewood, California. WDD's primary mission was to manage the Atlas program for development of the country's first ICBM. Capts. Denis J. Stanley and John J. Weaver, *An Air Force Command for R&D, 1949–1976: The History of ARDC/AFSC,* (Andrews Air Force Base, Maryland: Office of History, Headquarters, Air Force Systems Command, 1977) p 23.

‡ Both missile programs had existed for several years, but they were given increased importance as a result of the Killian Committee report of February 1955 which found that North America was vulnerable to surprise attack. The National Security Council adopted the tenets of the report in October 1955 and recommended that President Eisenhower assign highest priority to the development of both missile programs. In December he did so—to the ICBM (Atlas and Titan) and IRBM (Jupiter and Thor) programs. Robert Frank Futrell, *Ideas, Concepts, Doctrine: History of Basic Thinking in the United States Air Force, 1907–1964*, (Maxwell AFB, Alabama: Air University, 1974), pp 246–47.

By doing so, Quarles merely reflected the administration's overall national defense policy of deterrence based on "sufficiency," that total defensive and offensive structure of both nuclear and conventional weapons adequate to discourage a potential adversary from provoking war. This policy represented a complete reversal of the administration's previous position that the United States possessed the best Air Force in the world as well as the most advanced technology.[62]

Secretary Quarles's poor man's approach exemplified this reversal. President Eisenhower and Secretary Wilson had espoused earlier budget cuts, and Quarles had merely done his part to support them, at the expense, however, of sound relations between the OSAF and the Air Staff and commands. Their disagreements became public at Senator Symington's air power hearings during the spring and summer of 1956.

A Divergence of Views

In July 1956, SAC Commander, General Curtis E. LeMay, argued before the Symington Committee that the administration's defense economies would lead to the Soviet Union's attaining strategic air superiority over the United States, primarily in numbers of bombers, by 1960. Quarles denied LeMay's contention. He maintained that the B-47, missiles, and other forces would assure continuing U.S. domination of air power. The Air Secretary also challenged the assertion of Lt. Gen. Donald Putt, Deputy Chief of Staff (Research and Development), that the Air Force's research and development programs had been funded at the same level over the previous several years. Quarles emphasized that there had been a steady increase over the same period and that he had endorsed an additional $100 million. When Senator Symington suggested that Quarles's sworn testimony conflicted with that of the field commanders, the Air Secretary expressed resentment over the implication that he would make false statements.[63]

Quarles had staunchly supported the administration's position against the testimony of the Air Force's general officers. He was doubtless in a difficult position, and Secretary of Defense Wilson's activities did not help his cause. Wilson had reportedly labeled the Senate's attempts to increase the Air Force's budget as "phony." The Senate, which in late June had voted an $800 million increase in Air Force procurement for fiscal year 1957, was so offended by his statement that it considered asking for his resignation. Symington and Senator Richard Russell of Georgia, Chairman of the Senate Armed Services Committee, both demanded that Wilson be removed from office. Even Republicans such as former Chairman of the Senate Appropriations Committee, Styles Bridges of New Hampshire, called Wilson's pronouncement an "unwarranted slur on all senators." Democrats were incensed. Senator George Smathers of Florida stated that he could not recall when another government official had managed so often to insult not only his co-workers but members of Congress as well. Smathers characterized Wilson as a pedant, guilty of misleading the public and of too readily discarding the views of such experienced and dedicated officers as LeMay and Twining. Senator Dennis Chavez of New Mexico reminded Wilson that he was not running the General Motors Corporation but working for the public. "Every time he holds a conference," the senator remarked, "as the proverbial saying goes, he puts his foot in his mouth."[64]

Air Force Chief of Staff, General Twining, after a trip to the Soviet Union where he had witnessed an air show, submitted a detailed report which verified the truth of the convictions he had expressed during Senator Symington's hearings—that the Soviet Union was going "all out" building atomic air power and would succeed in gaining "world superiority" unless the United States intensified its efforts. Twining had, in effect, revealed the inaccuracies in many of Wilson's statements about the Soviet Union's intentions. Wilson's characterization in 1954 of the Soviet Union's Air Force as primarily defensive was negated by the appearance in 1955 of the twin-jet Badger, the four-jet Bison and the turboprop intercontinental Bear bomber. The existence of squadron-size formations of Badgers, Farmers (MiG-19s), Flashlights (Yak-25s), and other aircraft in 1955 disproved Wilson's belief that the new Soviet jet-fighters were "hand-built prototypes." Wilson's assertion that these new aircraft were imitations of American models was refuted by new delta designs, supersonic light bombers, and new Yakovlev supersonic all-weather fighters, which were quite different from western designs. General Twining reported specifically that Soviet aeronautical designers were pioneering "on their own in the field of modern aircraft development."[65]

The public airing of such divergent views created more tension among the services, the Secretary of Defense, and the Congress than had existed during the Symington-Forrestal-Truman era. What was most difficult for the Air Force to accept was that the President whose administration opposed the view articulated by LeMay, Twining, and others was headed by one of the most famous American military heroes of the 20th century, Dwight D. Eisenhower. The service naturally expected him to take its side if the situation was as serious as some airpower experts believed it to be. Two questions were crucial. Just how serious a threat was the Soviet Union? Did Quarles's definition of sufficiency mean the acceptance of the Soviet Union by the United States as an equal power? According to Quarles and other administration officials, the Soviet Union would be unable to achieve both the maintenance of a superior Air Force and the preservation of a stable economy.[66]

Arguments over the Soviet threat continued throughout the summer of 1956 and were fueled by former Assistant Secretary of the Air Force (Research and Development) Trevor Gardner. In an *Aviation Week* article he once again added spice to Senator Symington's air power investigation, charging that interservice competition within the United States wasted both talent and facilities and might very well allow the Soviet Union to win the race for the ICBM. He noted that high-caliber executives working on America's missile project spent less time actually running it than complaining about interservice squabbling. The three services had fifteen to twenty ballistic missile programs competing with each other for engines, engineers, and firing ranges.[67]

The administration's and the Air Force's arguments continued. At the August 1956 Air Force Association convention, Quarles became involved in a disagreement concerning a possible cut in the number of Air Force wings. He stated that the administration did not consider a 137-wing force permanent and indicated that 1958 might bring the beginning of a downward trend because of the increasing potency of the entire range of Air Force weapons and the Army's fast-growing ability with tactical missiles for close support.[68] His statements ignited the wrath of AFA veterans and active-duty officers in attendance. General LeMay challenged Quarles's assertion that U.S. air power could serve as an effective deterrent if it were not actually superior. Quarles held that the United States needed only enough force capable of delivering a devastating counterattack, and he maintained that neither side could hope to escape catastrophe in an atomic war. General LeMay disagreed with the Air Secretary, asserting, "you have to have more combat potential if you are going to be a deterrent force."[69]

The convention had become another arena within which the service's and the administration's opposing positions were hotly debated, and Quarles was caught in the middle. Indeed, when Defense Secretary Wilson heard that the AFA would honor two critics of the DOD, Stuart Symington and Trevor Gardner, he attempted to prevent Quarles from delivering his speech. Symington's selection as "Aviation's Man of the Year," for his work heading the Senate's air power study irritated the Secretary of Defense. Gardner's award truly angered him; the former Assistant Secretary had, upon quitting his office, delivered a scathing denunciation of the administration's attitude toward the funding of research and development. The AFA in turn hailed Gardner for his "courageous leadership." Quarles held to his commitment and spoke before the AFA against the wishes of his superior. However, he remained faithful to the administration's policy of restraint on defense spending and did not endear himself to his audience, which he likened to a college alumni association demanding that the school president or the football coach be fired.[70]

The following February, Senator Symington's committee completed its report of the Eisenhower administration's Air Force. The report presented twenty-three major conclusions, many of them harshly critical. Senator Leverett Saltonstall of Massachusetts declined to sign it, deeming its assessment of present and future U.S. air defense overly pessimistic. He argued that the committee had focused too much attention on the Eisenhower years and had disregarded the opinions of DOD civilian heads in favor of the views of the advocates of the Air Force.

The report contained three particularly damning charges against the DOD—(1) that it had failed to develop an adequate defense early warning sys-

Soviet Air Power. The threat posed by the Tupolev Tu-16 Badger *(above)*, the supersonic Mikoyan and Gurevich MiG-19 Farmer *(below)*, and other new Soviet aircraft preoccupied the Air Force and Congress in 1955.

tem; (2) that, with respect to Soviet air power, it had overemphasized U.S. air power's qualitative advantage to excuse its quantitative disadvantage; and (3) that it had allowed duplication and even triplification between the three services in missile development. The report, in spite of its political bias and its failure to offer solutions to the many problems it addressed, was widely regarded as the most comprehensive compilation of expert military opinions on the subject ever assembled for distribution to the general public.[71]

Quarles would continue to support the administration's goals for defense

161

spending against the arguments of the Air Staff. In March 1957, his testimony that the United States was substantially ahead of the Soviet Union in long-range strategic air capability and would remain so effectively stalled Congress's action to raise the Air Force's 1958 budget. Quarles assured the Air Force Subcommittee of the Senate Armed Services Committee that, according to his interpretation of intelligence on Soviet aircraft production, B-52 production, which at one time trailed the Bison's, had regained its lead. Senator Symington challenged the statement, noting that the Air Force's 1958 budget of nearly $2.5 billion over 1957's represented only a $66 million increase in real terms. Congress had raised the initial 1957 budget from $16.5 billion to $17.69 billion; the 1958 budget was listed as $17.75 billion. Symington had resigned as Secretary of the Air Force rather than preside over a service that he had firmly believed was funded too poorly at forty-eight groups to function as it should. Now, to his amazement and exasperation, Quarles was actually discouraging Congress's generosity.* The Air Secretary remained unwavering in his opinion that the administration's 1958 budget allowed the United States to confront any aggressor with an indestructible and inescapable retaliatory force.[72]

Quarles's and Symington's situations as Air Secretary differed greatly. Symington, unhampered by layers of authority within the OSD, had enjoyed with the other service secretaries near equality with the Secretary of Defense and had skillfully perfected his relationship with Congress. Quarles had devoted his attention to research and development and had proved in the brief period of twenty months that a scientist could competently lead and manage the Air Force. Quarles, like Symington, might have been the right man at the right time. The Air Force was developing missiles and supersonic bombers whose increasingly complex technologies he understood fully. He was unable, however, to confront President Eisenhower's administration the way Symington had confronted President Truman's. The two legislative acts of 1949 and 1953 had helped change the relationship of the Secretary of the Air Force to the Secretary of Defense. By 1953 the Secretary of Defense had a deputy and nine assistant secretaries who stood between him and the service secretaries. Quarles simply did not have the power that Symington had. He had to support the administration against the wishes of his own airmen and, if he aspired to higher office within the DOD, he had to toe Defense Secretary Wilson's line.

The intensity of the discord between the Air Secretary and the Air Staff would abate somewhat in April 1957 with the departure of Quarles for the OSD

---

* Quarles, in fact, as Assistant Secretary of Defense for Research and Development, drafted the nation's first space policy for the National Security Council and was privy to information concerning the U-2 reconnaissance program. Unbeknownst to Symington, Twining, and LeMay, the U-2 program had by early 1957 proved to administration leaders that no "bomber gap" existed and that the U.S. Air Force was superior to the Soviet Air Force, at least in numbers.

as Deputy Secretary of Defense. The subsequent selection of Under Secretary of the Air Force James Douglas as Secretary of the Air Force would calm the storm. As a former under secretary within the OSAF he had earned a favorable reputation with the Air Staff. Quarles, however, disturbed by the dissent that had marred his tenure as Air Secretary, ordered, before he left for the DOD, a study of the relationship between the OSAF and the Air Staff, the results of which would significantly affect dealings between the two bodies during the final years of the Eisenhower administration.

Chapter 7

The Air Staff and the OSAF

The mid-1950s saw radical changes in military weapon systems accompanied by interservice arguments about how they should be used and which service should control them. The Department of Defense (DOD) confronted an array of questions about tactical air support and airlift for Army ground forces, antimissile missiles, intermediate-range ballistic missiles (IRBMs), carrier versus land-based aviation, and its own ability to meet future problems.

While use and control were being debated, the relationship between the Office of the Secretary of the Air Force (OSAF) and the Air Staff was breaking down as the growing authority of the Office of the Secretary of Defense (OSD) complicated their interactions. The 1949 amendments to the National Security Act had added to the OSD a Deputy Secretary of Defense and three assistant secretaries. Reorganization Plan No. 6 in 1953 had added six more assistant secretaries. Gradually these new officials built up their own staffs and expertise within special functional areas. Stuart Symington could deal directly with the Secretary of Defense. His assistant secretaries and their Air Staff counterparts were the Air Force's acknowledged specialists in operations. The Air Secretary and the other service secretaries had now to contend with a completely new center of expertise and authority within the OSD. As the OSD became larger, its members tended to communicate directly with the Air Staff, bypassing the OSAF. The Air Staff had found that channelling its concerns through the OSAF was increasingly cumbersome and time-consuming.

Reorganization Plan No. 6 was complemented five years later by the Department of Defense Reorganization Act of 1958. This act completely removed the service secretaries from the operational chain of command of which they had been a part on a formal basis since the Reorganization Plan of 1953. Under the new act, control flowed directly from the President through the Secretary of Defense and the Joint Chiefs of Staff (JCS) to the unified and specified commands. The 1958 act merely confirmed reality. Secretaries Talbott, Quarles, Finletter, and Symington had all distanced themselves to varying degrees from day to day operational concerns. However, the responsibility for support functions in such areas as training and logistics remained with the service secretaries and the military chiefs.

The 1958 act authorized the JCS 400 officers as well as a more powerful chairman. It also granted the Secretary of Defense the discretion to allow orders to be issued to the military departments by the Assistant Secretaries of Defense. The service secretaries, their civilian assistants, and military personnel from the various service staffs were expected to cooperate fully with OSD personnel "in a continuous effort to achieve efficient administration of the Department of Defense and effectively to carry out the direction, authority, and control of the Secretary of Defense."[1] The service secretaries did retain the right under the 1958 act to present recommendations to Congress after first informing the Secretary of Defense. President Eisenhower and Secretary of Defense Neil H. McElroy regarded this right as "disruptive" and were disappointed by its retention. Congress, however, preserved it to avoid becoming isolated from military views on matters vital to national security.[2]

To determine the extent to which the lines of authority between the Air Staff and the OSAF had broken down and the feasibility of rebuilding them, Air Secretary Quarles requested in 1956 that the OSAF undertake a study, the results of which were published internally that fall under the title *The Secretary of the Air Force-Air Staff Relationship Study*. Subsequent related studies would be conducted throughout Air Secretary Douglas's tenure from May 1957 to December 1959. The initial study was most important and represented the first real analysis of the civilian-military relationship since the establishment of the OSAF in 1947. Its findings, although sometimes harsh, revealed several truths concerning the Air Staff's view of the OSAF. Both parties, however, were convinced that the source of their changing relationship could be found in the ever-expanding OSD.

The informal relationship between the Air Force Chief of Staff and the Secretary of the Air Force was, by the mid-1950s, becoming more complicated as their offices grew and their autonomy diminished under the OSD. No longer could most Air Staff-OSAF business be carried out on the personal first-name basis that had existed during Secretary Symington's tenure. The rapid spending surge unleashed by Congress in response to the Korean War expanded forty-eight wings in 1950 to ninety-five wings in 1951 and augmented both the OSAF and the Air Staff. The OSAF parceled out its additional responsibilities to newly created deputies (formerly special assistants). They, in turn, increased their staffs to meet the crisis. Wartime tasks increased so dramatically throughout the secretariat that they impeded personal contact between the Air Secretary and other members of his staff. The infrequency of such contact was pointed out in a study in 1951 by the Assistant Secretary of the Air Force (Management), Eugene Zuckert. Zuckert had been struck by the marked differences in his working relationships with Secretary Symington and Secretary Finletter. Finletter had communicated with the assistant secretaries far less frequently than Symington.[3]

The Eisenhower administration's emphasis on more civilian control of the DOD through the deputy system further muddied communications between the

Air Staff and the OSAF. The six new Assistant Secretaries of Defense and the General Counsel created under Reorganization Plan No. 6 were not supposed to be in the direct line of administrative authority over the three military departments. They were, however, strategically placed within the OSD. As the Secretary of Defense came to rely on their advice, which often countered the Air Force's, the status of the service secretaries declined. Reorganization Plan No. 6 accelerated the process that began with the 1949 amendments to the National Security Act under which additional assistant secretaries provided the OSD with new layers of authority and expertise in special areas.[4] The Air Staff and the OSAF found working through these new civilian offices burdensome and sometimes unnecessary.

As early as 1952 the Administrative Assistant to the Secretary of the Air Force, John J. McLaughlin, recognized that the situation within the OSAF had changed with a heavier workload. He noted in particular a lack of "complete" dissemination of information on any given action, observing that while it flowed to five individuals easily enough, it flowed to the five organizational segments of the OSAF haphazardly at best. The assistants or deputies, who once required only small staffs of two or three, now demanded much more support. McLaughlin wanted to limit the number of deputies reporting to statutory appointees—the Secretary of the Air Force and the assistant secretaries—to three or four, arguing that more merely slowed the coordination process and clogged appointment calendars. He cautioned Assistant Secretary Zuckert that the creation of additional deputies by the OSAF strained the centralized administrative and management services provided by his office. If more deputies were brought in, McLaughlin perhaps self-servingly warned, numerous small decentralized administrative empires within the OSAF would soon be established, a practice which, he predicted, would eventually cost more to run than his own centralized Office of the Administrative Assistant.[5]

In May 1953, in anticipation of President Eisenhower's reorganization of the DOD, McLaughlin recommended to the Air Secretary that a study of both the Air Staff and the OSAF receive top priority. Since he expected that the Rockefeller Committee, which had been developing Eisenhower's initiatives, would recommend increased responsibility for the Secretary of Defense but not for the service secretaries, he felt that the time for an "honest evaluation of how we do business or manage this business at the Seat of Government is now."[6] He believed that such an effort should focus on defining the missions of the Air Staff, that the numerous levels of review that accompanied many actions were, for the most part, unwarranted. In his view, neither the OSAF nor the Air Staff was equipped organizationally or otherwise to meet an "overnight mobilization situation. Iron-clad prerogatives of supervisory personnel at all echelons" dominated the Air Force and had driven it "toward stagnation of ideas, imagination, and fresh approaches to old problems."[7] McLaughlin's criticisms found some immediate support but his study would not be undertaken for three years.

Complaints about the lack of clear authority lines had circulated during Air Secretary Finletter's tenure, more recently during Talbott's tenure, and had intensified during Quarles's. Growing confusion frustrated workings between the OSAF and the Air Staff and had damaging effects on specific areas such as procurement. Seeking to improve the process by which the OSAF and the Air Staff communicated, Secretary Quarles in May 1956 justified his study officially as an attempt to trace the directives which governed the submission of procurement contracts for secretarial approval and to clarify how and to whom the authority for that approval had been delegated. Actually, he wished to restore the once easy access to each other that the OSAF and Air Force had enjoyed and to determine exactly why it had diminished.

Under Secretary of the Air Force James H. Douglas, Jr., welcomed the study as the first all-embracing review of the OSAF since its establishment in 1947. Douglas hoped that the effort would help decrease the amount of paperwork processed through the OSAF; that it would determine which matters the Air Staff could directly handle that involved outside offices; and that it would provide a better channel for the formal exchange of information affecting the several functional areas within the OSAF.[8]

John J. McLaughlin, selected by Secretary Quarles to supervise the study, recommended that it be expanded to include a special inventory of all matters processed through the OSAF. He decided to focus on how much of the time dedicated to program and operating reviews was generated by external as opposed to internal requirements. He ordered each office of the OSAF to furnish an inventory of its transactions with the Air Staff and each office of the the Air Staff to prepare a similar list of its dealings with the OSAF. McLaughlin planned for a combined OSAF-Air Staff group to evaluate the two inventories and make recommendations.

McLaughlin requested the Air Staff to evaluate the effectiveness of the OSAF as manager of the Air Force, rating the quality of its guidance and participation in staff activities as well as the quality of its contributions to policy making and problem solving. He wanted to determine which areas needed increased OSAF involvement and then to identify ways in which both offices could work more closely together to reduce overlapping responsibilities.

In October 1956, McLaughlin's study was completed. It included six major findings. The first was that the Air Staff could not decide exactly how the Secretary of the Air Force should exercise leadership or how much civilian involvement in operations was desirable. For example, the Air Staff's Directorate of Plans wanted less OSAF participation, while the Directorate of Materiel wanted more, especially in policy formulation.[9] Some of Quarles's colleagues within the OSAF felt that he sometimes delved too deeply into areas the Air Staff considered its own. Former Under Secretary of the Air Force Malcolm A. MacIntyre recalled that the Air Staff chafed under Quarles's demands for what it felt was too much detailed information on matters with which the Air

Secretary of the Air Force Donald A. Quarles presents Administrative Assistant John J. McLaughlin with the Exceptional Civilian Service award. McLaughlin had long supported the OSAF-Air Staff study that Quarles ordered carried out in 1956.

Secretary should not have been personally involved.[10] Perhaps some Air Staff elements felt pushed by his penchant for probing and hoped that he would eventually abandon the practice. None of them, however, should have been surprised that he would demonstrate a profound interest in their management of missile technology, his field of expertise. Quarles, more than likely aware of the Air Staff's attitude, concurred with McLaughlin that a study was necessary. Perhaps Secretary Talbott did not pursue one because he was preoccupied with the reenlistment issue and later with the personal difficulties that clouded his term.

Quarles had no illusions about his role and power as Secretary of the Air Force. He was responsible for the administration of the Department of the Air Force and looked to the Chief of Staff and the Air Staff for guidance on all operational issues. He acknowledged that the assistant secretaries' duties correlated with the duties of the respective Air Staff deputies, and, in his view, the assistant secretaries and the Air Staff deputies functioned best working closely with each other. He considered himself the service's spokesman before Congress and, in some cases, before the public, but he also considered himself subordinate to the Secretary of Defense. Quarles, much like Stuart Symington, left operational decisions to operational specialists.[11] It seems likely that the real impetus behind the study and the core of dissatisfaction arose from career bureaucrats within the OSAF and the Air Staff, from someone like McLaughlin, who had served the organization since its inception in 1947.

Opinions within the Air Staff about the role of the OSAF split along functional lines. Personnel offices preferred minimal OSAF participation in program planning. Budget offices, however, interacted with the OSAF almost daily and valued what they regarded as its substantial contribution to the preparation, review, and submission of estimated expenditures. The Air staff discovered that, in fact, some of its offices were closer to the OSAF than to the Chief of Staff. Thus the relationship between the Deputy Chief of Staff, Comptroller, and the Assistant Secretary (Financial Management) was a notable exception to the study's findings. Personnel offices within the OSAF maintained that the Air Staff had based too many decisions on its notions of "what the boss will buy" and had, in effect, deprived the Air Secretary of his usefulness and objectivity as a reviewing authority. They believed that the role of the OSAF was to review and evaluate and to apply any policy initiated directly to it by the OSD, unrouted through the Air Staff.[12]

The Air Staff generally agreed that, to varying extents, its involvement in policy development was important. Its civilian personnel offices held that the OSAF's participation in policy development should constitute little more than a "response" to the Air Staff's priorities. Its materiel offices however, balked at that approach. They believed that it would burden them with additional correspondence to confirm the consistency of Air Staff and Air Secretarial positions.

Much of the Air Staff believed that secretarial decision-making ought to be confined to supporting the headquarters on critical, controversial, or sensitive issues.[13] This might explain the rapport between the civilian and military budget preparers who shared tremendous responsibilities. Neither the OSAF nor the Air Staff wished to shoulder sole accountability when funding problems arose.

The study's second major finding revealed the significant degree to which the OSD shaped the relationship between the OSAF and the Air Staff. Of more than 6,000 pieces of correspondence transmitted to agencies outside the Air Force, half were destined for the OSD. Also, nearly 20 percent of all plans, programs, and policy directives sent by the Air Staff for OSAF approval were initiated by the OSD. When an Air Staff office had little or no business with the OSD, it also had few dealings with the OSAF. Study participants discovered that the Air Staff and the OSAF were not "masters in their own houses" and maintained that if the OSD curbed its direction of or involvement in the activities of the services by 50 percent, a corresponding reduction in contacts and transactions between the Air Staff and the Secretariat occurred.

Air Secretary Harold Talbott had expressed concern over the increasing power of the OSD and had sought to preserve the right of the military departments to negotiate with foreign countries for basing rights. He felt that it was unnecessary for the maintenance of effective policy control to shift responsibility for such an activity away from the services.[14]

In 1954 General Twining warned Secretary Quarles that a diminution of functions and responsibilities within the individual military departments and the JCS would concentrate excessive power within the OSD. There would be no assurance, he worried, that OSD decisions, made perhaps on the recommendations of the unified commanders or the joint agencies, would reflect the service's aims and programs. Centralization would decrease those occasions during which the three military departments and the JCS could present their views to the Secretary of Defense, the National Security Council, and the President. Twining believed that the Secretary of Defense risked isolating himself from an abundance of expert sources.[15]

The study's third major finding emphasized that because most contact between the Air Staff and the OSAF was conducted on a reactive basis, no channels had been established for the regular exchange and dissemination of information, particularly on policies and plans. The study acknowledged the close association between the Secretary of the Air Force and the Chief of Staff, and between the Under Secretary of the Air Force and the Vice Chief of Staff, but, in disagreement with Secretary Quarles, it faulted the far less frequent interaction between the Assistant Secretaries of the Air Force and the Deputy Chiefs of Staff and the Air Staff directors. The Air Staff reported that it was compelled repeatedly to question the OSAF, which provided no broad guidance, for direction on a host of issues.[16] Air Secretary Talbott, like Air Secretary Quarles, would have agreed that there were some close, efficient dealings between the Secretariat and the Air Staff. He was apparently satisfied by his rapport with the Chief and with the interactions between his statutory assistants and their counterparts in the Air Staff. He had not felt it necessary to eliminate the Chief of Staff from the reporting chain to his office on any subject—the budget, logistics, or research and development.[17] Talbott had wished to preserve the familiar system by which the Air Staff and the OSAF conducted business together before the Korean War.

The study recommended that the OSAF act more effectively as a guiding and stimulating force and sponsor regular meetings with the Deputy Chiefs of Staff and Air Staff directors to exchange ideas and to resolve questions. In addition, it recommended that the Staff Digest be modified to summarize major projects undertaken and completed, to convey policy statements, to serve as a voice for management leaders, and to eliminate staff duplication. In fairness, the study also recommended that the Air Staff keep the OSAF fully informed of its major activities.

The fourth major finding was that responsibility for Air Force-wide decisions had become concentrated in the Air Staff and that in most cases its recommendations were accepted by the OSAF without substantive change. Robert E. Hampton, who served within the OSAF as a civilian Assistant Deputy for Manpower, Personnel, and Organization in the mid-1950s, recalled that he left his position believing that the civilian segment of the OSAF "played second fiddle to the military staff and that recommendations emanating from our sources were not given the weight" that they merited.[18]

Some of the Air Staff believed that its lack of interaction with the OSAF diminished the effectiveness of the service's transactions with the OSD as well as with Congress and other agencies such as the Bureau of the Budget. Their notion presented the Air Staff with a dilemma, since some of its offices desired maximum OSAF support when dealing with outside agencies and minimal OSAF participation in internal matters. The Air Staff was aware that the two goals could not be achieved concurrently; the OSAF had to have knowledge of internal Air Force operations and activities to be of more use to the entire service.[19]

The fifth major finding raised several questions about what controls should be placed on the Air Staff's direct contacts with the OSD. Of the Air Staff's 14,800 contacts with the OSD during the period inventoried, most of which were by telephone, 94 percent had been handled directly by the Air Staff without referral to the OSAF. The Air Staff was against a general curb on its direct contacts with the OSD, if only to eliminate the administrative task of sending correspondence through the OSAF. It believed that it could resolve non-controversial, non-sensitive, and non-political matters with the OSD without having to consult with the Air Secretariat.

The study also noted that among the 163 working group committees for policy development on which elements of both the Air Staff and the OSD served, the OSAF had little or no interest in 141 of them. The Secretariat was represented on only 12 of the remaining 22 committees in which it should have a legitimate interest and was fully cognizant of only 10 Air Staff committees dealing directly with the OSD.

The study finally found that the DOD's encroachment on the operations of Air Force programs was continuing. Since the passage of Reorganization Plan Number 6 in June 1953, DOD directives to the Air Staff had nearly doubled. Even the House Appropriations Committee, when dealing with fiscal year 1957 funding, had expressed the view that the OSD was concerning itself too much with the issuance of detailed instructions and the constant review of actions proposed by the military departments. The study supported Congress's view, stating that the OSD was providing too much guidance on specific projects, often of minor importance, and conducting often time-consuming, unwarranted, and duplicative reviews. It also suggested that to diminish its administrative burden, the OSAF demonstrate greater initiative by delegating more actions to the Air Staff for processing. The study group estimated that at least 10 percent of all correspondence submitted to the OSAF could be signed in the Air Staff.[20]

In mid-1957, the study group made a preliminary presentation of its findings, held in the Office of the Assistant Vice Chief of Staff. Representatives of the Air Staff and the OSAF were among the attendees, nearly all of whom criticized the study group's effort as a "juvenile response" to the growing number of problems and discontents which had emerged in the months immediately following the study."[21] One idea seemed to underlie what were generally non-specific conclusions—that the Air Force would be better off without the Office of the Secretary of the Air Force.* The meeting adjourned with participants agreeing

* Eliminating the Air Secretariat was not feasible without a change to the National Security Act, if not the Air U.S. Constitution, which sustained civilian control over the military services.

that too many extraneous issues had been introduced into the study and that more analysis was needed.

More analysis was conducted and resulted in an October 1957 submission of seventy-five specific recommendations to the Chief of Staff. They concerned, primarily, delegating authority, both statutory and administrative, reducing the frequency of reports, and modifying certain OSD restrictions. Air Force Under Secretary James Douglas praised both the initial study and follow-up analysis as the first comprehensive attempt to streamline the overall operation of the Air Force's departmental organization, including its relationship with the OSD. Maj. Gen. Jacob Smart, the Assistant Vice Chief of Staff, praised them as well, although he faulted too many complaints and too few constructive remedies. The study and follow-up were worthwhile because they had clarified so many of the Air Staff's dissatisfactions.

The study sustained John McLaughlin's long-held view that communications between the Air Staff and the OSAF and within the OSAF itself were poorly systematized. He had frequently gone directly to the Air Staff for information that was, or should have been, available within the OSAF.

In January 1958, McLaughlin provided Under Secretary of the Air Force Malcolm A. MacIntyre with a list of proposed actions to improve interactions between the Air Staff and the OSAF and to insure that the OSAF actually functioned according to its assigned responsibility and authority. McLaughlin suggested that the Under Secretary find out from the Air Secretary, the Chief of Staff, deputy chiefs, chiefs of other major Air Staff offices, and all statutory appointees and civilian chiefs through a series of questions how his office could more significantly smooth communications within the Air Force. McLaughlin contended that a serious management problem existed and that a soul-searching self evaluation of the Secretariat was needed.[22]

One month later, in an apparent about-face he sent another memorandum to Under Secretary MacIntyre, stating that on the advice of the secretary to the Air Staff, Col. J. A. Brooks III, he had decided that for the time being such an evaluation need not be pursued. He also noted that the recommendations "in truth, consisted merely of those things that could have been changed or agreed upon unilaterally by the affected functional areas." *[23] Under Secretary MacIntyre, on the other hand, viewed the work relationship study as a valid point of departure for a continuing review of OSAF-Air Staff transactions.[24] McLaughlin might have concluded that in light of the DOD's preparations for another reorganization act whose passage was inevitable by 1958 and which would centralize even more control within the OSD, any further attempt to improve communications between the Air Staff and the OSAF would prove futile. He may have also have

---

* McLaughlin may have been directed by higher authorities within the Air Secretariat and the Air Staff to cease further study.

reasoned that he would have difficulty explaining to any new Air Secretary just how much power the OSAF had lost to the OSD since Stuart Symington's tenure. McLaughlin was one of the last who had served Symington still holding a prominent position within the Secretariat.*

The initial study revealed the extent to which the relationship between the OSAF and the Air Staff had deteriorated, particularly at lower levels. Remoteness now characterized what were once easy, informal interactions during the Symington era. The study also revealed that the Air Staff had expected perhaps too much from the OSAF regarding policy formulation and decision-making. The Secretariat had been organized since its inception so that each statutory position was assigned small supporting staffs which depended heavily on the Air Staff to carry out projects and investigations.[25] Responsibility for specific jobs remained ill-defined, if not confused, especially when new secretaries assumed office.

The study disclosed that, without a doubt, the new layers of authority vested within the OSD had complicated the communications process. The OSD had grown "in true bureaucratic fashion during the last four years," reported *Aviation Week* in August 1957, from a small advisory type group to a "gigantic paper mill laced with dozens of assistant secretaries of defense who now constitute one of the major bottlenecks [to] a Pentagon decision."[26]

The study identified a disease, but not a cure. However, by airing complaints, it allowed many offices within both the OSAF and the Air Staff the opportunity to recognize that they shared similar problems. The real difficulty, the encroachment of the OSD on areas formerly the domain of the services, remained. The brevity of Air Secretary Quarles's tenure prevented his improving matters. When he left office in April 1957 the creation of the Defense Reorganization Act was already underway. The study emphasized the importance of any effort by the OSAF and the Air Staff to improve relations and better coordinate their efforts in spite of increasing OSD authority.

The Defense Reorganization Act of 1958 gave the Secretary of Defense almost carte blanche to consolidate authority over the service secretaries. Complaints from the Air Staff about its dealings with the OSAF and interference by the OSD would not disappear but would, in fact, increase.

---

* Secretary Douglas felt that McLaughlin provided continuity for the OSAF while occupying a position of unusual responsibility and trust. Douglas regarded McLaughlin as his principal advisor and counsel to other statutory appointees and special assistants on all phases of internal administration and management policies within the OSAF. Memo, James H. Douglas to Civilian Personnel Division, Secretary of the Air Staff, Jun 12, 1959, RG 340, James H. Douglas, Jr., Chronological Files, 1957–1959, Box 19, NARA.

Chapter 8

Douglas and Sharp (1957–1961)

When James H. Douglas, Jr., took office as Secretary of the Air Force in May 1957, discord between the Office of the Secretary of the Air Force (OSAF) and the Air Staff eased somewhat, perhaps because both realized that the coming Reorganization Act of 1958 would further concentrate power within the Office of the Secretary of Defense (OSD). The OSAF and the Air Staff may have agreed to work more closely with each other to salvage some degree of autonomy.

A more likely reason for their rapprochement lay in Sputnik, whose dramatic launch by the Soviet Union on October 4, 1957, prompted the administration to increase across-the-board military spending. Prior to Sputnik, readjusting procurement schedules to meet new budget cuts had occupied much of Secretary Douglas's time. Sputnik helped reverse Congress's attitude toward military spending and actually aided some areas, such as missiles and research and development, to obtain additional funding. After Sputnik, Senators Stuart Symington and Henry Jackson charged that the administration's stringent fiscal policies had allowed the nation's satellite program to lag. They read into Sputnik's success alarming evidence that the Soviet Union was not only first in space but far ahead in missile development.[1]

Secretary Douglas testified frequently before Congress, outlining and defending the Air Force's goals, one of the most important of which was the completion of the Air Force Academy. He was also watchful of the Advanced Research Projects Agency (ARPA) and the National Aeronautics and Space Administration (NASA), making certain that their activities did not infringe on those of the Air Force. Douglas had helped the Air Force weather serious cuts in manpower dictated by Congress and the administration in early 1957 and stood ready to take advantage for the service of Sputnik's impact on congressional attitudes toward defense funding.

Dudley C. Sharp, who replaced James Douglas as Air Secretary in December 1959, would serve out the final year of the Eisenhower administration and would be complemented by Douglas's Chief of Staff, General Thomas D. White. Sharp realized that as a "lame duck" appointment he might never see his new policies yield results. Like Douglas, Sharp became involved in missile management problems, specifically, those relating to the Army's construction of intercontinental ballistic missile (ICBM) sites and to unfavorable reports on the performance of the Air Force missile program by the Government Accounting Office (GAO). Sharp also resisted what he believed were State Department intrusions into Air Force business. The trend in Congress toward greater military spending would continue throughout the final year of the Eisenhower administration as budget balancing became less important than developing new weapons and responding to world events. Dudley Sharp was not confronted with new cuts and, in fact, was satisfied with the budget for fiscal year 1961.

During Sharp's tenure, coincidentally, two studies, one by the Air Staff and the other by Senator Stuart Symington, were conducted on the organization of the Department of Defense (DOD). They both proposed the elimination of the service secretaries and more centralization of power within the OSD. Sharp disagreed with their conclusions. Any reorganization, however, would await the assessment of the next administration.

From 1957 to 1960, there was little continuity of leadership at the highest levels of the DOD. Secretary of Defense Charles E. Wilson left office in October 1957 and was succeeded by Neil H. McElroy who served for two years. McElroy was succeeded by Thomas S. Gates, Jr., former Secretary of the Navy. This turnover permitted neither McElroy nor Gates to imprint a style on the DOD. Each had to content himself with continuing the policies of the administration and dealing with various pressures for increased funding. James Douglas had some impact on the Air Force since he held office for over two years, but Dudley Sharp did not delude himself as his tenure spanned little more than one year. Despite the DOD's changing leadership, both Douglas and Sharp worked amicably with their respective Secretaries of Defense.

Perhaps because of their brief tenures neither McElroy nor Gates took full advantage of the powers granted them by the 1958 Defense Reorganization Act. While this act gave additional authority to the Secretary of Defense, it also granted more power to the Assistant Secretaries of Defense, further weakening the influence of the service secretaries. Neither Douglas nor Sharp felt the full affect of these newly vested powers. The act was not an issue for the OSAF during the closing years of the Eisenhower administration. (See Appendix 1, OSAF Organization Charts, pp. 268, 270.)

Douglas Takes Charge

On May 1, 1957, former Under Secretary of the Air Force James H. Douglas, Jr., became Secretary of the Air Force. Donald A. Quarles became Deputy Secretary of Defense, following the retirement of Ruben Robertson, Jr. Douglas worked well with military personnel, perhaps because of his World War II experiences, of which he spoke fondly, with the Army Air Forces (AAF).[2]

Secretary of Defense Wilson had asked Douglas to become Secretary of the Air Force after Harold Talbott's resignation in August 1955. Douglas had refused because of ill health but decided to continue as Under Secretary of the Air Force and recommended Donald Quarles to Secretary Wilson as a suitable replacement for Talbott. During his four years as under secretary, Douglas had attained a record of proven performance and was considered by some as the unsung workhorse of the OSAF.[3]

Quarles's elevation to Deputy Secretary of Defense gave hope to the Pentagon's supporters of basic research and development. They and many adherents believed in his abilities as a scientist. Although he had been criticized as Air Secretary for having sanctioned cuts in research and development budgets, Quarles, widely viewed as more appealing than Wilson, would work amicably with Douglas.[4]

Air Secretary Douglas's preference for briefings rather than detailed memoranda endeared him to the Air Staff. His own staff felt that those reporting to him would save themselves the time and the effort of developing written reports if they kept a list of important subjects and presented them to him orally when they had the opportunity. This *modus operandi* soon gained Secretary Douglas a reputation as the possessor of a remarkable memory.[5] He was, according to General Theodore R. Milton, his executive officer, held in great affection by the Chief of Staff and the Air Staff. Milton maintained that General White and Douglas got along extremely well and conferred with each other daily.

Filling Douglas's slot as Under Secretary of the Air Force was Malcolm A. MacIntyre, a lawyer and member of the New York firm of Debevoise, Plimpton and McLean. After attaining a law degree from Yale University in 1934, he was admitted to the New York bar and became affiliated with several firms until, during World War II, he was commissioned by the AAF as a first lieutenant in May 1942. He served with Air Transport Command Headquarters in Washington, D.C., and in various overseas theaters, reaching the rank of colonel before being discharged in January 1946. It was during the war that MacIntyre became friendly with Douglas. Afterwards, the pair teamed up as partners in the Washington, D.C., law firm of Douglas, Proctor, MacIntyre and Gates. MacIntyre returned to New York and Debevoise, Plimpton and McLean as a partner in 1948. It was Secretary Douglas who convinced MacIntyre to return to Washington, D.C., and accept a position in government as Under Secretary of the Air Force. MacIntyre was sworn into office on May 20, 1957.[6]

Weathering Cuts

James H. Douglas's reputation for getting along with the Air Force was soon tested when a large defense funding cutback instituted by the administration was announced by Secretary of Defense Wilson. In May 1957, Douglas informed the Assistant Secretary of Defense (Comptroller) W. S. McNeil, who supported the cuts, that he could not pare fourth quarter direct obligations for fiscal year 1957 by more than the already earmarked amount of $45 million. He gave the reduction issue his personal attention and instructed all responsible officials in the Air Force to do the same: "Wherever and whenever we find that we can reduce obligations and expenditures, in this or any fiscal year, without detriment to approved programs, we will do so."[7] A month later, Douglas was ordered by Wilson to cut the fiscal year 1958 budget by $1.2 billion to $17.6 billion. Douglas concluded that the entire reduction taken during 1958 would result in a sharp curtailment of the service's approved procurement program. He argued to Wilson that substantial reductions in force structure and programs would be required beyond those designated under the President's budget, bringing the Air Force's total number of wings to less than the end-of-1961 goal of 116. Douglas maintained that cuts in the procurement of new aircraft, missiles, and related items by as much as $1.2 billion in 1958 would require a reduction of nearly $4 billion in what had been already ordered or projected for order. Such cuts would also, the Air Secretary stressed, jeopardize the Air Force's combat capability and access to the latest technology. Douglas further noted that the Air Force would have to eliminate nearly 2,000 aircraft scheduled for procurement from 1956 through 1959 or else make substantial cuts in its highly emphasized missile program. Such a reduction would lower the labor force in major aircraft and missile contractors' plants from 275,000 to approximately 130,000 by December 1959. This estimate, he cautioned, did not take into account the impact of such a reduction on major sub-contractors and other suppliers.[8]

Air Force Chief of Staff General Thomas D. White was likewise alarmed by the projected cuts and also cautioned the Secretary of Defense that they

James H. Douglas, Jr., Under Secretary of the Air Force from 1953 to 1957 and fifth Secretary of the Air Force.

would imperil the Air Force's entire procurement program. If obligational authority were not forthcoming to meet contractual agreements, the service would be breaking faith with industry. He pointed out that contracts for nearly two-thirds of the weapon systems to be procured in 1958 had already been negotiated. Without that authority, he added, many contractors would drive up the costs of weapon system projects overall by adding to them the costs of production shutdown or disruption. They would also drive up costs when reopening suspended contracts and negotiating new ones.[9]

It remained the task of the OSAF and the Air Staff to create a plan for coping with less. By mid-July 1957, Secretary Douglas provided Secretary Wilson with a list of actions taken by the Air Force to control expenditures. These included postponing the outlay of $65 million for construction scheduled for 1958; reducing military personnel to 900,000 by the end of December 1957; cutting $20 million for the Air National Guard; deferring delivery to the second half of 1958 of items other than major aircraft; reducing inventories by 5 percent by November 30, 1957; and eliminating "alternate sources" by confining the number of contractors on certain components of ballistic missile programs to no more than one per component. The list also included extending the costs of programs to later years and terminating certain aircraft or missile projects.[10]

The Air Force met 1957's budgetary adjustments by holding production of both the B-52 and the KC-135 at fifteen aircraft per month; stretching out the programs of the F-100, the F-101B, and the F-104 and reducing their total numbers; and deleting the RF-104. These actions, particularly the fighter production stretch-outs, significantly affected J57 and J79 aircraft engine overhaul pro-

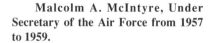

Malcolm A. McIntyre, Under Secretary of the Air Force from 1957 to 1959.

grams, created unanticipated capacity within the depots for J47 engine overhaul, and reduced the planned workload for the General Electric Company.[11]

Practically every Air Force program suffered cuts during 1957 and 1958. The OSAF and the Air Staff had to carefully readjust funding and program sizes. Accommodating to change became the norm. However, when, by July 1957, funding for new military construction had been scaled down to a "bare minimum," the Air Secretary complained to the Defense Secretary. Certain facilities were so urgently needed, he asserted, that he would accept no further decreases.[12]

Pilot procurement requirements were altered to meet personnel reductions, to increase the experience level of flight crews, and to save money.* Secretary Douglas felt it necessary to increase each new pilot's initial tour of duty from three to five years, since the number of new pilots had fallen by roughly one-third since 1954. New pilots had to undergo additional training to meet the demands of ever more powerful and complex aircraft. This new training necessitated the longer service obligation. In August 1957, the active duty reserve commitment for those volunteering for pilot training was extended to five years.† In December 1957, the same service commitment was expanded to include navigators.[13]

Speaking before the National Security Council (NSC) in November 1957 on the service's 1959 budget, Secretary Douglas outlined plans to be funded with a now slightly higher appropriation of $18.1 billion and a projected military personnel strength of 850,000 at the end of the fiscal year. The number of Strategic Air Command (SAC) bombers would be increased, but the Air Defense Command (ADC) would be reduced from thirty-two wings to twenty-six, and Tactical Air Command (TAC) forces from fifty-five wings to thirty-four wings—a reduction of approximately 1,800 aircraft in all. Douglas believed that the unavoidable reduction in ADC and TAC forces would be offset by the modernization of interceptors and fighter-bombers and increased reliance on atomic weapons. Other programs to which Douglas gave high priority were research and development, SAC alert and dispersal, ballistic missiles, ballistic missile detection, and modernization of combat aircraft.[14]

At the same time, Under Secretary MacIntyre spoke out whenever he could against lowering defense budgets and warned of repercussions. "Not doing what you may have planned to do but have not begun, while disappointing and perhaps

---

* Douglas's effort was part of a larger Air Force attempt to deter new applicants with marginal interest in the Air Force from applying for flight training, to use more effectively those who did attain their wings, and to encourage competent people not just to fulfill their minimum service obligation, but to make the Air Force a career.

† Secretary Douglas had to make an exception for Air Force Reserve Officers Training Corps (AFROTC) students. They had already signed three-year active duty contracts for both flying and non-flying duties in order to be assigned to advanced (junior & senior year) AFROTC and were given three options: (1) accept rated duties with a five-year active duty commitment, (2) accept non-rated duties with a three-year commitment, or (3) stand on the original contract for rated duties with a three-year obligation.

undesirable, is not fraught with the additional emotional and practical problems that go with undoing what you have already done."[15] MacIntyre often noted that a decision not to contract for a new product meant no additional hiring, but a decision to reduce or cut back an existing order meant immediate firing. Many pressures hindered the attainment of lower spending levels. Separating personnel from the service involved time and effort. Closing installations brought strong reactions from the communities in which they were located, and there were differing notions among the commands as to which units should be inactivated. The under secretary maintained that to stop spending at a level not yet attained was far easier than to cut spending back below a level already reached. Fluctuations in appropriations and expenditures might appear in the short run to save money or gain added defense, but such instability would disproportionately reduce defense. He warned of even deeper cuts should the lower level of appropriations maintained in 1958 be repeated by Congress in future years.[16]

Because of lower defense spending the Army unilaterally terminated its interservice support arrangements. Also faced with the prospect of greater funding reductions, the Army wanted to recover the costs of support services from the Air Force. Under Secretary MacIntyre urgently requested Defense Secretary Wilson to issue instructions on maintaining the status quo, at least until new arrangements for funding, manpower, and facilities could be made or a survey conducted. MacIntyre had become concerned about, an Army commander* in Japan who, in February and March of 1958, had informed his Air Force counterpart that he no longer had the resources to support a number of activities in the Tokyo area and planned to leave to the Air Force its own basic support responsibilities. MacIntyre argued that the Army's action was an arbitrary alteration of support agreements in effect since the separation of the Air Force from the Army. Under them the Air Force would receive a substantial amount of common items† from the Army Technical Services. The under secretary urged that clear instructions be given by the DOD to all three services that no existing support activities, whether based on directives, agreements, or custom be terminated or altered except by mutual consent or by authorization from the OSD with appropriate adjustments of funds, manpower, skills, and facilities.[17] The issue was eventually resolved,‡ but it was an example of the problems faced by the Air Secretary during the funding squeezes of the late 1950s.

---

* Neither the command nor the Army commander was specified in the document.

† Items common to two or more services include paints, dopes, metals, gases, petroleum products, chemicals, and office supplies.

‡ Under Secretary of the Air Force MacIntyre wrote to the Commanders, U.S. Air Forces in Europe (USAFE) and Pacific Air Force (PACAF) to confirm that efforts to stop the unilateral abandonment of cross support by any service were successful. Ltrs,

A Change of Mood

On October 4, 1957, the Soviet Union fired Sputnik, the world's first man-made satellite, into orbit. News of the event created near hysteria among some Americans over many frightful possibilities, especially the enhanced capability of the Soviet Union to continuously spy on and better direct an attack against the United States. In order to quiet anxieties, the administration undertook all necessary measures to accelerate the nation's missile and satellite programs. President Eisenhower himself had to modify his preference for low budgets, and he had to confront a Congress that favored increased federal spending for many defense and domestic programs. Sputnik jarred the United States out of its complacency—no longer could it bask in the illusion of technological superiority.[18]

For the Air Force, as well as the other services, Sputnik meant a Congress more receptive to increased defense spending. At appropriations hearings before Congress in June 1958 on funding for fiscal year 1959, Secretary Douglas and Air Force Chief of Staff General White requested a 43 percent increase in aircraft and missile support funds—from $1.63 billion for 1958 to $2.15 billion for 1959. Secretary Douglas noted that weapon systems had to be rigorously and frequently tested and kept ready for use when required. General White added that aircraft and missiles were no better than the caliber of the ground support equipment personnel required to operate and maintain them.*[19]

Sputnik was not the only driving force behind the hearings. Soviet air power was still the most serious and immediate threat to free nations. General White, like air leaders before him, advised Congress that to counter this threat, "we need an Air Force second to none with an offensive punch that the Soviets will fear."[20] While acknowledging the serious and growing threat represented by Soviet submarines, General White emphasized the importance of the U.S. Air Force's maintaining its capability to fight and win the battle for control of the air against Soviet satellites, ballistic missiles, and their great numbers of high performance aircraft. Satellites themselves were not the sole element of the Soviet threat, only a part of it. General White was confident that U.S. air power was superior in quality to the Soviet Union's but warned that the rapid rate of Soviet progress in many technical fields indicated a real growth of that threat. He believed that the projected reduc-

---

Malcolm A. MacIntyre to Gen Frank F. Everest, CINC, USAFE and Gen Laurence S. Kuter, CINC, PACAF, May 13, 1958, RG 340, Accession No 65A–3152, Jan 1958–Jun 1959, Box 7, NARA.

* During this period General White also settled a Strategic Air Command-Tactical Air Command struggle for funding and control. At issue was General LeMay's contention that TAC was using resources that could have been better spent on SAC. LeMay argued for combining SAC and TAC into an air offensive command. General White believed that a future limited war was more possible than a general war and decided in 1957 that TAC would remain a separate command.

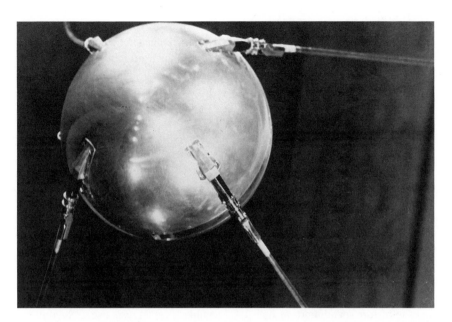

Sputnik. On October 4, 1957, the Soviet Union launched the first man-made object into orbit around the earth. It measured 22.8 inches in diameter, weighed 184 pounds, shocked the West, and inspired cartoons such as this in the November 9, 1957, issue of the *Washington Star.*

'That Does It . . . I'm Saucering Off to Mars!'

tion in the U.S. Air Force's structure to 105 wings by the end of 1959, mainly from tactical forces, would not jeopardize overall combat strength. White reasoned that quality would be maintained by higher performance aircraft.

Both Douglas and White testified to their belief in the importance of missiles. Douglas endorsed the Minuteman missile program as one of the most urgently needed by the Air Force. It was expected to produce a solid-propellant, long-range intercontinental ballistic missile (ICBM), a tremendous advance over the liquid-fuel missile and its attendant problems of transportation, maintenance, and operation. General White advised that a system of missiles and high-performance manned aircraft used in complementary and mutually supporting roles would best insure survival.

White told Congress that the Air Force's request of nearly $17.8 billion, down by $3 billion, for fiscal year 1959 was tight but was sufficient to meet immediate objectives. He also noted that rapid technological progress was bringing sudden and radical changes in equipment, methods, and concepts and thus some uncertainty.[21] He was assured by the Secretary of Defense that as new concepts and new capabilities developed, the OSD would promptly consider all new funding requirements. Congress significantly abated its pressure on the services to restrict spending from June 1957 to June 1958, in response to Sputnik. [22]

Secretary Douglas, years later, recalled that he felt confident that the Air Force would be adequately funded in every area except one—construction. Construction hearings were different from any others in his opinion. Instead of relying on the testimony of both uniformed and civilian service experts, members of Congress injected their own views on the kind of housing the Air Force needed. They thought they knew best which installation should receive new housing, how much that housing should cost, and where within the installation it should be built. The Air Secretary noted that at hearings on any other subject Congress presented few objections to Air Force budget requests. More generous defense funding would continue during Dudley Sharp's tenure as Air Secretary. Many Congressmen, led by Lyndon Johnson of Texas, were advocates of military programs.[23]

Secretary Sharp told Congress that the Air Force's budget for fiscal year 1961 of $17.7 billion was sufficient to balance the principal tasks in which the Air Force was engaged—operating and maintaining a strong effective and modern aerospace force and providing for the research and development which would shape the aerospace force of the future. It was also sufficient, he added, to provide a substantial increase in the free world's total defense capability, considering the vital contributions of the Army, the Navy, and the Marine Corps.*[24]

---

* Both Douglas and Sharp most likely exerted some influence on the Air Force's budget-making process. Air Force appropriations for fiscal years 1960 and 1961 increased considerably from $751.8 million in 1959 to $1.15 billion in 1960 and $1.55 billion in 1961. *Air Force Statistical Digest, Fiscal Year 1961*, p 436.

Douglas and the Air Force Academy

Congressional intervention in Air Force construction projects reached its greatest intensity over the Air Force Academy. Secretary Douglas had been affiliated with the academy since it was authorized in 1954 for construction in Colorado Springs, Colorado. As Under Secretary of the Air Force he had been closely involved in its planning with Lt. Gen. Hubert R. Harmon and had helped select the firm of Skidmore, Owings, Merrill, architects and engineers, to design it. As Secretary of the Air Force, he faced congressional questions on the cost and the design of its chapel. The chapel was intended to house under one roof separate areas representing the Protestant, Catholic, and Jewish faiths. Leaders of these faiths were consulted and gave the chapel's design their unqualified approval. In Secretary Douglas's opinion, the structure fit in well with the modern lines of the other buildings on campus and was, at the same time, strongly reminiscent of traditional Gothic architecture.[25]

House and Senate hearings on the academy revealed a decided lack of appreciation by some congressmen of the chapel's design. Douglas recalled receiving a letter from Senator Ralph Flanders of Vermont, which stated, "Your proposed chapel for the Air Force Academy is an insult to God."[26] Senator Willis Robertson of Virginia suggested that anyone who could propose a chapel "sheathed in aluminum on the slope of the Rocky Mountains was out of his mind."[27] Robertson later introduced a resolution to prohibit appropriations to the Air Force if any were spent on the chapel. Douglas recalled telling George Mahon, Congressman from Texas and Chairman of the House Appropriations Committee, of having to deal with the chapel's detractors. Mahon, regarded by Douglas as a friend of the Air Force, observed that "my committee is not going to make the slightest move to obstruct the chapel program, but it would be a great mistake for you to think that we are at all enthusiastic."[28]

Congress was as unenthusiastic about the academy's construction costs as it was about the chapel's configuration. As the press published congressional statements of displeasure, Douglas did much to defend the service's position. Writing in July 1958 to John T. O'Rourke of the *Washington Daily News*, Douglas noted that the editorialist's criticism was based on allegations contained in a House Appropriations Committee staff report and had overlooked information which the Air Force had supplied to the committee's Subcommittee on Military Construction. The Air Secretary took issue with O'Rourke's reference to a $300 million projected cost. He pointed out that costs associated with the academy, which was due to open in September 1958, would not exceed $135 million for land, buildings, and facilities. Douglas added that the Air Force's estimates of construction costs, including those for an airfield and certain other facilities not yet authorized, would not exceed $160 million. The Air Force had also estimated that the academy's total cost, including equipment and furnishings, would be no more than $190 million of its appropriated funds. The Air Secretary further commented that

The Air Force Academy, Colorado Springs, Colorado.
Congressional debate over the academy's location and the controversial design of its chapel was intense.

approximately $25 million of that total could be attributed to construction costs which had risen since the academy's authorization in 1954.[29]

The academy was the object of congressional inquiry even a year later because of a report by the U.S. Comptroller General. Again Douglas had to explain, this time to the House Armed Services Committee, that the Air Force had not exceeded the original ceiling set by Congress for the academy. He admitted, however, that the service had erred in not having informed Congress that it had transferred $6 million from family housing on other approved construction projects to cover part of the costs of two academy rectories and faculty offices. Again he argued that the original $126 million authorized for the Air Force Academy's construction was a lump sum authorization and not prepared in terms of line items. Until 1958, the academy's costs were at best only estimates, not based on final determinations as to specific requirements or final specifications and drawings. Since that time, Douglas contended, academy appropriations had been administered on a line item basis, as were subsequent funds granted for its construction.[30]

Douglas, ARPA, and NASA

Air Secretary Douglas had misgivings about the new Advanced Research Projects Agency (ARPA) and the National Aeronautics and Space Administration (NASA). He had to walk a thin line between the goals of the Air Force and the wishes of the administration. Would the services regard these offices as further intrusion by the OSD?

Both Sputnik and the Soviet's demonstration of ICBM capabilities in 1957 alarmed the press. For two years *Aviation Week* had criticized the administration's unwillingness to acknowledge the available evidence on Soviet missile firings. In January 1958, the magazine's editor, Robert Hotz, singled out the key decision-makers on military research and development as obstacles to U.S. superiority in the technological race with the Soviet Union. ARPA,* established by the new Secretary of Defense, Neil McElroy, in early February 1958 would, Hotz believed, prove to be merely another layer of bureaucracy in the already stifling research and development atmosphere. He also had misgivings about William Holaday, the agency's acting director, a man with a penchant for political compromise. Hotz argued that Holaday's decision to put both the Air Force's Thor and Army's Jupiter intermediate range ballistic missiles (IRBMs) into production indicated his inability to distinguish a weapon from a weapon system.†

---

* This agency was responsible for all military satellites, space research, and anti-ICBM's. Its existence was opposed by the Joint Chiefs of Staff, who regarded it as "just another agency."

† Apparently, Hotz felt that the two weapons, Jupiter and Thor, could do the same thing and that only one was necessary.

Hotz asserted that Deputy Defense Secretary Donald Quarles, another remnant of the "technically timid regime of former Defense Secretary Charles E. Wilson," had revealed in his public statements consistent underestimation of the pace of Soviet technical development. Hotz had little hope that ARPA could succeed under leadership that attempted to deny the existence of new Soviet weapons even when the facts on their performance were well known in the Pentagon.[31]

Air Secretary Douglas emphasized to Defense Secretary Wilson that ARPA represented another infringement on Air Force missions. Douglas thought it unnecessary that the agency be empowered with both contracting and directing authority. Such authority would, he argued, confuse existing relationships between the DOD and industry. ARPA would violate the National Security Act because a military mission would be assigned to a non-military agency. He wanted a weapon system from inception placed under the control of the using service. If the new office established laboratories or let contracts for research services, essential operating functions of the military departments would be transferred for the first time to a separate agency within the OSD.[32]

By contrast, the Air Secretary attempted to smooth the way for Air Force cooperation with NASA. Under the terms of the Space Act of 1958, signed by President Eisenhower on July 29, other departments and agencies were to make their "services, equipment, personnel and facilities available" to the new agency as required.[33] There was a grey area, however, between civilian and military interests, and only the President could determine which agency should have responsibility for a specific project.[34] Douglas wrote to NASA's new director, T. Keith Glennan, listing the contributions that the Air Force could make to new developments. He mentioned specifically the 1500K single chamber liquid rocket* and urged NASA to make the Air Force program manager for the project. Douglas noted that the Air Force had the specialized manpower and organization to work quickly and economically, as well as legal, procurement, and auditing staffs to monitor large contracts. He also mentioned that the Air Force had a rocket technical team at Wright Air Development Center (WADC) as well as test stand facilities at Edwards Air Force Base in California. Traditionally, the Air Force had joined with the National Advisory Committee for Aeronautics (NACA), NASA's predecessor,† in fostering aeronautical science. Douglas saw the 1500K engine development program as an excellent opportunity to present a forthright example of interagency cooperation.[35]

---

* It is not clear what system would contain this particular engine. Douglas might have been referring to an engine with 1.5 million pounds of thrust used to propel a follow-on to the Saturn rocket program.

† The National Aeronautics and Space Administration (NASA) was created by the Space Act of 1958 and replaced the National Advisory Committee for Aeronautics (NACA) founded in 1915. This same act also authorized the creation of the National Aeronautics And Space Council. Its membership consisted of the President of the United

A congressional provision also established a Civilian-Military Liaison Committee, which consisted of a chairman appointed by the President, and an unspecified number of DOD and NASA military and civilian officials. On October 16, 1958, Air Force Secretary Douglas attended a meeting in Deputy Defense Secretary Quarles's office with the service secretaries and the director of ARPA to discuss the draft charter of the committee. Army Secretary Wilber Brucker and Navy Secretary Thomas S. Gates felt that the charter was too general in that it did not assign the committee specific responsibilities. As did his counterparts, Secretary Douglas feared that the Liaison Committee would spend most of its time reporting to the National Aeronautics and Space Council rather than facilitating communication between NASA and the DOD, as it was intended to. Douglas and the other service secretaries objected to a single exclusive channel. He won approval of the idea that each military member be informed of all of the committee's activities and report back to his service. He dismissed as unwieldy Secretary Gates's proposal that each service have two representatives.[36]

Air Force Under Secretary Malcolm MacIntyre also participated in discussions on the Liaison Committee. In May 1959, he recommended that all programs having dual civilian-military potential be jointly financed. He wanted the responsibilities for both NASA and the DOD clarified and the Secretary of Defense to be able to proceed with development programs even though they might be useful for civilian purposes. He agreed that the President could assign a dual-purpose program to either of the two agencies. What MacIntyre sought was a policy which would allow the DOD to develop concurrently projects begun at NASA if they could become components of weapon systems or military vehicles.[37] Eventually, all of these matters would be resolved as the Air Force became more attentive to duplication of effort, and especially as the DOD gradually assumed a more important role in the space effort.

Over the next few years, the Air Force would work in harmony with NASA, even while harboring some concern that it might function as a monolithic space agency and a central supply point for all space equipment. The Air Force was pleased as long as NASA considered military needs and interests. The Army, Navy, and Air Force realized that they could not obtain enough funding for their own space needs and looked to NASA to complement their efforts.[38] An Air Force review of NASA's budget for fiscal year 1960 did not reveal any undesirable duplication between space programs. Yet, according to Under Secretary of the Air Force MacIntyre, some of NASA's proposed work would have military applications and therefore a place in later DOD programs.[39]

States, the Secretary of Defense, the Secretary of State, the NASA Administrator, and four additional members appointed by the President. Its function was to assist the President in surveying aeronautical and space activities and to provide for effective cooperation between NASA and the DOD. Futrell, *Ideas, Concepts, Doctrine*, p 298.

Douglas's and Sharp's Mutual Concerns

Both Douglas's and Sharp's tenures were marked by similarities in one particular area—civilian aviation. Douglas agreed with General Curtis E. LeMay, Vice Chief of Staff, that civil cargo airlift should be contracted for in peacetime to provide overseas logistical support. During his final year, Douglas wanted to contract for at least 10 percent of the total cargo capacity of commercial carriers and was worried that the percentage forecast by the Air Force for 1960 would decrease. He wanted that trend reversed.[40]

In an effort to comply with congressional and other studies, Douglas requested that the Air Force's prime contractors be urged to consider subcontracting to Canadian firms. He noted that Assistant Secretary of the Air Force (Materiel) Dudley Sharp, and other members of the Production Sharing Committee had been exploring means of participating in production tasks with Canada, particularly with regard to the Bomarc,* SAGE,† and heavy radar programs. Douglas believed that Canada's strategic position and relationship with the United States in continental defense necessitated some special arrangement. The Air Secretary pointed out to the Deputy Defense Secretary that statistics on reciprocal military purchasing between the United States and Canada for the previous eight years revealed that Canada had purchased more from the United States than the United States had from Canada. He thus recommended subcontracting the Bomarc wing and aileron assemblies to Canadair Limited.[41]

Sharp recalled that a consistent problem during his nearly six-year tenure with the OSAF concerned the insistence by commercial airlines that the Air Force's Military Air Transport Service (MATS) was interfering with their business.‡ Sharp attended many difficult congressional hearings at which the Air Force was charged with bureaucracy-building. He noted, however, that the accusation was squelched every time the airlines were asked whether they could guarantee their pilots' willingness to fly into combat zones. They could not.[42]

There were other issues related to MATS and commercial airlines. In February 1960, the Air Force was making the most economical use of the airlift capacity generated by MATS in its essential peacetime training. Secretary Sharp was against the specific earmarking of funds by Congress for commercial augmentation to meet total DOD airlift requirements because the Air Force was

---

* Bomarc derived its name from its inventors, Boeing and the Michigan Aeronautical Research Center. It was a long-range surface-to-air guided missile designed to hit invading aircraft and missiles at 80,000 feet and at a distance of 200 miles from its launch site.

† SAGE stands for Semiautomatic Ground Environment. It was an early warning and tracking defense system that provided instantaneous information needed for defensive air warfare.

‡ The airline industry looked upon the build-up of MATS as additional competition.

obliged to return its unspent portion to the Treasury.[43] He succeeded in keeping some funds for airlift requirements separate.

Both Douglas and Sharp had to confront the Army several times. In June 1957, Secretary Douglas challenged it for changing the name of its Antiaircraft Command at Colorado Springs, Colorado, to the Army Air Defense Command. The Air Secretary claimed that the redesignation violated the intent of the National Security Act of 1947 as well as the Air Force Organization Act of 1951. Douglas quoted for the Secretary of Defense, a statement of functions from Executive Order 9877, known as the "Functions Paper" (not included in the National Security Act of 1947), informing him that each service was to provide its own unique forces to the air defense of the continental United States. In the case of the Army, Douglas noted, these forces were described as Army antiaircraft artillery units. Since the functions statements had clearly designated air defense as a matter of primary interest to the Air Force, Douglas questioned the Army's identification with this function. Douglas felt that the Army's action was closely related to the long-standing controversy over Army responsibilities for air defense and was misleading. In discussing the matter with the Secretary of Defense, Douglas urged him to order the Army to change the name of its command so as not to imply possession of overall air defense capability, responsibility, or authority.[44] Douglas's efforts proved futile, as the Army's new designation for the former Army Antiaircraft Command would remain Army Air Defense Command for nearly eighteen years as part of the North American Air Defense Command (NORAD), until it was disestablished in January 1975.

During his brief tenure as Air Secretary, Sharp was involved with the Army over the construction of ICBM sites, wrote several letters to the U.S. Comptroller General protesting unfavorable GAO reports on Air Force missile management, and replied to many congressional inquiries concerning the Air Force's policies on construction of missile sites throughout the country.*

Sharp, speaking for the Air Force, which had already expressed its concerns to counterparts in the Army,† complained to the Secretary of the Army about awarding contracts to marginal performers for the construction of missile sites, especially near Offutt Air Force Base in Nebraska. He argued that some contractors had proved to be incompetent or lacked incentives to fulfill their contracts in a timely fashion. Sharp was not satisfied with the Army's attributing delays to unreasonable project schedules. According to the Air Secretary, in at

---

* The Air Force did not have the capacity to construct its own facilities and relied on the Army Corps of Engineers as its prime building contractor.

† Gen. Curtis E. LeMay, Vice Chief of Staff of the Air Force, had written to the Chief of Staff of the Army about the lag in the construction of technical facilities for the Atlas squadron at Offutt Air Force Base. Ltr, Vice Chief of Staff U.S. Air Force to Chief of Staff U.S. Army, subj: Construction Delays, ICBM Program, Nov 3, 1959, RG 340, Dudley C. Sharp, Chronological Files, NARA.

least one instance, an entire construction season had passed with little progress. Sharp contended that "well qualified and positively motivated firms should be capable of meeting established schedules."[45] He maintained that if the Army could not attract competent contractors under its bid-seeking system, the Air Force would support it if it chose to exercise its right, under Army Services Procurement Regulations, to negotiate with a selected list of bidders.[46]

Near the end of his term as Air Secretary, Douglas, looking to the future, called for a special review of the nation's ballistic missile program. He pointed to the Strategic Missiles Evaluation Committee whose excellent work in 1954 led to the radically reorganized ICBM project and the establishment of a new development-management agency with directive authority over it. The committee's recommendations were successfully carried out by the Air Force and resulted in the nation's most important weapons development effort, "a nationwide, multi-billion dollar, ballistic missile program."[47] There were several missile program reviews following Douglas's departure.

Douglas predicted that over the next decade, the Air Force's mission would remain substantially unchanged. He also predicted that because of increasingly complex electrical, mechanical, and hydraulic systems, as well as tools, the Air Force would be required to perform tasks calling for skills and versatility well beyond those deemed adequate in 1959. Training would become even more critical since modern weapon systems and components allowed considerably less latitude for error. As always, he stressed that no machine or device, however advanced, would be any better or safer than the people who operate and maintain it.

These people would need to acquire specialized skills, beyond the 850 officially listed, to help support future weapon systems. Douglas maintained that the Air Force's future would depend on progress in science, technology, and industry. Whatever the weapons of the future, they would, according to Douglas, have one basic failing: "They will not be able to think for themselves in an emergency situation. Thus, the human element will continue to remain foremost."[48]

Sharp's Turn

Douglas left office in December 1959 to replace Deputy Secretary of Defense Thomas S. Gates, Jr., who had followed Neil H. McElroy as Secretary of Defense. Dudley Sharp succeeded Douglas as Air Secretary on December 11, 1959. Sharp had served as Assistant Secretary of the Air Force (Materiel) from October 3, 1955, to January 31, 1959. He returned briefly to civilian life and his family concern, the Mission Manufacturing Company in Texas. With the resigna-

Neil H. McElroy *(left)* **and Thomas S. Gates, Jr., served short terms as Secretary of Defense from October 9, 1957, to December 1, 1959, and from December 2, 1959, to January 20, 1961, respectively.**

tion of Malcolm A. MacIntyre* as Under Secretary of the Air Force in July 1959, Secretary Douglas asked Sharp to return to public life as Under Secretary. Sharp agreed, but would hold that job for only four months until taking the oath as Secretary of the Air Force following Douglas's departure. As Under Secretary of the Air Force, Sharp served as principal assistant to the Air Secretary, to the Chairman of the Air Force Requirements Review Board, and to the DOD representative on the Department of Defense Federal Aviation Agency Advisory Committee.[49]

Dudley Sharp knew he was a lame duck. Addressing the USAF Commanders Conference in January 1960, he stated that he saw "some possibility that my tenure of office may not be for too many years."[50] Nine months into his term, invitations sent to the Air Secretary for speaking engagements and special appearances were still being addressed to former Secretary Douglas. In addition, his speeches did not receive national coverage.[51] Most press attention was being

---

* MacIntyre declared that he was offered the position of Secretary of the Air Force but refused, and when he resigned as Under Secretary of the Air Force, Douglas was supposed to move up as Deputy Secretary of Defense. MacIntyre said that he had neither the time nor the money to adjust to a new position and had also "no yen to become afflicted with Potomac fever." Intvw, Malcolm A. MacIntyre by author, Sep. 26, 1985, p 23.

focused on the upcoming national election and speculation about its outcome with respect to the DOD.

Sharp recalled that he had never in his life worked as hard as he did as both Assistant Secretary of the Air Force and Secretary of the Air Force. He said that everything was new to him—the names of contractors and the names of weapon systems. He rose almost every morning between 3:30 and 4:00 to prepare for the day's events. For at least four or five hours every day he was confronted with various visitors. He would spend an hour with a Minnesota contingent whose members wondered why the Air Force awarded a snow plow contract to a competitor; he would listen and then pretend he knew something about snowplows. Next, General Electric would demand to know why it lost an engine contract to Pratt & Whitney. Later, a delegation from a state in which an air base was scheduled to close would argue for its remaining open.[52]

Sharp introduced no major alterations to the programs and policies of the preceding four years. At the House appropriations hearings of February 1961, he described the tenor of the times and the 1961 budget period for the Air Force in terms of one word—change. He found change occurring in almost every area of Air Force activity and effort, most dramatically in the proportion of missiles to manned aircraft, with missiles clearly in the ascendant.[53]

One of Sharp's early accomplishments was his appointment of Joseph V. Charyk as Under Secretary of the Air Force. Charyk had formerly held the position of Chief Scientist of the Air Force from January to June 1959 and was Assistant Secretary of the Air Force (Research and Development) from June 1959 until his appointment as Under Secretary of the Air Force on January 28,

Dudley C. Sharp, Under Secretary of the Air Force in 1959 and sixth Secretary of the Air Force.

1960. Sharp hoped that Charyk's scientific credentials would prove that military space satellites could be as expertly controlled by the Air Force as by NASA. The control of satellites was, according to Sharp, being decided by some of the nation's most influential scientists, a kind of small fraternity. Joseph Charyk was one of them.[54]

New OSAF Faces under Douglas and Sharp

The 1958 Reorganization Act created some structural changes to the DOD, the most significant of which was, perhaps, the dissolution of the Office of the Assistant Secretary of Defense for Research and Development. This position was replaced by the Director of Defense for Research and Engineering who answered directly to the Secretary of Defense. Only the Deputy Secretary of Defense and the service secretaries preceded him in the organizational chain. The new director supervised all research and engineering activities within the DOD that the Secretary of Defense felt needed to be centrally managed. For the OSAF, the Office of the Assistant Secretary of the Air Force (Manpower, Personnel and Reserve Forces) was redesignated as Special Assistant for Manpower, Personnel and Reserve Forces on March 12, 1959. When David S. Smith left that post in January 1959 as the last assistant secretary, he felt sure that most of the projects with which he had been associated had been successfully concluded. Some of them included retraining career airmen; securing better personnel facilities, a mechanized assignment system, greater career motivation, training of scientific

Joseph V. Charyk, Assistant Secretary of the Air Force (Research and Development) from 1959 to 1960 and Under Secretary of the Air Force from 1960 to 1963.

and engineering personnel; and approving more high civilian grade positions. He recommended, on departing, that many of the tasks originating in his office be delegated to the Air Staff. They were, and his position was downgraded to special assistant. Smith remained in the Washington, D.C., area, returning to the practice of law, but he also continued his Air Force affiliation as a consultant.[55]

Replacing Joseph V. Charyk as Assistant Secretary of the Air Force (Research and Development), was Courtland D. Perkins, who took the position on February 25, 1960. Perkins had been affiliated with Princeton University as a professor and chairman of the department of aeronautical engineering. He was also a member of many technical committees on national defense, such as the Scientific Advisory Board, the Aero and Space Vehicles Panel, and the USAF Chief of Staff Committee on the Organization of the Scientific Advisory Board. He was also a member of the Scientific Advisory Committee on Research and Development Management. His most significant post was Chief Scientist of the Air Force from 1956 to 1957.[56]

Philip B. Taylor was appointed by James Douglas to replace Dudley Sharp as Assistant Secretary of the Air Force (Materiel) in April 1959. Older than most political appointees, Taylor had vast experience in the field of aircraft engine design. During World War I, as an employee of the Washington Navy Yard, he worked with the assembly and test of such engines as the Liberty, Curtiss, and Hispano-Suiza. After the war, receiving a Ph.D in mechanical engineering from Yale University, he went to work for the Wright Aeronautical Corporation, which later merged with the Curtiss Aeroplane and Motor Company to form the Curtiss-Wright Corporation. There he worked in various capacities until becoming chief engineer. During 1940 he helped develop and test the beginning series of the Cyclone engine. In 1944 he was promoted to acting general manager of the Wright Aeronautical Corporation. After the war he left Wright and worked as a consultant with several firms, formed his own, the Taylor Turbine Corporation, and was instrumental in obtaining the exclusive right to manufacture and sell the Rolls-Royce turbo-jet engine in the United States. In September 1949, he was appointed Chairman of the Committee on Aeronautics of the Research and Development Board and remained there until the board was dissolved in 1953. Like Perkins, Taylor served on the Air Force Scientific Advisory Board as a member of the Propulsion Panel. He also served on the Powerplants Committee of the National Advisory Committee for Aeronautics. He was prepared for the job as Assistant Secretary of the Air Force (Materiel) and worked closely with Secretaries Douglas and Sharp as well as the Commander of the Air Materiel Command, General Samuel E. Anderson. With them, he enlisted industry to hold down costs and instituted internal Air Force management and contractual procedures for the increased effectiveness of contract pricing and management.[57]

Courtland D. Perkins *(left)*, Assistant Secretary of the Air Force (Research and Development) from 1960 to 1961, and Philip B. Taylor, Assistant Secretary of the Air Force (Materiel) from 1959 to 1961.

Sharp Defends the Air Force

In April 1960, Sharp criticized a Government Accounting Office (GAO) draft report* on the Air Force's ballistic missile program for having slighted the service's extraordinary accomplishments. The draft failed, according to the Air Secretary, to mark the real measure of Air Force management and "our demonstrated success in realizing the primary program objective—to provide this nation and its allies with strategic ballistic missile capability in a time span limited only by technology."[58] The report denigrated Atlas, Sharp claimed, with the insupportable accusation that, because of adjustments in testing schedules, Initial Operational Capability (IOC) was achieved at the expense of performance and reliability.[59] Further, he faulted the report for concentrating on relatively minor incidents to the total exclusion of real management achievements which, in the "largest military development effort ever prosecuted by this nation, have met the free world's critical requirements for operational strategic ballistic missiles."[60]

Six months later the GAO still, in Sharp's opinion, had not achieved the proper balance in its treatment of the Atlas program, focusing too much on the failure of one test flight. Sharp chided the Comptroller General for allowing his auditors to state with an assurance that "our finest scientists and technicians cannot give" that the mishap could have been avoided by certain modifications to correct high-altitude turbopump difficulties.[61] Indeed, in many instances, Sharp noted, the auditors, despite pleading ignorance of issues not within their province,

---

* The GAO had begun working on the study of the Air Force's ballistic missile program in April 1958.

offered judgments on many complex scientific and technical questions. Sharp indicted the report as randomly critical rather than constructive, as too concerned with closed incidents, and as devoid of recommendations for corrective action. The Air Secretary emphasized to the Comptroller General his irritation with auditors who could not grasp the full import of the Air Force's tremendous accomplishment in developing a ballistic missile program with quality surpassing all expectations* in what could be described as record time. The Air Secretary then accused the auditors of having failed to examine the extensive public record on Thor, which the Air Force on numerous occasions had candidly discussed before Congress.[62]

Both General White and Under Secretary Charyk supported Secretary Sharp's argument in the case of the Atlas as well as other missiles. Charyk admitted that the Atlas had problems but noted that it had given the Air Force insights into developing other missiles, such as the Titan. Most of the Titan's problems, Charyk contended, were not with the missile itself, but with accessory equipment. White noted that, in his experience, every new aircraft had problems and that missiles were far more complex than aircraft.[63]

In August 1960, Sharp explained to Congress how the Air Force distributed the management of its missile sites. Writing to Congressman John W. McCormack of Massachusetts, Sharp explained that the Air Force had no intention of knowingly creating, sustaining, or encouraging monopolistic practices which were contrary to the accepted and respected philosophy of free enterprise and competition. The Air Force did not have to place research and development, missile manufacture, site construction, and maintenance under a single contractual authority, but had chosen to do so in its ballistic missile program. The airframe contractor was selected as the agent of the Air Force, below the level of the Air Force Ballistic Missile Division of the Space Technology Laboratories (STL), to act as captain of the team of contractors who built, installed, and modified a missile and checked out its ground environment. Sharp emphasized that this method was most desirable in view of the complexity of the program. Changes made to a missile during its test program required a multitude of corresponding changes made to its electronic and mechanical systems and in the construction of supporting facilities at its operational site. The Air Force had found that the airframe contractor was in the best position to assure that all resultant changes meshed.[64]

Congressman James C. Davis of Georgia declared that the Air Force had to develop more "in-house" scientific and technical capability within its missile program. Sharp felt otherwise, stating that the service had learned that private industry could efficiently provide the scientific and technical manpower required for a successful ballistic missile program. Pointing to the Atlas, Sharp noted that

---

* Sharp was exaggerating, since the Atlas did have serious problems. Early Atlas missiles had an 18 percent reliability factor.

despite many difficulties and failures, it reached operational status in 1959 within two months of the date originally projected by the Air Force five years earlier and from one to three years earlier than even independent experts believed possible. This was done, Sharp contended, through solid teamwork by the Air Force and industry.[65]

Other Issues

In July 1960, the Air Secretary informed the Defense Secretary of the Air Force's extreme reluctance to accept any reduction in its number of rated officers (pilots and navigators). Quoting his Chief of Staff, Sharp noted that General White had made it clear in his testimony before the Senate Committee on Appropriations in May that the grounding of a large number of rated officers would cause severe morale problems by denying the right to fly to many who wanted it. The Air Force had proposed to take its proportionate share of military spending cuts during fiscal year 1961 to effect cost reductions without drastic grounding actions. However, he wanted to make sure that the Air Force retained its share of the total number of rated officers in the DOD. The Air Force's share of the DOD rated inventory was established by Congress on December 31, 1959, at 70 percent. To meet even this standard, the Air Force would still have to ground at least 1,200 officers with complete loss of incentive pay.[66]

Sharp also called to the Secretary of Defense's attention a proposed presidential memorandum that would grant U.S. ambassadors the right in certain circumstances to to exercise control over U.S.-sponsored military activities overseas. The Air Secretary wanted no interference with the authority of unified commanders. He argued that the ambassador was responsible for overall foreign policy guidance but not for the operational direction of military activities. Further, he contended that a clear and direct line of command from the Secretary of Defense to the unified and specified commands was prescribed by law and should not be confused or diluted. Each military department was responsible for the administration of the forces assigned to such combatant commands. He urged that any memorandum relating to ambassadorial control over military personnel clearly specify the differences between U.S military personnel attached to diplomatic missions and other U.S. military personnel stationed abroad. Sharp argued against ambassadors assuming responsibility for the development, coordination, and administration of, for example, intelligence activities. Any new directive, in his view, should formulate effective working relationships between military and diplomatic functionaries.[67] The issue remained unsettled beyond Sharp's tenure.

In July 1960, Sharp requested of Congress that funds be released for several projects such as space satellite and airlift modernization, specifically development of new transport aircraft. After many heart-to-heart talks with General White, Sharp also requested funds for accelerated development of the B-70, although he was not as strong a supporter of the aircraft as his Chief of Staff. Sharp would eventually come to believe that its production would be in the highest national interest and supported its development for 1961. However, he did not want a full-scale development and production program, just the completion of a single B-70 for experimental or operational testing. This schedule would allow for a full production program if desired by early 1963. The B-70 production program would eventually have to be dealt with by Sharp's successor, Eugene M. Zuckert, but it is noteworthy that the bomber which would become so controversial during President Kennedy's administration was being quietly discussed during the last years of Eisenhower's.[68]

The "Black Book"

During Secretary Sharp's tenure, the Air Staff attempted an internal reorganization of the service. Having aired its complaints about the OSAF earlier in the OSAF-Air Staff Relationship Study, the Air Staff* in September 1960 unilaterally developed a reorganization document that became known as the Air Force's "Black Book." The Black Book called for radical reforms. While contending that the "full possibilities of the Reorganization Act of 1958 had not been realized," the Black Book called for the abolition of the JCS as well as the civilian service secretaries, and sought greater concentration of power within the OSD. Intended for internal use only, the document eventually found its way into such newspapers as the *Chicago Sun-Times* and the *Washington Post*. The Black Book argued against the DOD's including "the people and Congress" in any debate over its proposed reorganization because defense was, for the most part, a difficult and confusing subject to laymen. Any changes should be made by the Secretary of Defense. The document, which was not classified, but marked "Air Force Eyes Only," stressed the importance of speedy changes for the Air Force while it enjoyed a maximum of influence,† was equal to the other services in national military councils, and controlled the primary "survival weapon system." The Black Book recommended that the separate services be abolished and that a single service be created with the air element in the dominant position.‡ It argued that the division of the DOD into separate services invited civilian interference in military matters. The establishment of a single deciding authority and

---

* It is not clear which members of the Air Staff played a part in the creation of this document, or if it had been approved by the Chief of Staff.

† The question can then be raised, why would the Air Force want to give more power to the OSD? The Air Force believed that it would still be the lead service no matter what type of organization prevailed.

‡ *Aviation Week* reported in December 1960 that the Air Force expected to invade a province of NASA by proposing for itself manned space vehicles and large booster

a single national staff would maximize the prospect of military control over military matters.[69]

The single service, like civilian control, had been discussed at least since World War II. Both concepts had attained support within the Air Staff. Those in favor of a single service might have come to believe that the elimination of a level of civilian control would provide the Air Force with more autonomy. During the Symington air power hearings of 1956, Chief of Staff General Nathan F. Twining, had expressed a conflicting view of the single service. Although it might enable interservice issues to crystallize and be settled easily, he believed that the three services helped to check each other. A single service might, he warned, create a military dynasty which he felt would be a "mistake for the country."[70]

The Black Book, according to the press, was designed to provide the basis for extensive internal Air Force briefings throughout the country and to instruct key officers in how to present the service's view to the public.* It bore a striking parallel to a December 1960 report on defense reorganization requested by President-elect John F. Kennedy and prepared by a committee under the leadership of Stuart Symington. In 1960 Symington was a candidate for the Democratic presidential nomination, running on his recognized defense expertise and on the fact that, as he saw it, the DOD under Eisenhower needed restructuring. Everything the former Air Secretary had done prior to losing the nomination to Kennedy was more than likely colored by his presidential ambitions. He was influential enough, however, to secure a party plank to examine the DOD.

Symington's committee recommended greater concentration of power within the OSD, the replacement of the JCS with a Joint Staff headed by a single officer, and the elimination of the three military departments, along with the three civilian secretaries and their under secretaries and assistant secretaries in the DOD—a loss of twenty-two civilian positions in all. Other recommendations included the creation of two directorates, the first for research and engineering and the second for procurement and production, both of which would serve all three military branches; and the establishment of four major unified commands, Strategic, Tactical, Logistical, and Defense.[71]

It is possible that the Air Force's Black Book influenced Symington's committee. Its members included prominent former OSAF statutory appointees—its first two secretaries, Symington and Finletter, as well as Finletter's Air Force

---

development and that it intended to enter the communications satellite development field then being monitored by the Army. "Air Force Outlines Broad Space Plans," *Aviation Week,* vol 73, No 23, Dec 1960, p 26.

* Again, it appears that the Air Force's underlying view was that it should be the lead service when the service secretaries were eliminated.

Under Secretary, Roswell L. Gilpatric.* Gilpatric had strongly supported the scheme for DOD reorganization and was President-elect Kennedy's selection for Under Secretary of Defense. Before leaving office in 1952 as Under Secretary of the Air Force, he charged that waste and mismanagement at the Pentagon through duplication of effort were rampant. In 1953 he argued that Defense Secretary Charles Wilson was risking danger by cutting Air Force funds and downgrading research and development, that arguments over Air Force versus Navy air should have been resolved before Secretary Wilson's cuts in forces, and that duplication in newer weapons programs should have been prevented. He called Eisenhower's "new look" initiative inconsistent, since it cut the Air Force to bolster Navy ship building.[72] Both Symington and Finletter supported the report. It becomes difficult, however, to comprehend how the pair could have supported the dissolution of the OSAF, which they had worked so energetically to help build and within which they were the most prominent officials, unless they felt that they were doing what was best for the Air Force.

It is noteworthy that the departing Air Secretary, Dudley Sharp, advocated no drastic reorganization of the DOD. He believed strongly in civilian authority over the services and that the Secretary of Defense had acquired sufficient power over the service secretaries.[73]

The differences in perspective between Symington and Finletter on the one hand and Sharp on the other may have been aided by the stands of the two political parties, the Democrats, led by Symington, who wanted reform, and the retiring incumbents, the Republicans. The views of the former Air Secretaries diverged from those of the departing Air Secretary, perhaps along political lines, but they were in accord with those of the Air Staff.[74]

Sharp was placed in his various positions within the OSAF during a critical time for the Air Force, when it began its major transition from aircraft to missiles and space systems. And he felt that the Air Force had met the requirements demanded by that change admirably, a change that amounted to a technological revolution and, according to Sharp, had to be achieved at ever-lower costs in manpower.[75]

The OSAF under Secretaries Douglas and Sharp did not appear to be radically affected by the 1958 Defense Reorganization Act. The Air Secretary's power was dwindling to be sure, but there was no tyrannical hand within the OSD making life any more uncomfortable than it had been for Secretary Quarles. The final evaluation and implementation of the two reorganization acts of the

---

* There was most likely contact between the former Air Secretaries and key Air Force personnel. Newspaper reports did not identify specific participants. The study itself may have been prepared to help the Symington Committee. It may have been the Air Force's position on the subject of DOD reorganization.

1950s would be left to the next administration's Secretary of Defense, Robert S. McNamara. The Air Force's reaction to the full brunt of McNamara's attempts at further centralization of power within his office would be dealt with by the new Air Secretary, Eugene M. Zuckert.

An experimental Mach 3+ Boeing IM-99 Bomarc surface-to-air (SAM) missile is readied for launch from the Air Force Missile Test Center at Cape Canaveral, Florida. The rocket-boosted and ramjet-powered Bomarc, the most sophisticated long-range SAM of its time, resulted from long-standing Air Force interest in air defense missile systems and served with both American and Canadian forces.

Chapter 9

The Zuckert Era (1961–1965)

No Secretary of the Air Force ever assumed that office possessing as much knowledge about it as Eugene M. Zuckert in January 1961. Following World War II, he had served as an assistant to the Assistant Secretary of War for Air, Stuart Symington, and for over five years he had served Symington and Thomas Finletter as Assistant Secretary of the Air Force (Management). These assignments had left him with clear impressions of the way an Air Secretary should operate.

Unfortunately, times had changed, not all of Zuckert's experience was valid, and he found that the Secretary of the Air Force in a Department of Defense (DOD) run by Robert S. McNamara exercised infinitely less authority than one in a National Military Establishment (NME) and a DOD run by James V. Forrestal. McNamara was a dynamic man who took full advantage of the Reorganization Act of 1958 to enhance his authority over the service secretaries and the military departments. So overpowering was McNamara and his centralized system that Zuckert seriously considered resigning, but he decided not to, attempting instead to define a new role for the Air Secretary. He also sought to help the Air Force adapt to McNamara and to cope with the fact that it was no longer the dominant service that it had been in the 1950s.

In December 1960, President-elect John F. Kennedy and his Secretary of Defense-designate, Robert S. McNamara, outlined ambitious goals, agreeing that the nation's defense establishment must be second to none, that it must be cost-conscious and efficient yet strong enough to maintain peace, and that it must be organized to allow the most effective use of "our changing weapons technology."*[1] Organizing the DOD to manage these goals would become McNamara's special interest. Buoyed by the Reorganization Act of 1958, he

---

* President Lyndon B. Johnson did not change Kennedy's policies during Zuckert's tenure. Johnson would state in January 1965 that it was "our primary goal to maintain the most powerful military force in the world at the lowest possible cost . . . We must continue to make whatever changes are necessary in our defense establishment to increase its efficiency and insure that it keeps pace with the demands of an ever-changing world." "Principles of Defense Management Extracts from the President," *Aviation Week and Space Technology,* Jan 25, 1965, vol 82, no 4, p 17, Johnson's defense message delivered to Congress, Jan 18, 1965.

used the act's provisions by absorbing new powers within his office.

A 1937 Phi Beta Kappa and graduate of the University of California, McNamara earned a master's degree in business administration from Harvard University two years later. In 1940 he became an assistant professor of business administration there while acting as a consultant to the War Department on its project to install a statistical control system within the air arm. In 1943 he represented the War Department as a civilian consultant in England and later was commissioned an Army Air Forces (AAF) captain and stationed in China, then India, and finally the Pacific theater before his discharge as a lieutenant colonel. After the war, he formed a statistical control team with nine former AAF officers. They joined the Ford Motor Company as a group and became known as the "whiz kids." McNamara rose quickly at Ford from comptroller in 1949 to vice president and Ford division general manager in 1955. He was finally selected as president on November 9, 1960. In late 1960, he became Secretary of Defense at the age of forty-four, sacrificing $400,000 per year plus stock options for $25,000 per year. Money was not an issue to him. He had long regarded the Pentagon as a particularly fascinating challenge and informed President Kennedy that he intended to be very active in office and to undertake his responsibilities in his own way. Without compromising his own authority, President Kennedy acknowledged that his Secretary of Defense would be a policy maker as well as a manager, with broad authority for individual initiative.[2] McNamara's expertise in statistics, product planning, and finance, and his experience as a professional manager had accustomed him to basing budgetary decisions on close analyses of numerical data rather than on intuition. He had a reputation for studying all sides of a problem and defending his positions tenaciously.[3] He believed that overhauling the National Security Act was unnecessary, that it granted him sufficient authority to function as he wished according to his particular philosophy of active management. It was with this man and his office that the new Secretary of the Air Force, Eugene M. Zuckert, would have to deal.

Zuckert had first met McNamara in 1940 when both worked at Harvard University's Business School. Zuckert considered McNamara a remarkable man and credited him with building an excellent statistical control system for the AAF.* In 1952 Zuckert recommended that McNamara succeed him as Assistant Secretary of the Air Force (Management). As a member of the Atomic Energy Commission (AEC), Zuckert suggested that McNamara be appointed to that body's chairmanship. In December 1960, McNamara, the new Secretary of Defense, selected Zuckert as Secretary of the Air Force and offered him the

---

* During World War II, McNamara worked for Charles B. "Tex" Thornton. Thornton had been assigned to Harvard University by Assistant Secretary of War for Air Robert Lovett to establish a statistical control system for monitoring AAF records of production, supply, and shipment of material.

position. Zuckert, however, was embarrassed because he was supporting former Assistant Secretary of the Air Force (Civil Affairs) Harold C. Stuart, then being touted in the press as the most likely candidate. McNamara did not intend to name Stuart. Several days after Christmas, Zuckert accepted the position, but he soon learned that working with McNamara would not be easy.

McNamara wanted to institute a new approach to analyzing, synthesizing, and centralizing defense planning. In doing so he did not intend to substantially reorganize the DOD. He wished only to replace what he regarded as the intuitive judgment of military professionals with a rational decision-making process and directed that a major review of the DOD's entire program in relation to each of its elements be undertaken. As Secretary of Defense, McNamara would be active, always questioning, "suggesting alternatives, proposing objectives and stimulating progress."[4]

McNamara's initiatives toward centralization immediately provoked the service secretaries who argued against the "short circuiting" of their statutory functions. Acting under the President's direction to appraise defense strategy, to increase airlift capacity and mobility for conventional warfare, and to accelerate the intercontinental ballistic missile (ICBM) and Polaris submarine programs, McNamara bypassed the service secretaries. He established four study teams headed by his own assistant secretaries. Comptroller Charles J. Hitch, an economist from the Rand Corporation, headed a strategic weapon systems study to apply the budgeting theories he developed and explained in his 1960 book, *The Economics of Defense in the Nuclear Age.* Assistant Secretary for International Security Affairs, Paul H. Nitze, a former State Department planner and Democratic party adviser, reviewed U.S. commitments abroad and force requirements for limited wars; Research and Engineering Director Herbert F. York, on the job since 1958, headed a reappraisal of weapons research and development; and Assistant Secretary for Supply and Logistics Thomas D. Morris assessed the effectiveness and utility of U.S. bases at home and abroad. All four studies cut across service lines and were coordinated by McNamara.

The Secretary of Defense viewed the service secretaries as subordinates. To advance departmental centralization, he selected his replacements for the departing Secretaries of the Army and the Navy from the Office of the Secretary of Defense (OSD). Cyrus R. Vance, DOD General Counsel, succeeded Elvis Stahr as Secretary of the Army, and Paul Nitze, Assistant Secretary of Defense for International Security Affairs, succeeded Fred Korth as Secretary of the Navy. McNamara hoped that his assistant secretaries would deal openly and informally with their service counterparts. He himself favored informal exchanges of information among departments, particularly State, Commerce, and Justice.[5] Some of his lesser civilian appointees were like their boss, assertive and abrasive. They did not endear themselves to military leaders who increasingly resented taking orders from a growing legion of civilians. But the Secretary of Defense, who, Zuckert felt, had absolute confidence in his own abilities, left no doubt about who was in charge.

Zuckert's Team

Zuckert was determined to surround himself with a bright and capable staff of his own choosing. The only appointee he did not select was Joseph Charyk, who had been Assistant Secretary of the Air Force (Research and Development) since June 10, 1959. McNamara wanted him to stay with the service's super secret "black programs" to preserve continuity in important national initiatives. After consulting with McNamara, Zuckert agreed to make Charyk his under secretary. Charyk would leave in March 1963 to take over COMSAT (Communications Satellite, Inc.), much to the dismay of Zuckert who was then heavily involved with the hearings on the Air Force's latest experimental tactical fighter, the TFX.

Although Zuckert regarded Charyk's departure as poorly timed, he was pleased by the adept performance of his replacement, Brockway McMillan, a former Assistant Secretary of the Air Force (Research and Development). McMillan was familiar with many of the programs that Charyk had managed and Zuckert thought it logical to promote him. McMillan, a mathematician, had earned a Ph.D. from the Massachusetts Institute of Technology in 1939 and had worked since 1946 at Bell Laboratories, where he became director of military research in 1959. McMillan was involved in more than just secret projects. According to Zuckert, he stood up to Attorney General Robert Kennedy, who wanted the Air Force to help fight the desegregation battles in the South.*

Eugene M. Zuckert, seventh Secretary of the Air Force.

---

* A policy of boycotting businesses that discriminated, especially in rental housing, was eventually put into effect, and the Air Force abided by it.

Kennedy demanded that Air Force personnel boycott establishments that did not adhere to the administration's racial integration policies. Both McMillan and Zuckert positioned themselves against Kennedy, although, Zuckert maintained, McMillan showed "more guts" in the way he did so. Neither man believed that such use of the Air Force was appropriate. Even though his stance made him unpopular with the administration, McMillan was credited by Zuckert with holding firm. McMillan stayed with the OSAF for two years as Zuckert's under secretary. He returned to industry in September 1965. Alexander H. Flax, vice president and technical director of the Cornell Aeronautical Laboratory in Buffalo, New York, replaced McMillan as Assistant Secretary of the Air Force (Research and Development). Widely known and respected as an aeronautical engineer, he had been the Air Force's Chief Scientist from 1959 to 1961 and a long-time member of its Scientific Advisory Board. He had served with many governmental advisory groups, including the President's Science Advisory Committee. Zuckert regarded Flax as eminently qualified and recommended him to Secretary McNamara for the post. Flax would occupy it until March 1969.

Zuckert sought the advice of his long time friend, Jack Glover from Harvard Business School, before filling his old position, Assistant Secretary of the Force (Financial Management). Glover, who had completed several studies for Zuckert and the OSAF through the years, recommended Neil E. Harlan, his colleague at Harvard since the early 1950s. Harlan replaced the knowledgeable long-time incumbent, Lyle S. Garlock (who had left office in 1961), in January 1962, but before assuming the post, he and Zuckert agreed that he should devote the first few months to familiarizing himself with how weapon system managers

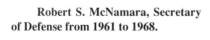

Robert S. McNamara, Secretary of Defense from 1961 to 1968.

209

plan and control the acquisition, installation, and operation of their programs. He traveled to the field to educate himself, left the major management of his office to subordinates, and sent important correspondence for signature to other appointees like Brockway McMillan. (See Appendix 1, OSAF Organization Charts, p. 272.)

Harlan left his position for the more lucrative business world two years later. But before leaving, he recommended another graduate of Harvard Business School, Leonard Marks, Jr., as his replacement. A professor of finance at Stanford University's School of Business, Marks remained as assistant secretary until December 1967. Zuckert was highly satisfied with both Harlan and Marks and observed that because the DOD's assistant secretaries had become involved in activities once handled primarily by the OSAF, their job had changed considerably in the years since he held it under Symington. Zuckert found himself as Air Secretary concerned far more with management problems than Stuart Symington. Symington had tended to concentrate on several large issues, assigning most management tasks to Zuckert. To Zuckert, the Assistant Secretary of the Air Force (Financial Management) had become more an overseer of the Comptroller and budget problems.

Zuckert selected his former deputy, Joseph S. Imirie, as Assistant Secretary (Materiel). During the Symington years, Zuckert worked very closely with Imirie, whom he first met while serving as assistant to the Under Secretary of the Air Force, Arthur S. Barrows. Imirie had left the OSAF in 1952 to join the Carborundum Company in Niagara Falls, New York, as assistant to its president, but became disillusioned there and periodically solicited Zuckert to help him find more suitable employment. Zuckert brought him to the attention of "Tex" Thornton, who headed Litton Industries, but Thornton confused him with someone he disliked with a similar name and did not hire him. When, in April 1961, Imirie was asked by Zuckert to be Assistant Secretary of the Air Force (Materiel), he jumped at the chance. According to Zuckert, during Imirie's two-and-one-half years of service, the Air Force markedly improved its stock control, storage, and distribution processes with reductions in costs and better service. The Air Force also improved its procurement process, but not as significantly as the Air Secretary had hoped it would. For that he did not fault Imirie.

Imirie's departure disappointed Zuckert as well as many in the OSAF and the Air Staff who had worked with him. He returned to Litton Industries to run its microwave division. Zuckert replaced him with a former law school acquaintance, Robert H. Charles. The new Assistant Secretary (Materiel) came highly recommended by James Webb, the former Director of the Bureau of the Budget and head of the National Aeronautics and Space Administration (NASA). Charles had worked for McDonnell Aircraft Corporation in St. Louis, Missouri, from 1941 to 1960 in various capacities until moving up to become executive vice president. In 1960 he became a director of the Universal Match Corporation. Zuckert, impressed by his scholarly background, assigned him the job of procuring the large transport aircraft, the C-5A. It was in Charles's office that the only major OSAF reorganization during Zuckert's tenure occurred. In February 1964, the functions of the Office of the Special Assistant for Installations were combined with the Office of the Assistant Secretary (Materiel) to form the Office of the Assistant Secretary (Installations and Logistics).*6

Zuckert's Style

Zuckert described a typical day as one on which he got up, rode in "that damned Cadillac," tore down Rock Creek Parkway before daybreak, spotted McNamara's car about eight lengths ahead on the Memorial Bridge, and raced to beat his boss to the elevator in the Pentagon. The squawk box in his office would be ringing and "McNamara would be wanting some information . . . right away." After routine contacts with his staff, Zuckert would hold "a systems management group meeting at ten o'clock, a working lunch followed by a couple of afternoon briefings, and possibly a staff meeting . . . " Zuckert maintained that in a day filled with so many meetings he barely had time to contemplate larger issues such as arms control. He felt, he said, "like a traffic cop directing the flow of work. It was just one damned thing after another until six-thirty or seven in the evening" when he would be brought all correspondence requiring his signature. He made a special effort to respond to at least ten congressional letters each day. Zuckert usually met with his under secretary and assistant secretaries at least once a week but talked to them every day by intercom. He sought to preserve active communications with them and made sure that he knew what their main projects were.[7] There were exceptions to his schedule, especially when he had to testify before Congress or travel to Air Force installations. The TFX hearings, for example occupied nearly 60 percent of his time during the summer of 1963.

Zuckert worked very closely with three Chiefs of Staff during his tenure. General Thomas D. White served until June 1961. General Curtis E. LeMay served from June 1961 until January 1965. General John P. McConnell replaced LeMay and remained after Zuckert's departure. In 1962 Zuckert realized that since the service secretaries had been excluded from the chain of operational command following the Reorganization Act of 1958, the chiefs could use the Joint Chiefs of Staff (JCS) as a vehicle to block any policies they rejected. General LeMay agreed to keep him informed on all positions the Air Force brought before the JCS. Thus Zuckert was able to exert influence despite the existence of a separate organizational chain. Before attending his regular

---

* Zuckert could not recall why this reorganization took place but speculated that his work on installations when he was Assistant Secretary of the Air Force might have led him to regard them as important enough to merit their own assistant secretary.

Tuesday morning meeting with McNamara, the Chief of Staff briefed Zuckert on JCS business or stopped by his office in the evening. To keep himself up-to-date, Zuckert also acquired a military assistant to gain a direct line to Air Force plans and operations.[8]

Zuckert had known General White since the 1940s, had been instrumental in bringing him to Washington, and had recommended him to Assistant Vice Chief of Staff General McKee as the OSAF's Director of Legislation and Liaison. White remained at that post from July 1948 to May 1950. By late 1961, Zuckert felt that only under strong leadership would the Air Force make convincing stands for its needs against McNamara's efforts to centralize authority. He believed that General LeMay would make an excellent Air Force Chief of Staff when General White retired.

Both Zuckert and McNamara valued LeMay as an expert in military operations, an innovator who had, for example, ahead of his contemporaries, supported the establishment of counterinsurgency units in the Air Force. They also valued his sense of humor. Zuckert went reluctantly to work one Sunday and dressed down for the occasion, wearing the least business-like clothes he could find: a red shirt, an inexpensive pair of slacks and some Spanish riding boots. General LeMay arrived impeccably dressed, his outfit enhanced by a Harris tweed jacket and a vest. The general looked the Air Secretary up and down and asked, "Where's your motorcycle?"[9] Zuckert was confident that LeMay, as Chief of Staff, would be a strong, unifying advocate for the Air Force.

Zuckert played a part in selecting LeMay's replacement, General McConnell. He had known General McConnell since the late 1940s. At that time the general was Chief of the Reserve and National Guard Division at Air Force Headquarters in Washington, D.C. McConnell had served as LeMay's Vice Chief of Staff. His vast experience in the Far East during World War II and afterwards might have given him the advantage as LeMay's possible successor, in light of America's growing involvement in southeast Asia. People who were surprised by his selection had reservations about him and doubted that he was the best qualified candidate. Others, including Zuckert, pointed to McConnell's long Air Force career and his ability to get along well with people. McConnell had manifested such promising leadership qualities as a student that he became first captain of the Corps of Cadets at the U.S. Military Academy in the class of 1932.[10]

Zuckert earnestly believed that keeping Congress fully informed of Air Force issues was vitally important. He kept in frequent contact with members whose responsibilities included oversight of the military departments or whose districts contained Air Force installations. He would invite newly elected representatives and senators to visit various sites such as Air Force Systems Command (AFSC) Headquarters, Strategic Air Command (SAC) Headquarters, North American Air Defense (NORAD) Command, and the Air Force Academy. He would invariably invite them to ride on the Special Mission Boeing VC-137, the type used by the President. Zuckert, perhaps influenced by his former boss,

Zuckert's Team. *Clockwise from above left*: **Under Secretary of the Air Force Brockway McMillan; Assistant Secretary of the Air Force (Research and Development) Alexander H. Flax; Assistant Secretary of the Air Force (Financial Management) Neil E. Harlan and his successor, Leonard Marks, Jr.; Assistant Secretary of the Air Force (Materiel) Joseph S. Imirie and his successor, Robert H. Charles.**

Stuart Symington, kept cordial relations with Congress, although McNamara seemed not to understand why he did so. Zuckert soon gained the reputation in Congress as an excellent manager.[11]

Throughout his tenure, he dealt with many congressmen, as well as state and local contingents regarding Air Force installation closings within their jurisdictions.* Zuckert was keenly aware that such closings often caused political turmoil. He had participated in many as Assistant Secretary of the Air Force with General McKee. One particularly sensitive action involved the Rome Air Development Center at Griffiss Air Force Base in New York. Early in his tenure, McNamara stated his intention to close a number of bases in an efficiency drive. The Air Staff proposed to Zuckert that the Air Force move its electronics laboratory in Rome to supposedly better facilities in Cambridge, Massachusetts. Zuckert remembered that in 1952 the laboratory had been moved from Cambridge to Rome for exactly the same reason. He did nothing about it even though he was approached by the Air Staff on a biweekly basis. When McNamara pressed for likely closings, Zuckert offered, among others, Griffiss Air Force Base, including the Rome Air Development Center. This offer pleased members of the Air Staff but not the people of Rome, New York. They complained to their Democratic representative who was a close friend of President Kennedy. Zuckert went to Capitol Hill with Roswell Gilpatric to meet with a New York delegation which wanted him to go to New York and explain in a public forum the reason for his selection. He sent a subordinate who "had to have a state police guard to get there." The base was not closed. Most likely the administration, the DOD, and Congress had second thoughts about their decision. As Zuckert was fond of saying, "Rome was not closed in a day."[12]

Zuckert found it difficult to accept the fact that the Air Secretary had been removed from operations and deprived of the opportunity to directly challenge the Secretary of Defense. He was wedded to Symington's approach and contemplated resigning to protest what he viewed as the usurpation of his authority by the OSD. He and the other service secretaries initiated management studies to determine their own roles. Secretary of the Army Elvis T. Stahr, who resigned in 1961, later blasted McNamara for "overreaching" and concentrating too much power in the hands of too few people within a bureaucracy as large as the DOD.

Zuckert's studies revealed what had happened to the OSAF in relation to the OSD during the 1950s. DOD Assistant and Deputy Assistant Secretaries, widening their spheres of influence, had increasingly bypassed the service secretaries. They contacted their civilian and military counterparts directly or circumvented the military chiefs by dealing with action officers on military staffs or in the field.[13] Zuckert characterized some members of McNamara's staff as incompe-

---

* Base closings were recommended by the President to save money and by the Secretary of Defense to centralize and consolidate functions.

tents and sycophants who "put their fingers up in the hall to find out which way the McNamara wind was blowing" and acted accordingly.[14] The Air Staff was as unenthusiastic about some of the "whiz kids," as the Air Secretary. Zuckert charged that most of McNamara's staff, including the assistant secretaries, lacked practical experience. Although their theories on strategic weapons seemed sound enough, their analyses of conventional forces, guns, men, and aircraft did not.

General White, an avid reader who was fluent in several languages, was profoundly apprehensive of "the pipe-smoking, tree full of owls type of so-called professional defense intellectuals who have been brought into this nation's capital." He doubted that many of these "often overconfident, sometimes arrogant young professors, mathematicians, and other theorists [had] sufficient worldliness or motivation to stand up to the kind of enemy we face."[15]

General LeMay accused McNamara and his staff of failing to listen to the military experts. He judged them too soft and naive to deal with the threat of international Communism and viewed their pursuit of parity instead of strategic superiority as foolish. LeMay likened McNamara to a hospital administrator who dabbles in brain surgery.[16] McNamara himself, according to Lt. Gen. Glen W. Martin, Zuckert's military assistant, had, despite his undoubted mental capacity, the knack "of arriving at the wrong conclusions in a spectacular fashion with great implications and repercussions."[17]

As a result of McNamara's effort to centralize authority within his office, most DOD studies in the spring of 1961 recommended cutting back the authority of the military services. It was becoming increasingly clear to both uniformed and civilian personnel within the DOD that the services would lose their influence over policy. Zuckert visited the White House that spring to present his views on Air Force operations in Laos,* should the United States intervene in the conflict in southeast Asia. Such visits were, by the time he became Air Secretary however, unusual. Eventually his policy-making role in operations ceased.

In December 1961, after deciding against resignation to protest DOD policies, Air Secretary Zuckert called together key air commanders at Homestead Air Force Base in Florida to discuss strategy. He noted that McNamara had consistently "pestered" the services for one- and two-page comments on changes he had made in their budget requests. These "snowflakes," as the commentaries

---

* In 1961 the United States seriously considered attempting to stop Communist infiltration from North Vietnam through Laos to the northern and central highlands of South Vietnam. McNamara believed that the United States had to decide whether to intervene to end the fighting between Laotian government forces and the pro-Communist Pathet Lao. General LeMay believed that a cease-fire in Laos was impossible without U.S. intervention. General Emmett O'Donnell, Commander of the Pacific Air Force (PACAF), estimated that his air forces could undertake a "small war" with conventional weapons. Robert F. Futrell, *The Advisory Years to 1965: The United States Air Force in Southeast Asia* (Washington: Office of Air Force History, 1981), pp 63–65.

were called, had become a blizzard. Position papers (longer reports) were another of McNamara's favorite requests during his first few months in office, and they became so numerous that they were labeled "the 76 trombones" after a popular song from the musical comedy, *The Music Man*. By May 1961, *Aviation Week* noted that requests for position papers had increased until "McNamara's band now had 146 trombones." General Martin suspected that McNamara's motive was to keep the military services too busy developing position papers to counter any of his proposals.

At Homestead, Zuckert urged that the Air Force, no longer the dominant service with the sole strategic mission, face up to a new era. He argued that it was losing to McNamara and his budget cuts and that in response it should improve the quality of its position papers and briefings to the DOD.[18] He emphasized to the Chief of Staff that clear, persuasive arguments were essential to the Air Staff's successful dealings with the OSAF and, more important, with the OSD which, Zuckert believed, had been unimpressed by the position papers and briefings it had received.[19] Zuckert consulted with several management specialists to help the Air Force strengthen its writing skills. Among the most prominent was Dr. Edward Learned from Harvard University's Business School. Learned had worked on developing better management practices for the OSAF, and Zuckert knew of his consulting work for the Chief of Staff dating back to General Arnold's time. He believed that the professor might be especially useful, since McNamara held him in high regard.[20]

In November 1961, General LeMay became particularly frustrated by budget projections for 1963 and what was becoming a losing battle against McNamara. The Chief of Staff noted that the Air Force had not done well on its funding for future strategic forces. It lost some planned-for B-52s, received inadequate funding for the B-70, insufficient numbers of hardened and dispersed Minuteman missiles, and saw its Mobile Minuteman missile canceled.[21]

The aviation press had noticed the trend in funding cuts. *Aviation Week*, a supporter of spending for the aerospace industry, reported its disgust with a "dismal pattern" that had been continued by Secretary of Defense McNamara and his decision to withhold $780 million voted by Congress for various Air Force programs. The magazine's editor, Robert Hotz, noted that the pattern of withholding funds had historically cut across party lines under Secretary of Defense Louis A. Johnson and President Truman (Democrats), as well as under Secretaries of Defense Charles E. Wilson and Neil A. McElroy and President Eisenhower (Republicans). McNamara's cuts, he asserted, were indefensible because they were made despite the views of the services as well as Congress.[22]

An example of Zuckert's philosophy emerged at the Homestead meeting when he reviewed the Air Force's December 1961 appeal for an additional $245 million to cover Atlas and Titan base construction. Zuckert was apprehensive about this cost, especially since it had nearly doubled in a month. McNamara, replying, had ordered an independent audit. The Air Secretary warned that

Congress would be no less disturbed in light of the fact that the overrun represented a 25 percent increase over figures presented six months earlier. He felt that statistics alone would not justify the request; a detailed narrative setting forth the reasons for the extraordinary escalation would be necessary. He also wanted a "white paper" concerning the entire program that detailed its problems and what had been done to overcome them. The paper was to present the Air Force's case and to answer anticipated questions. At stake was the Air Force's very credibility.[23] Presumably, Zuckert obtained a more communicative paper since the Air Force was granted additional funding.

At the beginning of his tenure as Air Secretary, Zuckert had taken several initiatives to improve interaction between the OSD and the Air Force. To keep himself better informed, he ordered his executive assistants to submit weekly digests to him as well as to each major agency within the OSAF. This measure enhanced communication within the OSAF and aided the OSAF in coordinating its dealings with the OSD. He monitored documentation between the Air Force and the OSD to ascertain what changes in control, amount of information flow, and lines of communication were needed. He also directed that over the course of a week all headquarters personnel having contacts with the OSD supply him with brief memoranda for the record.*[24]

Zuckert was constantly analyzing management practices between the OSAF and the Air Staff and was willing to tinker with them to establish clear authority. He believed that frequent studies of management practices within Air Force Headquarters would lead to a general improvement in staff operations without reductions in personnel. His major goal was to determine "what we do in Headquarters USAF, how we do it, and why we do it here."[25] On the whole, he succeeded.

Secretary Zuckert remained dissatisfied throughout his tenure with Air Force program analyses and the quality of special studies, those generated within the Air Staff as well as those directed by OSD. He believed that the Air Staff was competent enough to produce respectable analyses but was handicapped by an unwillingness to reexamine its established positions. In November 1963, the Air Secretary sought General LeMay's comments on the situation, suggesting that he consider broadening the participation of his own staff in developing studies and analyses. Vice Chief of Staff, General William F. McKee, responding for his chief, assured Zuckert that improvements could be made without altering staff interaction and that the participation of the chief's staff could be broadened.

On January 7, 1964, Zuckert held a meeting in his office with his staff and Admiral Draper L. Kauffman, who directed the Navy's Office of Program Appraisal. Kauffman explained how his office worked with the Office of the

---

* Zuckert claimed that his efforts were at times successful. He had often, however, to remind the Air Staff to prepare clearer papers.

Chief of Naval Operations Program Planning to review programs, analyze systems, and produce special studies. Zuckert held a subsequent meeting with his own staff and Neil Harlan, Assistant Secretary of the Air Force (Financial Management), to evaluate the Navy system and to determine how it could be applied to the Air Force. According to Harlan, no formal structure existed within which the OSAF could routinely assess problems and exchange ideas to determine policy and guidance. Nor did a formal structure exist within which the Air Staff could conduct comprehensive management review for the OSAF. There was not even a single Air Staff office that coordinated information and briefings for the Secretary of Defense. There was also no office to probe organizational or procedural weaknesses within the OSAF and no office to provide guidance for developing management concepts at the secretarial level. Harlan urged that Zuckert approve in principle a proposal to establish an Office of Program Appraisal within the OSAF. Eventually, instead of an Office of Program Appraisal, a study group was created with Zuckert's military assistant providing coordination between the Air Staff and the OSAF.[26] A few months later, an Office of Analytical Studies was established under the Vice Chief of Staff to provide services to the Chief of Staff and to the Secretary of the Air Force.

Zuckert Tries To Regain Lost Ground

Zuckert was not passive in the face of the OSD's encroachment into areas that once belonged to the service secretaries. He attempted to recapture lost ground by offering Air Force assistance where appropriate. From his earliest months as Air Secretary he had sought a specific role for his office. In early 1961, he suggested to Paul Nitze, Assistant Secretary of Defense for International Security Affairs (who would play a significant role in strategic military planning), that air power could play a special role in the maintenance of security and U.S. prestige throughout the free world. Zuckert claimed that the Air Force through its world-wide commitments and foreign bases had developed professional competence in international relations among a core of officers who had specialized in specific regions and areas.[27] He offered their expertise to Nitze, whose staff had included officers from all of the services. It is not certain, however, that any increase of Air Force officers on Nitze's staff occurred because of Zuckert's proposal.

In June 1961, Zuckert also warned Nitze that the United States, to counter any attempts by the Sino-Soviet Bloc to gain economic control of the undeveloped world, should establish air transport, particularly in remote areas. Seeking to interest Nitze, he suggested that the United States train the military forces of the nations of Africa to help advance air transport. Africa, he observed, lacked modern surface transport. Its roads were generally poor and many became impassable where there were long rainy seasons. Therefore, he argued, air transport represented the best means for shipping equipment, merchandise, produce, and people between coastal markets and interior production areas. And it could move internal security forces to subdue tribal disturbances and resolve border disputes among nomadic peoples. He suggested that the United States supply aircraft, ground transport, communications equipment and facilities, spare parts, and instructor personnel for pilot and ground school training and training in transport operations, maintenance and related fields. Zuckert recommended a joint DOD-State Department plan to emphasize economic development in future U.S. military assistance programs.[28] In following months, the State Department studied the subject, and the Air Force became more involved with African countries. Whether these activities can be directly attributed to Zuckert's suggestions is difficult to determine. The important point is that Zuckert tried to penetrate the upper layer of DOD authority to seek a more prominent role for the Air Force.

That same month he also took issue with Defense Secretary McNamara's assessment that the country had greater strategic capability (bombers capable of delivering nuclear warheads) than needed and that U.S. estimates of future Soviet strategic missile strength were too high. While advocating additional bombers, Zuckert had taken a special interest in strategic forces. In his view, the Air Force's most important task was to bring ICBMs into the operational inventory. Conceding that the country might acquire more strategic strength than necessary, the Air Secretary nonetheless noted, "Our situation today could be far different if we had not maintained a distinct superiority in strategic forces."[29] He acknowledged that calculations of enemy missiles, which nearly always led to some disagreement within the national security community, were uncertain at best. He deemed it wise to err on the high side.[30]

Crucial to the evaluation of U.S. strategic missile capabilities was the statistical relationship between reliability and response.* The lack of meaningful data rendered evaluation difficult and essentially futile, according to Zuckert, because too few missiles were tested. General White concurred with the Air Secretary, stating that the reliability of missiles would remain doubtful for at least five more years. He, nonetheless, recommended that missiles be emplaced in the ground and in submarines. Zuckert and White demanded that more detailed analyses of missile firings be undertaken and that particular attention be paid to the correlation between reliability and response before any speculation about numbers of operational missiles was attempted.[31]

Air Secretary Zuckert continued to chip away at DOD centralization policies that neglected Air Force participation. In August 1961, he complained bitterly to Roswell Gilpatric, Deputy Secretary of Defense, about the treatment of the Air

---

* The relationship between reliability and response was expressed by a formula for the number of missiles in inventory that were operational. Some missiles did not work during testing. Thus Zuckert preached caution when speaking of numbers of missiles stockpiled.

Three USAF Chiefs of Staff, General Thomas D. White *(above)* **General Curtis E. LeMay** *(above, right)* **and General John P. McConnell** *(right)* **served during Eugene M. Zuckert's term as Secretary of the Air Force.**

Force by the Office of the Director of Research and Engineering (ODR&E) under Harold Brown regarding DOD-NASA negotiations on missile test range operations. Zuckert demanded to know why the Air Force had not been included on the deliberating team and learned of the DOD's allegations that the Air Force would interfere with discussions. Zuckert was dismayed by what he regarded as a poor beginning to a joint venture, especially since the Air Force, with its experience in missile testing, would be the lead managing agency. He argued that the Air Force should have a direct voice in negotiations and the opportunity at the outset to help ensure the best possible terms between itself and NASA. Zuckert bristled under what he believed was condescension at its worst and cautioned against the establishment of such an ugly precedent lest it color the spirit of cooperation between the Air Force and ODR&E.[32] Eventually, the Air Force participated.

The dissemination of information from the DOD soon became a troublesome issue between McNamara and the service secretaries. McNamara was shocked by the release of what he believed was an unacceptable amount of security information from each of the services and, with the support of the Senate Armed Services Committee, set about to stop it. He assigned Lt. Gen. Joseph F. Carroll, Air Force Inspector General, to lead a monitoring effort against unwarranted "leaks," such as several from the Air Force. One which had particularly upset McNamara related to Secretary of State Dean Rusk's advocacy of stronger conventional forces and less reliance on strategic weapons. Another leak by an unidentified Air Force major general revealed in a press dispatch the operational date of a new weapon.[33] Yet another was published in a *Chicago Sun-Times* report in early 1961 alleging that General LeMay had advocated at a Pentagon briefing that the United States launch a preventive atomic attack to stop Communist infiltration of Laos. LeMay called the story false and a calculated attempt to discredit him in public to his civilian superiors. Under Secretary of the Air Force Joseph Charyk, like McNamara, was concerned that there had been far too much publicity regarding the Air Force and the space program, and he saw to it that NASA's public relations functions were in consonance with those of the Air Force and the DOD.[34]

As part of the DOD's crackdown during the spring of 1961, Defense Secretary McNamara proposed to centralize all public relations functions through the Deputy Secretary of Defense. Air Secretary Zuckert had previously agreed that the military services needed policy direction. However, he qualified his total support for McNamara's initiative by arguing that they also could not operate effectively "if every detail of daily activities has to be ordered and supervised directly from the level of the Office of the Secretary of Defense."[35] Merely one high echelon public affairs office could not, in his view, answer all DOD inquiries. He argued that responsibility for the public information function should reside at the operating levels of each service with control and guidance flowing from the Secretary of Defense through the Office of the Assistant Secretary of Defense for Public Affairs to each service.[36] Zuckert would have his way. The services managed to preserve control over their public affairs activities. Nevertheless, closer lines of communication between the public information function and the OSD were established. The atmosphere at the Pentagon reflected McNamara's tighter controls over public information, which, according to some cynics, gave new meaning to the term "cleared for unclassified."[37] Zuckert himself established the Office of the Special Assistant for Public Affairs to which, on March 21, 1961, he appointed Edward R. Trapnell.*[38]

----

* This office was redesignated Special Assistant for Public and Legislative Affairs on March 15, 1965. It was abolished in 1969 in budget cuts. Its functions would be carried out by the Office of the Director of Information and the Office of the Director of Legislative Liaison.

Nearly a year after the leaks, Arthur Sylvester, Assistant Secretary of Defense for Public Affairs, was able to report to the Senate Armed Services Committee's subcommittee investigating censorship of military officers that the DOD and the Air Force had succeeded in improving the protection of sensitive information. Sylvester had, for example, not divulged the dates and locations of missile test firings to prevent the acquisition of developmental chronologies, the photographing of weapons and facilities, and the emplacing of data-gathering instruments by enemy intelligence agents. He had kept certain aspects of the space program secret as well.[39]

Periodic attempts by Sylvester to gain more control over public affairs continued, and the subject of consolidation surfaced again when a 1963 Government Accounting Office (GAO) study recommended the establishment of a defense information office to replace the separate service offices. The GAO predicted that centralization would save $12 million and cut what was perceived as duplication of effort with the elimination of 112 jobs. It also projected an uneven work load when different crises such as accidents affected only one service. Naturally, the services took issue with the study, arguing that the centralization of public affairs would delay clearance of non-sensitive aerospace industry information for release. Industry too, had long complained of the tediousness of DOD procedures for clearing its press releases, photographs, films, brochures, speeches, and corporate annual statements. It blamed Sylvester for the new reorganization effort and for any further withholding of information to the public.[40]

McNamara's persistent efforts to control the news were causing embarrassing repercussions within the Pentagon. In August 1961, Zuckert complained to McNamara of Sylvester's penchant for briefing the press ahead of the service information chiefs and cautioned that the chiefs as well as the service secretaries were feeling increasingly isolated from what he characterized as "incomplete" DOD internal communications. Doubts about whether the views of the Secretary of Defense were being accurately reflected to the public were circulating throughout the OSAF. Zuckert had to inform Sylvester in October of that year that no Air Force official had been responsible for the publication of inaccurate statements from United Press International in several newspaper articles relating to ICBM site activations. In attempting to overcome the obstacles impinging on the service secretaries which had been built into the DOD's new communications control function, Zuckert had to be vigilant in bringing to both McNamara's and Sylvester's attention problems with the dissemination of Air Force information from the Office of the Assistant Secretary of Defense for Public Affairs.[41]

Zuckert tirelessly defended the role of the service secretaries. In July 1961, he responded to a draft plan of yet another of Defense Secretary McNamara's efforts at consolidation—the establishment of a Defense Intelligence Agency (DIA). The Air Secretary criticized the plan as so broad that it appeared to encompass almost every facet of the DOD's intelligence activities. He feared that the plan might deprive the service secretaries, commanders, and chiefs of the ability to direct intelligence activities that properly belonged to them by transferring their specialists to the new center. In outlining his objections to the formation of a DIA, Zuckert cited the example of research and development. He reasoned that specialists in the scientific aspects of intelligence acquisition and analysis were best employed when they worked closely with the military services to advance technical capabilities. Zuckert was wary of any proposal to shift all of that knowhow from the services to the DIA and he advised against it.[42] He succeeded in holding the line on the issue. The services managed to retain their own operational intelligence function despite the fact that a new centralized DIA was created in August 1961.

While Zuckert was trying to recapture some measure of the influence once exercised by the OSAF and to urge caution regarding the scope of McNamara's centralization program, he was also exercising the talents that had brought him to the attention of government in the first place. His experience administering Stuart Symington's Management Control through Cost Control initiative had thoroughly prepared him to take on the challenge of managing the costs of systems and equipment. One of his first initiatives in 1963 was to develop, with the Air Staff, a methodology for comprehensively evaluating major Air Force contractors. Zuckert devised a series of Industrial Management Assistance Surveys with which a special team was able to determine the effects of Air Force management on contractor performance. Zuckert's main objective was to help contractors and their Air Force monitors by identifying project problems and deficiencies, by recommending improvements, and by sharing outstanding practices throughout the aerospace industry. The team, comprised of thirty-five field grade officers drawn from the Air Staff and major commands, along with the Air Force Inspector General, usually spent six weeks at selected plants analyzing policies, procedures, and management practices. By January 1963, they had completed twelve Industrial Management Assistance Surveys, pinpointing clearly where immediate improvements were possible.

Encouraged by the success of his survey initiative, the Air Secretary attempted to introduce it to the Navy. Noting that most of the large industries studied were under contract to both the Navy and the Air Force, Zuckert suggested that a joint survey would offset some of the many complaints that had surfaced about different service procurement practices and would lead to greater interservice cooperation.[43] The Navy did participate in several joint surveys, many of which continued after Zuckert left office.

Zuckert remained consistent in his attempts to achieve cost reductions and when he did, was not above sharing the credit. The final report of the Air Force Cost Reduction Program* for 1965 revealed that the Air Force had accounted for nearly half of the total $4.6 billion DOD savings reported by Secretary

---

* The impetus for the Cost Reduction Program came from McNamara's office.

McNamara to President Johnson. Secretary Zuckert sent a special letter of commendation to all Air Force personnel who had contributed to so laudable an effort. The Air Force had examined every significant mission and had tested the necessity and effectiveness of every aspect of organization, manning, administration, and deployment. Pleased, McNamara noted that the Air Force Cost Reduction Program's results had exceeded his expectations.[44]

Non-Profit Companies

The Air Force had traditionally depended on its prime contractors and private industry for scientific and technical guidance in the development of major weapon systems. In the case of ballistic missile development, however, the Air Force believed that it would obtain a greater degree of objectivity from independent sources—those with no responsibility for and thus no occasion to profit from the production of hardware. In 1954 the Air Force engaged the services of the California-based Ramo-Wooldridge Corporation for systems engineering and technical direction. The Air Force stipulated that the corporation, to avoid conflict of interest, be prohibited from developing and manufacturing any missiles and their components.

The Air Force had recognized from the outset of its relationship with Ramo-Wooldridge that certain misgivings, particularly among its associate contractors, about the corporation's profit-seeking status would not easily be dispelled. The Air Force's associate contractors were reluctant to cooperate with a company that might one day be able to benefit financially from information that originated with them. Ramo-Wooldridge attempted to quiet growing industry as well as government criticism by separating from its Guided Missile Research Division, renamed Space Technology Laboratories (STL), in December 1957. Associate contractors remained uneasy about sharing information with STL and about Ramo-Wooldridge as STL's parent. They also feared that its holding company, Thompson Products of Ohio, might monopolize the supply of missile parts. In October 1958, Thompson-Ramo-Wooldridge (TRW) was established through a merger and STL became a wholly owned subsidiary of the new corporation. The Air Force prohibited the production of hardware by both TRW and STL.

Two studies, one by Congress in 1959 and another by the Air Force in 1960, found that industry's suspicions concerning potential competition would be most effectively mitigated with the formation of a non-profit civil contractor responsible for advanced planning, systems design, and technical evaluation of programs. This arrangement would better fulfill the Air Force's requirement for independent scientific and technical advice. Thus, in 1960 STL was converted to the Aerospace Corporation to help support and advance the government's scientific activities and projects."[45]

Early in 1961, however, the press began accusing the Air Force of using non-profit companies to circumvent government salary schedules. In March of that year Secretary Zuckert had to answer an inquiry from Senator J. Glenn Beall of Maryland relating to allegations in the *Washington Post* that the Aerospace Corporation in particular was paying exorbitant salaries. He explained the history of the corporation, pointing out that the Air Force's relationship with Ramo-Wooldridge and STL had helped produce outstanding results in the Thor, Atlas, Titan, and Minuteman missile programs. These results, in his view, had more than justified the Air Force's new management approach with non-profit corporations.

Zuckert informed the senator that government salary schedules were not applicable to these companies. He also maintained that Aerospace offered salaries comparable with those of private industry with only a handful of its leading scientist-executives earning $40,000 per year. The highest salary among non-executives, he contended, was no more than $30,000. In fact, only 3 percent of the corporation's employees were paid in excess of $19,000.[46]

Zuckert was not without reservations about non-profit corporations, although he defended them. He believed that they were insensitive to the fact that their status as hybrids—part public, part private—set them apart. They did not have to adhere to civil service hiring practices. On the rare occasion when the Air Force complained to them about over-charges for independent research and development, their officers invariably responded that they were being "stifled" and predicted that "barbarians and cavemen would soon take over the United States." Zuckert got little sympathy from representatives of profit-making corporations in many heated meetings on the subject of compensation.

During hearings in 1965 on Aerospace's activities, Congress criticized expenditures on such luxuries as parties and lawn maintenance at corporate headquarters. The Air Secretary was constrained to defend Aerospace and praised the quality of its work, but was annoyed that the corporation sometimes seemed to go too far. He later recalled that the same people who had shown the temerity to demand that the Air Force ship a boat belonging to an Aerospace executive from New York to California through the Panama Canal "had the nerve" to tell him that he "was suffocating the development of Air Force technology by not giving them money to play with as they wanted."[47] Zuckert felt that periodic independent reviews of relations with Air Force-sponsored non-profit corporations were necessary, and such reviews were eventually carried out.

The B-70

No single debate enabled Zuckert to define a more substantive role for the Secretary of the Air Force than that surrounding the development of the B-70 bomber—despite the fact that his views and the administration's were opposed. Because the debate, during many lengthy congressional budget hearings,

The controversial North American XB-70 Valkyrie bomber.

exposed the longstanding argument within the Air Force over missiles versus manned bombers, Zuckert became convinced that the Air Staff must learn to justify its positions more compellingly. Congressman Carl Vinson of Georgia, who headed the House Appropriations Committee's inquiry, made the debate a test in the ongoing power struggle between the executive and legislative branches of government.

The B-70 bomber, intended as the successor to the B-52, was designed to achieve a speed of mach-3 (2,000 miles per hour) and an altitude of 70,000 feet. However, its history of delays necessitated several reprogrammings. The Air Force had initiated the first studies and plans in 1953 and awarded a contract to North American Aviation, Inc. in 1957 for the production of fifty-nine aircraft by 1968. In January 1958, the contract was amended to stipulate an operational first wing by August 1964. By the autumn of 1958, however, the Air Force's 1960 budget submission had reduced the program, stretching out its production schedule for an additional year to August 1965. During the autumn of 1959, the Secretary of Defense decided to terminate the B-70 program with the production of just one prototype.

President Eisenhower did not support the B-70. He nonetheless sanctioned additional funding for its development when it became a political issue in the 1960 presidential campaign. In fact, in 1960 Eisenhower approved the appropriation of $420 million to reinstitute a limited development program and to complete the first wing by the autumn of 1966. His final budget, submitted in January 1961, approved the expenditure of $358 million for a combat wing by August 1968. In March 1961, however, President Kennedy and Defense Secretary McNamara approved only the production of a single model so that the technical possibilities of its structure and complex and costly subsystems for bombing, navigation, environment, automatic flight, air traffic, and defense could be demonstrated at high speeds and altitudes. Because the subsystems would not render the aircraft completely invulnerable to enemy missiles, McNamara could not defend production beyond the prototype.[48]

Zuckert echoed the Air Force's contention that the B-70 was a necessary weapon system and a worthy replacement for the B-52. As to vulnerability, he argued that the B-70, trailing ballistic missiles to their targets, could take advantage of a stricken enemy's damaged defenses and, unlike ICBMs, swiftly attack specific sites. Acknowledging the importance of strategic missiles, Zuckert, nonetheless, reminded Congress that their reliability had not been proven and cautioned against overdependence on them. He supported the development of a mach-3 bomber when the necessary technology became available, advocating as diversified an array of weapon systems as possible to complicate enemy defense strategies. Fond of analogies to football, Zuckert contended that a good running back could be contained unless his team possessed a solid passing threat to spread the opposing defense and thus use both running and passing attacks more effectively. Zuckert's view was very much at odds with that of McNamara and his logicians.[49]

General White agreed with Secretary Zuckert. Testifying in April 1961 before the Senate Appropriations Subcommittee, he recommended that the B-70 program be accelerated because missiles, unlike bombers, did not have the flexibility that would be required in nuclear war. General LeMay praised the aircraft's ability to carry missiles and perform a wide range of wartime missions. He regarded no technological problem associated with the production of the B-70 as insurmountable.[50]

Zuckert's arguments for the B-70 received a favorable congressional reception throughout the hearings, but, as he later recalled, the Air Force's arguments did not. They seemed based more on institutional prejudices than on facts and logic. In the summer of 1961, the administration announced its intention to cut the B-70 program and was consequently vilified in the press. Zuckert lost no time in seeking and gaining on August 3 a private meeting with President Kennedy. He informed the President that certain administration officials had urged him to defend the official position in public statements. The Air Secretary had naturally refused in view of his recent pro-B-70 testimony before Congress. Zuckert explained to the President that he would lose credibility as Air Secretary if he supported the administration in the matter of the B-70 when only weeks before he had not. He asked the President whether he should resign his office. Kennedy said "not at all" and, responding with a quick smile, told Zuckert he was satisfied with his performance and was delighted to have chatted with him.[51] The B-70 issue intensified Zuckert's belief in his role as an advocate for the Air Force's basic programs even though he represented the administration. He saw himself as "the man in the middle," fighting for what he supported.

The Missile Age. *Left to right*: **the liquid-fuel Atlas, Titan II, Thor, and the solid-fuel Minuteman were among the Air Force's new weapon systems of the 1960s.**

Shortly after leaving office, Zuckert admitted that, on reflection, he had erred in promoting the B-70 because as time passed its vulnerability to enemy defenses became increasingly difficult to dismiss. He added that he favored a manned strategic bomber to replace the B-52, but not the B-70. It had been dealt the fatal blow, he believed, by too many stops and starts in its development schedule. A successor to the B-52 would be pursued after Zuckert's administration in the form of two experimental aircraft. The first flight of the XB-70A-1 took place on September 21, 1964. The XB-70A-2 made its first mach-3 flight at 70,000 feet on January 3, 1967. The following June it was destroyed in a mid-air collision with an F-104 on its forty-sixth flight. In March 1967, the XB-70 project was transferred to NASA for high altitude, high speed testing. Two years later the remaining aircraft was installed in the Air Force Museum at Wright-Patterson Air Force Base in Ohio.[52]

TFX-Tactical Fighter, Experimental

The most trying and controversial debate of Zuckert's tenure concerned the TFX, a tactical fighter-bomber designed and built for both the Air Force and the

Navy. In this case Zuckert sided with the administration against the Air Force. In so doing, he strained his relationship with the Air Force and lost a measure of the confidence it had placed in him.

Secretary McNamara had envisioned a single advanced fighter aircraft to replace the Air Force's F-105s and the Navy's F-4s. Both the Navy and the Air Force balked at the idea of a joint fighter-bomber, arguing for more than a year that their missions were too divergent to be joined in a single plane. The Air Force needed a plane weighing as much as 75,000 pounds. The Navy, however, needed one weighing less than 55,000 to operate from carriers. McNamara disregarded such basic differences. In June 1961, he ordered Secretary Zuckert to develop the TFX for both services, thus bringing to a head the issues of interservice and military-civilian decision-making. The Air Force became frustrated during Senate investigative hearings on the award of contract by what it regarded as incessant and unwarranted probing, and it complained that such proceedings were hurting Air Force morale. The hearings represented the first significant congressional challenge to McNamara's judgment. His reversal of the Air Force-Navy Source Selection Board's decision was not, in Congress's view, adequately substantiated.

Competition for the TFX contract became complicated by the new biservice approach to weapon system development. The TFX had to satisfy both the Air Force and the Navy in, for example, weight and bomb load. The field of bidders soon narrowed to the Boeing Aircraft Company of Washington, and the General Dynamics Corporation of Texas, the latter proposing to subcontract some work to

Grumman Aircraft Company of New York. During 1961 and 1962, Boeing and General Dynamics revised their proposals four times. At first the services leaned toward Boeing. But the fourth evaluation report submitted by a technical team of 169 military and civilian experts* indicated that competition had ended in a tie.

A Source Selection Board composed of service representatives from the Navy and three Air Force commands—Systems, Tactical Air, and Logistics—evaluated the technical team reports and recommended that Boeing be awarded the contract. The Air Force Council† then reviewed the decision. The council, which included the five Deputy Chiefs of Staff, the Surgeon General and the Inspector General of the Air Force, was led by Vice Chief of Staff General William F. McKee. On November 8, the council, in agreement with the Air Force-Navy Source Selection Board, recommended Boeing and submitted its decision to the Chief of Staff, who approved it and forwarded it to Secretary Zuckert. On November 24, 1962, Secretary McNamara announced that a $439 million contract for twenty-two F-111s (TFXs) had been awarded to General Dynamics. He had overruled the unanimous recommendation of a colonel, four major generals, six lieutenant generals, five generals, five rear admirals, and one admiral.[53]

Zuckert maintained that he had decided in favor of General Dynamics, uninfluenced and unpressured by McNamara, by studying every detail of the fourth evaluation report and soliciting the advice of his military experts and his staff. According to General McKee, never before had a decision made by the Source Selection Board and upheld by the Air Force Council been overruled by an Air Secretary. General LeMay, to whom the TFX was "no goddam good as a strategic bomber,"[54] and the Air Staff were disappointed in Zuckert, believing that he had lied about the way he reached his decision. McNamara did not routinely consult the Air Staff on many issues and rarely sought the advice of the service secretaries. The agreement of the service secretaries, particularly the Secretary of the Navy, and McNamara was, Zuckert believed, coincidental.[55] The Air Secretary had investigated the TFX on his own, assessed the needs of the Air Force against those of the administration as fairly as he could, and had chosen to reject the advice of his military experts, something he had not done in the B-70 debate. Once again he was the man in the middle.

---

* A technical team varied in size according to weapon system and was usually divided into four sections: management, operational, technical, and logistics. Seventy percent of the TFX team worked in the technical area. Robert J. Art, *The TFX Decision: McNamara and the Military* (Boston: Little, Brown and Company, 1968), p 58; Senate Committee on Government Operations, Hearings before the Permanent Subcommittee, *TFX Contract Investigation,* 88th Cong., 1st sess., 1963. Part 1, p 1975.

† The Air Force Council provides guidance on policy to the Chief of Staff and the Air Staff and monitors the Air Force as it carries out its assigned missions. The council is composed of the Vice Chief of Staff, Deputy Chiefs of Staff, and the Inspector General.

The TFX decision immediately snowballed into a political issue. Senator Henry Jackson, a Democrat of Boeing's home state, questioned the award. General Dynamics was situated in Texas, and its major TFX subcontractor, Grumman, was headquartered in New York. Vice President Lyndon Johnson was a Texan. Texas and New York had supported John Kennedy during the 1960 presidential election. Washington and Kansas had not. New York and Texas represented sixty-nine electoral votes, Washington represented nine, and Kansas, where the plane would have been built at Boeing's Wichita plant, represented eight. Also, Deputy Secretary of Defense Roswell L. Gilpatric had performed a considerable amount of legal work for General Dynamics before entering federal service. Navy Secretary Fred Korth, from Ft. Worth, where the TFX would be built, had headed a bank through which General Dynamics had secured several loans. Later TFX hearings revealed that both Korth and Gilpatric should have disqualified themselves from the contract award process. Both subsequently resigned their positions with the government. According to General McKee, most of the Air Force believed that President Kennedy himself, to reward loyal constituents, had induced McNamara to favor General Dynamics. McKee, however, admitted that he could not confirm the truth of that suspicion.

A month following the contract award, Zuckert was questioned in his office by two investigators from the Permanent Subcommittee of the Senate Committee on Government Operations headed by Senator John L. McClellan of Arkansas. He emphasized that he had reached his decision completely free of political duress. Although the Source Selection Board and the Air Force Council had found Boeing's version of the TFX operationally superior, Zuckert declared that it was not "so substantially better that its superiority should dominate the selection." He had considered several factors. One of McNamara's express wishes was the greatest possible commonality of aircraft parts. Boeing's proposal showed sixty percent common parts; General Dynamics' showed eighty-five. The investigators then asked Zuckert to review his actions of November 1962. He told them that he had spent a great deal of time studying all available data and consulting with various Air Force technical specialists from around the country. On November 21, he completed his final recommendation and submitted it to Defense Secretary McNamara. It was announced on November 24. Zuckert's cooperation with the investigators stopped at their request to examine his personal TFX files before he could examine them fully himself.[56]

During the spring of 1963, Zuckert was approached several times by examiners from the GAO who wanted additional information for the McClellan Committee on TFX costs. The Air Secretary was gratified that the examiners, one of whom had read the entire fourth evaluation report, affirmed that the selection in favor of General Dynamics was a sound one.[57]

Formal hearings on the TFX began on February 26, 1963, and were concluded on August 7. More than ninety witnesses representing all facets of the weapon systems development community and the DOD testified before Senator

**General William F. McKee, USAF
Vice Chief of Staff from July 1962
through July 1964.**

McClellan's subcommittee. Among DOD notables were Secretary of Defense McNamara, Secretary of the Navy Fred Korth, Secretary of the Air Force Zuckert, and Director of Defense, Research, and Engineering Harold Brown. McNamara was unyielding on his selection of General Dynamics. In his view, the company promised higher dependability and lower costs.

LeMay based his support for Boeing primarily on operational advantages. He believed that the company was more knowledgeable of what the Air Force required in this case than General Dynamics and that its aircraft would perform better on unprepared airfields. He believed firmly that the Air Force's recommendations on the TFX were the most authoritative of all. Like his Vice Chief, General McKee, LeMay was truly stung by Zuckert's rejection of Boeing.[58]

McKee cautioned that the low position of the engine air scoops on General Dynamics' version could lead to high maintenance costs, frequent repairs, and engine failure. Their much higher location on Boeing's version would minimize the ingestion of foreign material and lessen the possibility of engine damage. In general, the Air Force chose the design with the extras. Boeing's use of titanium, lighter than steel, promised better wing performance and a lighter aircraft which would satisfy the Navy. Boeing's use of thrust reversers to slow or stop an aircraft during landing by diverting external exhaust gases forward promised greater braking power than General Dynamics' spoilers and drag chutes.[59]

The Air Secretary got his chance to speak in late July and August. He referred to a memorandum of November 21, 1963, to Secretary McNamara in which he had outlined his reasons for supporting the award of contract to General Dynamics. He had weighed the risks and the costs associated with any

232

system that existed on paper only and decided that Boeing's proposal left him more doubtful than General Dynamics'. It contained many technical innovations that were, in his opinion, questionable. One, which located the engine air scoops atop the fuselage, apparently lessened the danger of damage from foreign objects and reduced the likelihood of engine flameouts from missile exhaust ingestion. However, it imposed a serious performance limitation during supersonic flight. Tests revealed that the air scoops' position caused an airflow distortion that exceeded engine specifications and decreased stability and control.*[60]

Another innovation involved the use of titanium for the wings instead of standard materials. Zuckert acknowledged that titanium certainly reduced aircraft weight. Any problems occurring because of it, however, would, according to the technical team, necessitate the substitution of materials and the redesign of a heavier aircraft and would impede program progress, create delays, and greatly increase costs. General Dynamics' proposal did not call for the use of titanium.

Yet another Boeing innovation involved the placement of the thrust reversers near the horizontal and vertical control surfaces. Zuckert consulted with Joseph Charyk, his under secretary, who informed him that this adaptation might be one more cause of instability. The Air Secretary cited expressions of extreme caution contained in the fourth evaluation report from some Air Force engineers about the adaptation. They had faulted Boeing for not projecting sufficient flight time within which to test and assess the adaptation and for not providing a backup system if it proved unworkable. General Dynamics had incorporated conventional speed brakes that had been tested and proven.[61] Air Force leaders, however, again argued that Boeing's thrust reversers, although untried on combat aircraft, would impart greater braking power than General Dynamics' spoilers and drag chutes.

Zuckert next turned to the principle of commonality to keep changes in the TFX required by the Air Force's and Navy's tactical missions to a minimum. From the start, both services had opposed the TFX but were forced by McNamara to accept it. In arriving at an acceptable aircraft, they had made real concessions, although General LeMay declared repeatedly that an aircraft designed specifically for the Air Force would have performed better than either Boeing's or General Dynamics'. The fourth evaluation report convinced Zuckert that General Dynamics' design had come closer to meeting the requirements of both services.

In justifying his approval of General Dynamics' approach, the Air Secretary pointed to cost as the final determinant. Boeing's thrust reversers alone cost $400 million, far more than General Dynamics' conventional deceleration devices.

---

* This actually happened to General Dynamics' version of the TFX: it required redesign and the installation of splitter plates to direct the flow of air into the jet engine. Without them, air flowed unevenly at high speeds, and the engine stalled.

Zuckert maintained that until the technical problems in applying the reversers to tactical and supersonic aircraft were solved, there could be no accurate estimate of cost. For Zuckert, Boeing's expensive extras, lower technical rating, and greater development risk gave Boeing's offering the "significantly higher inherent cost." Zuckert discussed the cost evaluations with his advisers, whose views coincided with his own. Charyk was amazed by Boeing's estimates which he believed were particularly understated. Assistant Secretary of the Air Force (Financial Management) Neil Harlan warned that costs could fluctuate markedly in a program as large as the TFX. Others on Zuckert's staff calculated that Boeing had based its estimates on those of its bombers, heavy transports, and Bomarc missiles. Its manufacturing and tooling estimates were low. Compared with "actual performance in the fighter industry, its costs were unrealistic."[62] The Air Force insisted on Boeing's proposal despite the cost.

Zuckert concluded his testimony on August 21, 1963, by stating that in the absence of a profound qualitative difference between the two proposals, he came to prefer General Dynamics' because of its reliance on proven technology and established processes to keep development risks low, because of its recommendation of the use of conventional materials, and because of its more credible assurance of on-time delivery to the operational forces.[63]

The Air Secretary also created controversy by admitting that before Pentagon officials, both military and civilian, read the fourth evaluation report, the TFX contract decision was made and revealed to President Kennedy. The report gave an edge in operational superiority to Boeing, but awarded General Dynamics a higher total score. Zuckert conceded that he and Navy Secretary Korth sent a memorandum to McNamara on November 13, 1962, one day before they received the final report, notifying him of their tentative choice of General Dynamics. The fourth evaluation report merely confirmed their views. The features that the Air Force praised for providing extra performance were those features that the civilians criticized for raising risks and costs.

The investigation continued for some time, and by October 1964, any controversy had subsided since the subcommittee had taken longer to investigate the contractor than the contractor had taken to build the aircraft. Zuckert, in spite of the decision, credited LeMay with mobilizing the Air Staff to aid him with his testimony. LeMay had behaved like a good soldier. Zuckert was confident that LeMay had realized the importance to the Air Force as an organization of his standing behind the Air Secretary. To LeMay, a rift between the Air Staff and Zuckert had been formed. He remained convinced that Zuckert had been influenced by McNamara. The TFX decision probably wiped out any hope among military leaders that the service secretaries could recapture control of their own departments, for in LeMay's mind at least, it was the Secretary of Defense who was in charge.[64]

Skybolt

The cancellation of the Skybolt missile program in December 1962 found the Air Secretary and the Air Staff allied as they had been during the B-70 debate against the Secretary of Defense and the administration. The Air Force wanted to be able, by mating a ballistic missile and a B-52, to strike potential targets 1,500 miles away. Just when it seemed that some of the program's many daunting technical problems would be solved, McNamara canceled it.[65] Zuckert later admitted that while Skybolt's developer, the Douglas Aircraft Company, did a "lousy job," the program itself was unusual and posed a truly difficult challenge.

The missile was supposed to be the Air Force's answer to the Navy's Polaris. As an air-to-ground missile with a range in excess of 1,000 miles, it would be launched outside enemy territory, safe from attack. It was also intended to help prolong the life of the bomber fleet. The British were impressed by the idea behind the program and sought to mate a missile with a Vulcan bomber in lieu of developing their own expensive system. McNamara, with President Kennedy's blessing, decided to cancel the program with little regard to political implications. He was more concerned with technical problems and rising costs. What were the Americans going to give the British to replace the Skybolt? The British press picked up the issue and accused the Americans of betrayal. A British politician called it "the greatest double cross since the Last Supper."[66]

To quiet the storm, President Kennedy, Secretary McNamara, and British Prime Minister Harold Macmillan met at Nassau in the Bahamas for four days in December where they agreed that the British would receive the Polaris missile as compensation for the loss of the Skybolt missile but would build their own submarines and warheads. However, complications developed during deliberations when the Air Force held its sixth Skybolt test and declared it a success. While Kennedy and McNamara were busy convincing the British otherwise, the Air Force was demonstrating that the Skybolt could work.

Zuckert had held a staff meeting that month just before leaving for a trip to Japan and asked General Thomas P. Gerrity, Deputy Chief of Staff for Systems and Logistics, about the chances for success of the upcoming Skybolt test. General Gerrity had assured Zuckert that he was 97 percent certain of success in reaching a target 1,500 miles away. Zuckert then asked McNamara, prior to the meeting in Nassau, whether he wanted to cancel the test since he had already moved to cancel the program. McNamara muttered complaints about the "God damned Air Force," but did not cancel the test.[67]

The Air Force's announcement angered President Kennedy and brought to the surface the recurring debate over who should control DOD news. Kennedy had spent a good deal of his time at Nassau attempting to convince Macmillan that there were too many technical difficulties to warrant further development of the Skybolt. McNamara probably wished that the OSD had

The experimental Skybolt air-to-surface missile mounted under the wing of a B-52. The Skybolt program, which married bomber and missile, was beset by technical difficulties and was ultimately cancelled.

President John F. Kennedy and British Prime Minister Harold Macmillan confer over the Skybolt missile program, Nassau, December 1962.

demonstrated tighter control over its public relations function. On December 22, the Air Force reported that the Skybolt had impacted in a target area hundreds of miles downrange. However, hitting the target was not a test objective. The Air Force wanted to check loading, launching, firing, staging, and guidance. The Assistant Secretary of Defense for Public Affairs Arthur Sylvester took issue with the Air Force's presentation of the tests to the public and reported on December 28 that the Skybolt had no re-entry nose cone and had actually burned up in the air. A Defense Department spokesman maintained that all the Air Force could really conclude was that "if it had been fired, if it had had a nose cone, and if there had been a lot of other things on it, then maybe it would have landed some place."[68] Sylvester confronted the Air Force, asserting that he had understood that the Air Force had agreed to clear all Skybolt information through his office. Air Force officials declared that no special information clearance was required for that particular test. Both Under Air Force Secretary Charyk and Deputy Defense Secretary Gilpatric had considered canceling or postponing the test because of the Nassau meeting but did not do so. The press release was poorly timed and did not endear the Air Force to McNamara and the President, both of whom had been acutely embarrassed.[69]

Project Forecast

One idea of Secretary Zuckert's that was positively received by both the OSD and the Air Force was Project Forecast. This study, initiated in March 1963, was prompted by Zuckert's observation that the Air Force ought to look at the technologies that would bear on future military operations. Uninterested in a "party line" product, he ordered that the study present a reasonable set of assumptions regarding, specifically, threats, constraints, and arms control and a justification based on those assumptions of the Air Force's projected requirements for the 1970s. He was concerned particularly with weapon systems. After consulting with General LeMay, Zuckert appointed General Bernard A. Schriever, Commander, Air Force Systems Command, to lead the study, which was completed during the fall of 1963.

The Chief of Staff was generally supportive of the study's focus, but the Secretary of Defense had reservations, preferring a broader look at proposals for the entire DOD. He had more than a few suggestions. He was concerned about the DOD's ability to locate and destroy enemy covert communications nets (intelligence and spying techniques) and wanted to know if any new techniques in counterinsurgency would be explored. He hoped that the study would project what would be needed to transport specialists to remote sites, equipped and ready for action. McNamara also wanted to know how to build airfields more quickly. Most of his interests were included in the various technology panels represented in the final report which, when completed in the fall of 1963, was very carefully distributed. Zuckert was proud of Project Forecast and called it the most valuable "conceptual thing" that he had contributed as Secretary of the Air Force.[70]

Project Forecast recommended that the Air Force emphasize revolutionary technological advances, specifically new propulsion systems that would help make the VTOL (Vertical Take Off and Landing) possible. The project also recommended that the variable wing concept, said to enable a plane to operate effortlessly at various speeds and altitudes, be studied. New, improved air-to-surface missiles and better operating ICBM guidance systems were other possible products of future scientific breakthroughs that merited close attention. Large cargo logistic aircraft and VTOL strike reconnaissance aircraft, manned orbital laboratories, reusable space landing vehicles, and hypersonic aircraft were other systems that Project Forecast predicted could be operational between 1970 and 1975. Many of these ideas would be realized in the following decades, and Project Forecast itself would become a model for other future-oriented studies.

Final Years

By the end of his tenure, Eugene Zuckert was still concerned with overall OSAF-Air Staff functions. He was pleased with his permanent staff and with his own appointees. All, he believed, were proficient and made a good team. But he acknowledged that no one could ever be entirely satisfied with the management of an organization as huge and complex as the Air Force. The curse of bigness denied many problems attention at the highest organizational levels. The increase in OSD actions requiring Air Force study and response had caused the OSAF to become fixated on details. He felt it was the responsibility of the Air Staff to prepare preliminary background and detailed objective analysis for the OSD. Secretary Zuckert certainly recognized that the OSAF needed to be informed, but he also wished that the OSAF could concentrate on more significant Air Force issues, such as the B-70 and the TFX. He thus urged that Under Secretary Brockway McMillan and Assistant Secretaries Leonard Marks, Jr. (Financial Management), Alexander H. Flax (Research and Development), and Robert H. Charles (Installations and Logistics), review both organization and functions to allow the OSAF more time for matters of importance to the Air Force.[71]

Zuckert anticipated an increase in reports on growing U.S. Air Force activity in southeast Asia. He had appeared before Congress many times during 1964 to answer specific questions about why the Air Force's newest aircraft were not yet being sent into Vietnam. He wanted to accommodate Congress but was hampered, he believed, by a lack of adequate combat reporting from the field. His concern for up-to-date, accurate reporting was not new. It went back to his World War II experience in statistical analysis. Problems associated with reporting from Vietnam had intensified with the increased tempo of operations there, and he feared that the Air Force had not at that time overcome all of them. He strongly suggested that the acquisition by the Air Staff of the latest information and its presentation in the form of detailed analyses by the Chief of Staff to Congress become the most immediate, highest priority objective.*[72]

Zuckert also took an interest in logistical planning for the heightening Vietnam conflict. He wanted logistics to stay ahead of operational requirements. He informed General LeMay that he would take a personal interest in any logistical problems relative to Southeast Asia. It was important to Secretary Zuckert to review constantly why critical ordnance and equipment were required. In 1965 he appointed an ad hoc committee of experienced logisticians to advise him of potential problem areas. Always cautious of his relationship with the Air Staff, the Air Secretary wanted to avoid duplicating or interfering with any similar activity that the Chief of Staff might have already begun. Zuckert's primary purpose was to prevent the Air Force from being caught unprepared.[73]

What served as Zuckert's ballast against the tide of many disappointments was his sense of humor. He maintained that it was possible to have fun in the job, and he believed that he would have "gone crazy" without some light moments in such activities as the "Pinky Thompson Award" and the "Leany Meany Program." The Air Secretary believed that staff members were getting too fat, so he established the "Leany Meany Program" (which was published in the *Wall Street Journal),* whereby staffers would weigh in once a week. Those who had not lost weight or had added weight had to pay a fine, which went to charity. Brig. Gen. Brian S. Gunderson, Zuckert's executive officer, who kept track of staff poundage, recalled that he heard all types of excuses which he secretly recorded. When the Air Secretary terminated the program, he held a party. The tapes were played to the amusement of the entire gathering.

Louis S. Thompson had worked for former Secretary of the Air Force Dudley Sharp as Special Assistant for Manpower, Personnel and Reserve Forces. Thompson was known for traveling a great deal on the job. When one of Zuckert's staff associates would travel too much, the staff would give out the "Pinky Thompson Award." Though regarded with contempt by Zuckert's "intellectual friends on the third floor" (OSD), these frivolities helped morale considerably within the OSAF and the Air Staff.[74]

By the end of 1964, Zuckert believed that he had carved out a significant role for the Secretary of the Air Force. Planning strategy and determining force levels had become centralized within the OSD and the JCS. He no longer spoke of the service secretary's dual role as agent to the President and civilian spokesman of

---

* As the war in Vietnam progressed, various statistical summaries were maintained by the Air Force, including a USAF Management Summary of Southeast Asia, and an HQ/PACAF Summary of Air Operations in Southeast Asia.

his department. He now had to consider the Secretary of Defense and the chain of command. Defense budgeting was centralized within the DOD. Joint and unified combat commands reported to the Secretary of Defense through the JCS with a single commander in the field controlling aerospace, land, and sea elements.

McNamara's centralization left no doubt that the authority of the military departments and their secretaries had been diminished over the past seventeen years. The Air Secretary was no longer responsible for combat operations. This must have become clear during the Bay of Pigs fiasco of April 1961—an unsuccessful invasion of Cuba by anti-Castro forces from the United States that were supported by U.S. naval forces—and the Cuban missile crisis of October 1962 when President Kennedy faced down Premier Nikita Khrushchev by holding firm for the removal of Soviet missiles from Cuba. In both instances Zuckert was kept out of policy formulation but remained involved in logistical duties and calling up the reserves. While he still saw his role as spokesman for the Air Force, he felt that his primary duty was to create combat-ready forces for the unified commanders. This task allowed for creativity, independent thinking, and decision making, not only in operations, but also in logistics and research and development. Although Zuckert believed that centralization had benefited planning, budgeting, and operational command, he would not support a single service. He felt that the objectives of centralized planning and operational control as well as a balance of forces to meet any threat had been achieved without destroying the identities of the three military departments. To Zuckert, the service secretaries were much like the heads of Chevrolet, Pontiac, and Oldsmobile who were managers within the General Motors Corporation. The service secretaries answered to the Secretary of Defense in much the same way corporate managers answered to corporate chiefs.[75]

Zuckert found several reasons to continue supporting separate departments of the Army, Navy, and Air Force, and during 1964 and 1965, he mentioned them frequently. Military professionals were necessary to manage large and instantly ready combat forces and to man complicated weapon systems.* Competition between the services engendered new ideas and forced the critical examination of methods. Just as it would be unwise to merge Ford, Chrysler, and General Motors to build a better automobile, the Air Secretary maintained that it would not be wise to merge the military departments to produce better military thought and performance. There were some functions such as military training, administration, logistics support, and research and development that could be managed better by each military department in terms of the type of warfare on which it focused. He further believed that each of the three services created and maintained a high esprit de corps when it existed as an identifiable

---

* Zuckert realized that each service had complicated weapon systems, and he felt that it would have been difficult for a single service to manage them all.

group. The spirit of unity was enhanced by tradition, pride in one's organization, and by a distinctive uniform.[76]

Shortly after resigning as Secretary of the Air Force on September 30, 1965, Zuckert stressed that the DOD was simply too large to be managed efficiently from one central point. He felt that he had done all he could do, and he was tired. He was convinced that management responsibility had to be parceled out to the service secretaries. To him, the service secretaries had a key role to perform. He opposed creating Under Secretaries of Defense for the Army, Navy, and Air Force (which had been suggested by various unification studies, including the 1960 Symington Committee). Downgrading the service secretaries upset their balancing function as advisers to the Secretary of Defense and as "advocates of service interests" at the OSD level. The service secretaries, in Zuckert's opinion, seemed to bring an objectivity to debate at the OSD level that the Chiefs of Staff did not.*[77] If the service secretaries were in future to be appointed from among the ranks of first-rate candidates, their status had to be maintained, if not raised.

Zuckert maintained that the service secretaries had expert managerial roles to accomplish in personnel, procurement, logistics, training, and research and development. In those areas the job of the service secretary would not overlap that of the Secretary of Defense.[78] Zuckert stated that he sometimes got "pushed around" by decision makers below and above, but his job was nevertheless exciting—sometimes frustrating, sometimes rewarding, but never dull. His responsibility was to weigh resources management in relation to combat readiness, and as a defense manager to evaluate the position of the scientist, mathematician, economist, and analyst.[79] Blame stopped in the Office of the Secretary of the Air Force while credit passed either up or down. Most crises came in three categories—ordinary, secondary, and "colossal." However, he noted that most did not emanate from a momentous event, but rather from "the windblown pop fly, a piece of bad luck, a goof by somebody" followed by the "replication of the principle that when things are bad they especially get worse."[80]

In assessing his own performance, Zuckert complained that he never really had the time to think about the great issues of the day, such as arms control. He felt he would never be considered a great secretary because of this. He did believe, however, that he was the proper man for the job when he held it. He felt that he helped the Air Force adapt from its status as the dominant service of the 1950s to one among three equals in the 1960s. He believed that the Air Force had become more aware of the need for military forces to meet limited war and insurgent threats while maintaining superiority in nuclear deterrent forces. He had seen an increase in the number of operational ICBMs and a doubling of air-

---

* The Chiefs of Staff were too preoccupied with operations since most of their time was devoted to their roles on the JCS.

lift capacity with the introduction of the C-141. Overall, in Zuckert's judgment, the Air Force was better balanced in weapon systems, better equipped, trained, and educated; more flexible, responsive, and secure; more efficiently managed; more willing to question its own concepts.[81]

In 1965 the Air Force was not the service it had been in the 1950s. The Navy's Polaris missile had become a formidable mobile weapon, while the Army was developing its own missiles. Regaining that lost prominence would have been impossible for any Air Secretary serving under McNamara's centralization effort. Zuckert did well to save what he did. He himself was not the Secretary that he wished he could have been. As he sought a role for the Air Secretary he found that he sometimes alienated either the leaders of the Air Staff or the Secretary of Defense. He was like a boxer fighting two opponents—the OSD, and the Air Force, and it was impossible to please all the time. He was a spokesman for the Air Force, but not its champion in the manner of Stuart Symington. Symington dealt with Forrestal almost as an equal. Zuckert dealt with McNamara's entourage of Assistant Secretaries of Defense at times with less than equal status. Symington stayed out of operational matters by choice because of his lack of expertise. Zuckert stayed out of operational and policy matters because the law required him to. Yet he, too, respected the opinions and abilities of his military staff. It was the new layer of authority within the OSD that showed the least respect for the military specialists and the service secretaries. The service secretary had declined from co-chairman of the board under Forrestal to group vice president under McNamara. Zuckert might never have recovered from that shock. He would admit after leaving office that he had exercised more power as an Assistant Secretary of the Air Force in the 1940s than he had as Secretary of the Air Force in the 1960s.

Three pieces of legislation deprived the service secretary of the privilege of confronting the Defense Secretary on equal terms—the 1949 amendments to the National Security Act; Reorganization Plan No. 6 of 1953; and the Defense Reorganization Act of 1958. No Defense Secretary had ever wielded the power of Robert McNamara, who was involved even in foreign policy. Because of his standing with Presidents Kennedy and Johnson, McNamara had more influence than any of his predecessors. To Lt. Gen. Glen W. Martin, who served as Zuckert's military assistant and had known him since Symington's time, he was one of the best, if not the best, Secretary of the Air Force. Zuckert did not receive the recognition he deserved, Martin argued, because he happened to be Secretary of the Air Force under McNamara; and McNamara overshadowed everyone else.[82]

McNamara did not deal amicably with Congress, and he missed an opportunity to gain support for his programs and the administration's national security policies. His disdain for Congress clearly brought to a head the question of who controlled defense affairs, Congress or the Secretary of Defense. McNamara perhaps should have followed Zuckert's example, but he chose to be combative.

He had a knack for frustrating Congress. In April 1964, he irritated Congressman Melvin R. Laird by releasing to the press copies of a letter intended for his receipt. Laird, a ranking member of the Defense Appropriations Committee and chairman of the 1964 Republican Party Platform Committee, was visibly annoyed and led the attack on McNamara during House hearings on the military budget. Laird criticized McNamara for listing dollar amounts in the letter to justify the classification of each weapon system as major. Using that criterion, Laird argued, perhaps "we should classify the war on poverty as a major new weapon system."[83] Laird was so perturbed about the release of the letter that he even considered introducing an amendment to the DOD's appropriations bill forbidding such a practice. Another Republican congressmen, Earl Wilson, who enjoyed attacking McNamara, carried a "grudge chart" with him which detailed alleged wastes in DOD procurement. Wilson would drag the chart with him every day onto the House floor hoping to use it whenever he got a chance to speak on the topic.[84]

In 1965 Congressman F. Edward Hebert, a Democrat and one-time New Orleans newspaper editor, who headed the House Armed Services Subcommittee on Reserve Forces, had mobilized for what he called a showdown with McNamara. At issue was McNamara's failure to consult with Congress on the legality of proposed decisions. Hebert claimed that Pentagon press agents had built up McNamara as a modern St. George killing the dragon of waste. In reality, Hebert maintained, McNamara was Merlin the magician, "befuddling the people with economic legerdemain taken from computer machines."[85] He acknowledged that the Defense Secretary while brilliant, reflected little realization of the fact that the DOD was "a creature of Congress" rather than the other way around. "This is a government of law not of men," the Congressman cautioned, and the threat posed by McNamara and his growing power is "one man, one button, one missile . . . Don't worry about the man in uniform," Hebert added, "worry about the man in mufti."[86]

Zuckert dealt with Congress, on the other hand, to the benefit of the Air Force and earned its respect. Despite differences over the TFX, General LeMay and his staff generally appreciated what Zuckert had done for the Air Force on the Hill. At the time of his retirement from office, many congressmen testified to the Air Secretary's accomplishments. Democratic Senator Mike Mansfield of Montana, noting that Zuckert would be greatly missed, credited the high state of combat readiness and strength of the U.S. Air Force to Zuckert's effective leadership over four and one-half years. Mansfield added that he was reassured to know that while Secretary Zuckert successfully stressed cost control and improved efficiency, he had not lost sight of the object of full military strength. Mansfield also praised Zuckert's never-failing appreciation of the importance of people.[87] President Johnson also praised Zuckert for his years of public service. "Your personal concern for our men and women in uniform," Johnson said, "played an important role in improving the housing, pay, promotion and medical care of Air

Force personnel."[88] Zuckert himself felt privileged to have witnessed first-hand the tremendous advances that had been made in missiles, aircraft, and space technology. He attributed that significant progress to the professionalism of Air Force personnel.[90] True to form at the end, he took the opportunity to distribute the plaudits.

Chapter 10

Conclusion

The history of the Office of the Secretary of the Air Force (OSAF) from 1947 to 1965 reveals a decline in the authority and influence of the OSAF within the National Military Establishment (NME) and, subsequently, the Department of Defense (DOD). The effect of weapons technology—in the wake of the nuclear age, the drive by the DOD to control when and how new weapons would be used was intense—as well as three pieces of legislation accelerated the diminishment of the influence of the service secretaries: the 1949 amendments to the National Security Act of 1947, Reorganization Plan No. 6 of June 30 1953, and the Defense Reorganization Act of 1958. The 1949 legislation increased the authority of the Secretary of Defense and created a Deputy Secretary of Defense and three Assistant Secretaries of Defense. The service secretaries lost their seats on the National Security Council and thus their executive branch status. The Secretary of Defense now spoke for all three services at the National Security Council and gained more authority over the budget by the creation of a Department of Defense Comptroller.

As part of his policy to institute clearer lines of authority within the DOD and to foster better service cooperation and greater civilian control, President Eisenhower supported Reorganization Plan No. 6. This plan added six additional Assistant Secretaries of Defense and a General Counsel to the Office of the Secretary of Defense (OSD). It firmly established civilian control with a line of authority from the President to the Secretary of Defense, creating further layers of authority between the service secretaries and the Secretary of Defense. The 1953 Plan also reduced service autonomy by eliminating various investigative boards and agencies of which representatives of the armed services had been members. The 1958 Reorganization Act removed the service secretaries from the chain of command with regard to unified and specified commands and authorized the Assistant Secretaries of Defense—who were reduced to seven—to issue non-operational orders through the service secretaries by written authority of the Secretary of Defense. The 1958 act placed the service secretaries in a subordinate position within the OSD.

An assessment of the tenures of the secretaries of the Air Force—from Symington's (September 1947–April 1950) to Zuckert's (January 1961–September 1965), including Robert A. Lovett's wartime service (April 1941–December 1945) and Symington's post-war term (February 1946–September 1947) as Assistant

Secretary of War for Air—reveals several common areas. One concerns the relationship of the Air Secretary to the Chief of Staff of the Air Force and the Air Staff and, paralleling that, the relationship between the OSAF and the Air Staff. There is no doubt that the personality of each Air Secretary played an important part in interactions between the OSAF and the Air Staff.

Robert A. Lovett worked extremely closely with Secretary of War Henry L. Stimson, Army Chief of Staff General George C. Marshall, and Commander of the Army Air Forces (AAF) General Henry H. Arnold. He operated with a very small staff. Because he was well liked and respected, he commanded the confidence of military and political leaders. He was often involved in discussions of major wartime policy decisions at the highest level. He had a tremendous amount of influence despite his status as an "Assistant" Secretary of War for Air. Lovett was more of a probing intellectual than his successor, W. Stuart Symington, and would often generate huge amounts of paperwork in pursuit of facts. Stuart Symington was also a thinker, but he acted more quickly than Lovett. One general officer who had served both Symington and Lovett observed that Lovett was a pitcher always winding up and never throwing, whereas Symington was throwing all the time in all directions. Lovett had to write many point papers to influence key decision makers, whereas Symington had much more authority vested in his office.

When he became the first Secretary of the Air Force, Stuart Symington continued to be the forceful and respected leader within the National Military Establishment (NME) that he had been as Assistant Secretary of War for Air. He was an exceptionally attractive leader, charming and gifted with an easy congeniality and a keen perception of people. He deferred to the military leaders in operational matters—specifically, his successive chiefs of staff, Generals Carl A. Spaatz and Hoyt S. Vandenberg—and devoted himself primarily to promoting the goals of the Air Force on Capitol Hill. Symington had problems with the first Secretary of Defense, James V. Forrestal. Their views often diverged over budgetary matters and the manner in which Symington should present such subjects before Congress. Forrestal wanted the Air Secretary to stand with the administration, but Symington felt that he should represent the needs of the Air Force regardless of Forrestal and President Truman. The Air Force respected Symington for benefitting it during its infancy. He was interested in the most minute subjects within the OSAF. His political astuteness allowed him to help the Air Force present a positive image to Congress, the administration, and the public. He emphasized his Management Control through Cost Control program to prove that the Air Force, although young, was a serious, responsible organization, although program specifics were never clear even to its formulators.

Symington's greatest challenges came when he attempted to thwart the Navy's charges of corruption against the Air Force and himself over the B-36 and when he attempted to convince the administration and Congress of the need for a 70-group Air Force. Disappointed by not having achieved a larger Air

Force, he resigned his office because he did not want to preside over a service he believed was funded too poorly to fulfill its missions. His forceful nature and sometimes stubborn stances would not be duplicated by any succeeding Air Secretary, partially because of personality, but mostly because the authority of the position would gradually decline. Stuart Symington set the precedent for civilian leadership of the armed services for future Air Secretaries in the DOD until the era of Defense Secretary Robert S. McNamara.

Thomas K. Finletter was not the leader that his predecessor was. Whereas Symington was more open to discussion and the solutions of others, Finletter was less disposed to delegate. His lack of rapport with military leaders was colored by his difficult relationship with the Chief of Staff, General Vandenberg. Finletter operated in a closed circle; not even his assistant secretaries really knew what he was thinking or wanted. He appeared not to be interested in the day-to-day operations and details of the Air Force—he was not, for instance, interested in enlisted personnel and their problems. His attentions were focused on what he considered to be larger issues such as the North Atlantic Treaty Organization (NATO), the uses of nuclear weapons, and massive retaliation. If he was politically motivated it was not for public office but for appointed office. He did not have the personality to be a successful politician. During Finletter's tenure the Air Force gained more than twice the number of wings that it had under Symington, but this was due more to congressional reaction to the Korean War than to any effort on the part of the Air Secretary. Like Symington, he primarily presented the Air Force's case before Congress. The seeds of any breakdown in relations between the OSAF and the Air Staff were planted by Finletter and were due more to his nature and manner of administering than to specific issues.

Before Finletter's term ended, newly elected President Dwight D. Eisenhower initiated some changes within the DOD;* and in June 1953, Reorganization Plan No. 6 added six new Assistant Secretaries of Defense who added new layers of authority between the service secretaries and the Secretary of Defense. The new assistant secretaries also complicated communications between the OSAF and the Air Staff by dealing directly with the Air Staff and bypassing the OSAF.

Harold E. Talbott became Eisenhower's first Air Secretary. He was a forceful businessman who at times reacted before deliberating. For the most part, he got along well with the military establishment and he sought its advice on many issues. He was particularly interested in the concerns of the man and woman in uniform. Through his efforts, all ranks were given better housing and pay raises. He did much to solve one of the Air Force's major problems at the time—its inability to attract and retain competent personnel. Talbott was forced to resign

---

* The National Military Establishment became the Department of Defense as part of the August 10, 1949, amendments to the National Security Act.

after holding office for two and one-half years because he used his position as Air Secretary to gain a business advantage for a friend. Had it not been an election year he might well have escaped with a verbal chastisement from the President instead of a dismissal. His firing did not hasten the decline of the OSAF, but his reputation as an Air Force Secretary and as a public servant was tarnished.

Talbott's successor, Donald A. Quarles, was a scientist who had been the Assistant Secretary of Defense for Research and Development. He came to office with preconceived ideas about which research and development projects should be undertaken and how research and development funding should be appropriated. Although the Air Force respected him, it disliked his probing too deeply into activities that they regarded as theirs rather than his. Perhaps feeling the Air Force's animosity, Quarles ordered a study on the relationship between his office and the Air Staff which revealed that communication between them was confused and getting worse because of the six new Assistant Secretaries of Defense. Quarles was not in office long enough to institute many changes, and he moved up in April 1957 to become Deputy Secretary of Defense, leaving former Under Secretary of the Air Force, James H. Douglas, Jr. as his successor.

Douglas, a lawyer, helped to improve communication between the Air Staff and OSAF. His World War II experiences with the AAF and his four-year service as Under Secretary of the Air Force gave him an understanding of the way the Air Staff and the OSAF coordinated their activities. Like Talbott, Douglas was interested in the lower echelons of the Air Force. In 1957 Douglas had to endure cuts in his military budgets, but the launch of Sputnik by the Soviet Union in the autumn of 1957 pressured the opponents of greater spending into rethinking their position and opening congressional coffers. The United States could no longer bask in the belief that it led the world in research and development. Douglas's job, therefore, was made easier, although the 1958 Reorganization Act further lessened his authority. The Assistant Secretaries of Defense could, under the act, issue orders to the service secretaries with the Secretary of Defense's approval. The 1958 act increased the distance and decreased direct communications between the service secretaries and the Secretary of Defense, but the full use of its authority was not pursued by either Secretary of Defense McElroy or Secretary of Defense Gates, perhaps because of the brevity of their tenures. With Quarles's sudden death in April 1959, Douglas moved up to become Deputy Secretary of Defense. He was replaced by Dudley C. Sharp, who had served with him in the OSAF as Assistant Secretary of the Air Force (Materiel), and as Under Secretary of the Air Force. Sharp freely admitted that he was a lame duck and continued the policies of Douglas.

The first Secretary of Defense to take full advantage of the new powers granted by the Defense Reorganization Act of 1958 was Robert S. McNamara. He sought to centralize the DOD to better control it. As part of his consolidation effort, he created two new defense agencies—the Defense Intelligence Agency and the Defense Logistics Agency. Eugene M. Zuckert, former Assistant Secretary of the Air Force for both Secretaries Symington and Finletter, became McNamara's new Secretary of the Air Force. Zuckert was shocked by the rigid controls that the OSD had imposed on the military departments. Although he would sometimes speak of McNamara positively, calling him the "only real Secretary of Defense," Zuckert objected to the DOD's oppressive control system. He had enjoyed more power as an Assistant Secretary of the Air Force under Symington than as Secretary of the Air Force under McNamara. Zuckert thought briefly about resigning but felt he could help the Air Force reexamine its place and adjust to its less dominant role. Zuckert supported McNamara and opposed the Air Force on the question of the TFX, but he supported the Air Force against McNamara on the question of the B-70. Despite his differences with the Air Force over the TFX, Zuckert was generally respected by the Air Force for his knowledge of and dedication to the service's programs.

Zuckert was the only Air Secretary who possessed personal insight into how the OSAF had evolved since 1947. Only he could ascertain from actual experience the degree to which the authority of the service secretaries had declined since Symington. He could not stand up to McNamara the way Symington had stood up to Forrestal. In fact, Zuckert could rarely get near the Secretary of Defense. The additional Assistant Secretaries of Defense represented a formidable barrier. McNamara could issue memos and demand answers from the service secretaries and their staffs while making policy by himself. Zuckert believed that he should help prepare the Air Force for what would become the unified and specified commands. Symington chose to stay out of operational matters; Zuckert had no such luxury. McNamara usually got his way. He succeeded in having the B-70 cancelled against the will of the Air Force and its Air Secretary; and he pushed the TFX "down the throats" of the Air Force and the Navy—although not without the Air Secretary's support, which alienated the Air Force. Zuckert saw his position more clearly than others. The service secretaries had become like the vice presidents of large corporations. Part of Zuckert's uniqueness as Secretary of the Air Force was that he represented a link between what the OSAF had been and what it would become.

The press played a significant role in the conduct of all of the Air Secretaries. Barton Leach, Harvard Business School professor and long-time Air Force consultant, maintained that the working press represented the service secretaries' access to the taxpayer and should thus be handled carefully. A favorable press was critical to the Air Force. Robert A. Lovett had particularly good contacts in the field and he used them constantly for the benefit of the AAF. A consistent point of friction between the press and the service secretaries was security. The press always feared being cut off from information because of what it regarded as unnecessary classification—for political expediency rather than for national security.

On the other hand, Symington was enraged by the release of information about the X-1 rocket plane's breaking of the sound barrier. He cautioned the editor of *Aviation Week*, the journal that published the news. Instead of bringing charges, the Air Secretary arranged a luncheon with the editor at which the two discussed the necessity of keeping such leaks classified in future. Symington, who understood the power of the press, hired a specialist, Stephen F. Leo, as Director of Information. Leo instituted a workable arrangement with the press. If the Air Force did not want information immediately released, then he would ask the press to withhold it from publication until a later date.

During Finletter's tenure, the press was preoccupied with the Korean War. Always gracious to journalists, Finletter appeared several times on the television program, "Meet the Press." The press most likely knew of the breach in relations between the Air Secretary and his Chief of Staff as well as Finletter's closed-door management style, but did not feel that they were worth publicizing. Like Symington, Finletter went out of his way to set straight reporters whom he felt had expressed inaccuracies in print. He was wise enough to see that the "fear of flying" issue, raised by General LeMay, was also a public relations issue. He disagreed with LeMay, who wanted to punish those air crews who had refused to fly in Korea. Finletter believed that harshness would bring unwelcome attention to the Air Force. He also handled the news of substandard living conditions at Lackland Air Force Base in Texas very skillfully.

When Harold Talbott used official stationery to aid a friend in securing a job at companies with Air Force contracts, the press picked up the story, not so much to damage Talbott as to embarrass President Eisenhower, who was running for reelection. Nevertheless, because of his misuse of office, Talbott's resignation was unavoidable and unfortunate for someone who had done so much for Air Force personnel. He should have known, however, that he could not do many of the things in public office that he had done in private enterprise; and perhaps he should have had a more realistic view of the power of the press.

Secretary Quarles had made his mark as Assistant Secretary of Defense for Research and Development. The press respected his scientific expertise, and he provided them with a great deal of material. The deteriorating relationship between the Air Staff and the OSAF remained largely unnoticed by the press while Quarles was Air Secretary. Perhaps internal rumblings were not loud enough or dramatic enough or important enough to report. Overall, Quarles with his sometimes grim bearing did not hurt the Air Force's relations with the press, perhaps because he did not purposely withhold information.

James Douglas's staff had difficulties over the release of critical information. Douglas tried, like the other Air Secretaries, to walk a fine line between the release of critical information and its manipulation. Generally, he kept a low profile and did not allow many interviews. Like Symington during the B–36 hearings, Douglas sought to tighten security around military news.

Zuckert tended to indulge and, in general, had excellent relations with, the press. Periodically, he would become involved in writing a rebuttal to a journal or newspaper in an effort to correct some factual error. He respected the way

Symington had handled the press and sought to be friendly. In general, the Air Secretaries and their staffs sought to make an ally of the press by sharing news, then asking its cooperation when necessary. But again, individual personalities played a role. Symington could charm the press in a way that Finletter could not. Talbott was not careful, Quarles was too direct. While Douglas was reticent, Zuckert was ebullient. It was easy for the press to exploit these personality differences.

The Air Secretaries' ability to select competent subordinates to ensure continuity after they had departed office, as well as their ability to deal with Congress, differed markedly. Both Symington and Finletter felt that they should express the military point of view because they realized that military careerists were restricted by Congress from speaking freely in public. Both Symington and Finletter selected as under secretaries men who were not of their own political party, such as Arthur S. Barrows and John L. McCone. This gave the Air Secretaries leverage in Congress when they attempted to promote certain legislation. Neither Democrats nor Republicans felt that they were the outside party when dealing with the Air Force under Symington and Finletter. Symington needed the support of both political parties during the B-36 hearings, and during Finletter's tenure, the 143-wing Air Force program was co-sponsored by Republican Senator Henry Cabot Lodge and Democratic Congressman Carl Vinson.

Talbott was not as shrewd when dealing with Congress. He was often blunt and disliked both the Congress's and the press's probing methods. This left him with little support when the press seized the news that he had used his position improperly. As his under secretary, Talbott chose Douglas, a lawyer from the midwest who knew and was liked by the Air Force. He represented for them a welcome contrast to the gruff Talbott and his successor, the often meddlesome Donald A. Quarles. Douglas would later encourage Dudley Sharp, who had resigned as Assistant Secretary of the Air Force (Materiel), to return as his under secretary, thereby providing some continuity within the OSAF. This move insured that during the last year of Eisenhower's administration the Air Force had an experienced civilian at the helm.

Symington, Finletter, Douglas, and Zuckert with excellent staff appointments excelled at keeping continuity of civilian leadership between administrations. They all maintained good relations with Congress, the press, and the military services. Each Air Secretary was unique. Some more than others had to cope with less power conferred upon their office; their stewardship was a product of the issues, individuals, and the character of the office at any particular time.

Could Symington and Finletter have survived Secretary of Defense McNamara, or could Zuckert and Douglas have stood up to Secretary of Defense Forrestal the way Symington had? Of all the Air Secretaries, only Symington had political ambitions that ultimately resulted in four terms as senator and a candidacy for the Democratic presidential nomination in 1960. He was of all the Air Secretaries by far the most charismatic leader and the strongest representative of civilian control. Symington was astute enough to stay out of operational matters, and he was not the most technologically knowledgeable of the secretaries. In areas of technology and weapon system acquisition, Donald A. Quarles was superior to the rest. However, Quarles was not the best or the most effective manager; he chose not to leave systems acquisition to the military specialists. Douglas restored better relations with uniformed personnel but the 1958 Reorganization Act removed him and his counterparts in the Army and the Navy from the operational chain of command.

Zuckert had to convince the Air Force that it was no longer the leading service that it had been in the 1950s. At the same time, he helped the Air Force preserve its share of the military budget. Zuckert was deeply involved in acquisition, supporting the Air Staff on the B-70, opposing the Air Staff on the TFX. It can be argued that Zuckert did "more with less" and he did so against the strongest-minded Secretary of Defense since the passage of the National Security Act, Robert McNamara. In spite of a decade of legislation that curtailed the power of the service secretaries, Zuckert managed to preserve and even raise to a degree the prominence of his office by sometimes resisting the powerful McNamara. Like Symington, Zuckert provided the Air Force with a strong model of civilian leadership. He maintained that it took at least eighteen months to learn the job and become effective.

Symington, Douglas, Zuckert, and Sharp brought with them to the OSAF backgrounds that had given them real comprehension of the needs of the Air Force. Dudley Sharp—who had served a total of four years and eight months in the OSAF, but only one year and one month as Air Secretary—did not have time to influence policy. Stuart Symington had served for one year and seven months as Assistant Secretary of War for Air when the Air Force was making the transition from war to peace and in its status from a branch of the U.S. Army to an independent air department. He had gained from that office valuable experience. The National Security Act of 1947 provided him increased stature and power, and he used it extensively.

James Douglas had served for four years and one month as Under Secretary of the Air Force under two controversial air secretaries, Harold Talbott and Donald Quarles. He would serve for two years and seven months as Air Secretary before moving up to the OSD. Douglas brought a calm to the relationship between the OSAF and the Air Staff. His prior experience helped him to recognize the importance of good relations between the two offices.

Eugene Zuckert had six years' experience with the OSAF, including a year and seven months as an assistant to the Assistant Secretary of War for Air. His duties helped him to understand how the status of the Air Secretary had slipped since the time of Symington and Finletter. He stayed longer in office than any other Air Secretary—four years and eight months. He was in some ways as much a help to the Air Force as Symington was, despite his disagreement with the Air Staff over the TFX.

The Air Secretaries from Symington through Zuckert held office through some tumultuous years—from the dawn of the atomic age to the space age. All contributed to helping the Air Force overcome major obstacles and adjust to the policy changes of different administrations. And they all served to uphold the principle of civilian control of the armed services as expressed in the National Security Act of 1947.

Appendices

Appendix 1

Air Secretariat Organizational Charts

Office of the Assistant Secretary of War for Air, 1946

Office of the Secretary of the Air Force, April 1948

Office of the Secretary of the Air Force, November 1951

Office of the Secretary of the Air Force, September 1953

Office of the Secretary of the Air Force, August 1955

Office of the Secretary of the Air Force, July 1957

Office of the Secretary of the Air Force, September 1960

Office of the Secretary of the Air Force, September 1963

(over)

Office of the Assistant Secretary of War for Air

1946

ASSISTANT SECRETARY OF WAR FOR AIR

FUNCTIONS: The Assistant Secretary of War for Air advises and represents the Secretary of War on aviation matters, including supervision of matters pertaining to the Army Air Forces and contacts with other agencies, governmental and private, on policy matters of interest to the War Department.

EXECUTIVE OFFICER

FUNCTIONS: (a) To relieve the Assistant Secretary of War for Air of detail by assuming the responsibility of approving, processing and deciding on matters of routine and minor policy and procedure; to refer matters of major policy and controversial questions to the Assistant Secretary for decision.

(b) To coordinate and expedite the work of the various office components and follow up to insure the efficient accomplishment of the mission and the instructions of the Assistant Secretary; to keep the Assistant Secretary informed as to work status and progress.

(c) To assume additional responsibilities and activities of the Assistant Secretary of War for Air in the absence of the Assistant Secretary as assigned from time to time.

(d) To give general supervision to internal office service activities, including office procedures, personnel, equipment and special assignments; office supplies and facilities; files, records and reports; personnel actions and records; and necessary liaison with other War Department offices and other agencies of the Government in connection with these activities.

RECORDS SECTION

Maintains in such a form as to be readily available a current file of all records and correspondence pertaining to the Office of the Assistant Secretary of War for Air and pertinent current regulations and publications of the War Department and the Army Air Forces as directed.

SPECIAL ASSISTANT TO THE SECRETARY OF WAR

FUNCTIONS: (a) Assists in the performance of the functions of the Office of the Assistant Secretary of War for Air by monitoring all Army Air Force activities falling within the functional assignment of Program Monitoring, Statistical Control Budget & Fiscal Office, and Information Services, as outlined in Army Air Forces Regulations of the 20 Series, including the analysis and processing of all projects and correspondence in connection therewith found appropriate or referred to the Assistant Secretary of War for Air, as necessary to provide the Executive with completed staff work in each instance. Monitors Army Air Forces organization planning activity.

(b) Performance of special assignments as designated by the Assistant Secretary of War for Air or his Executive.

ASSISTANT EXECUTIVE (A)

FUNCTIONS: (a). Assists in the performance of the functions of the Office of the Assistant Secretary of War for Air by monitoring all Army Air Force activities falling within the functional assignment of Assistant Chiefs of Air Staff -1, -3, and -4, and Deputy Chief of Air Staff for Research and Development, as outlined in Army Air Forces Regulations of the 20 Series, including the analysis and processing of all projects and correspondence in connection therewith found appropriate or referred to the Assistant Secretary of War for Air, as necessary to provide the Executive with completed staff work in each instance.

(b) Performance of special assignments as designated by the Assistant Secretary of War for Air or his Executive.

ASSISTANT EXECUTIVE (B)

FUNCTIONS: (a) Assists in the performance of the functions of the Office of the Assistant Secretary of War for Air by monitoring all Army Air Force activities falling within the functional assignment of Assistant Chiefs of Air Staff -2, and -5, as outlined in Army Air Forces Regulations of the 20 Series, including the analysis and processing of all projects and correspondence in connection therewith found appropriate or referred to the Assistant Secretary of War for Air, as necessary to provide the Executive with completed staff work in each instance.

(b) Performance of special assignments as designated by the Assistant Secretary of War for Air or his Executive.

ASSISTANT EXECUTIVE (C)

FUNCTIONS: (a) Assists in the performance of the functions of the Office of the Assistant Secretary of War for Air by monitoring the legal aspects of the activities pertaining to the mission of the Office of the Assistant Secretary of War for Air with special reference to legislation proposed, modification of existing legislation, Army Air Forces contracts, drafting and interpretation of directives, policies and other control documents.

(b) Performance of special assignments as designated by the Assistant Secretary of War for Air or his Executive.

Source: Record Group 107, Records of the Office of the Secretary of War, Files of the Assistant Secretary of War for Air, 020.

Office of the Secretary of the Air Force

April 1948

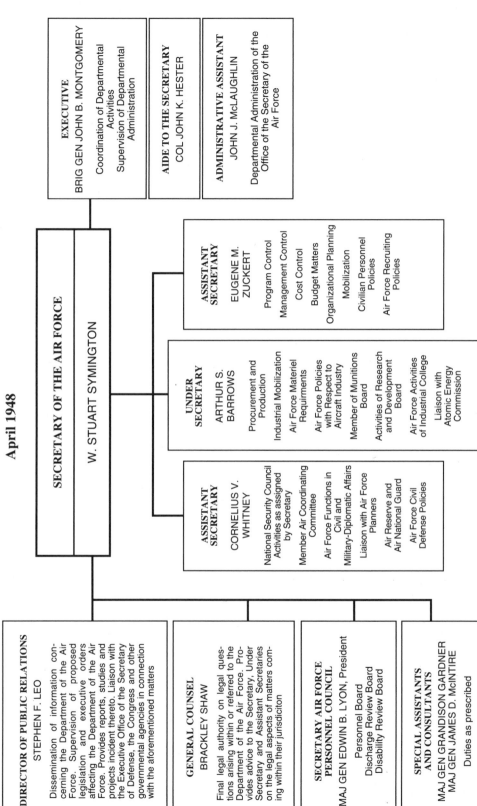

SECRETARY OF THE AIR FORCE

W. STUART SYMINGTON

EXECUTIVE

BRIG GEN JOHN B. MONTGOMERY

Coordination of Departmental Activities
Supervision of Departmental Administration

AIDE TO THE SECRETARY

COL JOHN K. HESTER

ADMINISTRATIVE ASSISTANT

JOHN J. McLAUGHLIN

Departmental Administration of the Office of the Secretary of the Air Force

ASSISTANT SECRETARY

EUGENE M. ZUCKERT

Program Control
Management Control
Cost Control
Budget Matters
Organizational Planning
Mobilization
Civilian Personnel Policies
Air Force Recruiting Policies

UNDER SECRETARY

ARTHUR S. BARROWS

Procurement and Production
Industrial Mobilization
Air Force Materiel Requirements
Air Force Policies with Respect to Aircraft Industry
Member of Munitions Board
Activities of Research and Development Board
Air Force Activities of Industrial College
Liaison with Atomic Energy Commission

ASSISTANT SECRETARY

CORNELIUS V. WHITNEY

National Security Council Activities as assigned by Secretary
Member Air Coordinating Committee
Air Force Functions in Civil and Military-Diplomatic Affairs
Liaison with Air Force Planners
Air Reserve and Air National Guard
Air Force Civil Defense Policies

DIRECTOR OF PUBLIC RELATIONS

STEPHEN F. LEO

Dissemination of information concerning the Department of the Air Force. Supervision of proposed legislation and executive orders affecting the Department of the Air Force. Provides reports, studies and projects incident thereto. Liaison with the Executive Office of the Secretary of Defense, the Congress and other governmental agencies in connection with the aforementioned matters

GENERAL COUNSEL

BRACKLEY SHAW

Final legal authority on legal questions arising within or referred to the Department of the Air Force. Provides advice to the Secretary, Under Secretary and Assistant Secretaries on the legal aspects of matters coming within their jurisdiction

SECRETARY AIR FORCE PERSONNEL COUNCIL

MAJ GEN EDWIN B. LYON, President

Personnel Board
Discharge Review Board
Disability Review Board

SPECIAL ASSISTANTS AND CONSULTANTS

MAJ GEN GRANDISON GARDNER
MAJ GEN JAMES D. McINTIRE

Duties as prescribed

Source: Office of the Secretary of the Air Force Organizational and Functional Charts 1947–1984 (Washington: Office of Air Force History, 1985).

Office of the Secretary of the Air Force

November 1951

SECRETARY OF THE AIR FORCE
THOMAS K. FINLETTER

The Secretary of the Air Force is the head of the Department of the Air Force and is responsible for all matters pertaining to its operation and for the performance of such duties as may be prescribed by law or enjoined upon him by the President and the Secretary of Defense

EXECUTIVE ASSISTANT
COL WILLIAM G. HIPPS

UNDER SECRETARY
ROSWELL L. GILPATRIC

Deputy to the Secretary. Shares with Secretary responsibility for the general supervision and operation of the department. Responsible to the Secretary for procurement, production; supply, maintenance and transportation; industrial security; contract negotiation and contract appeals. Member Research and Development Board. Member Air Coordinating Committee. Member Munitions Board

EXECUTIVE
COL JOHN H. BELL

GENERAL COUNSEL

JAMES T. HILL, JR

Final determination on all legal questions, legal advice and opinions. Loyalty-security program

---

DIRECTOR OF LEGISLATION & LIAISON

BRIG GEN ROBERT E.L. EATON

Legislative program, liaison for executive office

ADMINISTRATIVE ASSISTANT

JOHN J. McLAUGHLIN

Organization and management; administrative services; Office of Record Contingency Administration; Claims and Pecuniary Liability Appeals

---

DEPUTY FOR PROCUREMENT & MATERIEL PROGRAMS

JOSEPH S. IMIRIE

DIRECTOR AIR FORCE DIVISION ARMED SERVICES RENEGOTIATION BOARD

THOMAS COGGESHALL

CHAIRMAN AIR FORCE PANEL ARMED FORCES CONTRACT APPEALS BOARD

ROSWELL M. AUSTIN

SPECIAL ASSISTANT (BASE NEGOTIATIONS)
HOWARD J. NEWMARK

Negotiations Relative to Overseas Facilities

EXECUTIVE
COL DANIEL K. PHIPPEN

ASSISTANT SECRETARY (MANAGEMENT)
EUGENE M. ZUCKERT

Organization - Manpower
Budget - Fiscal - Cost Control
Civilian - Military Personnel
Reserve Forces
Board for Correction of Military Records
Member Management Committee
Member Reserve Forces Policy Board
Member Personnel and Manpower
Council

EXECUTIVE
COL KENNETH O. DESSERT

DEPUTY FOR FINANCIAL & PROGRAM MGMT
GEORGE E. MOORE

DEPUTY FOR CONTRACT FINANCING
C. D. SEFTENBERG

DEPUTY FOR MANPOWER & ORGANIZATION
WILLIAM E. SWEENEY

DEPUTY FOR PERSONNEL MGMT
JAMES P. GOODE

DEPUTY FOR RESERVE FORCES
COL F.T. McCOY, JR

DIRECTOR SECRETARY OF THE AIR FORCE PERSONNEL COUNCIL
MAJ GEN E.B. LYON

ASSISTANT SECRETARY (MATERIEL)
EDWIN V. HUGGINS

Command Installations - Real Estate,
Family Housing, MDAP

EXECUTIVE
COL GUSTAV A. NUEBERG

DEPUTY FOR FAMILY HOUSING
L. R. REYNOLDS, JR

DEPUTY FOR INSTALLATIONS
EDWARD T. DICKENSON

SPECIAL ASSISTANT
WILLIAM A.M. BURDEN

Research and Development; Civil
Air Matters; Civil Defense;
Alternate Member Research and
Development Board; Member Air
Coordinating Committee

EXECUTIVE
LT COL VINCENT T. FORD

DEPUTY FOR RESEARCH & DEVELOPMENT
JAMES C. EVANS

DEPUTY FOR CIVIL AVIATION
J. PARKER VAN ZANDT

Source: Office of the Secretary of the Air Force Organizational and Functional Charts 1947–1984 (Washington: Office of Air Force History, 1985).

Office of the Secretary of the Air Force

September 1953

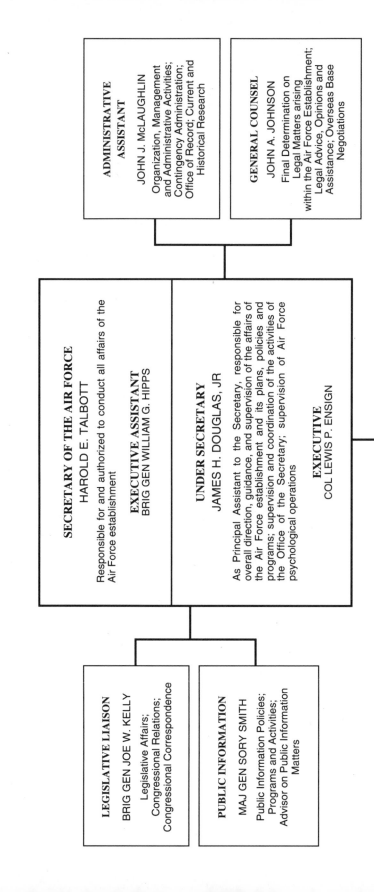

ADMINISTRATIVE ASSISTANT

JOHN J. McLAUGHLIN

Organization, Management and Administrative Activities; Contingency Administration; Office of Record; Current and Historical Research

GENERAL COUNSEL

JOHN A. JOHNSON

Final Determination on Legal Matters arising within the Air Force Establishment; Legal Advice, Opinions and Assistance; Overseas Base Negotiations

SECRETARY OF THE AIR FORCE

HAROLD E. TALBOTT

Responsible for and authorized to conduct all affairs of the Air Force establishment

EXECUTIVE ASSISTANT
BRIG GEN WILLIAM G. HIPPS

UNDER SECRETARY

JAMES H. DOUGLAS, JR

As Principal Assistant to the Secretary, responsible for overall direction, guidance, and supervision of the affairs of the Air Force establishment and its plans, policies and programs; supervision and coordination of the activities of the Office of the Secretary; supervision of Air Force psychological operations

EXECUTIVE
COL LEWIS P. ENSIGN

LEGISLATIVE LIAISON

BRIG GEN JOE W. KELLY

Legislative Affairs; Congressional Relations; Congressional Correspondence

PUBLIC INFORMATION

MAJ GEN SORY SMITH

Public Information Policies; Programs and Activities; Advisor on Public Information Matters

ASSISTANT SECRETARY (MATERIEL)

ROGER LEWIS

Industrial Resources, Security and Mobilization; Procurement; Production; Supply and Maintenance; Transportation and Communications; Contract Appeals; Civil Aviation; Mutual Security Assistance Program

EXECUTIVE
COL DONALD W. GRAHAM

DEPUTY FOR PROCUREMENT & PRODUCTION
MAX GOLDEN

DEPUTY FOR MATERIEL PROGRAMS
MYRON A. TRACY

DEPUTY FOR MUTUAL SECURITY ASSISTANCE AFFAIRS
CHARLES H. SHUFF

DEPUTY FOR CIVIL AVIATION
BRADLEY D. NASH

CHAIRMAN AIR FORCE PANEL BOARD OF CONTRACT APPEALS
ROSWELL M. AUSTIN

SPECIAL ASSISTANT FOR INTELLIGENCE

FREDERICK AYER, JR

Analysis and Interpretation of Intelligence Reports; Appraisal of Intelligence Programs

---

ASSISTANT SECRETARY (MANAGEMENT)

H. LEE WHITE

Manpower; Personnel; Organization; Budget; Finance; Accounting; Contract Financing; Reserve and ROTC; Personnel Security; Civil Defense; Correction of Military Records; Travel and per diem Allowances

EXECUTIVE
COL KENNETH O. DESSERT

DEPUTY FOR CONTRACT FINANCING
CHESTER D. SEFTENBERG

DEPUTY FOR ACCOUNTING & FINANCIAL MANAGEMENT
ROBERT D. BENSON

DEPUTY FOR BUDGET & PROGRAM MANAGEMENT
HYDE GILLETTE

DEPUTY FOR MANPOWER, PERSONNEL & UTILIZATION
JAMES P. GOODE

DEPUTY FOR RESERVE & ROTC AFFAIRS
CHESTER D. SEFTENBERG

DIRECTOR SECRETARY OF THE AIR FORCE PERSONNEL COUNCIL
MAJ GEN JOHN F. McBLAIN

SPECIAL ASSISTANT FOR INSTALLATIONS

JOHN M. FERRY

EXECUTIVE
LT COL DAVID S. CHAMBERLAIN

Installations; Real Estate; Construction; Family Housing

SPECIAL ASSISTANT FOR RESEARCH & DEVELOPMENT

TREVOR GARDNER

EXECUTIVE
LT COL VINCENT T. FORD

Research and Development; Qualitative Requirements; Integration of Technology with Military Requirements and Procurement Planning

---

Source: Office of the Secretary of the Air Force Organizational and Functional Charts 1947–1984 (Washington: Office of Air Force History, 1985).

Office of the Secretary of the Air Force

August 1955

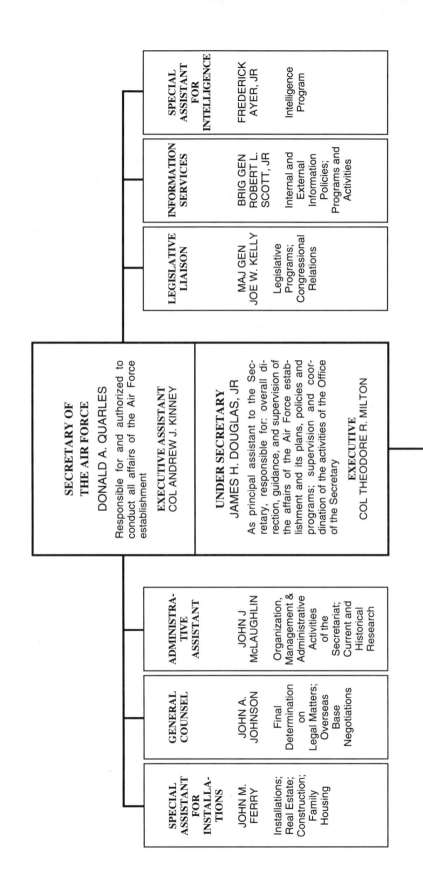

SECRETARY OF THE AIR FORCE

DONALD A. QUARLES

Responsible for and authorized to conduct all affairs of the Air Force establishment

EXECUTIVE ASSISTANT
COL ANDREW J. KINNEY

UNDER SECRETARY
JAMES H. DOUGLAS, JR

As principal assistant to the Secretary, responsible for: overall direction, guidance, and supervision of the affairs of the Air Force establishment and its plans, policies and programs; supervision and coordination of the activities of the Office of the Secretary

EXECUTIVE
COL THEODORE R. MILTON

SPECIAL ASSISTANT FOR INTELLIGENCE

FREDERICK AYER, JR

Intelligence Program

INFORMATION SERVICES

BRIG GEN ROBERT L. SCOTT, JR

Internal and External Information Policies; Programs and Activities

LEGISLATIVE LIAISON

MAJ GEN JOE W. KELLY

Legislative Programs; Congressional Relations

ADMINISTRATIVE ASSISTANT

JOHN J McLAUGHLIN

Organization, Management & Administrative Activities of the Secretariat; Current and Historical Research

GENERAL COUNSEL

JOHN A. JOHNSON

Final Determination on Legal Matters; Overseas Base Negotiations

SPECIAL ASSISTANT FOR INSTALLATIONS

JOHN M. FERRY

Installations; Real Estate; Construction; Family Housing

ASSISTANT SECRETARY (MATERIEL)	ASSISTANT SECRETARY (FINANCIAL MANAGEMENT)	ASSISTANT SECRETARY (MANPOWER & PERSONNEL)	ASSISTANT SECRETARY (RESEARCH & DEVELOPMENT)
ROGER LEWIS	LYLE S. GARLOCK	DAVID S. SMITH	TREVOR GARDNER
Industrial Resources, Security and Mobilization; Procurement; Production; Supply and Maintenance; Transportation and Communications; Contract Appeals; Civil Aviation; Mutual Security Assistance Program	Budgeting; Accounting; Financing; Progress & Statistical Reporting; Management Analysis; Management Engineering Services; Auditing; Contract Financing	Manpower, Personnel, Reserve and ROTC; Organization; Military, Civilian, Industrial Personnel Security Programs; Management Improvement Program; Civil Defense; Correction of Military Records	Research & Development; Qualitative Requirements; Integration of Technology with Military Requirements and Procurement Planning
EXECUTIVE COL ROY W. GUSTAFSON	EXECUTIVE COL EDWARD P. FOOTE	EXECUTIVE COL HERBERT G. BENCH	EXECUTIVE COL RAYMOND A. BALLWEG, JR
DEPUTY FOR PROCUREMENT & PRODUCTION MAX GOLDEN	DEPUTY FOR CONTRACT FINANCING ORMAND MILTON	DEPUTY FOR MANPOWER PERSONNEL & ORGANIZATION JAMES P. GOODE	DEPUTY FOR PROGRAMS
DEPUTY FOR MATERIEL PROGRAMS DONALD R. JACKSON	DEPUTY FOR BUDGET & PROGRAM MANAGEMENT HYDE GILLETTE	DEPUTY FOR SECURITY PROGRAMS JOHN J. GRADY	DEPUTY FOR REQUIREMENTS RICHARD E. HORNER
DEPUTY FOR MUTUAL SECURITY ASSISTANCE AFFAIRS LEWIS S. THOMPSON	DEPUTY FOR ACCOUNTING & FINANCIAL MANAGEMENT ROBERT D. BENSON	DEPUTY FOR RESERVE ROTC AFFAIRS JOHN I. LEROM	
DEPUTY FOR CIVIL AVIATION BRADLEY D. NASH		DIRECTOR SECRETARY OF THE AIR FORCE PERSONNEL COUNCIL MAJ GEN JOHN F. McBLAIN	
CHAIRMAN AIR FORCE PANEL BOARD OF CONTRACT APPEALS ROSWELL M. AUSTIN			

Source: Office of the Secretary of the Air Force Organizational and Functional Charts 1947–1984 (Washington: Office of Air Force History, 1985).

Office of the Secretary of the Air Force

July 1957

SECRETARY OF THE AIR FORCE

JAMES H. DOUGLAS, JR

Responsible for and has the authority to conduct all affairs of the Department of the Air Force

EXECUTIVE ASSISTANT
COL THEODORE R. MILTON

UNDER SECRETARY
MALCOLM A. MacINTYRE

As principal assistant to the Secretary, acts with full authority of the Secretary on all affairs of the department, is responsible for: overall direction, guidance, and supervision of the affairs of the Department and its Plans, Policies and Programs; supervises and coordinates the activities of the Office of the Secretary; Chairman of the Requirements Review Board

EXECUTIVE
COL ROBERT F. BURNHAM

DEPUTY FOR REQUIREMENTS REVIEW

PHILIP F. HILBERT

Programming and Progress Reporting; Coordination of Analysis and Review of Requirements for Manpower, Materiel and Facilities

---

INFORMATION SERVICES

BRIG GEN ARNO H. LUEHMAN

Internal and External Information Policies; Programs and Activities

---

LEGISLATIVE LIAISON

MAJ GEN JOE W. KELLY

Legislative Program; Congressional Relations

ADMINISTRATIVE ASSISTANT

JOHN J. McLAUGHLIN

Organization, Management & Administrative Activities of the Secretariat; Current and Historical Research

---

GENERAL COUNSEL

JOHN A. JOHNSON

Final determination on Legal Matters; Overseas Base Negotiations

---

SPECIAL ASSISTANT FOR INSTALLATIONS

JOHN M. FERRY

Installations; Real Estate; Construction; Maintenance of Real Property; Family Housing

ASSISTANT SECRETARY (FINANCIAL MANAGEMENT)

LYLE S. GARLOCK

Budgeting; Accounting; Financing; Progress & Statistical Reporting; Management Analysis; Management Engineering Services; Auditing; Contract Financing

EXECUTIVE
LT COL JACK REED

DEPUTY FOR ACCOUNTING & FINANCIAL MANAGEMENT
ROBERT D. BENSON

DEPUTY FOR CONTRACT FINANCING
ORMAND MILTON

SPECIAL ASSISTANT
CLEMENT G. MALONEY

ASSISTANT SECRETARY (MANPOWER, PERSONNEL & RESERVE FORCES)

DAVID S. SMITH

Manpower, Personnel; Reserve and ROTC; Organization; Military, Civilian, Industrial Personnel Security Programs; Management Improvement Program; Civil Defense; Correction of Military Records

EXECUTIVE
LT COL WINSTON P. ANDERSON

DEPUTY FOR MANPOWER PERSONNEL & ORGANIZATION
JAMES P. GOODE

DEPUTY FOR SECURITY PROGRAMS
JOHN J. GRADY

DEPUTY FOR RESERVE & ROTC AFFAIRS
DONALD J. STRAIT

DIRECTOR SECRETARY OF THE AIR FORCE PERSONNEL COUNCIL
MAJ GEN LEWIS R. PARKER

ASSISTANT SECRETARY (MATERIEL)

DUDLEY C. SHARP

Industrial Resources, Security and Mobilization; Procurement; Production; Supply and Maintenance; Transportation and Communications; Contract Appeals; Civil Aviation; Mutual Security Assistance Progam

EXECUTIVE
COL EDWIN P. SCHMID

DEPUTY FOR PROCUREMENT & PRODUCTION
MAX GOLDEN

DEPUTY FOR MATERIEL PROGRAMS
DONALD R. JACKSON

DEPUTY FOR MILITARY ASSISTANCE PROGRAMS
LEWIS S. THOMPSON

DEPUTY FOR CIVIL & MILITARY AIR TRANSPORTATION
GILBERT C. GREENWAY

CHAIRMAN AIR FORCE PANEL BOARD OF CONTRACT APPEALS
ROSWELL M. AUSTIN

ASSISTANT SECRETARY (RESEARCH & DEVELOPMENT)

RICHARD E. HORNER

Research & Development; Qualitative Requirements Integration of Technology with Military Requirements & Procurement Planning

DEPUTY ASSISTANT SECRETARY

EXECUTIVE
COL BENTLEY H. HARRIS, JR

DEPUTY FOR REQUIREMENTS
DALE E. OYSTER

DEPUTY FOR RESEARCH & DEVELOPMENT OPERATIONS
WILLIAM WEITZEN

DEPUTY FOR PROGRAMS

Source: Office of the Secretary of the Air Force Organizational and Functional Charts 1947–1984 (Washington: Office of Air Force History, 1985).

Office of the Secretary of the Air Force

September 1960

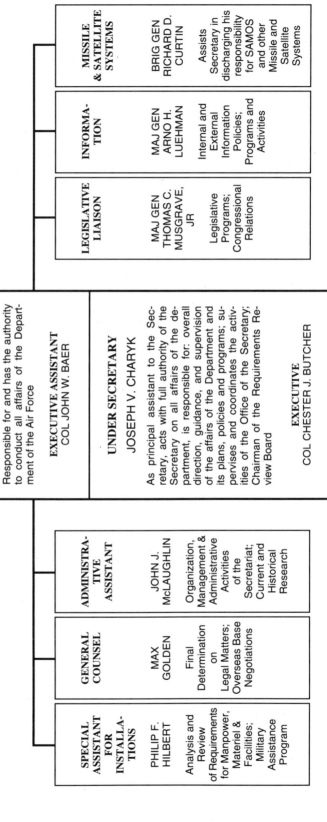

SECRETARY OF THE AIR FORCE

DUDLEY C. SHARP

Responsible for and has the authority to conduct all affairs of the Department of the Air Force

EXECUTIVE ASSISTANT

COL JOHN W. BAER

UNDER SECRETARY

JOSEPH V. CHARYK

As principal assistant to the Secretary, acts with full authority of the Secretary on all affairs of the department, is responsible for: overall direction, guidance, and supervision of the affairs of the Department and its plans, policies and programs; supervises and coordinates the activities of the Office of the Secretary; Chairman of the Requirements Review Board

EXECUTIVE

COL CHESTER J. BUTCHER

SPECIAL ASSISTANT FOR INSTALLATIONS

PHILIP F. HILBERT

Analysis and Review of Requirements for Manpower, Materiel & Facilities; Military Assistance Program

GENERAL COUNSEL

MAX GOLDEN

Final Determination on Legal Matters; Overseas Base Negotiations

ADMINISTRATIVE ASSISTANT

JOHN J. McLAUGHLIN

Organization, Management & Administrative Activities of the Secretariat; Current and Historical Research

LEGISLATIVE LIAISON

MAJ GEN THOMAS C. MUSGRAVE, JR

Legislative Programs; Congressional Relations

INFORMATION

MAJ GEN ARNO H. LUEHMAN

Internal and External Information Policies; Programs and Activities

MISSILE & SATELLITE SYSTEMS

BRIG GEN RICHARD D. CURTIN

Assists Secretary in discharging his responsibility for SAMOS and other Missile and Satellite Systems

SPECIAL ASSISTANT FOR MANPOWER, PERSONNEL & RESERVE FORCES

LEWIS S. THOMPSON

Manpower, Personnel, Reserve and ROTC Civil Air Patrol; Military, Civilian Industrial Personnel Security; Correction of Military Records

EXECUTIVE
COL DANIEL K. PHIPPEN

DEPUTY FOR MANPOWER PERSONNEL & ORGANIZATION
JAMES P. GOODE

DEPUTY FOR SECURITY PROGRAMS
JOHN E. WHALAN JR

DEPUTY FOR RESERVE & ROTC AFFAIRS
WILLIAM P. WRIGHT JR

DIRECTOR PERSONNEL COUNCIL
MAJ GEN STANLEY T. WRAY

ASSISTANT SECRETARY (RESEARCH & DEVELOPMENT)

COURTLAND D. PERKINS

Research & Development; Qualitative Requirements; Integration of Technology with Military Requirements & Procurement Planning

EXECUTIVE
COL LEE V. GOSSICK

DEPUTY FOR RESEARCH
HARRY DAVIS

DEPUTY FOR DEVELOPMENT
WILLIAM WEITZEN

DEPUTY FOR REQUIREMENTS
FRANKLIN J. ROSS

ASSISTANT SECRETARY (FINANCIAL MANAGEMENT)

LYLE S. GARLOCK

Budget; Accounting; Financing; Progress & Statistical Reporting; Management Analysis; Management Engineering Services; Auditing; Contract Financing

DEPUTY ASSISTANT SECRETARY
ROBERT D. BENSON

EXECUTIVE
COL JACK F. PRATHER

DEPUTY FOR CONTRACT FINANCING
P. ORMAND MILTON

SPECIAL ASSISTANT
LEWIS TURNER

ASSISTANT SECRETARY (MATERIEL)

PHILIP B. TAYLOR

Industrial Resources; Mobilization; Procurement; Production; Supply & Maintenance; Transportation & Communications; Contract Appeals; Civil Aviation

EXECUTIVE
COL JONAS L. BLANK

DEPUTY FOR MATERIEL PROGRAMS
DONALD R. JACKSON

DEPUTY FOR PROCUREMENT & PRODUCTION
AARON J. RACUSIN

DEPUTY FOR TRANSPORTATION & COMMUNICATIONS
EDWARD J. DRISCOLL

CHAIRMAN OF PANEL BOARD OF CONTRACT APPEALS
GEORGE W. CRAWFORD

SPECIAL ASSISTANT FOR INSTALLATIONS

JOHN M. FERRY

Installations; Real Estate; Construction; Maintenance of Real Property; Family Housing

DEPUTY SPECIAL ASSISTANT
GEORGE S. ROBINSON

EXECUTIVE
LT COL H. W. HOUSTON

DEPUTY FOR MAINTENANCE
JOHN J.B. ROCKFELLER

DEPUTY FOR PLANNING & PROGRAMMING
JACK RILEY

Source: Office of the Secretary of the Air Force Organizational and Functional Charts 1947–1984 (Washington: Office of Air Force History, 1985).

Office of the Secretary of the Air Force

September 1963

SECRETARY OF THE AIR FORCE
EUGENE M. ZUCKERT

EXECUTIVE ASSISTANT TO SECRETARY
COL BUDDY R. DAUGHTREY

SPECIAL ASSISTANT TO SECRETARY FOR PUBLIC AFFAIRS
EDWARD R. TRAPNELL

UNDER SECRETARY
BROCKWAY McMILLAN

MILITARY ASSISTANT TO SECRETARY
COL ROBERT W. SHICK

EXECUTIVE TO UNDER SECRETARY
COL JOHN H. STRAND

The Secretary of the Air Force is responsible for and has the authority to conduct all affairs of the Department of the Air Force. The Under Secretary of the Air Force acts with full authority of the Secretary on all affairs of the Department and in addition supervises the Reserve Components of the Air Force, serves as a Member of the Reserve Forces Policy Board, supervises Air Force participation in the Military Assistance Program, supervises the Analysis and Review of Air Force Requirements,

---

DEPUTY FOR REQUIREMENTS REVIEW

PHILIP F. HILBERT

Analysis and Review of Requirements and the Plans and Programs from which they derive; Military Assistance Program and other assigned International Activities

---

GENERAL COUNSEL

GERRITT W. WESSELINK
(Acting)

MAJ JAMES L. GAGNIER
(Executive)

Final Determination on Legal Matters; Overseas Base Negotiations

---

ADMINISTRATIVE ASSISTANT

JOSEPH P. HOCHREITER
(Acting)

LT COL FRANK J. SIMOKAITIS
(Executive)

Organization, Management and Administrative Activities of the Secretariat; Current and Historical Research

---

LEGISLATIVE LIAISON

MAJ GEN PERRY M. HOISINGTON, II
(Director)

BRIG GEN THOMAS G. CORBIN
(Deputy Director)

MAJ JACK R. BENSON
(Executive)

Legislative Programs, Congressional Relations

INFORMATION

MAJ GEN WILLIAM K. MARTIN
(Director)

COL MAURICE F. CASEY
(Deputy Director)

LT COL KENNETH L. SANDVIG
(Executive)

Internal and External Information Policies, Programs and Activities

---

SPACE SYSTEMS

BRIG GEN JOHN L. MARTIN, JR
(Director)

LT COL ROBERT A. VAN ARSDALL
(Executive)

Space Systems Supervision

Source: Office of the Secretary of the Air Force Organizational and Functional Charts 1947–1984 (Washington: Office of Air Force History, 1985).

SPECIAL ASSISTANT FOR MANPOWER, PERSONNEL & RESERVE FORCES

BENJAMIN W. FRIDGE

EXECUTIVE
COL BIRDENE E. FORREST

Principal Staff Assistant to the Secretary of the Air Force relative to: Manpower and Organization, Military and Civilian Personnel including Health, Welfare, Morale, and Equal In-House Employment Opportunities, Reserve Components, the Air National Guard and the Air Force Reserve Officers Training Corps (this responsibility is exercised under the supervision of the Under Secretary), Civil Air Patrol, Military and Civilian Personnel Security Programs, Informational, International, Physical and Personnel aspects of Industrial Security Program Training, Management Principles and Techniques including the Management Improvement Program, Contracts for Personal Services and Training, Travel and Per Diem Allowances Board for the Correction of Military Records, Member Secretary of the Air Force Personnel Council and its Component Boards

DEPUTY FOR MANPOWER PERSONNEL & ORGANIZATION
JAMES P. GOODE

DEPUTY FOR SECURITY PROGRAMS
JOHN E. WHALAN, JR

DEPUTY FOR RESERVE & ROTC AFFAIRS
JOHN A. LANG, JR

DIRECTOR PERSONNEL COUNCIL
MAJ GEN TURNER C. ROGERS

ASSISTANT SECRETARY (MATERIEL)

JOSEPH S. IMIRIE

DEPUTY ASSISTANT SECRETARY
DONALD R. JACKSON

EXECUTIVE
COL ALLEN B. GASTON

Principal Staff Assistant to the Secretary of the Air Force relative to: Aviation including the Department of Defense, Federal Aviation Agency Advisory Group and the Interagency Group for International Aviation Matters, Procurement Activities including Required Determinations and Findings, Contracting and Administration and Termination of Contracts, Supply Management including Requirements, Determinations, Storage, Distribution and Disposal of all Materiel, Production and Contract Management of Weapon Systems, Equipment Maintenance and Modification Management, Transportation, Communications, and other Service Activities, Production, Contractors Equal Employment Opportunities, Materiel and Logistics Planning and Programming, Industrial Defense Program, Industrial Resources and Readiness, Cost Reduction Program, Renegotiation Affairs, Contract Appeals, and Related Activities, Economic Utilization Policy, Civil Aviation

DEPUTY FOR PROCUREMENT MANAGEMENT
AARON J. RACUSIN

DEPUTY FOR SUPPLY & MAINTENANCE
HUGH E. WITT

DEPUTY FOR TRANSPORTATION & COMMUNICATIONS
JOHN W. PERRY (Acting)

ASSISTANT SECRETARY (FINANCIAL MANAGEMENT)

NEIL E. HARLAN

DEPUTY ASSISTANT SECRETARY
ROBERT D. BENSON

EXECUTIVE
LT COL WILLIAM D. CONKLIN

Principal Staff Assistant to the Secretary of the Air Force relative to: The Air Force Programming Processes and the Preparation and Validation of all Program Documentation including Program Change Proposals and other Adjustments, Budgeting, Budget Review of Air Force Requirements and Budget Presentations, Accounting and Accounting Systems, Finance including Disbursement and Collection of Funds, Progress and Statistical Reporting and Interpretation of such Management Data, Management Analysis and Special Program Status Reports, Contracts for Management Engineering Services, Auditing, Contract Financing. Responsible for Directing and Supervising the Comptroller of the Air Force. While the Comptroller is directly responsible to the Assistant Secretary (Financial Management), he has concurrent responsibility to the Chief of Staff

DEPUTY FOR FINANCIAL ANALYSIS
JOHN J. HOLLERAN (Acting)

DEPUTY FOR CONTRACT FINANCING
P. ORMAND MILTON

DEPUTY FOR MANAGEMENT SYSTEMS

ASSISTANT SECRETARY (RESEARCH & DEVELOPMENT)

ALEXANDER H. FLAX

EXECUTIVE
LT COL RICHARD L. JOHNSON

Principal Staff Assistant to the Secretary of the Air Force relative to: Scientific and Technical Matters, Basic and Applied Research, Exploratory Development and Advanced Technology, Integration of Technology with and Determination of Qualitative Air Force Requirements, Research, Development, Test and Evaluation of Weapons, Weapons Systems, and Defense Materiel, Technical Management of Systems Engineering and Integration

DEPUTY FOR DEVELOPMENT
JOE C. JONES

DEPUTY FOR REQUIREMENTS
FRANKLIN J. ROSS

DEPUTY FOR RESEARCH
HARRY DAVIS

DEPUTY FOR ENGINEERING
THOMAS H. DALEHITE

SPECIAL ASSISTANT FOR INSTALLATIONS

ALAN I. McCONE

DEPUTY SPECIAL ASSISTANT
GEORGE S. ROBINSON

EXECUTIVE
LT COL HUBERT O. JOHNSON

Principal Staff Assistant to the Secretary of the Air Force relative to: Installations Planning and Programming, Acquisition and Disposal of Real Estate, Construction of Bases and Facilities, Family Housing, Maintenance of Real Property

DEPUTY FOR PLANNING & PROGRAMMING
JACK RILEY

DEPUTY FOR MAINTENANCE
CARL W. ANDERSON

Appendix 2

Office of the Secretary of the Air Force
September 1947 to September 1965

Secretaries of the Air Force

W. Stuart Symington	Sep 18, 1947	to	Apr 24, 1950
Thomas K. Finletter	Apr 24, 1950	to	Jan 20, 1953
Harold E. Talbott	Feb 4, 1953	to	Aug 13, 1955
Donald A. Quarles	Aug 15, 1955	to	Apr 30, 1957
James H. Douglas, Jr.	May 1, 1957	to	Dec 10, 1959
Dudley C. Sharp	Dec 11, 1959	to	Jan 20, 1961
Eugene M. Zuckert	Jan 23, 1961	to	Sep 30, 1965

Under Secretaries of the Air Force

Arthur S. Barrows	Sep 26, 1947	to	Apr 21, 1950
John A. McCone	Jun 15, 1950	to	Oct 12, 1951
Roswell L. Gilpatric	Oct 19, 1951	to	Feb 5, 1953
James H. Douglas, Jr.	Mar 3, 1953	to	Apr 30, 1957
Malcolm A. MacIntyre	Jun 5, 1957	to	Jul 31, 1959
Dudley C. Sharp	Aug 3, 1959	to	Dec 10, 1959
Joseph V. Charyk	Jan 28, 1960	to	Mar 1, 1963
Brockway McMillan	Jun 12, 1963	to	Sep 30, 1965

Assistant Secretaries of the Air Force (Management)*

Eugene M. Zuckert	Sep 26, 1947	to	Feb 24, 1953
James T. Hill	Jul 5, 1952	to	Jan 20, 1953
H. Lee White	Feb 16, 1953	to	Jul 2, 1954

* Position redesignated Assistant Secretary of the Air Force (Financial Management) and Assistant Secretary of the Air Force (Manpower, Personnel, and Reserve Forces) Aug 1, 1954.

Appendix 3

Air Force Chiefs of Staff
September 1947 to September 1965

General Carl A. Spaatz	Sep 26, 1947	to Apr 29, 1948
General Hoyt S. Vandenberg	Apr 30, 1948	to Jun 29, 1953
General Nathan F. Twining	Jun 30, 1953	to Jun 30, 1957
General Thomas D. White	Jul 1, 1957	to Jun 30, 1961
General Curtis E. LeMay	Jun 30, 1961	to Jan 31, 1965
General John P. McConnell	Feb 1, 1965	to Jul 31, 1969

Air Force Vice Chiefs of Staff
September 1947 to September 1965

General Hoyt S. Vandenberg	Oct 10, 1947	to Apr 28, 1948
General Muir S. Fairchild	May 27, 1948	to May 17, 1950
General Nathan F. Twining	Oct 10, 1950	to Jun 30, 1953
General Thomas D. White	Jun 30, 1953	to Jun 30, 1957
General Curtis E. LeMay	Jul 1, 1957	to Jun 30, 1961
General Frederic H. Smith, Jr.	Jul 1, 1961	to Jun 30, 1962
General William F. McKee	Jul 1, 1962	to Jul 31, 1964
General John P. McConnell	Aug 1, 1964	to Jan 31, 1965
General William H. Blanchard	Feb 19, 1965	to May 31, 1966

Appendix 4

Secretaries of Defense
September 1947 to September 1965

James V. Forrestal	Sep 18, 1947	to	Mar 27, 1949
Louis A. Johnson	Mar 28, 1949	to	Sep 19, 1950
George C. Marshall	Sep 21, 1950	to	Sep 12, 1951
Robert A. Lovett	Sep 17, 1951	to	Jan 20, 1953
Charles E. Wilson	Jan 28, 1953	to	Oct 8, 1957
Neil H. McElroy	Oct 9, 1957	to	Dec 1, 1959
Thomas S. Gates, Jr.	Dec 2, 1959	to	Jan 20, 1961
Robert S. McNamara	Jan 21, 1961	to	Feb 29, 1968

Appendix 5

OSAF/Air Staff Authorized Strength, 1948 to 1963

Year	Total	Category	OSAF	Air Staff
1948	4,339	Officer	130	1,527
		Enlisted	18	406
		Civilian	228	2,030
1949	6,507	O	107	2,157
		E	31	579
		C	286	3,347
1950	6,575	O	99	1,798
		E	30	483
		C	269	3,107
1951	8,950	O	131	2,381
		E	59	731
		C	422	4,354
1952	8,811	O	138	2,445
		E	32	703
		C	320	4,315
1953	8,679	O	124	2,480
		E	32	718
		C	307	4,235
1954	8,864	O	121	2,489
		E	35	729
		C	290	4,434
1955	9,074	O	158	2,610
		E	40	711
		C	348	4,836

(over)

Year	Total	Category	OSAF	Air Staff
1956	9,589	Officer	146	2,267
		Enlisted	37	667
		Civilian	353	5,040
1957	9,843	O	150	2,263
		E	37	653
		C	353	5,038
1958	8,821	O	141	2,367
		E	33	609
		C	330	4,399
1959	9,122	O	141	2,365
		E	36	607
		C	325	4,471
1960	8,343	O	151	2,161
		E	39	541
		C	323	3,947
1961	8,357	O	175	2,140
		E	44	515
		C	342	3,885
1962	8,254	O	190	2,186
		E	55	496
		C	350	4,112
1963	6,870	O	185	2,086
		E	26	369
		C	334	3,097
1964	6,960	O	189	2,117
		E	30	381
		C	352	2,971
1965	6,773	O	174	2,094
		E	20	285
		C	344	2,848

Appendix 6

The National Security Act of 1947

[61 Stat.]

PUBLIC LAW 253—July 26, 1947

Public Law 253   Chapter 343

AN ACT

To promote the national security by providing for a Secretary of Defense; for a National Military Establishment; for a Department of the Army, a Department of the Navy, and a Department of the Air Force; and for the coordination of the activities of the National Military Establishment with other departments and agencies of the Government concerned with the national security.

BE IT ENACTED BY THE SENATE AND HOUSE OF REPRESENTATIVES OF THE UNITED STATES OF AMERICA IN CONGRESS ASSEMBLED,

Short Title

That this Act may be cited as the "National Security Act of 1947".

Table of Contents

Title III - Miscellaneous

Declaration of Policy

Sec. 2. In enacting this legislation, it is the intent of Congress to provide a comprehensive program for the future security of the United States; to provide for the establishment of integrated policies and procedures for the departments, agencies, and functions of the Government relating to the national security; to provide three military departments for the operation and administration of the Army, the Navy (including naval aviation and the United States Marine Corps), and the Air Force, with their assigned combat and service components; to provide for their authoritative coordination and unified direction under civilian control but not to merge them; to provide for the effective strategic direction of the armed forces and for their operation under unified control and for their integration into an efficient team of land, naval, and air forces.

TITLE I - COORDINATION FOR NATIONAL SECURITY

National Security Council

Sec. 101. (a) There is hereby established a council to be known as the National Security Council (hereinafter in this section referred to as the "Council").

The President of the United States shall preside over meetings of the Council: PROVIDED, That in his absence he may designate a member of the Council to preside in his place.

The function of the Council shall be to advise the President with respect to the integration of domestic, foreign, and military policies relating to the national security so as to enable the military services and the other departments and agencies of the Government to cooperate more effectively in matters involving the national security.

The Council shall be composed of the President; the Secretary of State; the Secretary of Defense, appointed under section 202; the Secretary of the Army, referred to in section 205; the Secretary of the Navy; the Secretary of the Air Force, appointed under section 207; the Chairman of the National Security Resources Board, appointed under section 103; and such of the following named officers as the President may designate from time to time: The Secretaries of the executive departments, the Chairman of the Munitions Board appointed under section 213, and the Chairman of the Research and Development Board appointed under section 214; but no such additional member shall be designated until the advice and consent of the Senate has been given to his appointment to the office the holding of which authorizes his designation as a member of the Council.

(b) In addition to performing such other functions as the President may direct, for the purpose of more effectively coordinating the policies and functions of the departments and agencies of the Government relating to the national security, it shall, subject to the direction of the President, be the duty of the Council—

> (1) to assess and appraise the objectives, commitments, and risks of the United States in relation to our actual and potential military power, in the interest of national security, for the purpose of making recommendations to the President in connection therewith; and
>
> (2) to consider policies on matters of common interest to the departments and agencies of the Government concerned with the national security, and to make recommendations to the President in connection therewith.

(c) The Council shall have a staff to be headed by a civilian executive secretary who shall be appointed by the President, and who shall receive compensation at the rate of $10,000 a year. The executive secretary, subject to the direction of the Council, is hereby authorized, subject to the civil-service laws and the Classification Act of 1923, as amended, to appoint and fix the compensation of such personnel as may be necessary to perform such duties as may be prescribed by the Council in connection with the performance of its functions.

(d) The Council shall, from time to time, make such recommendations, and such other reports to the President as it deems appropriate or as the President may require.

Central Intelligence Agency

Sec. 102. (a) There is hereby established under the National Security Council a Central Intelligence Agency with a Director of Central Intelligence, who shall be the head thereof. The Director shall be appointed by the President, by and with the advice and consent of the Senate, from among the commissioned officers of the armed services or from among individuals in civilian life. The Director shall receive compensation at the rate of $14,000 a year.

(b) (1) If a commissioned officer of the armed services is appointed as Director then —

(A) in the performance of his duties as Director, he shall be subject to no supervision, control, restriction, or prohibition (military or otherwise) other than would be operative with respect to him if he were a civilian in no way connected with the Department of the Army, the Department of the Navy, the Department of the Air Force, or the armed services or any component thereof; and

(B) he shall not possess or exercise any supervision, control, powers, or functions (other than such as he possesses, or is authorized or directed to exercise, as Director) with respect to the armed services or any component thereof, the Department of the Army, the Department of the Navy, or the Department of the Air Force, or any branch, bureau, unit or division thereof, or with respect to any of the personnel (military or civilian) of any of the foregoing.

(2) Except as provided in paragraph (1), the appointment to the office of Director of a commissioned officer of the armed services, and his acceptance of and service in such office, shall in no way affect any status, office, rank, or grade he may occupy or hold in the armed services, or any emolument, perquisite, right, privilege, or benefit incident to or arising out of any such status, office, rank, or grade. Any such commissioned officer shall, while serving in the office of Director, receive the military pay and allowances (active or retired, as the case may be) payable to a commissioned officer of his grade and length of service and shall be paid, from any funds available to defray the expenses of the Agency, annual compensation at a rate equal to the amount by which $14,000 exceeds the amount of his annual military pay and allowances.

(c) Notwithstanding the provisions of section 6 of the Act of August 24, 1912 (37 Stat. 555), or the provisions of any other law, the Director of Central Intelligence may, in his discretion, terminate the employment of any officer or employee of the Agency whenever he shall deem such termination necessary or advisable in the interests of the United States, but such termination shall not affect the right of such officer or employee to seek or accept employment in any other department or agency of the Government if declared eligible for such employment by the United States Civil Service Commission.

(d) For the purpose of coordinating the intelligence activities of the several Government departments and agencies in the interest of national security, it shall be the duty of the Agency, under the direction of the National Security Council—

(1) to advise the National Security Council in matters concerning such intelligence activities of the Government departments and agencies as relate to the national security;

(2) to make recommendations to the National Security Council for the coordination of such intelligence activities of the departments and agencies of the Government as relate to the national security;

(3) to correlate and evaluate intelligence relating to the national security, and provide for the appropriate dissemination of such intelligence within the Government using where appropriate existing agencies and facilities: PROVIDED, That the Agency shall have no police, subpoena, law-enforcement powers, or internal-security functions: PROVIDED FURTHER, That the departments and other agencies of the Government shall continue to collect, evaluate, correlate, and disseminate departmental intelligence: AND PROVIDED FURTHER, That the Director of Central Intelligence shall be responsible for protecting intelligence sources and methods from unauthorized disclosure;

(4) to perform, for the benefit of the existing intelligence agencies, such additional services of common concern as the National Security Council determines can be more efficiently accomplished centrally;

(5) to perform such other functions and duties related to intelligence affecting the national security as the National Security Council may from time to time direct.

(e) To the extent recommended by the National Security Council and approved by the President, such intelligence of the departments and agencies of the Government, except as hereinafter provided, relating to the national security shall be open to the inspection of the Director of Central Intelligence, and such intelligence as relates to the national security and is possessed by such departments and other agencies of the Government, except as hereinafter provided, shall be made available to the Director of Central Intelligence for correlation, evaluation, and dissemination: PROVIDED, HOWEVER, That upon the written request of the Director of Central Intelligence, the Director of the Federal Bureau of Investigation shall make available to the Director of Central Intelligence such information for correlation, evaluation, and dissemination as may be essential to the national security.

(f) Effective when the Director first appointed under subsection (a) has taken office—

(1) the National Intelligence Authority (11 Fed. Reg. 1337, 1339, February 5, 1946) shall cease to exist; and

(2) the personnel, property and records of the Central Intelligence Group are transferred to the Central Intelligence Agency, and such Group shall cease to exist. Any unexpended balances of appropriations, allocations, or other funds available or authorized to be made available for such Group shall be available and shall be authorized to be made available in like manner for expenditure by the Agency.

National Security Resources Board

Sec. 103. (a) There is hereby established a National Security Resources Board (hereinafter in this section referred to as the "Board") to be composed of the Chairinan of the Board and such heads or representatives of the various executive departments and independent agencies as may from time to time be designated by the President to be members of the Board. The Chairman of the Board shall be appointed from civilian life by the President, by and with the advice and consent of the Senate, and shall receive compensation at the rate of $14,000 a year.

(b) The Chairman of the Board, subject to the direction of the President, is authorized, subject to the civil-service laws and the Classification Act of 1923, as amended, to appoint and fix the compensation of such personnel as may be necessary to assist the Board in carrying out its functions.

(c) It shall be the function of the Board to advise the President concerning the coordination of military, industrial, and civilian mobilization, including—

(1) policies concerning industrial and civilian mobilization in order to assure the most effective mobilization and maximum utilization of the Nation's manpower in the event of war;

(2) programs for the effective use in time of war of the Nation's natural and industrial resources for military and civilian needs, for the maintenance and stabilization of the civilian economy in time of war, and for the adjustment of such economy to war needs and conditions;

(3) policies for unifying, in time of war, the activities of Federal agencies and departments engaged in or concerned with production, procurement, distribution, or transportation of military or civilian supplies, materials, and products;

(4) the relationship between potential supplies of, and potential requirements for, manpower, resources, and productive facilities in time of war;

(5) policies for establishing adequate reserves of strategic and critical material, and for the conservation of these reserves;

(6) the strategic relocation of industries, services, government, and economic activities, the continuous operation of which is essential to the Nation's security.

(d) In performing its functions, the Board shall utilize to the maximum extent the facilities and resources of the departments and agencies of the Government.

TITLE II-THE NATIONAL MILITARY ESTABLISHMENT

Establishment of the National Military Establishment

Sec. 201. (a) There is hereby established the National Military Establishment, and the Secretary of Defense shall be the head thereof.

(b) The National Military Establishment shall consist of the Department of the Army, the Department of the Navy, and the Department of the Air Force, together with all other agencies created under title II of this Act.

Secretary of Defense

Sec. 202. (a) There shall be a Secretary of Defense, who shall be appointed from civilian life by the President, by and with the advice and consent of the Senate: PROVIDED, That a person who has within ten years been on active duty as a commissioned officer in a Regular component of the armed services shall not be eligible for appointment as Secretary of Defense. The Secretary of Defense shall be the principal assistant to the President in all matters relating to the national security. Under the direction of the President and subject to the provisions of this Act he shall perform the following duties:

(1) Establish general policies and programs for the National Military Establishment and for all of the departments and agencies therein;

(2) Exercise general direction, authority, and control over such departments and agencies;

(3) Take appropriate steps to eliminate unnecessary duplication or overlapping in the fields of procurement, supply, transportation, storage, health, and research;

(4) Supervise and coordinate the preparation of the budget estimates of the departments and agencies comprising the National Military Establishment; formulate and determine the budget estimates for submittal to the Bureau of the Budget; and supervise the budget programs of such departments and agencies under the applicable appropriation Act: PROVIDED, That nothing herein contained shall prevent the Secretary of the Army, the Secretary of the Navy, or the Secretary of the Air Force from presenting to the President or to the Director of the Budget, after first so informing the Secretary of Defense, any report or recommendation relating to his department which he may deem necessary: AND PROVIDED FURTHER, That the Department of the Army, the Department of the Navy, and the Department of the Air Force shall be administered as individual executive departments by their respective Secretaries and all powers and duties relating to such departments not specifically conferred upon the Secretary of Defense by this Act shall be retained by each of their respective Secretaries.

(b) The Secretary of Defense shall submit annual written reports to the President and the Congress covering expenditures, work, and accomplishments of the National Military Establishment, together with such recommendations as he shall deem appropriate.

(c) The Secretary of Defense shall cause a seal of office to be made for the National Military Establishment, of such design as the President shall approve, and judicial notice shall be taken thereof.

Military Assistants to the Secretary

Sec. 203. Officers of the armed services may be detailed to duty as assistants and personal aides to the Secretary of Defense, but he shall not establish a military staff.

Civilian Personnel

Sec. 204. (a) The Secretary of Defense is authorized to appoint from civilian life not to exceed three special assistants to advise and assist him in the performance of his duties. Each such special assistant shall receive compensation at the rate of $10,000 a year.

(b) The Secretary of Defense is authorized, subject to the civil-service laws and the Classification Act of 1923, as amended, to appoint and fix the compensation of such other civilian personnel as may be necessary for the performance of the functions of the National Military Establishment other than those of the Departments of the Army, Navy, and Air Force.

Department of the Army

Sec. 205. (a) The Department of War shall hereafter be designated the Department of the Army, and the title of the Secretary of War shall be changed to Secretary of the Army. Changes shall be made in the titles of other officers and activities of the Department of the Army as the Secretary of the Army may determine.

(b) All laws, orders, regulations, and other actions relating to the Department of War or to any officer or activity whose title is changed under this section shall, insofar as they are not inconsistent with the provisions of this Act, be deemed to relate to the Department of the Army within the National Military Establishment or to such officer or activity designated by his or its new title.

(c) The term "Department of the Army" as used in this Act shall be construed to mean the Department of the Army at the seat of government and all field headquarters, forces, reserve components, installations, activities, and functions under the control or supervision of the Department of the Army.

(d) The Secretary of the Army shall cause a seal of office to be made for the Department of the Army, of such design as the President may approve, and judicial notice shall be taken thereof.

(e) In general the United States Army, within the Department of the Army, shall include land combat and service forces and such aviation and water transport as may be organic therein. It shall be organized, trained, and equipped primarily for prompt and sustained combat incident to operations on land. It shall be responsible for the preparation of land forces necessary for the effective prosecution of war except as otherwise assigned and, in accordance with integrated joint mobilization plans, for the expansion of peacetime components of the Army to meet the needs of war.

Department of the Navy

Sec. 206. (a) The term "Department of the Navy" as used in this Act shall be construed to mean the Department of the Navy at the seat of government; the headquarters, United States Marine Corps; the entire operating force of the United States Navy, including naval aviation, and of the United States Marine Corps, including the reserve components of such forces; all field activities, headquarters, forces, bases, installations, activities, and functions under the control or supervision of the Department of the Navy; and the United States Coast Guard when operating as a part of the Navy pursuant to law.

(b) In general the United States Navy, within the Department of the Navy, shall include naval combat and services forces and such aviation as may be organic therein. It shall be organized, trained, and equipped primarily for prompt and sustained combat incident to operations at sea. It shall be responsible for the preparation of naval forces necessary for the effective prosecution of war except as otherwise assigned, and, in accordance with integrated joint mobilization plans, for the expansion of the peacetime components of the Navy to meet the needs of war.

All naval aviation shall be integrated with the naval service as part thereof within the Department of the Navy. Naval aviation shall consist of combat and service and training forces, and shall include land-based naval aviation, air transport essential for naval operations, all air weapons and air techniques involved in the operations and activities of the United States Navy, and the entire remainder of the aeronautical organization of the United States Navy, together with the personnel necessary therefor.

The Navy shall be generally responsible for naval reconnaissance, antisubmarine warfare, and protection of shipping.

The Navy shall develop aircraft, weapons, tactics, technique, organization and equipment of naval combat and service elements; matters of joint concern as to these functions shall be coordinated between the Army, the Air Force, and the Navy.

(c) The United States Marine Corps, within the Department of the Navy, shall include land combat and service forces and such aviation as may be organic therein. The Marine Corps shall be organized, trained, and equipped to provide fleet marine forces of combined arms, together with supporting air components, for service with the fleet in the seizure or defense of advanced naval bases and for the conduct of such land operations as may be essential to the prosecution of a naval campaign. It shall be the duty of the Marine Corps to develop, in coordination with the Army and the Air Force, those phases of amphibious operations which pertain to the tactics, technique, and equipment employed by landing forces. In addition, the Marine Corps shall provide detachments and organizations for service on armed vessels of the Navy, shall provide security detachments for the protection of naval property at naval stations and bases, and shall perform such other duties as the President may direct: PROVIDED, That such additional duties shall not detract from or interfere with the operations for which the Marine Corps is primarily organized. The Marine Corps shall be responsible, in accordance with integrated joint mobilization plans, for the expansion of peacetime components of the Marine Corps to meet the needs of war.

Department of the Air Force

Sec. 207. (a) Within the National Military Establishment there is hereby established an executive department to be known as the Department of the Air Force, and a Secretary of the Air Force, who shall be the head thereof. The Secretary of the Air Force shall be appointed from civilian life by the President, by and with the advice and consent of the Senate.

(b) Section 158 of the Revised statutes is amended to include the Department of the Air Force and the provisions of so much of Title IV of the Revised Statutes as now or hereafter amended as is not inconsistent with the Act shall be applicable to the Department of the Air Force.

(c) The term "Department of the Air Force" as used in this Act shall be construed to mean the Department of the Air Force at the seat of government and all field headquarters, forces, reserve components, installations, activities, and functions under the control or supervision of the Department of the Air Force.

(d) There shall be in the Department of the Air Force an Under Secretary of the Air Force and two Assistant secretaries of the Air Force, who shall be appointed from civilian life by the President by and with the advice and consent of the senate.

(e) The several officers of the Department of the Air Force shall perform such functions as the Secretary of the Air Force may prescribe.

(f) So much of the functions of the Secretary of the Army and of the Department of the Army, including those of any officer of such Department, as are assigned to or under the control of the commanding General, Army Air Forces, or as are deemed by the Secretary of Defense to be necessary or desirable for the operations of the Department of the Air Force or the United States Air Force, shall be transferred to and vested in the Secretary of the Air Force and the Department of the Air Force: PROVIDED,That the National Guard Bureau shall, in addition to the functions and duties performed by it for the Department of the Army, be charged with similar functions and duties for the Department of the Air Force, and shall be the channel of communication between the Department of the Air Force and the several States on all matters pertaining to the Air National Guard: AND PROVIDED FURTHER, That in order to permit an orderly transfer, the Secretary of Defense may, during the transfer period hereinafter prescribed, direct that the Department of the Army shall continue for appropriate periods to exercise any of such functions, insofar as they relate to the Department of the Air Force, or the United States Air Force or their property and personnel. Such of the property, personnel, and records of the Department of the Army used in the exercise of functions transferred under this subsection as the Secretary of Defense shall determine shall be transferred or assigned to the Department of the Air Force.

(g) The Secretary of the Air Force shall cause a seal of office to be made for the Department of the Air Force, of such device as the President shall approve, and judicial notice shall be taken thereof.

United States Air Force

Sec. 208. (a) The United States Air Force is hereby established under the Department of the Air Force. The Army Air Forces, the Air Corps, United States Army, and the General Headquarters Air Force (Air Force Combat Command), shall be transferred to the United States Air Force.

(b) There shall be a Chief of Staff, United States Air Force, who shall be appointed by the president, by and with the advice and consent of the Senate, for a term of four years from among the officers of general rank who are assigned to or commissioned in the United States Air Force. Under the direction of the Secretary of the Air Force, the Chief of Staff, United States Air Force, shall exercise Command over the United States Air Force and shall be charged with the duty of carrying into execution all lawful orders and directions which may be transmitted to him. The functions of the Commanding General, General Headquarters Air Force (Air Force Combat Command), and of the Chief of the Air corps and of the Commanding General, Army Air Forces, shall be transferred to the Chief of Staff, United States Air Force. When such transfer becomes effective, the offices of the Chief of the Air Corps, United States Army, and Assistants to the Chief of the Air Corps, United States Army, provided for by the Act of June 4, 1920, as amended (41 Stat. 768), and Commanding General, General Headquarters Air Force, provided for by section 5 of the Act of June 16, 1936 (49 Stat. 1525), shall cease to exist. While holding office as Chief of Staff, United States Air Force, the incumbent shall hold a grade and receive allowances equivalent to those prescribed by law for the Chief of Staff, United States Army. The Chief of Staff, United States Army, the Chief of Naval Operations, and the Chief of Staff, United States Air Force, shall take rank among themselves according to their relative dates of appointment as such, and shall each take rank above all other officers on the active list of the Army, Navy, and Air Force: PROVIDED, That nothing in this Act shall have the effect of changing the relative rank of the present Chief of Staff, United States Army, and the present Chief of Naval Operations.

(c) All commissioned officers, warrant officers, and enlisted men, commissioned, holding warrants, or enlisted, in the Air Corps, United States Army, or the Army Air Forces, shall be transferred in branch to the United States Air Force. All other commissioned officers, warrant officers, and enlisted men, who are commissioned, hold warrants, or are enlisted, in any component of the Army of the United States and who are under the authority or command of the Commanding General, Army Air Forces, shall be continued under the authority or command of the Chief of Staff, United States Air Force, and under the jurisdiction of the Department of the Air Force. Personnel whose status is affected by this subsection shall retain their existing commissions, warrants, or enlisted status in existing components of the armed forces unless otherwise altered or terminated in accordance with existing law; and they shall not be deemed to have been appointed to a new or different office or grade, or to have vacated their permanent or temporary appointments in an existing component of the armed forces, solely by virtue of any change in status under this subsection. No such change in status shall alter or prejudice the status of any individual so assigned, so as to deprive him of any right, benefit, or privilege to which he may be entitled under existing law.

(d) Except as otherwise directed by the Secretary of the Air Force, all property, records, installations, agencies, activities, projects, and civilian personnel under the jurisdiction, control, authority, or command of the Commanding General, Army Air Forces, shall be continued to the same extent under the jurisdiction, control, authority, or command, respectively, of the Chief of Staff, United States Air Force, in the Department of the Air Force.

(e) For a period of two years from the date of enactment of this Act, personnel (both military and civilian), property, records, installations, agencies, activities, and projects may be transferred between the Department of the Army and the Department of the Air Force by direction of the Secretary of Defense.

(f) In general the United States Air Force shall include aviation forces both combat and service not otherwise assigned. It shall be organized, trained, and equipped primarily for prompt and sustained offensive and defensive air operations. The Air Force shall be responsible for the preparation of the air forces necessary for the effective prosecution of war except as otherwise assigned and, in accordance with integrated joint mobilization plans, for the expansion of the peacetime components of the Air Force to meet the needs of war.

Effective Date of Transfers

Sec. 209. Each transfer, assignment, or change in status under section 207 or section 208 shall take effect upon such date or dates as may be prescribed by the Secretary of Defense.

War Council

Sec. 210. There shall be within the National Military Establishment a War Council composed of the Secretary of Defense, as Chairman, who shall have power of decision; the Secretary of the Army; the Secretary of the Navy; the Secretary of the Air Force; the Chief of Staff, United States Army the Chief of Naval Operations; and the Chief of Staff, United States Air Force. The War Council shall advise the Secretary of Defense on matters of broad policy relating to the armed forces, and shall consider and report on such other matters as the Secretary of Defense may direct.

Joint Chiefs of Staff

Sec. 211. (a) There is hereby established within the National Military Establishment the Joint Chiefs of Staff, which shall consist of the Chief of Staff, United States Army; the Chief of Naval Operations; the Chief of Staff, United States Air Force; and the Chief of Staff to the Commander in Chief, if there be one.

(b) Subject to the authority and direction of the President and the Secretary of Defense, it shall be the duty of the Joint Chiefs of Staff—

(1) to prepare strategic plans and to provide for the strategic direction of the military forces;

(2) to prepare joint logistic plans and to assign to the military services logistic responsibilities in accordance with such plans;

(3) to establish unified commands in strategic areas when such unified commands are in the interest of national security;

(4) to formulate policies for joint training of the military forces;

(5) to formulate policies for coordinating the education of members of the military forces;

(6) to review major material and personnel requirements of the military forces, in accordance with strategic and logistic plans; and

(7) to provide United States representation on the Military Staff Committee of the United Nations in accordance with the provisions of the Charter of the United Nations.

(c) The Joint Chiefs of Staff shall act as the principal military advisers to the President and the Secretary of Defense and shall perform such other duties as the President and the Secretary of Defense may direct or as may be prescribed by law.

Joint Staff

Sec. 212. There shall be, under the Joint Chiefs of Staff, a Joint Staff to consist of not to exceed one hundred officers and to be composed of approximately equal numbers of officers from each of the three armed services. The Joint Staff, operating under a Director thereof appointed by the Joint Chiefs of Staff, shall perform such duties as may be directed by the Joint Chiefs of Staff. The Director shall be an officer junior in grade to all members of the Joint Chiefs of Staff.

Munitions Board

Sec. 213. (a) There is hereby established in the National Military Establishment a Munitions Board (hereinafter in this section referred to as the "Board").

(b) The Board shall be composed of a Chairman, who shall be the head thereof, and an under Secretary or Assistant Secretary from each of the three military departments, to be designated in each case by the Secretaries of their respective Departments. The Chairman shall be appointed from civilian life by the President, by and with the advice and consent of tbe Senate, and shall receive compensation at the rate
$14,000 a year.

(c) It shall be the duty of the Board under the direction of the Secretary of Defense and in support of strategic and logistic plans prepared by the Joint Chiefs of Staff—

(1) to coordinate the appropriate activities within the National Military Establishment with regard to industrial matters, including the

procurement, production, and distribution plans of the departments and agencies comprising the Establishment;

(2) to plan for the military aspects of industrial mobilization;

(3) to recommend assignment of procurement responsibilities among the several military services and to plan for standardization of specifications and for the greatest practicable allocation of purchase authority of technical equipment and common use items on the basis of single procurement;

(4) to prepare estimates of potential production, procurement, and personnel for use in evaluation of the logistic feasibility of strategic operations;

(5) to determine relative priorities of the various segments of the military procurement programs;

(6) to supervise such subordinate agencies as are or may be created to consider the subjects falling within the scope of the Board's responsibilities;

(7) to make recommendations to regroup, combine, or dissolve existing interservice agencies operating in the fields of procurement, production, and distribution in such manner as to promote efficiency and economy;

(8) to maintain liaison with other departments and agencies for the proper correlation of military requirements with the civilian economy, particularly in regard to the procurement or disposition of strategic and critical material and the maintenance of adequate reserves of such material, and to make recommendations as to policies in connection therewith;

(9) to assemble and review material and personnel requirements presented by the Joint Chiefs of Staff and those presented by the production, procurement, and distribution agencies assigned to meet military needs, and to make recommendations thereon to the Secretary of Defense; and

(10) to perform such duties as the Secretary of Defense may direct.

(d) When the Chairman of the Board first appointed has taken office, the Joint Army and Navy Munitions Board shall cease to exist and all its records and personnel shall be transferred to the Munitions Board.

(e) The Secretary of Defense shall provide the Board with such personnel and facilities as the Secretary may determine to be required by the Board for the performance of its functions.

Research and Development Board

Sec. 214. (a) There is hereby established in the National Military Establishment a Research and Development Board (hereinafter in this section referred to as the "Board"). The Board shall be composed of a Chairman, who shall be the head thereof, and two representatives from each of the Departments of the Army, Navy, and Air Force, to be designated by the Secretaries of their respective Departments. The Chairman shall be appointed from civilian life by the President, by and with the advice and consent of the Senate, and shall receive compensation at the rate of $14,000 a year. The purpose of the Board shall be to advise the Secretary of Defense as to the status of scientific research relative to the national security, and to assist him in assuring adequate provision for research and development on scientific problems relating to the national security.

(b) it shall be the duty of the Board, under the direction of the Secretary of Defense—

(1) to prepare a complete and integrated program of research and development for military purposes;

(2) to advise with regard to trends in scientific research relating to national security and the measures necessary to assure continued and increasing progress;

(3) to recommend measures of coordination of research and development among the military departments and allocation among them of responsibilities for specific programs of joint interest;

(4) to formulate policy for the National Military Establishment in connection with research and development matters involving agencies outside the National Military Establishment;

(5) to consider the interaction of research and development and strategy, and to advise the Joint Chiefs of Staff in connection therewith; and

(6) to perform such other duties as the Secretary of Defense may direct.

(c) When the Chairman of the Board first appointed has taken office the Joint Research and Development Board shall cease to exist and all its records and personnel shall be transferred to the Research and Development Board.

(d) The Secretary of Defense shall provide the Board with such personnel and facilities as the Secretary may determine to be required by the Board for the performance of its functions.

TITLE III-MISCELLANEOUS

Compensation of Secretaries

Sec. 301. (a) The Secretary of Defense shall receive the compensation prescribed by law for heads of executive departments.

(b) The Secretary of the Army, the Secretary of the Navy, and the Secretary of the Air Force shall each receive the compensation prescribed by law for heads of executive departments.

Under Secretaries and Assistant Secretaries

Sec. 302. The Under Secretaries and Assistant Secretaries of the Army, the Navy, and the Air Force shall each receive compensation at the rate of $10,000 a year and shall perform such duties as the Secretaries of their respective Departments may prescribe.

Advisory Committees and Personnel

Sec. 303. (a) The Secretary of Defense, the Chairman of the National Security Resources Board, and the Director of Central Intelligence are authorized to appoint such advisory committees and to employ, consistent with other provisions of this Act, such part-time advisory personnel as they may deem necessary in carrying out their respective functions and the functions of agencies under their control. Persons holding other offices or positions under the United States for which they receive compensation while serving as members of such committees shall receive no additional compensation for such service. Other members of such committees and other part-time advisory personnel so employed may serve without compensation or may receive compensation at a rate not to exceed $35 for each day of service, as determined by the appointing authority.

(b) Service of an individual as a member of any such advisory committee, or in any other part-time capacity for a department or agency hereunder, shall not be considered as service bringing such individual within the provisions of section 109 or 113 of the Criminal Code (U.S.C., 1940 edition, title 18, secs. 198 and 203), or section 19 (e) of the Contract Settlement Act of 1944, unless the act of such individual, which by such section is made unlawful when performed by an individual referred to in such section, is with respect to any particular matter which directly involves a department or agency which such person is advising or in which such department or agency is directly interested.

Status of Transferred Civilian Personnel

Sec. 304. All transfers of civilian personnel under this Act shall be without change in classification or compensation, but the head of any department or agency to which such a transfer is made is authorized to make such changes in the titles and designations and prescribe such changes in the duties of such personnel commensurate with their classification as he may deem necessary and appropriate.

Saving Provisions

Sec. 305. (a) All laws, orders, regulations, and other actions applicable with respect to any function, activity, personnel, property, records, or other thing transferred under this Act, or with respect to any officer, department, or agency, from which such transfer is made, shall, except to the extent rescinded, modified, superseded, terminated, or made inapplicable by or under authority of law, have the same effect as if such transfer had not been made; but, after any such transfer, any such law, order, regulation, or other action which vested functions in or otherwise related to any officer, department, or agency from which such transfers was made shall, insofar as applicable with respect to the function, activity, personnel, property, records or other thing transferred and to the extent not inconsistent with other provisions of this Act, be deemed to

298

have vested such function in or relate to the officer, department, or agency to which the transfer was made.

(b) No suit, action, or other proceeding lawfully commenced by or against the head of any department or agency or other officer of the United States, in his official capacity or in relation to the discharge of his official duties, shall abate by reason of the taking effect of any transfer or change in title under the provisions of this Act; and, in the case of any such transfer, such suit, action, or other proceeding may be maintained by or against the successor of such head or other officer under the transfer, but only if the court shall allow the same to be maintained on motion or supplemental petition filed within twelve months after such transfer takes effect, showing a necessity for the survival of such suit, action, or other proceeding to obtain settlement of the questions involved.

(c) Notwithstanding the provisions of the second paragraph of section 5 of title I of the First War powers Act, 1941, the existing organization of the War Department under the provisions of Executive Order Numbered 9082 of February 28, 1942, as modified by Executive Order Numbered 9722 of May 13, 1946, and the existing organization of the Department of the Navy under the provisions of Executive Order Numbered 9635 of September 29, 1945, including the assignment of functions to organizational units within the War and Navy Departments, may, to the extent determined by the Secretary of Defense, continue in force for two years following the date of enactment of this Act except to the extent modified by the provisions of this Act or under the authority of law.

Transfer of Funds

Sec. 306. All unexpended balances of appropriations, allocations, nonappropriated funds, or other funds available or hereafter made available for use by or on behalf of the Army Air Forces or officers thereof, shall be transferred to the Department of the Air Force for use in connection with the exercise of its functions. Such other unexpended balances of appropriations, allocations, nonappropriated funds, or other funds available or hereafter made available for use by the Department of War or the Department of the Army in exercise of functions transferred to the Department of the Air Force under this Act, as the Secretary of Defense shall determine, shall be transferred to the Department of the Air Force for use in connection with the exercise of its functions. Unexpended balances transferred under this section may be used for the purposes for which the appropriations, allocations, or other funds were originally made available, or for new expenditures occasioned by the enactment of this Act. The transfers herein authorized may be made with or without warrant action as may be appropriate from time to time from any appropriation covered by this section to any other such appropriation or to such new accounts established on the books of the Treasury as may be determined to be necessary to carry into effect provisions of this Act.

Authorization for Appropriations

Sec. 307. There are hereby authorized to be appropriated such sums as may be necessary and appropriate to carry out the provisions and purpose of this Act.

Definitions

Sec. 308. (a) As used in this Act, the term "function" includes functions, powers and duties.

(b) As used in this Act, the term "budget program" refers to recommendations as to the apportionment, to the allocation and to the review of allotments of appropriate funds.

Separability

Sec. 309. If any provisions of this Act or the application thereof to any person or circumstances is held invalid, the validity of the remainder of the Act and of the application of such provision to other persons and circumstances shall not be affected thereby.

Effective Date

Sec. 310. (a) The first sentence of section 202 (a) and sections 1, 2, 307, 308, 309, and 310 shall take effect immediately upon the enactment of this Act.

(b) Except as provided in subsection (a), the provisions of this Act shall take effect on whichever of the following days is the earlier: The day after the day upon which the Secretary of Defense first appointed takes office, or the sixtieth day after the date of the enactment of this Act.

Succession to the Presidency

Sec. 311. Paragraph (1) of subsection (d) of section 1 of the Act entitled "An Act to provide for the performance of the duties of the office of President in case of the removal, resignation, death, or inability both of the President and Vice President", approved July 18, 1947, is amended by striking out "Secretary of War" and inserting in lieu thereof "Secretary of Defense", and by striking out "Secretary of the Navy".

Approved July 26, 1947.

Appendix 7

The National Security Act Amendments of 1949

[63 Stat.]

PUBLIC LAW 216—August 10, 1949

Public Law 216   Chapter 412

AN ACT

To reorganize fiscal management in the National Military Establishment to promote economy and efficiency, and for other purposes.

Be it enacted by the Senate and House of Representatives of the United States of America in Congress assembled.

SHORT TITLE

Section 1. This Act may be cited as the "National Security Act Amendments of 1949".

Sec. 2. Section 2 of the National Security Act of 1947 is amended to read as follows:

"Sec. 2. In enacting this legislation, it is the intent of Congress to provide a comprehensive program for the future security of the United States; to provide for the establishment of integrated policies and procedures for the departments, agencies, and functions of the Government relating to the national security; to provide three military departments, separately administered, for the operation and administration of the Army, the Navy (including naval aviation and the United States Marine Corps), and the Air Force, with their assigned combat and service components; to provide for their authoritative coordination and unified direction under civilian control of the Secretary of Defense but not to merge them; to provide for the effective strategic direction of the armed forces and for their operation under unified control and for their integration into an efficient team of land, naval, and air forces but not to establish a single Chief of Staff over the armed forces nor an armed forces general staff (but this is not to be interpreted as applying to the Joint Chiefs of Staff or Joint Staff)."

CHANGE IN COMPOSITION OF THE NATIONAL SECURITY COUNCIL

Sec. 3. The fourth paragraph of section 101 (a) of the National Security Act of 1947 is amended to read as follows: "The Council shall be composed of-

"(1) the President;

"(2) the Vice President;

"(3) the Secretary of State;

"(4) the Secretary of Defense;

"(5) the Chairman of the National Security Resources Board; and

"(6) The Secretaries and Under Secretaries of other executive departments and of the military departments, the Chairman of the Munitions Board, and the Chairman of the Research and Development Board, when appointed by the President by and with the advice and consent of the Senate, to serve at his pleasure."

CONVERSION OF THE NATIONAL MILITARY ESTABLISHMENT INTO AN EXECUTIVE DEPARTMENT

Sec. 4. Section 201 of the National Security Act of 1947 is amended to read as follows:

"Sec. 201. (a) There is hereby established, as an Executive Department of the Government, the Department of Defense, and the Secretary of Defense shall be the head thereof.

(b) There shall be within the Department of Defense (1) the Department of the Army, the Department of the Navy, and the Department of the Air Force, and each such department shall on and after the date of enactment of the National Security Act Amendments of 1949 be military departments in lieu of their prior status as Executive Departments, and (2) all other agencies created under title II of this Act.

"(c) Section 158 of the Revised Statutes, as amended, is amended to read as follows:

"'Sec. 158. The provisions of this title shall apply to the following Executive Departments:

"'First. The Department of State.

"'Second. The Department of Defense.

"'Third. The Department of the Treasury.

"'Fourth. The Department of Justice.

"'Fifth. The Post Office Department.

"'Sixth. The Department of the Interior.

"'Seventh. The Department of Agriculture.

"'Eighth. The Department of Commerce.

"'Ninth. The Department of Labor.'

"(d) Except to the extent inconsistent with the provisions of this Act, provisions of title IV of the Revised Statutes as now or hereafter amended should be applicable to the Department of Defense."

THE SECRETARY OF DEFENSE

Sec. 5. Section 202 of the National Security Act of 1947, as amended, is further amended to read as follows:

"Sec. 202. (a) There shall be a Secretary of Defense, who shall be appointed from civilian life by the President, by and with the advice and consent of the Senate: Provided, That a person who has within ten years been on active duty as a commissioned officer in a Regular component of the armed services shall not be eligible for appointment as Secretary of Defense.

"(b) The Secretary of Defense shall be the principal assistant to the President in all matters relating to the Department of Defense. Under the direction of the President, and subject to the provisions if this Act, he shall have direct authority, and control over the Department of Defense.

"(c) (1) Notwithstanding any other provision of this Act, the combatant functions assigned to the military services by sections 205 (e), 206 (b), 206 (c), and 208 (f) hereof shall not be transferred, reassigned, abolished, or consolidated.

"(2) Military personnel shall not be so detailed or assigned as to impair such combatant functions.

(3) The Secretary of Defense shall not direct the use and expenditure of funds of the Department of Defense in such manner as to effect the results prohibited by paragraphs (1) and (2) of this subsection.

"(4) The Departments of the Army, Navy, and Air Force shall be separately administered by their respective Secretaries under the direction, authority, and control of the Secretary of Defense.

"(5) Subject to the provisions of paragraph (1) of this subsection no function which has been or is hereafter authorized by law to be performed by the Department of Defense shall be substantially transferred, reassigned, abolished or consolidated until after a report in regard to all pertinent details shall have been made by the Secretary of Defense to the Committees on Armed Services of the Congress.

"(6) No provision of this Act shall be so construed as to prevent a Secretary of a military department or a member of the Joint Chiefs of Staff from presenting to the Congress on his own initiative, after first so informing the Secretary of Defense, any recommendation relating to the Department of Defense that he may deem proper.

"(d) The Secretary of Defense shall not less often than semiannually submit written reports to the President and the Congress covering expenditures, work and accomplishments of the Department of Defense, accompanied by (1) such recommendations as he shall deem appropriate, (2) separate reports from the military departments covering their expenditures, work and accomplishments, and (3) itemized statements showing the savings of public funds and the eliminations for unnecessary duplications and overlappings that have been accomplished pursuant to the provisions of this Act.

"(e) The Secretary of Defense shall cause a seal of office to be made for the Department of Defense, of such design as the President shall approve, and judicial notice shall be taken thereof.

"(f) The Secretary of Defense may, without being relieved of his responsibility therefor, and unless prohibited by some specific provision of this Act or other specific provision of law, perform any function vested in him through or with the aid of such officials or organizational entities of the Department of Defense as he may designate."

THE DEPUTY SECRETARY OF DEFENSE; ASSISTANT SECRETARIES OF DEFENSE; MILITARY ASSISTANTS; AND CIVILIAN PERSONNEL

Sec. 6 (a) Section 203 of the National Security Act of 1947 is amended to read as follows:

"Sec. 203. (a) There shall be a Deputy Secretary of Defense, who shall be appointed from civilian life by the President, by and with the advice and consent of the Senate: Provided, That a person who has within ten years been on active duty as a commissioned officer in a Regular component of the armed services shall not be eligible for appointment as Deputy Secretary of Defense. The Deputy Secretary shall perform such duties and exercise such powers as the Secretary of Defense may prescribe and shall take precedence in the Department of Defense next after the Secretary of Defense. The Deputy Secretary shall act for, and exercise the powers of the Secretary of Defense during his absence or disability.

"(b) There shall be three Assistant Secretaries of Defense, who shall be appointed from civilian life by the President, by and with the advice and consent of the Senate. The Assistant Secretaries shall perform such duties and exercise such powers as the Secretary of Defense may prescribe and shall take precedence in the Department of Defense after the Secretary of Defense, the Deputy Secretary of Defense, the Secretary of the Army, the Secretary of the Navy, and the Secretary of the Air Force.

"(c) Officers of the armed services may be detailed to duty as assistants and personal aides to the Secretary of Defense, but he shall not establish a military Staff other than that provided for by section 211 (a) of this Act."

"(b) Section 204 of the National Security Act of 1947 is amended to read as follows:

"Sec 204. The Secretary of Defense is authorized, subject to the civil service laws and the Classification Act of 1923, as amended, to appoint and fix the compensation of such civilian personnel as may be necessary for the performance of the functions of the Department of Defense other than those of the Departments of the Army, Navy, and Air Force."

CREATING THE POSITION OF CHAIRMAN OF THE JOINT CHIEFS OF STAFF AND PRESCRIBING HIS POWERS AND DUTIES

Sec. 7. (a) Section 210 of the National Security Act of 1947 is amended to read as follows:

"Sec. 210. There shall be within the Department of Defense an Armed Forces Policy Council composed of the Secretary of Defense, as Chairman, who shall have power of decision; the Deputy Secretary of Defense; the Secretary of the Army; The Secretary of the Navy; the Secretary of the Air Force; the Chairman of the Joint Chiefs of Staff; the Chief of Staff, United States Army; the Chief of Naval Operations; and the Chief of Staff, United States Air Force. The Armed Forces Policy Council shall advise the Secretary of Defense on matters of broad policy relating to the armed forces and shall consider and report on such other matters as the Secretary of Defense may direct."

"(b) Section 211 of the National Security Act of 1947 is amended to read as follows:

"Sec 211. (a) There is hereby established within the Department of Defense the Joint Chiefs of Staff, which shall consist of the Chairman, who shall be the presiding officer thereof but who shall have no vote; the Chief of Staff, United States Army, the Chief of Naval Operations: and the Chief of Staff, United States Air Force. The Joint Chiefs of Staff shall be the principal military advisers to the President, the National Security Council, and the Secretary of Defense.

"(b) Subject to the authority and direction of the President and the Secretary of Defense, the Joint Chiefs of Staff shall perform the following duties, in addition to such other duties as the President or the Secretary of Defense may direct:

"(1)   preparation of strategic plans and provision for the strategic direction of the military forces;

"(2)   preparation of joint logistic plans and assignment to the military services of logistic responsibilities in accordance with such plans;

"(3)   establishment of unified commands in strategic areas;

"(4)   review of major material and personnel requirements of the military forces in accordance with strategic and logistic plans;

"(5)   formulation of policies for joint training of the military forces;

"(6)   formulation of policies for coordinating the military education of members of the military forces; and

"(7)   providing United States representation on the Military Staff Committee of the United Nations in accordance with the provisions of the Charter of the United Nations.

"(c) The Chairman of the Joint Chiefs of Staff (hereinafter referred to as the 'Chairman') shall be appointed by the President, by and with the advice and consent of the Senate from among the Regular officers of the armed services to serve at the pleasure of the President for a term of two years and shall be eligible for one reappointment, by and with the advice and consent of the Senate, except in time of war hereafter declared by the Congress when there shall be no limitation on the number of such reappointments. The Chairman shall receive the basic pay and basic and personal money allowances prescribed by law for the Chief of Staff, United States Army, and such special pays and hazardous duty pays to which he may be entitled under other provisions of law.

"(d) The Chairman, if in the grade of general, shall be additional to the number of officers in the grade of general provided in the third proviso of section 504 (b) of the Office Personnel Act of 1947 (Public Law 381,

Eightieth Congress) or, of [*sic*] in the rank of admiral, shall be additional to the number of officers having the rank of admiral provided in section 413 (a) of such Act. While holding such office he shall take precedence over all other officers of the armed services: Provided, That the Chairman shall not exercise military command over the Joint Chiefs of Staff or over any of the military services.

"(e) In addition to participating as a member of the Joint Chiefs of Staff in the performance of the duties assigned in sub-section (b) of this section, the Chairman shall, subject to the authority and direction of the President and the Secretary of Defense, perform the following duties:

"(1) serve as the presiding officer of the Joint Chiefs of Staff;

"(2) provide agenda for meetings of the Joint Chiefs of Staff and assist the Joint Chiefs of Staff to prosecute their business as promptly as practicable; and

"(3) inform the Secretary of Defense and, when appropriate as determined by the President or the Secretary of Defense, the President, of those issues upon which agreement among the Joint Chiefs of Staff has not been reached."

"(c) Section 212 of the National Security Act of 1947 is amended to read as follows:

"Sec. 212. There shall be, under the Joint Chief of Staff, a Joint Staff to consist of not to exceed two hundred and ten officers and to be composed of approximately equal numbers of officers appointed by the Joint Chiefs of Staff from each of the three armed services. The Joint Staff, operating under a Director thereof appointed by the Joint Chiefs of Staff, shall perform such duties as may be directed by the Joint Chiefs of Staff. The Director shall be an officer junior in grade to all members of the Joint Chiefs of Staff."

CHANGING THE RELATIONSHIP OF THE SECRETARY OF DEFENSE TO THE MUNITIONS BOARD

Sec. 8. Section 213 of the National Security Act of 1947 is amended to read as follows:

"Sec. 213. (a) There is hereby established in the Department of Defense a Munitions Board (hereinafter in this section referred to as the 'Board').

"(b) The Board shall be composed of a Chairman, who shall be the head thereof and who shall, subject to the authority of the Secretary of Defense and in respect to such matters authorized by him, have the power of decision upon matters falling within the jurisdiction of the Board, and an Under Secretary or Assistant Secretary from each of the three military departments, to be designated in each case by the Secretaries of their respective departments. The Chairman shall be appointed from civilian life by the President, by and with advice and consent of the Senate, and shall receive compensation at the rate of $14,000 a year.

"(c) Subject to the authority and direction of the Secretary of Defense, the Board shall perform the following duties in support of strategic and logistic plans and in consonance with guidance in those fields provided by the Joint

Chiefs of Staff, and such other duties as the Secretary of Defense may prescribe:

"(1) coordination of the appropriate activities with regard to industrial matters, including the procurement, production, and distribution plans of the Department of Defense;

"(2) planning for the military aspects of industrial mobilization;

"(3) assignment of procurement responsibilities among the several military departments and planning for standardization of specifications and for the greatest practicable allocation of purchase authority of technical equipment and common use items on the basis of single procurement;

"(4) preparation of estimates of potential production, procurement, and personnel for use in evaluation of the logistic feasibility of strategic operations;

"(5) determination of relative priorities of the various segments of the military procurement programs;

"(6) supervision of such subordinate agencies as are or may be created to consider the subjects falling within the scope of the Board's responsibilities;

"(7) regrouping, combining, or dissolving of existing interservice agencies operating in the fields of procurement, production, and distribution in such manner as to promote efficiency and economy;

"(8) maintenance of liaison with other departments and agencies for the proper correlation of military requirements with the civilian economy, particularly in regard to the procurement or disposition of strategic and critical material and the maintenance of adequate reserves of such material, and making of recommendations as to policies in connection therewith; and

"(9) assembly and review of material and personnel requirements presented by the Joint Chiefs of Staff and by the production, procurement, and distribution agencies assigned to meet military needs, and making of recommendations thereon to the Secretary of Defense.

"(d) When the Chairman of the Board first appointed has taken office, the Joint Army and Navy Munitions Board shall cease to exist and all its records and personnel shall be transferred to the Munitions Board.

"(e) The Secretary of Defense shall provide the Board with such personnel and facilities as the Secretary may determine to be required by the Board for the performance of its functions."

CHANGING THE RELATIONSHIP OF THE SECRETARY OF DEFENSE TO THE RESEARCH AND DEVELOPMENT BOARD

Sec. 9. Section 214 of the National Security Act of 1947 is amended to read as follows:

"Sec 214. (a) There is hereby established in the Department of Defense a Research and Development Board (hereinafter in this section referred to as the 'Board'). The Board shall be composed of a Chairman, who shall be the head thereof and who shall, subject to the authority of the Secretary of Defense and in respect to such matters authorized by him, have the power of decision on matters falling within the jurisdiction of the Board, and two representatives from each of the Departments of the Army, Navy, and Air Force, to be designated by the Secretaries of their respective Departments. The Chairman shall be appointed from civilian life by the president, by and with the advice and consent of the Senate, and shall receive co npensation at the rate of $14,000 a year. The purpose of the Board shall be to advise the Secretary of Defense as to the status of scientific research relative to the national security, and to assist him in assuring adequate provision for research and development on scientific problems relating to the national security.

"(b) Subject to the authority and direction of the Secretary of Defense, the Board shall perform the following duties and such other duties as the Secretary of Defense may prescribe:

"(1) preparation of a complete and integrated program of research and development for military purposes;

"(2) advising with regard to trends in scientific research relating to national security and the measures necessary to assure continued and increasing progress;

"(3) coordination of research and development among the military departments and allocations among them of responsibilities for specific programs;

"(4) formulation of policy for the Department of Defense in connection with research and development matters involving agencies outside the Department of Defense; and

"(5) consideration of the interaction of research and development and strategy, and advising the Joint Chiefs of Staff in connection therewith.

"(c) When the Chairman of the Board first appointed has taken office, the Joint Research and Development Board shall cease to exist and all its records and personnel shall be transferred to the Research and Development Board.

"(d) The Secretary of Defense shall provide the Board with such personnel and facilities as the Secretary may determine to be required by the Board for the performance of its functions."

COMPENSATION OF THE SECRETARY OF DEFENSE, DEPUTY SECRETARY OF DEFENSE, SECRETARIES OF MILITARY DEPARTMENTS, AND CONSULTANTS

Sec. 10. (a) Section 301 of the National Security Act of 1947 is amended to read as follows:

"Sec. 301. (a) The Secretary of Defense shall receive the compensation prescribed by law for heads of executive departments.

"(b) the Deputy Secretary of Defense shall receive compensation at the rate of $14,000 a year, or such other compensation plus $500 a year as may hereafter be provided by law for under secretaries of executive departments. The Secretary of the Army, the Secretary of the Navy, and the Secretary of the Air Force shall each receive compensation at the rate of $14,000 a year, or such other compensation as may hereafter be provided by law for under secretaries of executive departments."

(b) Section 302 of the National Security Act of 1947 is amended to read as follows:

"Sec. 302. The Assistant Secretaries of Defense and the Under Secretaries and Assistant Secretaries of the Army, the Navy and the Air Force shall each receive compensation at the rate of $10,330 a year or at the rate hereafter prescribed by law for assistant secretaries of executive departments and shall perform such duties as the respective Secretaries may prescribe."

(c) Section 303 (a) of the National Security Act of 1947 is amended to read as follows:

"(a) The Secretary of Defense, the Chairman of the National Security Resources Board, the Director of Central Intelligence, and the National Security Council, acting through its Executive Secretary, are authorized to appoint such advisory committees and to employ, consistent with other provisions of this Act, such part-time advisory personnel as they may deem necessary in carrying out their respective functions and the functions of agencies under their control. Persons holding other offices or positions under the United States for which they receive compensation, while serving as members of such committees, shall receive no additional compensation for such service. Other members of such committees and other part-time advisory personnel so employed may serve without compensation or may receive compensation at a rate not to exceed $50 for each day of service, as determined by the appointing authority."

REORGANIZATION OF FISCAL MANAGEMENT TO PROMOTE ECONOMY AND EFFICIENCY

Sec. 11. The National Security Act of 1947 is amended by inserting at the end thereof the following new title:

. . . .

[Ed. Note] Material omitted (Title IV) can be found in: Alice C. Cole, et al, eds., *The Department of Defense: Documents on Establishment and Organization, 1944–1978* (Washington, D.C.: Office of the Secretary of Defense, Historical Office, 1978), pp. 100–106, or in: *Joint Army and Air Force Bulletin*, No. 22, August 22, 1949.

Appendix 8

President Eisenhower's Message of April 30, 1953

President Dwight D. Eisenhower, after reviewing the report of the Committee on Department of Defense Organization, submitted his recommendations for changes in the Department of Defense organization on 30 April 1953 in a message transmitting Reorganization Plan No. 6 of 1953.

To the Congress of the United States:

I address the Congress on a subject which has been of primary interest to me throughout all the years of my adult life-the defense of our country.

As a former soldier who has experienced modern war at first hand, and now as President and Commander in Chief of the Armed Forces of the United States, I believe that our Defense Establishment is in need of immediate improvement. In this message I indicate actions which we are taking and must yet take, to assure the greater safety of America.

Through the years our Nation has warded off all enemies. We have defended ourselves successfully against those who have waged war against us. We enjoy, as a people, a proud tradition of triumph in battle.

We are not, however, a warlike people. Our historic goal is peace. It shall ever be peace—peace to enjoy the freedom we cherish and the fruits of our labors. We maintain strong military forces in support of this supreme purpose, for we believe that in today's world only properly organized strength may altogether avert war.

Because we are not a military-minded people, we have sometimes failed to give proper thought to the problems of the organization and adequacy of our Armed Forces. Past periods of international stress and the actual outbreaks of wars have found us poorly prepared. On such occasions we have had to commit to battle insufficient and improperly organized military forces to hold the foe until our citizenry could be more fully mobilized and our resources marshaled. We know that we cannot permit a repetition of those conditions.

Today we live in a perilous period of international affairs. Soviet Russia and her allies have it within their power to join with us in the establishment of a true peace or to plunge the world into global war. To date they have chosen to conduct themselves in such a way that these are years neither of total war nor total peace.

We in the United States have, therefore, recently embarked upon the definition of a new, positive foreign policy. One of our basic aims is to gain again for the free world the initiative in shaping the international conditions under which freedom can thrive. Essential to this endeavor is the assurance of an alert, efficient, ever-prepared Defense Establishment.

Today our international undertakings are shared by the free peoples of other nations. We find ourselves in an unparalleled role of leadership of free men everywhere. With this leadership have come new responsibilities. With the basic purpose of assuring our own security and economic viability, we are helping our friends to protect their lives and liberties. And one major help that we may give them is reliance upon our own Military Establishment.

Today also witnesses one of history's times of swiftest advance in scientific achievements. These developments can accomplish wonders in providing a healthier and happier life for us all. But—converted to military uses—they threaten new, more devastating terrors in war. These simple, inescapable facts make imperative the maintenance of a defense organization commanding the most modern technological instruments in our arsenal of weapons.

In providing the kind of military security that our country needs, we must keep our people free and our economy solvent. We must not endanger the very things we seek to defend. We must not create a nation mighty in arms that is lacking in liberty and bankrupt in resources. Our armed strength must continue to rise from the vigor or a free people and a prosperous economy.

Recognizing all these national and international demands upon our Military Establishment, we must remain ever mindful of three great objectives in organizing our defense.

First: Our Military Establishment must be founded upon our basic constitutional principles and traditions. There must be a clear and unchallenged civilian responsibility in the Defense Establishment. This is essential not only to maintain democratic institutions, but also to protect the integrity of the military profession. Basic decisions relating to the military forces must be made by politically accountable civilian officials. Conversely, professional military leaders must not be thrust into the political arena to become the prey of partisan politics. To guard these principles, we must recognized and respect the clear lines of responsibility and authority which run from the President, through the Secretary of Defense and the Secretaries of the military departments, over the operations of all branches of the Department of Defense.

Second: Effectiveness with economy must be made the watchwords of our defense effort. To maintain an adequate national defense for the indefinite future, we have found it necessary to devote a larger share of our national resources than any of us have heretofore anticipated. To protect our economy, maximum effectiveness at minimum cost is essential.

Third: We must develop the best possible military plans. These plans must be sound guides to action in case of war. They must incorporate the most competent and considered thinking from every point of view—military, scientific, industrial, and economic.

To strengthen civilian control by establishing clear lines of accountability, to further effectiveness with economy, and to provide adequate planning for military purposes—these were primary objectives of the Congress in enacting the National Security Act of 1947 and strengthening it in 1949.

Now much has happened which makes it appropriate to review the workings of those basic statutes. Valuable lessons have been learned through 6 years of trial by experience. Our top military structure has been observed under changing conditions. The military action in Korea, the buildup of our forces everywhere, the provision of military action in Korea, the buildup of our forces everywhere, the provision of military aid to other friendly nations, and the participation of United States Armed Forces in regional collective security arrangements, such as those under the North Atlantic Treaty Organization—all these have supplied sharp tests of our military organization. Today, in making my specific recommendations, I have also had the benefit of the report prepared by the Committee on Department of Defense Organization established by the Secretary of Defense 3 months ago.

The time is here, then, to work to perfect our Military Establishment without delay.

I

The first objective, toward which immediate actions already are being directed, is clarification of lines of authority within the Department of Defense so as to strengthen civilian responsibility.

I am convinced that the fundamental structure of our Department of Defense and its various component agencies as provided by the National Security Act, as amended, is sound. None of the changes I am proposing affects that basic structure, and this first objective can and will be attained without any legislative change.

With my full support, the Secretary of Defense must exercise over the Department of Defense the direction, authority, and control which are vested in him by the National Security Act. He should do so through the basic channels of responsibility and authority prescribed in that act—through the three civilian Secretaries of the Army, the Navy, and the Air Force, who are responsible to him for aspects of the respective military departments (except for the legal responsibility of the Joint Chiefs of Staff to advise the President in military matters). No function in any part of the Department of Defense, or in any of its component agencies, should be performed independent of the direction, authority, and control of the Secretary of Defense. The Secretary is the accountable civilian head of the Department of Defense, and, under the law, my principal assistant in all matters relating to the Department. I want all to know that he has my full backing in that role.

To clarify a point which has led to considerable confusion in the past, the Secretary of Defense, with my approval, will shortly issue a revision of that portion of the 1948 memorandum commonly known as the Key West agreement, which provides for a system of designating executive agents for unified commands. Basic decisions with respect to the establishment and direction of unified commands are made by the President and the Secretary of Defense, upon the recommendation of the Joint Chiefs of Staff in their military planning and advisory role. But the provision of the Key West agreement, under the Joint Chiefs of Staff designate one of their members as an executive agent for each unified command, has led to considerable confusion and misunderstanding with respect to the relationship of the Joint Chiefs of Staff to the Secretary of Defense, and the relationship of the military chief of each service to the civilian Secretary of his military department.

Hence, the Secretary of Defense, with my approval, is revising the Key West agreement to provide that the Secretary of Defense shall designate in each case a military department to serve as the executive agent for a unified command. Under this new arrangement the channel of responsibility and authority to a commander of a unified command will unmistakably be from the President to the Secretary of Defense to the designated civilian Secretary of a military department. This arrangement will fix responsibility along a definite channel of accountable civilian officials as intended by the National Security Act.

It will be understood, however, that, for the strategic direction and operational control of forces and for the conduct of combat operations, the military chief of the designated military department will be authorized by the Secretary of Defense to receive and transmit reports and orders and to act for that department in its executive agency capacity. This arrangement will make it always possible to deal promptly with emergency or wartime situations. The military chief will clearly be acting in the name and by the direction of the Secretary of Defense. Promulgated orders will directly state that fact.

By taking this action to provide clearer lines of responsibility and authority for the exercise of civilian control, I believe we will make significant progress toward increasing proper accountability in the top levels of the Department of Defense.

II

Our second major objective is effectiveness with economy. Although the American people, throughout their history, have hoped to avoid supporting large military forces, today we must obviously maintain a strong military forces to ward off attack, at a moment's notice, by enemies equipped with the most devastating weapons known to modern science. This need for immediate preparedness makes it all the more imperative to see that the Nation maintains effective military forces in the manner imposing the minimum burden on the national economy.

In an organization the size of the Department of Defense, true effectiveness with economy can be attained only by decentralization of operations, under flexible and effective direction and control from the center. I am impressed with the determination of the Secretary of Defense to administer the Department on this basis and to look to the Secretaries of the three military departments as his principal agents for the management and direction of the entire defense enterprise.

Such a system of decentralized operations, however, requires, for sound management, flexible machinery at the top. Unfortunately, this is not wholly possible in the Department of Defense as now established by law. Two principal fields of activity are rigidly assigned by law to unwieldy boards which—no matter how much authority may be centralized in their respective chairmen—provide organizational arrangements too slow and too clumsy to serve as effective management tools for the Secretary. In addition, other staff agencies have been set up in the Office of the Secretary of Defense and their functions prescribed by law, thus making it difficult for the Secretary to adjust his staff arrangements to deal with new problems as they arise, or to provide for flexible cooperation among the several staff agencies.

Accordingly, I am transmitting today to the Congress a reorganization plan which is designed to provide the Secretary of Defense with a more efficient staff organization. The plan calls for the abolition of the Munitions Board, the Research and Development Board, the Defense Supply Management Agency, and the office of Director of Installations and vests their functions in the Secretary of Defense. At the same time the plan authorizes the appointment of new Assistant Secretaries of Defense to whom the Secretary of Defense intends to assign the functions now vested in the agencies to be abolished and certain other functions now assigned to other officials. Specifically, the reorganization plan provides for 6 additional Assistant Secretaries, 3 to whom the Secretary will assign the duties now performed by the 2 Boards (based on a redistribution of staff functions), 2 who will be utilized to replace individual officials who presently hold other titles, and 1 to be assigned to a position formerly but no longer filled by an Assistant Secretary. The new Assistant Secretary positions are required in order to make it possible to bring executives of the highest type to the Government service and to permit them to operate effectively and with less personnel than at present. In addition, the plan also provides that, in view of the importance of authoritative legal opinions and interpretations, the office of General Counsel be raised to a statutory position with rank substantially equivalent to that of an Assistant Secretary.

The abolition of the present statutory staff agencies and the provision of the new Assistant Secretaries to aid the Secretary of Defense will be the key to the attainment of increased effectiveness at low cost in the Department of Defense. These steps will permit the Secretary to make a thorough reorganization of the nonmilitary staff agencies in his office. He will be able to establish truly effective and vigorous staff units under the leadership of the Assistant Secretaries. Each Assistant Secretary will function as a staff head within an assigned field of responsibility.

Without imposing themselves in the direct lines of responsibility and authority between the Secretary of Defense and the Secretaries of the three military departments, the Assistant Secretaries of Defense will provide the Secretary with a continuing review of the programs of the Defense Establishment and help him institute major improvements in their execution. They will be charged with establishing systems, within their assigned fields, for obtaining complete and accurate information to support recommendations to the Secretary. The Assistant Secretaries will make frequent inspection visits to our farflung installations and check for the Secretary the effectiveness and efficiency of operations in their assigned fields.

Other improvements are badly needed in the Departments of the Army, the Navy, and the Air Force. Accordingly, the Secretary of Defense is initiating studies by the three Secretaries of the military departments of the internal organization of their departments with a view toward making those Secretaries truly responsible administrators, thereby obtaining greater effectiveness and attaining economies wherever possible. These studies will apply to the organization of the military departments some of the same principles of clearer lines of accountability which we are applying to the Department of Defense as a whole.

Immediate attention will also be given to studying improvements of those parts of the military departments directly concerned with the procurement and distribution of munitions and supplies and the inventory and accounting systems within each military department. We must take every step toward seeing that our Armed Forces are adequately supplied at all times with the materials essential for them to carry on their operations in the field. Necessary to this effort is a reorganization of supply machinery in the military departments. These studies of the organization of the military departments have my full support.

One other area for improved effectiveness is civilian and military personnel management. In this area certain specialized studies and actions are desirable. Accordingly, I have directed the Secretary of Defense to organize a study of the problems of attracting and holding competent career of this study, an examination of the Office Personnel Act of 1947 and its practical administration will be undertaken to see if any changes are needed. I am directing that this study also include a review of statutes governing the retirement of military officers aimed at eliminating those undesirable provisions which force the early retirement of unusually capable officers who are willing to continue on active service.

The Secretary of Defense, with my approval, is issuing revised orders relating to the preparing and signing of efficiency reports for military personnel who serve full time in the Office of the Secretary, and new instructions to the military departments to guide selection boards in their operations. These actions are aimed at giving full credit to military officers serving in the Office of the Secretary of Defense for their work for the Department of Defense as a whole. Henceforth, civilian officials who have military officers detailed to their offices on a full-time basis will be responsible for filling out and signing the formal efficiency reports for such officers for the period of such service. In the case of officers serving in the Office of the Secretary of Defense, no other efficiency reports for such service will be maintained. The Secretary of each military department is being instructed to direct the boards convened in his department for the selection of military officers for promotion, to give the same weight to service in the Office of the Secretary of Defense and the efficiency reports from that Office as to service in the military department staff and to efficiency reports of departmental officers. These actions are desirable in order to reward military officers equally for service on behalf of the Department of Defense and service on the staff of a military department.

These actions and others which will be undertaken are aimed at a more effective and efficient Department of Defense; indeed, actions toward this objective will be continuous.

The impact of all these measures will be felt through the whole structure of the Department of Defense, its utilization of millions of personnel and billions of dollars. A simple token testimony to this is this fact: in the Office of the Secretary of Defense alone a staff reduction of approximately 500 persons will be effected.

III

Our third broad objective is to improve our machinery for strategic planning for national security. Certain actions toward this end may be taken administratively to improve the organization and procedures within the Department of Defense. Other changes are incorporated in the reorganization plan transmitted to the Congress today.

The Joint Chiefs of Staff, as provided in the National Security Act of 1947, are not a command body but are the principal military advisers to the President, the National Security Council, and the Secretary of Defense. They are responsible for formulating the strategic plans by which the United States will cope with the challenge of any enemy. The three members of the Joint Chiefs of Staff who are the military chiefs of their respective services are responsible to their Secretaries for the efficiency of their services and their readiness for war.

These officers are clearly overworked, and steps must be devised to relieve them of time-consuming details of minor importance. They must be encouraged to delegate lesser duties to reliable subordinate individuals and agencies in both the Joint CHiefs of Staff structure and in their military-department staffs. One of our aims in making more effective our strategic planning machinery, therefore, is to improve the organization and procedures of the supporting staff of the Joint Chiefs of Staff so that the Chiefs, acting as a body, will be better able to perform their roles as strategic planners and military advisers.

Our military plans are based primarily on military factors, but they must also take into account a wider range of policy and economic factors as well as the latest developments of modern science. Therefore, our second aim in assuring the very best strategic planning is to broaden the degree of active participation of other persons and units at the staff level in the consideration of matters before the Joint Chiefs of Staff and to bring to bear more diversified and expert skills.

The reorganization plan transmitted to the Congress today is designed—without detracting from the military advisory functions of the Joint Chiefs of Staff as a group—to place upon the Chairman of the Joint Chiefs of Staff greater responsibility for organizing and directing the subordinate structure of the Joint Chiefs of Staff in such a way as to help the Secretary of Defense and the Joint Chiefs of Staff discharge their total responsibilities.

Specifically, the reorganization plan makes the Chairman of the Joint Chiefs of Staff responsible for managing the work of the Joint Staff and its Director. The Joint Staff, is or course, a study-and-reporting body serving the Joint Chiefs of Staff. The plan makes the service of the Director of the Joint Staff subject to the approval of the Secretary of Defense. It also makes the service of officers on the Joint Staff subject to the approval of the Chairman of the Joint Chiefs of Staff. These new responsibilities of the Chairman are in consonance with this present functions of serving as the presiding officer of the Joint Chiefs of Staff, providing agenda for meetings, assisting the Joint Chiefs of Staff to perform their duties as promptly as practicable, and keeping the Secretary of Defense and the President informed of issues before the Joint Chiefs of Staff. In addition, the proposed changes will relieve the Joint Chiefs of Staff. In addition, the proposed changes will relieve the Joint Chiefs of Staff, as a body, of a large amount of administrative detail involved in the management of its subordinate committee and staff structure.

In support of our second aim, broadened participation in strategic planning, the Secretary of Defense will direct the Chairman of the Joint Chiefs of Staff to arrange for the fullest cooperation of the Joint Staff and the subcommittees of the Joint Chiefs of Staff with other parts of the Office of the Secretary of Defense in the early stages of staff work on any major problem. If necessary, to aid in this additional burden, an Assistant or Deputy Director of the Joint Staff will be designated to give particular attention to this staff collaboration. Thus, at the developmental stages of important staff studies by the subordinate elements of the Joint Chiefs of Staff, there will be a proper integration of the views and special skills of the other staff agencies of the Department, such as those responsible for budget, manpower, supply, research, and engineering. This action will assure the presentation of improved staff products to the Joint Chiefs of Staff for their consideration.

Also, special attention will be given to providing for the participation of competent civilian scientists and engineers within the substructure of the Joint Chiefs of Staff. Such participants will be able to contribute a wide range of scientific information and knowledge to our strategic planning.

Only by including outstanding civilian experts in the process of strategic planning can our military services bring new weapons rapidly into their established weapons systems, make recommendations with respect to the use of new systems of weapons in the future war plans, and see that the whole range of scientific information and knowledge of fundamental cost factors are taken into account in strategic planning.

Taken together, the changes included in the reorganization plan and the several administrative actions should go a long way toward improving the strategic planning machinery of the Joint Chiefs of Staff, and lead to the development of plans based on the broadest conception of the overall national interest rather than the particular desires of the individual services.

I transmit herewith Reorganization Plan No. 6 of 1953 is necessary to accomplish one or more of the purposes set forth in section 2 (a) of the Reorganization Act of 1949, as amended.

I have found and hereby declare that it is necessary to include in the accompanying reorganization plan, by reason of reorganizations made thereby, provisions for the appointment and compensation of six additional Assistant Secretaries of Defense and a General Counsel of the Department of Defense. The rates of compensation fixed for these officers are those which I have found to prevail in respect of comparable officers in the executive branch of the Government.

The statutory authority for the exercise of the function of guidance to the Munitions Board in connection with strategic and logistic plans, abolished by section 2 (d) of the reorganization plan, is section 213 (c) of the National Security Act of 1947, as amended.

The taking effect of the reorganizations included in Reorganization Plan No. 6 of 1953 is expected to result in a more effective, efficient, and economical performance of functions in the Department of Defense. It is impracticable to specify or itemize at this time the reduction of expenditures which it is probable will be brought about by such taking effect.

The Congress is a full partner in actions to strengthen our Military Establishment. Jointly we must carry forward a sound program to keep America strong. The Congress and the President, acting in their proper spheres, must perform their duties to the American people in support of our highest traditions. Should, for any reason, the national military policy become a subject of partisan politics, the only loser would be the American people.

We owe it to all the people to maintain the best Military Establishment that we know how to devise. There are none, however, to whom we owe it more than the soldiers, the sailors, the marines, and the airmen in uniform whose lives are pledged to the defense of our freedom.

DWIGHT D. EISENHOWER

THE WHITE HOUSE
APRIL 30, 1953

Appendix 9

Reorganization Plan No. 6 of 1953

Prepared by the President and transmitted to the Senate and the House of Representatives in Congress assembled, April 30, 1953, pursuant to the provisions of the Reorganization Act of 1949, approved June 20, 1949, as amended.

Department of Defense

Section 1. Transfers of functions.—(a) All functions of the Munitions Board, the Research and Development Board, the Defense Supply Management Agency and the Director of Installations are hereby transferred to the Secretary of Defense.

(b) The selection of the Director of the Joint Staff by the Joint Chiefs of Staff, and his tenure, shall be subject to the approval of the Secretary of Defense.

(c) The selection of the members of the Joint Staff by the Joint Chiefs of Staff, and their tenure, shall be subject to the approval of the Chairman of the Joint Chiefs of Staff.

(d) The functions of the Joint Chiefs of Staff with respect to managing the Joint Staff and the Director thereof are hereby transferred to the Chairman of the Joint Chiefs of Staff.

Sec. 2. Abolition of agencies and functions.—(a) There are hereby abolished the Munitions Board, the Research and Development Board, and the Defense Supply Management Agency.

(b) The offices of Chairman of the Munitions Board, Chairman of the Research and Development Board, Director of the Defense Supply Management Agency, Deputy Director of the Defense Supply Management Agency and Director of Installations are hereby abolished.

(c) The Secretary of Defense shall provide for winding up any outstanding affairs of the said abolished agency, boards, and offices, not otherwise provided for in this reorganization plan.

(d) The function of guidance to the Munitions Board in connection with strategic and logistical plans as required by section 213 (c) of the National Security Act of 1947, as amended, is hereby abolished.

Sec. 3. Assistant Secretaries of Defense.—Six additional Assistant Secretaries of Defense may be appointed from civilian life by the President, by and with the advice and consent of the Senate. Each such Assistant Secretary shall perform such functions as the Secretary of Defense may from time to time prescribe and each shall receive compensation at the rate prescribed by law for assistant secretaries of executive departments.

Sec. 4. General Counsel.—The President may appoint from civilian life, by and with the advice and consent of the Senate, a General Counsel of the Department of Defense who shall be the chief legal officer of the Department, and who shall perform such functions as the Secretary of Defense may from time to time prescribe. He shall receive compensation at the rate prescribed by law for assistant secretaries of executive departments.

Sec. 5. Performance of functions.—The Secretary of Defense may from time to time make such provisions as he shall deem appropriate authorizing the performance by any other officer, or by any agency or employee, of the Department of Defense of any function of the Secretary, including any function transferred to the Secretary by the provisions of this reorganization plan.

Sec. 6. Miscellaneous provisions.—(a) The Secretary of Defense may from time to time effect such transfers within the Department of Defense of any of the records, property, and personnel affected by this reorganization plan, and such transfers of unexpended balances (available or to be made available for use in connection with any affected function or agency) of appropriations, allocations, and any other funds of such Department, as he deems necessary to carry out the provisions of this reorganization plan.

(b) Nothing herein shall affect the compensation of the Chairman of the Military Liaison Committee (63 Stat. 762).

Appendix 10

The Department of Defense Reorganization Act of 1958

[72 Stat.]

PUBLIC LAW 85-599—August 6, 1958

Public Law 85-599

AN ACT

To promote the national defense by providing for reorganization of the Department of Defense, and for other purposes.

Be it enacted by the Senate and House of Representatives of the United States of America in Congress assembled, That this Act may be cited as the "Department of Defense Reorganization Act of 1958".

AMENDING THE DECLARATION OF POLICY

Sec. 2. Section 2 of the National Security Act of 1947, as amended (50 U.S.C. 401), is further amended to read as follows:

"Sec. 2. In enacting this legislation, it is the intent of Congress to provide a comprehensive program for the future security of the United states; to provide for the establishment of integrated policies and procedures for the departments,agencies, and functions of the Government relating to the national security; to provide a Department of Defense, including the three military Departments of the Army, the Navy (including naval aviation and the United States Marine Corps), and the Air Force under the direction, authority, and control of the Secretary of Defense; to provide that each military department shall be separately organized under its own Secretary and shall function under the direction, authority, and control of the Secretary of Defense; to provide for their unified direction under civilian control of the Secretary of Defense but not to merge these departments or services; to provide for the establishment of unified or specified combatant commands, and a clear and direct line of command to such commands; to eliminate unnecessary duplication in the Department of Defense, and particularly in the field of research and engineering by vesting its overall direction and control in the Secretary of Defense; to provide more effective, efficient, and economical administration in the Department of Defense; to provide for the unified strategic direction of the combatant forces, for their operation under unified command, and for their integration into an efficient team of land, naval, and air forces but not to establish a single Chief of Staff over the armed forces nor an overall armed forces general staff."

STRENGTHENING THE DIRECTION, AUTHORITY, AND CONTROL OF THE SECRETARY OF DEFENSE

Sec. 3. (a) Section 202(c) of the National Security Act of 1947, as amended (5 U.S.C. 171a(c), is amended to read as follows:

"(c) (1) Within the policy enunciated in section 2, the Secretary of Defense shall take appropriate steps (including the transfer, reassignment, abolition, and consolidation of functions) to provide in the Department of Defense for more effective, efficient, and economical administration and operation and to eliminate duplication. However, except as otherwise provided in this subsection, no function which has been established by law to be performed by the Department of Defense, or any officer or agency thereof, shall be substantially transferred reassigned, abolished, or consolidated until the expiration of the first period of thirty calendar days of continuous session of the Congress following the date on which the Secretary of Defense reports the pertinent details of the actin to be taken to the Armed services committees of the Senate and of the House of Representatives.

If during such period a resolution is reported by either of the said committees stating that the proposed action with respect to the transfer, reassignment, abolition, or consolidation of any function should be rejected by the resolving House because (1) it contemplates the transfer, reassignment, abolition, or consolidation of a major combatant function now or hereafter assigned to the military services by section 3062 (b), 5012, 5013, or 8062 (c) of title 10 of the United States Code, and (2) if carried out it would in the judgment of the said resolving House tend to impair the defense of the United States, such transfer, reassignment, abolition, or consolidation shall take effect after the expiration of the first period of forty calendar days of continuous session of the Congress following the date on which such resolution is reported; but only if, between the date of such reporting in either House and the expiration of such forty-day period such resolution has not been passed by such House.

(2) For the purposes of paragraph (1)—

"(A) continuity of session shall be considered as broken only by an adjournment of the Congress sine die: but

"(B) in the computation of the thirty-day period or the forty-day period there shall be excluded the days on which either House is not in session because of an adjournment of more than three days to a day certain.

"(3) (A) The provisions of this paragraph are enacted by the Congress—

"(i) as an exercise of the rulemaking power of the Senate and the House of Representatives; and as such they shall be considered as part of the rules of each House, respectively, and such rules shall supersede other rules only to the extent that they are inconsistent therewith; and

"(ii) with full recognition of the constitutional right of either House to change such rules (so far as relating to the procedure in such

House) at any time, in the same manner and to the same extent as in the case of any other rule of such House.

"(B) For the purposes of this paragraph, any resolution reported to either House pursuant to the provisions of paragraph (1) hereof, shall for the purpose of the consideration of such resolution by either House be treated in the same manner as a resolution with respect to a reorganization plan reported by a committee within the meaning of the Reorganization Act of 1949 as in effect on July 1, 1958 (5 U.S.C. 133z et seq.) and shall be governed by the provisions applicable to the consideration of any such resolution by either House of the Congress as provided by sections 205 and 206 of such Act.

"(4) Notwithstanding the provisions of paragraph (1) hereof, the Secretary of Defense has the authority to assign, or reassign, to one or more departments or services, the development and operational use of new weapons or weapons systems.

"(5) Notwithstanding other provisions of this subsection, if the President determines that it is necessary because of hostilities or imminent threat of hostilities, any function, including those assigned to the military services by sections 3062 (b), 5012, 5013, and 8062 (c) of title 10 of the United States Code, may be transferred, reassigned, or consolidated and subject to the determination of the President shall remain so transferred, reassigned, or consolidated until the termination of such hostilities or threat of hostilities.

"(6) Whenever the Secretary of Defense determines it will be advantageous to the Government in terms of effectiveness, economy, or efficiency, he shall provide for the carrying out of any supply or service activity common to more than one military department by a single agency or such other organizational entities as he deems appropriate. For the purposes of this paragraph, any supply or service activity common to more than one military department shall not be considered a "major combatant function" within the meaning of paragraph (1) hereof.

"(7) Each military department (the Department of the Navy to include naval aviation and the United states Marine Corps) shall be separately organized under its own Secretary and shall function under the direction, authority, and control of the Secretary of Defense. The Secretary of a military department shall be responsible to the Secretary of Defense for the operation of such department as well as its efficiency. Except as otherwise specifically provided by law, no Assistant Secretary of Defense shall have authority to issue orders to a military department unless (1) the Secretary of Defense has specifically delegated in writing to such an Assistant Secretary the authority to issue such orders with respect to a specific subject area, and (2) such orders are issued through the Secretary of such military department or his designee. In the implementation of this paragraph it shall be the duty of each such Secretary, his civilian assistants, and the military personnel in such department to cooperate fully with personnel of the Office of the Secretary of Defense in a continuous effort to achieve efficient administration of the Department of Defense and effectively to carry out the direction, authority, and control of the Secretary of Defense.

"(8) No provision of this Act shall be so construed as to prevent a Secretary of a military department or a member of the Joint Chiefs of Staff from presenting to the Congress, on his own initiative, after first so informing the Secretary of Defense, any recommendations relating to the Department of Defense that he may deem proper."

(b) Section 202 (d), of the National Security Act of 1947, as amended (5 U.S.C. 171a (d)), is further amended to read as follows:

"(d) The Secretary of Defense shall annually submit a written report to the President and the Congress covering expenditures work, and accomplishments of the Department of Defense, accompanied by (1) such recommendations as he shall deem appropriate, (2) separate reports from the military departments covering their expenditures, work, and accomplishments, and (3) itemized statements showing the savings of public funds and the eliminations of unnecessary duplications and overlappings that have been accomplished pursuant to the provisions of this Act."

(c) Section 2201 of title 10, United States Code, is repealed and the analysis of chapter 131 of title 10 is amended by striking out the following item: "2201. General functions of Secretary of Defense."

(d) Section 2351 of title 10, United States Code, is repealed and the analysis of chapter 139 of title 10 is amended by striking out the following item: "2351. Policy, plans, and coordination."

CLARIFYING THE CHAIN OF COMMAND OVER MILITARY OPERATIONS

Sec. 4. (a) section 3034 (d) (4) of title 10, United States Code, is amended to read as follows:

"(4) exercise supervision over such of the members and organizations of the Army as the Secretary of the Army determines. Such supervision shall be exercised in a manner consistent with the full operational command vested in unified or specified combatant commanders pursuant to section 202 (j) of the National Security Act of 1947, as amended."

(b) Section 5081 (c) of title 10, United States Code, is amended to read as follows:

"(c) Under the direction of the Secretary of the Navy, the Chief of Naval Operations shall exercise supervision over such of the members and organizations of the Navy and the Marine Corps as the Secretary of the Navy determines. Such supervision shall be exercised in a manner consistent with the full operational command vested in unified or specified combatant commanders pursuant to section 202 (j) of the National Security Act of 1947, as amended."

(c) Section 5201 of title 10, United States Code, is amended by adding at the end thereof a new subsection (d) to read as follows:

"(d) Under the direction of the Secretary of the Navy, the Commandant of the Marine Corps shall exercise supervision over such of the members and organizations of the Marine Corps and Navy as the Secretary of the Navy determines. Such supervision shall be exercised in a manner consistent with the full operational command vested in unified or specified combatant commanders pursuant to section 202 (j) of the National Security Act of 1947, as amended."

(d) clause (5) of section 8034 (d) of title 10, United States Code, is renumbered "(4)" and amended to read as follows:

"(4) exercise supervision over such of the members and organizations of the Air Force as the Secretary of the Air Force determines. Such supervision shall be exercised in a manner consistent with the full operational command vested in unified or specified combatant commanders pursuant to section 202 (j) of the National Security Act of 1947, as amended."

(e) Section 8034 (d) is amended by striking out clause (4) and by renumbering clauses (6) and (7) as clauses "(5)" and "(6)", respectively.

(f) (1) Section 8074 (a) of title 10, United States Code, is amended to read as follows:

"(a) The Air Force shall be divided into such organizations as the Secretary of the Air Force may prescribe."

(2) Subsections (b) and (c) of section 8074 of title 10, United States Code, are repealed, and subsection (d) is redesignated as subsection "(b)".

(g) Section 3032 (b) (1) of title 10, United States Code, is amended to read as follows:

"(1) prepare for such employment of the Army, and for such recruiting, organizing, supplying, equipping, training, serving, mobilizing, and demobilizing of the Army, as will assist in the execution of any power, duty, or function of the Secretary or the Chief of Staff;".

(h) Section 8032 (b) (1) of title 10, United States Code, is amended to read as follows:

"(1) prepare for such employment of the Air Force, and for such recruiting, organizing, supplying, equipping, training, serving, mobilizing, and demobilizing of the Air Force, as will assist in the execution of any power, duty, or function of the Secretary or the Chief of Staff;".

CLARIFYING THE ORGANIZATION AND DUTIES OF THE JOINT STAFF

Sec. 5. (a) Section 143 of title 10, United States Code, is amended to read as follows:

"§ 143. Joint Staff

"(a) There is under the Joint chiefs of staff a Joint staff consisting of not more than 400 officers selected by the Joint Chiefs of Staff with the approval of the Chairman. The Joint Staff shall be selected in approximately equal numbers from

"(1) the Army;

"(2) the Navy and the Marine Corps; and

"(3) the Air Force.

The tenure of the members of the Joint staff is subject to the approval of the Chairman of the Joint Chiefs of Staff, and except in time of war, no such tenure of duty may be more than three years. Except in time of war, officers completing a tour of duty with the Joint Staff may not be reassigned to the Joint staff for a period of not less than three years following their previous tour of duty on the Joint staff, except that selected officers may be recalled to Joint staff duty in less than three years with the approval of the Secretary of Defense in each case. The number of such officers recalled to Joint staff duty in less than three years shall not exceed 30 serving on the Joint Staff at any one time.

"(b) The Chairman of the Joint Chiefs of Staff in consultation with the Joint Chiefs of Staff, and with the approval of the Secretary of Defense, shall select the Director of the Joint Staff. Except in time of war, the tour of duty of the Director may not exceed three years. Upon the completion of a tour of duty as Director of the Joint staff, the Director, except in time of war, may not be reassigned to the Joint staff. The Director must be an officer junior in grade to each member of the Joint Chiefs of Staff.

"(c) The Joint Staff shall perform such duties as the Joint Chiefs of Staff or the Chairman prescribes. The Chairman of the Joint Chiefs of Staff manages the Joint Staff and its Director, on behalf of the Joint Chiefs of Staff.

"(d) The Joint Staff shall not operate or be organized as an overall Armed Forces General staff and shall have no executive authority. The Joint Staff may be organized and may operate along conventional staff lines to support the Joint Chiefs of Staff in discharging their assigned responsibilities."

(b) Section 202 of the National Security Act of 1947, as amended, is amended by adding at the end thereof the following new subsection:

"(j) With the advice and assistance of the Joint Chiefs of Staff the President, through the Secretary of Defense, shall establish unified or specified combatant commands for the performance of military missions, and shall determine the force structure of such combatant commands to be composed of forces of the Department of the Army, the Department of the Navy, the Department of the Air Force, which shall then be assigned to such combatant commands by the departments concerned for the performance of such military missions. Such combatant commands are responsible to the President and the Secretary of Defense, with the approval of the President. Forces assigned to such unified combatant commands or specified combatant commands shall be under the full operational command of the commander of the unified combatant command or the commander of the specified combatant command. All forces not so assigned remain for all purposes in their respective departments. Under the direction, authority, and control of the Secretary of Defense each military department shall be responsible for the administration of the forces assigned from its department to such combatant commands. The responsibility for the support of forces assigned to combatant commands shall be vested in one or more of the military departments as may be directed by the Secretary of Defense. Forces assigned to such unified or specified combatant commands shall be transferred therefrom only by authority of and under procedures established by the Secretary of Defense, with the approval of the President."

. . . .

[Ed. Note] Material deleted can be found in Public Law 85-599 (72 Stat. 514).

(d) Section 8035 of title 10, United States Code, is amended by adding at the end thereof a new subsection (d) to read as follows: "(d) The Vice Chief of Staff has such authority and duties with respect to the Department of the Air Force as the Chief of Staff, with the approval of the Secretary of the Air Force, may delegate to or prescribe for him. Orders issued by the Vice Chief of Staff in performing such duties have the same effect as those issued by the Chief of Staff."

CLARIFYING THE RULE Of THE CHAIRMAN OF THE JOINT CHIEFS OF STAFF

Sec. 7. Section 141 (a) (1) of title 10, United States Code, is amended by striking out the words ", who has no vote".

REDUCING THE NUMBER OF ASSISTANT SECRETARIES OF MILITARY DEPARTMENTS

. . . .
[Ed. Note] Material deleted can be found in Public Law 85-599 (72 Stat. 514).

(c) Section 8013 (a) of title 10, United States Code, is amended to read as follows:
"(a) There are an Under Secretary of the Air Force and three Assistant Secretaries of the Air Force in the Department of the Air Force. They shall be appointed from civilian life by the President, by and with the advice and consent of the Senate."

ESTABLISHING THE DIRECTOR OF DEFENSE RESEARCH AND ENGINEERING

Sec. 9. (a) Section 203 of the National Security Act of 1947, as amended, is amended by redesignating subsections "(b)" and "(c)" as subsections "(c)" and "(d)", respectively, and by inserting a new subsection "(b)" as follows:
(b) (1) There shall be a Director of Defense Research and Engineering who shall be appointed from civilian life by the President, by and with the advice and consent of the Senate, who shall take precedence in the Department of Defense after the Secretary of Defense, the Deputy Secretary of Defense, the Secretary of the Army, the Secretary of the Navy, and the Secretary of the Air Force. The Director performs such duties with respect to research and engineering as the Secretary of Defense may prescribe, including, but not limited to, the following: (i) to be the principal adviser to the Secretary of Defense on scientific and technical matters: (ii) to supervise all research and engineering activities in the Department of Defense; and (iii) to direct and control (including their assignment or reassignment) research and engineering activities that the Secretary of Defense deems to require centralized

management. The compensation of the Director is that prescribed by law for the Secretaries of the military departments.

"(2) The Secretary of Defense or his designee, subject to the approval of the President, is authorized to engage in basic and applied research projects essential to the responsibilities of the Department of Defense in the field of basic and applied research and development which pertain to weapons systems and other military requirements. The Secretary or his designee, subject to the approval of the President, is authorized to perform assigned research and development projects: by contract with private business entities, educational or research institutions, or other agencies of the Government, through one or more of the military departments, or by utilizing employees and consultants of the Department of Defense.

"(3) There is authorized to be appropriated such sums as may be necessary for the purposes of paragraph (2) of this subsection."

(b) Section 7 of Public Law 85-325, dated February 12, 1958, is amended to read as follows:

"Sec. 7. The Secretary of Defense or his designee is authorized to engage in such advanced projects essential to the Defense Department's responsibilities in the field of basic and applied research and development which pertain to weapons systems and military requirements as the Secretary of Defense may determine after consultation with the Joint Chiefs of Staff: and for a period of one year from the effective date of this Act, the Secretary of Defense or his designee is further authorized to engage in such advanced space projects as may be designated by he President.

"Nothing in this provision of law shall preclude the Secretary of Defense from assigning to the military departments the duty of engaging in research and development of weapons systems necessary to fulfill the combatant functions assigned by law to such military departments.

"The Secretary of Defense shall assign any weapons systems developed to such military department or departments for production and operational control as he may determine."

(c) Section 171 (a) of title 10, United States Code, is amended by renumbering clauses "(6)", "(7)", "(8)", and "(9)" as clauses "(7)", "(8)", "(9)", and "(10)", respectively, and inserting the following new clause (6) after clause (5):

"(6) The Director of Defense Research and Engineering;".

REDUCING THE NUMBER OF ASSISTANT SECRETARIES OF DEFENSE

Sec. 10. (a) Subsection (c) of section 203 of the National Security Act of 1947, as amended (5 U.S.C. 171c), as redesignated by section 9 (a) of this act, is amended as follows:

(1) By striking out the word "three" and inserting the word "seven" in place thereof.

(2) By striking out the word "and" after the word "Navy,".

(3) By inserting the words ", and the Director of Defense Research and Engineering" after the words "Air Force".

(b) Section 3 of Reorganization Plan No. 6 of 1953 (67 Stat. 638) is repealed.

AUTHORIZING THE TRANSFER OF OFFICERS BETWEEN THE ARMED FORCES

Sec. 11. Chapter 41 of title 10, United States Code, is amended as follows:

(1) By adding the following new section at the end:

"§ 716. Commissioned officers: transfers between Army, Navy, Air Force, and Marine Corps."

"Notwithstanding any other provision of law, the President may, within authorized strengths, transfer any commissioned officer with his consent from the Army, Navy, Air Force, or Marine Corps to, and appoint him in, any other of those armed forces. The Secretary of Defense shall establish, by regulations approved by the President, policies and procedures for such transfers and appointments. No officer transferred pursuant to this authority shall be assigned precedence or relative rank higher than that which he held on the day prior to such transfer."

NATIONAL GUARD BUREAU

Sec. 12. Section 3015 of title 10, United States Code, is amended by redesignating subsections "(a)", "(b)", and "(c)" as subsections "(b)", "(c)", and "(d)", respectively, and by inserting a new subsection (a) to read as follows:

"(a) There is a National Guard Bureau, which is a Joint Bureau of the Department of the Army and the Department of the Air Force, headed by a chief who is the adviser to the Army Chief of Staff and the Air Force Chief of Staff on National Guard matters. The National Guard Bureau is the channel of communication between the departments concerned and the several States, Territories, Puerto Rico, the Canal Zone, and the District of Columbia on all matters pertaining to the National Guard, the Army National Guard of the United States, and the Air National Guard of the United States."

EFFECTIVE DATE

Sec. 13. Sections 8 and 10 of this Act shall become effective six months after the date of enactment of this Act.

Approved August 6, 1958.

Notes

Notes

Archival repositories are abbreviated as follows: NARA (National Archives and Records Administration), LC (Library of Congress), HSTL (Harry S. Truman Library), AFHRC (USAF Historical Research Center), CAFH (Center for Air Force History), and its former designation, AFCHO (Office of Air Force History). Record Group is abbreviated RG.

Preface

1. Samuel P. Huntington, "Strategic Programs and the Political Process," *American Defense Policy*, ed Associates in Political Science, U.S. Military Academy, Wesley W. Posvar et al (Baltimore: Johns Hopkins Press, 1965), pp 140–41.

2. Stanley Falk and Harry B. Yoshpe, *The Economics of National Security: Organization for National Security* (Washington, D.C.: Industrial College of the Armed Forces, 1963), p 17.

3. *Ibid*, p 17.

4. Walter Millis, *Arms and the State: Civil-Military Elements in National Policy* (New York: The Twentieth Century Fund, 1958), pp 178–79.

5. *Ibid.*

6. Falk and Yoshpe, *The Economics of National Security*, pp 21–22.

7. *Ibid*, pp 29–30.

8. Alice C. Cole et al, eds, *The Department of Defense: Documents on Establishment and Organization, 1944–1978* (Wash-

ington, D.C.: Office of the Secretary of Defense Historical Office, 1978), p 43.

9. Harry H. Ransom, "Department of Defense: Unity or Confederation?" *American Defense Policy*, ed Associates in Political Science, U.S. Military Academy, Wesley W. Posvar et al (Baltimore: Johns Hopkins Press, 1965), pp 172–73.

10. Falk and Yoshpe, *The Economics of National Security*, pp 35–37; Cole et al, *Department of Defense Documents*, pp 157–58.

11. Ransom, "Unity or Confederation?" p 173; Falk and Yoshpe, *The Economics of National Security*, p 38.

12. Cole et al, eds, Apr 3, 1958, Message by President Eisenhower to Congress, *Department of Defense Documents*, p 177.

13. Ransom, "Unity or Confederation?" p 175.

14. Falk and Yoshpe, *The Economics of National Security*, p 49.

Chapter 1

Precedent for an Air Secretary

1. James E. Hewes, Jr., *From Root to McNamara: Army Organization and Administration, 1900–1963* (Washington, D.C.: Center of Military History, U.S. Army, 1975), p 36; John F. Shiner, *Foulois and the U.S. Army Air Corps, 1931–1935* (Washington, D.C.: Office of Air Force History, 1983), p 17.

2. Assistant Chief of the Air Staff,

Intelligence, *U.S. Army Air Forces Historical Studies: No. 25, Organization and Military Aeronautics, 1907–1935* (Washington, D.C.: Air Staff Historical Division, Dec 1944), p 51.

3. *Ibid*, p 79; memo, Asst Secys War Hanford MacNider and F. Trubee Davison to Secy War Dwight F. Davis, subj: Division of Duties of the Two Assistant Sec-

retaries of War, Oct 4, 1926, RG 107, File 020, Jul 1926–Jun 1929, NARA; Hewes, *From Root to McNamara*, pp 36, 54–55; Irving Brinton Holley, Jr., *Buying Aircraft: Matériel Procurement For the Army Air Forces*, United States Army in World War II (Washington, D.C.: Office of the Chief of Military History, Department of the Army, 1964), pp 46–53.

4. Two-page biography of F. Trubee Davison, Jul 16, 1926, RG 107, File 020.2, NARA; R. Earl McClendon, *Autonomy of the Air Arm* (Research Studies Institute, Air University, Maxwell AFB, Ala, Jan 1954), p 92 n 31; Unclassified Testimony before the President's Air Policy Commission, Sep 15–Dec 3, 1947 (Typescript form, 6 vols, 1947), pp 2644–45, AFHRC, Maxwell AFB, Ala; Shiner, *Foulois and the Air Corps*, pp 81–83.

5. McClendon, *Autonomy of the Air Arm*, p 107.

6. Harold B. Hinton, *Air Victory: The Men and the Machines* (New York: Harper & Bros, Publishers, 1948), p 20; *Who's Who in America* (Chicago: Marquis Who's Who, Inc, 1972); Forrest C. Pogue, *George C. Marshall: Ordeal and Hope, 1939–1942* (New York: Viking Press, 1965), pp 43–44.

7. Jonathan F. Fanton, "Robert A. Lovett: The War Years," PhD dissertation, Yale Univ, 1978, pp 18–21.

8. *Ibid*, pp 21–24.

9. Pogue, *Ordeal and Hope*, pp 43–44; Henry L. Stimson and McGeorge Bundy, *On Active Service in Peace and War* (New York: Harper & Bros, Publishers, 1948), pp 324–44.

10. Stimson and Bundy, *On Active Service in Peace and War*, pp 324–44; Pogue, *Ordeal and Hope*, pp 43–44.

11. Fanton, "Robert A. Lovett," pp 56, 60–61.

12. Memo, Col George A. Brownell to Julius H. Amberg, subj: Functions and Activities of the Assistant Secretary of War for Air, Nov 8, 1944, Brownell Collection, AFHRC, Maxwell AFB, Ala.

13. H. H. Arnold, *Global Mission* (New York: Harper & Bros, Publishers, 1949), pp 266–67; Holley, *Buying Aircraft*, pp 474–75; James Lea Cate and Kathleen Williams, "The Air Corps Prepares for War," The Army Air Forces in World War II, vol 1, *Plans and Early Operations*, ed Wesley Frank Craven and James Lea Cate (Washington, D.C.: Office of Air Force History, 1983), p 115; Walter Isaacson and Evan Thomas, *The Wise Men: Six Friends and the World They Made* (New York: Simon & Schuster Inc, 1986), p 337.

14. Elting E. Morison, *Turmoil and Tradition: A Study of the Life and Times of Henry L. Stimson* (Boston: Houghton Mifflin Co, 1960), pp 492–93.

15. Pogue, *Ordeal and Hope*, p 44.

16. Ltr, Lt Gen H. H. Arnold, Commanding Gen, AAF, to Robert A. Lovett, Dec 23, 1941, Arnold Collection, Box 16, Gen Corresp 1939–1946, LC Manuscript Div.

17. Memo, Lt Gen H. H. Arnold to Gen George C. Marshall, Chief of Staff, subj: Request for Appointment in the Air Corps Reserve, Oct 30, 1944, Arnold Collection, Box 16, Gen Corresp 1939–1946, LC Manuscript Div.

18. Memo, Col Thetus C. Odom to Deputy Chief of Staff, Jan 12, 1946, RG 340, Corresp Control Div Gen File by Org and Subj Jan 1947–Jan 1953, Box 120, Chron File Sep 1945–Dec 1948, NARA.

19. Memo, Robert A. Lovett to Adjutant Gen through Commanding Gen, AAF, subj: Recommendation for the Award of the Distinguished Service Medal to Brig Gen George A. Brownell, Nov 18, 1945, RG 107, NARA.

20. Memo, Robert A. Lovett to Col Ward, Jun 12, 1941, RG 107, File 320.2, NARA.

21. Ltr, Under Secy War (Acting Secy War) Robert P. Patterson to Robert R. Reynolds, Chmn, Ctee on Military Affairs, U.S. Senate, Sep 4, 1941, RG 107, File 320.2, NARA.

22. Memo, Robert A. Lovett to Secy and Under Secy War, subj: Army Air Forces Post-War Plans, Nov 8, 1943, RG 107, File 388, Post-War, NARA; ltr, Robert A. Lovett to Lt Gen Ira C. Eaker, Commanding Gen, Eighth AF, Nov 8, 1943, RG 107, File 373.11, Item 63, NARA.

23. Statement by Robert A. Lovett, Assistant Secretary of War for Air, before the House Select Committee on Post-War

Military Policy, Apr 26, 1944, RG 107, File 381(9), NARA; ltr, Robert A. Lovett to L.F.V. Drake, Apr 29, 1944, with congressional testimony concerning military org, Apr 29, 1944, RG 107, File 381(2), NARA.

24. Fanton, "Robert A. Lovett," p 60; *Legislative History of the AAF and the USAF, 1941–1951*, Historical Study no 84 (Research Studies Institute, Air University, Maxwell AFB, Ala, Sep 1955), pp 24–25.

25. Joseph P. Lash, *Roosevelt and Churchill, 1939–1941: The Partnership that Saved the West* (New York: W. W. Norton & Co, Inc, 1976), p 81.

26. Memo, Robert A. Lovett to Under Secy War Robert P. Patterson, subj: Review of Air Program, Dec 30, 1940, RG 107, File 381, NARA.

27. Memo, Brig Gen H. H. Arnold, Acting Deputy Chief of Staff, to Gen George C. Marshall, subj: Review of Air Program, Jan 9, 1941, RG 107, File 381, NARA.

28. Memo, Robert P. Patterson to Robert A. Lovett, Jan 22, 1941, RG 107, File 381, NARA.

29. Memo, Robert A. Lovett to Secy War Henry L. Stimson, Feb 24, 1941; ltr, Robert A. Lovett to Harry L. Hopkins, Mar 19, 1941; both sources from RG 107, File 381, NARA.

30. Memo, Robert A. Lovett to Gen George C. Marshall, Mar 21, 1941, RG 107, File 452.l, Misc, NARA.

31. Fanton, "Robert A. Lovett," pp 67–68.

32. *Ibid*, p 69.

33. *Ibid*, p 75.

34. Ltr, Gen A. H. Self, British Air Commission Dir, to Henry L. Stimson, May 5, 1941, RG 107, File 452.l, England, NARA.

35. Memo, Robert A. Lovett to Maj Gen H. H. Arnold, May 10, 1941, RG 107, File 452.l, England (5–10–41), NARA.

36. *Ibid*.

37. Ltr, Robert A. Lovett to Air Marshal A. T. Harris, RAF Delegation in Washington, Oct 21, 1941, RG 107, File 381, NARA.

38. Memo, his ofc to Maj Gen H. H. Arnold, subj: Plan for the Trans-Atlantic Ferry of Aircraft, Mar 28, 1941; memos, Robert A. Lovett to Maj Gen H. H. Arnold, Apr 1, 1941; all sources from RG 107, File 373.41, Ferrying Command, NARA.

39. Msg, Prime Min of Iceland to Pres Roosevelt, Jul 7, 1941; msg, Pres Roosevelt to Prime Min of Iceland, Jul 7, 1941; memo for record by Robert A. Lovett, subj: Iceland, Jul 8, 1941; all sources from RG 107, File 381, Preparations for War, NARA.

40. Memo, Robert A. Lovett to Henry L. Stimson, subj: Big Bomber Program, Jul 2, 1941, RG 107, File 452.l, NARA.

41. Memo, Robert A. Lovett to Secy War through Chief of Staff, subj: Recapture of Aircraft Now on Docks Awaiting Shipment to Russia, Dec 8, 1941, RG 107, NARA; Samuel Eliot Morison, *The Battle of the Atlantic, September 1939–May 1943* (Boston: Little, Brown and Co, 1950), pp 30–33.

42. Memo, Robert A. Lovett to Henry L. Stimson, Dec 13, 1941, RG 107, NARA.

43. Memo, Robert A. Lovett to Henry L. Stimson, subj: Need for Protection of West African Bases and Africa Below the Great Desert, Dec 18, 1941, RG 107, NARA.

44. Fanton, "Robert A. Lovett," pp 143–44.

45. Memo, Robert A. Lovett to Maj Gen Dwight D. Eisenhower, Chief, War Plans Div, subj: Strategy of Scarcity, Mar 9, 1942, RG 107, File 381, NARA.

46. *Ibid*.

47. Fanton, "Robert A. Lovett," p 155, from Stimson Diary, Jul 28, 1942.

48. Memo, Robert A. Lovett to Lt Gen H. H. Arnold, Deputy Chief of Staff, Feb 25, 1942, RG 107, File 381, NARA.

49. *Ibid*.

50. Memo, Lt Gen H. H. Arnold to Robert A. Lovett, subj: Defense of East and West Coasts Against Submarine Attacks, Feb 26, 1942, RG 107, File 381, NARA.

51. Fanton, "Robert A. Lovett," p 81.

52. *Ibid*, p 85.

53. Memo, Robert A. Lovett to Lt Gen H. H. Arnold, Commanding Gen, AAF, Oct 14, 1942, RG 107, File 452.1(7), Production, Item 11a, NARA.

54. *Ibid*.

55. Memo, Robert P. Patterson to Lt Gen H. H. Arnold, Oct 17, 1942, RG 107, File 452.1(7), Production, Item 11a, NARA.

56. Memo, Lt Gen H. H. Arnold to Robert A. Lovett, subj: Aircraft Production for 1943, Oct 20, 1942, RG 107, File 452.1(7), Production, Item 11a, NARA.

57. *Ibid.*

58. *Ibid.*

59. Ltr, Robert A. Lovett to Harry L. Hopkins, Mar 25, 1943, RG 107, File 452.1(9), Materials, Item 143, NARA.

60. Ltr, Robert A. Lovett to Edsel Ford, Nov 30, 1942; memo, Robert A. Lovett to Lt Gen H. H. Arnold, Nov 24, 1942, RG 107, File 320.4, Manpower, NARA.

61. Memo, Robert A. Lovett to Henry L. Stimson, Apr 2, 1943, RG 107, File 327, NARA.

62. Fanton, "Robert A. Lovett," pp 92, 101–2.

63. Memo, Robert A. Lovett to Brig Gen Clayton L. Bissell, Commanding Gen, Tenth AF, Jan 3, 1943, with attachment from Gardner Ackley, Chief, Military Supplies, Ofc of Strategic Serv, Jan 3, 1944; memo, Brig Gen Thomas D. White, Asst Chief, Air Staff, Intelligence, to Robert A. Lovett, subj: Target Information from POWs, Jan 11, 1944; all sources from RG 107, NARA.

64. Memo, Robert A. Lovett to Maj Gen George E. Stratemeyer, Chief, Air Staff, Feb 9, 1943, RG 107, File 319.1, NARA.

65. Ltr, Robert A. Lovett to Maj Gen Ira C. Eaker, Jun 18, 1943, RG 107, File 373.11(2), General Eaker, NARA.

66. *Ibid.*

67. Isaacson and Thomas, *The Wise Men*, p 92.

68. Ltr, Robert A. Lovett to Maj Gen Ira C. Eaker, Aug 21, 1943, RG 107, File 373.11(2), Sec 1(2), NARA.

69. *Ibid.*

70. Ltr, Lt Gen Ira C. Eaker, Commanding Gen, MAAF, to Robert A. Lovett, Jan 23, 1944, RG 107, NARA; Herman S. Wolk, *Strategic Bombing: The American Experience* (Manhattan, Kansas: MA/AH Publishing, 1981), p 24; Dewitt S. Copp, *Forged in Fire: Strategy and Decision in the Air War Over Europe, 1940–1945* (New York: Doubleday & Co, 1982), pp 449–52.

71. Ltr, Robert A. Lovett to Maj Gen Ira C. Eaker, Commanding Gen, Eighth AF, Sep 19, 1943, RG 107, File 373.11(2), Sec 1(2), NARA; ltr, Gen H. H. Arnold to Maj Gen Ira C. Eaker, Jun 29, 1943, letter no. 83, Arnold Collection, pp 449–52, CAFH.

72. Ltr, Robert A. Lovett to Maj Gen Ira C. Eaker, Sep 19, 1943; ltr, Gen H. H. Arnold to Maj Gen Ira C. Eaker, Jun 29, 1943; Fanton, "Robert A. Lovett," p 178.

73. Ltr, Robert A. Lovett to Lt Gen Carl A. Spaatz, Commanding Gen, US SAFE, Jul 25, 1944, Spaatz Diary Personal, Jul 1944/15, LC Manuscript Div.

74. *Ibid*; Copp, *Forged in Fire*, pp 455–65.

75. Ltr, Robert A. Lovett to Lt Gen Carl A. Spaatz, Sep 18, 1944, Spaatz Diary Personal, Oct 1944/16, LC Manuscript Div.

76. Ltr, Robert A. Lovett to Lt Gen Carl A. Spaatz, Nov 27, 1944, Spaatz Diary Personal, Dec 1944/16, LC Manuscript Div.

77. *Ibid.*

78. Memo, Col George A. Brownell to Robert A. Lovett, Dec 14, 1944, Brownell Collection, AFHRC, Maxwell AFB, Ala.

79. Memo, personal, Robert A. Lovett to Gen H. H. Arnold, Jan 9, 1945, RG 107, File 311, NARA.

80. Ltr, Robert A. Lovett to L. Welch Pogue, Civil Aeron Board, Commerce Dept, Jan 26, 1943; memo, Robert A. Lovett to Asst Chief of Staff, Plans, subj: Army Air Forces Policy in Regard to Post-War International Civil Aviation, Dec 13, 1943; both sources from RG 107, File 334, Ctee on Internat Aviation, NARA.

81. Ltr, Robert A. Lovett to Asst Secy Navy for Air John L. Sullivan, Aug 20, 1945; ltr, John L. Sullivan to Robert A. Lovett, Aug 18, 1945; both sources from RG 107, Post V-J Day Production, NARA.

82. Memo, Robert A. Lovett to Lt Gen Ira C. Eaker, Chief of Air Staff, subj: Surplus Property, Possible Reduction of Spare Parts, Inventory, Jul 3, 1945, RG 107, Post V-J Day Production, NARA.

83. Staff Study on the Importance of the Air Coordinating Committee, RG 340,

Nov 1947–Dec 1949, vol 1, NARA.

84. John R. M. Wilson, *Turbulence Aloft: The Civil Aeronautics Administration Amid Wars and Rumors of Wars, 1938–1953* (Washington, D.C.: U.S. Department of Transportation, Federal Aviation Administration, 1979), p 159.

85. Ltr, Gen H. H. Arnold to Robert A. Lovett, Dec 21, 1945, Arnold Collection, Box 16, Gen Corresp 1939–1946, LC Manuscript Div; Arnold, *Global Mission*, pp 195–96; ltr, Gen H. H. Arnold to Robert A. Lovett, Dec 8, 1945, Brownell Collection, AFHRC, Maxwell AFB, Ala.

86. Ltr, Gen H. H. Arnold to Robert A. Lovett on Lovett's retirement as Asst Secy War for Air, Dec 8, 1945, Brownell Collection, AFHRC, Maxwell AFB, Ala.

Chapter 2

The Interlude (1946–1947)

1. Herman S. Wolk, *Planning and Organizing the Postwar Air Force, 1943–1947* (Washington, D.C.: Office of Air Force History, 1984), pp 112–16; memo, Col R. C. Moffatt, Chief, Spec Planning Div, to Asst Secy War for Air, to Commanding Gen, AAF, to Deputy Cmdr, AAF, to Chief of Air Staff et al, subj: Assumptions and Ground Rules Pertaining to the Interim and Peacetime Air Forces Plans, Dec 26, 1945, RG 18, U.S. Army Air Forces, File 381, Air Adjutant Gen, Post-War 1945, NARA.

2. Ltr, W. Stuart Symington to J. H. Whitney, Oct 30, 1946, Box 14, Symington Papers, HSTL.

3. Ltr, Brig Gen George A. Brownell to Lt Gen Ira C. Eaker, Jan 7, 1946; memo, Brig Gen George A. Brownell to Gen H. H. Arnold, Jan 4, 1946; both sources from Brownell Collection, Chron File, AFHRC, Maxwell AFB, Ala.

4. Memo, Brig Gen George A. Brownell to his ofc, Dec 11, 1945; memo, Brig Gen George A. Brownell to Asst Secy War Howard C. Petersen, Dec 11, 1945; both sources from Brownell Collection, Chron File, AFHRC, Maxwell AFB, Ala; memo, Col Thetus C. Odom to W. Stuart Symington, subj: Functions of the Assistant Secretary of War for Air, Mar 5, 1946, RG 107, File 020, NARA.

5. Memo, Col Thetus C. Odom to Deputy Chief of Staff, subj: Estimate of Personnel Requirements, Second Quarter Calander Year 1946, RG 340, Box 102, Chron File Jan–Apr 1946, NARA.

6. Memo, Col Thetus C. Odom to W. Stuart Symington, subj: Functions of the Assistant Secretary of War for Air, Mar 6, 1946, RG 340, File 020, Ofc of the Admin Asst, Box 106, NARA.

7. Ofc memo no 4, Col Thetus C. Odom, subj: Hours of Work, Apr 1, 1946, RG 340, File 020, Ofc of the Admin Asst, Box 106, NARA.

8. Memo, Col Thetus C. Odom to Howard C. Petersen, Jan 28, 1946, with Summary of Matters of Prime Importance to the Asst Secy War for Air in 1946, RG 107, File 020, Box 178, NARA.

9. *Ibid.*

10. Paul I. Wellman, *Stuart Symington: Portrait of a Man With a Mission* (New York: Doubleday & Co, 1960), pp 99–133; *Who's Who in America* (Chicago: A.N. Marquis Co, 1950), p 2699.

11. Ltr, Charles H. Lipsett (private citizen of New York) to Charles Ross, Secy to President, Jan 19, 1946, RG 107, File 020, Box 178, NARA.

12. Intvw, W. Stuart Symington by author, Oct 21, 1981, USAF Oral History Collection, AFHRC file K239.0512–1343, AFHRC, Maxwell AFB, Ala.

13. *Ibid.*

14. Intvw, Eugene M. Zuckert by Jerry N. Hess, Sep 27, 1971, HSTL; intvw, W. Stuart Symington by Hugh N. Ahmann and Herman S. Wolk, May 2, 1978, Dec 12, 1978, USAF Oral History Collection, AFHRC file K239.0512–1039, AFHRC, Maxwell AFB, Ala.

15. Memo, W. Stuart Symington to Gen Carl A. Spaatz, Commanding Gen, AAF,

subj: Surplus Property in the Air Force Depots, Dec 30, 1946, RG 340, Asst Secy AF (Management), Mar 1946–Oct 1952, Zuckert Chron File, Box 179, NARA.

16. Memo, Under Secy War Kenneth C. Royall to W. Stuart Symington, subj: Disposal of Surplus Property from Robins Air Depot, Warner Robins Field, Georgia, Dec 24, 1946, RG 340, Asst Secy AF (Management), Mar 1946–Oct 1952, Zuckert Chron File, Box 179, NARA.

17. Memo, W. Stuart Symington to Gen Carl A. Spaatz, subj: Surplus Property in the Air Force Depots, Dec 30, 1946.

18. Ltr, W. Stuart Symington to R. R. Deupree, Exec Chmn, Army-Navy Munitions Board, Jun 25, 1946, RG 340, Asst Secy AF (Management), Mar 1946–Oct 1952, Zuckert Chron File, Box 179, NARA.

19. Ibid.

20. Memo, W. Stuart Symington to Secy War Robert P. Patterson, Sep 16, 1946, Symington Papers, Box 10, Patterson Corresp, HSTL.

21. Memo, Brig Gen Turner A. Sims, Jr., USAF (Ret.) to W. Stuart Symington, May 29, 1947, RG 340, Numeric Files 1947–1949, File 4A, Box 4; telephone intvw, Gen Turner A. Sims by author, Aug 19, 1981, author's files.

22. Memo, W. Stuart Symington to Gen Carl A. Spaatz, Jul 11, 1947, Symington Papers, Box 12, Spaatz folder, HSTL.

23. Memo, Robert A. Lovett to Gen of the Army H. H. Arnold, subj: (a) Need for Improved and Increased Management Procedures (b) Solution through Establishment of the Office of Air Comptroller General, Oct 5, 1945, RG 18, File 322, 11-7-45, NARA.

24. Memo, W. Stuart Symington to Robert P. Patterson, Jan 9, 1947, Symington Papers, Box 10, Patterson Corresp, HSTL.

25. Ibid.

26. Memo, W. Stuart Symington to Lt Gen Ira C. Eaker, Chief of Air Staff, May 8, 1946, RG 107, File 020, NARA; memo, W. Stuart Symington, subj: Management Control Through Cost Control for the Army Air Forces, Jul 24, 1947, Symington Papers, Box 8, Memoranda and Drafts, HSTL.

27. Eugene M. Zuckert, "U.S. Air Force Cost Control Program," Army-Navy Journal, Sep 11, 1948, article requested for Air Force Day issue, RG 340, Asst Secy AF (Management), Mar 1946–Oct 1952, Zuckert Chron File, Box unknown, NARA.

28. Ltr, Eugene M. Zuckert to author, Sep 2, 1987, author's files.

29. Ibid.

30. Ltr, W. Stuart Symington to J. H. Whitney, Oct 30, 1946, Symington Papers, Box 14, HSTL.

31. Statement of the Secretary of the Air Force before the House Military Appropriations Subcommittee, Mar 18, 1948, RG 340, Special Interest Files, Special File 14, Corresp Oct 1947–Oct 1948, NARA.

32. Ibid.

33. Annual Report of the Secretary of the Air Force for Fiscal Year 1948 (Washington, D.C.: GPO, Dec 1948), p 7; NME Dept AF, Washington, press release, Jan 9, 1949, RG 340, Special Interest Files, Special File 14, Staff Action, Budget, NARA.

34. Wolk, Planning and Organizing the Postwar Air Force, pp 154–55.

35. Statement of W. Stuart Symington, Assistant Secretary of War for Air, War Department, Washington, D.C., presented by Eugene M. Zuckert, Special Assistant to the Secretary of War, in Hearings before the Committee on Armed Services, U.S. Senate, 80th Cong, 1st sess, Mar 18, 1947, pp 86–88; remarks by W. Stuart Symington before the Economic Club of Detroit, Michigan, Jun 17, 1946, CAFH.

36. Ltr, W. Stuart Symington to Gen George C. Kenney, Commanding Gen, SAC, May 30, 1947, Symington Papers, HSTL.

37. Ibid.

38. Joint ltr on Army and Navy unification, Secys Robert P. Patterson and James V. Forrestal to Pres Truman, May 31, 1946, RG 340, Special Interest Files, Special File 4A, Unification, NARA.

39. Ibid.

40. Wolk, Planning and Organizing the Postwar Air Force, p 150.

41. Ltr on Army and Navy unification, Secys Robert P. Patterson and James V. Forrestal to Pres Truman, May 31, 1946.

Chapter 3

Separate and Equal: The First Secretariat

1. Report of the Secretary of the Air Force to the Secretary of Defense for Fiscal Year 1948, pp 277–79, CAFH; "History of the Office of the Secretary of the Air Force: Sep 18, 1947 to Jun 30, 1950," (hereafter, "History Secy AF"), unpublished manuscript, vol 1, pp 1–2, CAFH.

2. Remarks by W. Stuart Symington, Secretary of the Air Force, on Armistice Day before the Aviation Post of the American Legion, New York, New York, Nov 11, 1947, CAFH.

3. Presentation by Mr. Eugene M. Zuckert, Assistant Secretary of the Air Force, before the Eberstadt Committee, Aug 11, 1948, RG 340, Ofc of Admin Asst, Corresp Control Div Gen File by Org and Subj 1947–Jan 1953, NARA; paper (14 pp) concerning organization of AF, Nov 27, 1951, pp 1–2, no author (probably from OSAF Admin Asst John J. McLaughlin), RG 340, Acces no 63-A1749, Box 3, folder marked 1949-1954 Organization and Functional Manual, OSAF, NARA.

4. Presentation by Mr. Eugene M. Zuckert, Assistant Secretary of the Air Force, Before the Eberstadt Committee, Aug 11, 1948; 14-page paper concerning organization of AF, Nov 27, 1951, pp 1–2; intvw, W. Stuart Symington by author, Oct 21, 1981.

5. *Time* magazine, Jan 19, 1948, pp 24–25.

6. "History Secy AF," vol 1, pp 4–5.

7. *Ibid*, p 5; Report of the Secretary of the Air Force to the Secretary of Defense for Fiscal Year 1948, pp 280–81; Lt Gen E. W. Rawlings, Report on the Comptrollership within the Air Force, 1946–1950, no date, probably 1951, p 1.

8. Attachment to memo for Col J.B. Montgomery, Admin Asst to Secy Army, Sep 23, 1947, RG 340, Ofc of Admin Asst, Corresp and Control Div Gen File by Org and Subj, 1947–Jan 1953, Budget Estimates and Justifications 1948–1954, Box 249, NARA; memo, OSAF Admin Asst John J. McLaughlin to Mr. Hill, Aug 1, 1952, RG 340, Acces no 60–A1055, Box 27, R. L.

Gilpatric, Misc Files 1951–1953, folder marked Responsib Mr. Gilpatric, NARA.

9. Memo, Eugene M. Zuckert to W. Stuart Symington, Nov 6, 1947, RG 340, Ofc of Admin Asst, Corresp and Control Div Gen File by Org and Subj, 1947–Jan 1953, Budget Estimates and Justifications 1948–1954, Box 249, NARA.

10. Memo, W. J. McNeil to W. Stuart Symington, subj: Civilian Personnel Ceiling for the Third Quarter Fiscal Year 1949, Jan 5, 1949, RG 340, Ofc of Admin Asst, Corresp and Control Div Gen File by Org and Subj, 1947–Jan 1953, Budget Estimates and Justifications 1948–1954, Box 249, NARA.

11. "History Secy AF," vol 2, Appendix, Doc 1.

12. "History Secy AF," vol 1, sections concerning Ofc of the Gen Counsel; Directorate, Public Rel; and Directorate, Legis and Liaison.

13. Barton Leach, Summary of the Meyers Case, Nov 19, 1947; ltr, W. Stuart Symington to Homer Ferguson, U.S. Senate, Nov 19, 1947; memo, Gen H. H. Arnold to Brig Gen Kenneth C. Royall, Ofc of Under Secy War, subj: Status of Maj Gen Bennett E. Meyers, Jun 30, 1945; ltr, W. Stuart Symington to Isaiah Matlack, Dept of Justice, Nov 15, 1946; all sources from RG 340, Special Interest Files, Box 13, NARA.

14. Ltr, W. Stuart Symington to Homer Ferguson, U.S. Senate, Nov 19, 1947; Statement by W. Stuart Symington, Secretary of the Air Force, before the Subcommittee of the Special Senate Committee Investigating the National Defense Program, Nov 24, 1947; both sources from RG 340, Special Interest Files, Box 13, NARA.

15. Memo, W. Stuart Symington to Col Desmond O'Keefe, Air Judge Advoc, Dec 1, 1947, Spaatz Collection, Box 264, Folder 2, LC Manuscript Div.

16. Intvw, W. Stuart Symington by author, Oct 21, 1981, pp 21–22; memo, W. Stuart Symington to Secy Army Kenneth C. Royall, Nov 19, 1947, Spaatz Collec-

tion, Box 264, Folder 2, LC Manuscript Div; *Evening Star* (Washington, D.C.), Mar 18, 1949, p 6.

17. Memo, Col Desmond O'Keefe to W. Stuart Symington, subj: Weekly Report, Maj Gen Bennett E. Meyers; memo, Maj Gen Reginald C. Harmon, Judge Advoc Gen, USAF, to W. Stuart Symington, Nov 24, 1948; Presidential Order by Harry S. Truman, Jul 16, 1948; all sources from RG 340, Special Interest Files (9), Box 12, Symington's personal Meyers file, NARA; *Journal Herald* (Dayton, Ohio), Apr 4, 1972, p 29.

18. Statement by W. Stuart Symington, Secretary of the Air Force, Upon Recent Testimony Before the Subcommittee of the Special Senate Committee Investigating the National Defense Program, Nov 24, 1947, RG 340, Special Interest Files, Box 13, Symington's personal Meyers file, NARA.

19. *Ibid.*

20. *Ibid*; intvw, W. Stuart Symington by author, Oct 21, 1981; "History of the Air Force Office of Special Investigations" (draft), History Ofc, AF Ofc of Special Investigations.

21. Ltr, Robert F. Boger, Publisher, *Aviation Week*, to W. Stuart Symington, Sep 23, 1947; ltr, James H. McGraw Jr., President, McGraw-Hill Publishing Co, Inc, to W. Stuart Symington, Sep 23, 1947; memo, Stephen F. Leo, Dir, Public Rel, OSAF, to W. Stuart Symington, Oct 1, 1947; ltr, W. Stuart Symington to James H. McGraw Jr., Oct 3, 1947; all sources from RG 340, Special Interest Files, Special File 4, Box 9, McGraw-Hill Corresp, *Aviation Week*, NARA.

22. Sworn Testimony of Mr Stephen F. Leo, Director of Public Relations, Department of the Air Force, Regarding the Visit to Mr Robert J. Wood, Editor of *Aviation Week* and Mr Robert F. Boger, Publisher of *Aviation Week*, Dec 31, 1947, RG 340, Special Interest Files, Special File 4, Box 9, McGraw-Hill Corresp, *Aviation Week*, NARA.

23. Memo, W. Stuart Symington to Secy Defense James V. Forrestal, Jan 14, 1948, RG 340, Special Interest Files, Special File 4, Box 9, McGraw-Hill Corresp, *Aviation Week*, NARA.

24. John L. O'Brian, Arthur W. Pare, and Roane Waring, Report of the Board on Flying Pay and Submarine Pay, Dec 10, 1947; memo, W. Stuart Symington to James V. Forrestal, Dec 22, 1947; both sources from RG 340, Special Interest Files, Folder 6, Box 9, O'Brian Board Report (Hook Board) Corresp, NARA.

25. Memo, Asst Secy AF (Civil, Military, and Diplomatic) Cornelius V. Whitney to James V. Forrestal, subj: Report of the Board on Flying Pay and Submarine Pay, Dec 10, 1947; detailed comments on report of O'Brian Board with exhibits 1, 2, and 3, Feb 4, 1948; both sources from RG 340, Special Interest Files, Folder 6, Box 9, O'Brian Board Report (Hook Board) Corresp, NARA.

26. Memo, W. Stuart Symington to Advisory Commission on Service Pay, subj: Air Force Comments on Tentative Recommendations of Pay Advisory Commission, Nov 10, 1948, RG, 340, Special Interest Files, Folder 6, Box 9, O'Brian Board Report (Hook Board) Corresp, NARA.

27. Memo, W. Stuart Symington to James V. Forrestal, Jan 26, 1948, RG 340, Gen Corresp File .032, NARA.

28. Memo, W. Stuart Symington to Gen Carl A. Spaatz, Sep 25, 1947, Symington Papers, Box 12, Spaatz folder, HSTL.

29. Ltr, Glen Martin to Eugene M. Zuckert, Jun 10, 1982; intvw, Eugene M. Zuckert by author, Apr 27, 1982, USAF Oral History Collection, AFHRC file K239. 0512–1348, AFHRC, Maxwell AFB, Ala.

30. Ltr, Glen Martin to Eugene M. Zuckert, Jun 10, 1982; intvw, Eugene M. Zuckert by author, Apr 27, 1982; intvw, W. Stuart Symington by author, Oct 21, 1981.

31. Intvw, Eugene M. Zuckert by author, Apr 27, 1982; intvw, W. Stuart Symington by author, Oct 21, 1981.

32. Memo, James V. Forrestal to Secys AF and Navy, Mar 10, 1948, RG 340, Gen Corresp 1947–1948, File 452.1, NARA.

33. Memo, W. Stuart Symington to James V. Forrestal, Mar 24, 1948, RG 340, Gen Corresp 1947–1948, File 452.1, NARA.

34. Memo, Maj Gen Frederic H. Smith,

Jr., to W. Stuart Symington, Apr 15, 1948, RG 340, Gen Corresp 1947–1948, File 452.1, NARA.

35. Jacob Neufeld, *Turbojet Engine Development: A Brief Historical Synopsis* (Washingtom, D.C.: Office of Air Force History, 1974), pp 2–8.

36. Ltr, Under Secy AF Arthur S. Barrows to Under Secy State Robert A. Lovett, Apr 2, 1948; memo to Under Secy AF and Asst Deputy Chief of Staff, Materiel, subj: British Gas Turbine Engines, Apr 5, 1948; memo, James V. Forrestal to W. Stuart Symington, Apr 14, 1948; all sources from RG 340, Gen Corresp 1947–1948, File 452.1, NARA.

37. Note, W. Stuart Symington to Carl Hinshaw, U.S. House of Representatives, Mar 31, 1948; memo, Gen Carl A. Spaatz to W. Stuart Symington, subj: Use of Jet Planes and Long Range Propeller Fighters, Mar 26, 1948; ltr (confid), W. Stuart Symington to Carl Hinshaw, U.S. House of Representatives, Apr 24, 1948; all sources from RG 340, Gen Corresp 1947–1948, File 452.1, NARA.

38. Ltr (secret), W. Stuart Symington to Secy State George C. Marshall, Oct 16, 1947, RG 340, Gen Corresp 1947–1948, File 452.1, NARA.

39. Ltr (secret), Acting Secy State Robert A. Lovett to W. Stuart Symington, Dec 18, 1947, RG 340, Gen Corresp 1947–1948, File 452.1, NARA.

40. Ltr, W. Stuart Symington to Carl T. Hayden, U.S. Senate, Dec 31, 1947; Statement of W. Stuart Symington, Secretary of the Air Force, before the Committee on Armed Services, House of Representatives, Concerning HR 3434, Authorizing Unitary Plan for Construction of Transonic and Supersonic Wind-Tunnel Facilities and Establishment of Air Engineering Development Center; both sources from RG 340, Special Interest Files, Special File 29A, Air Engineering Devel Ctr, 1948, NARA.

41. Ltr, W. Stuart Symington to Carl T. Hayden, U.S. Senate, Dec 31, 1947; Statement of W. Stuart Symington Concerning HR 3434; both sources from RG 340, Special Interest Files, Special File 29A, Air Engineering Devel Ctr, 1948,

NARA.

42. Memo, W. Stuart Symington to James V. Forrestal, subj: Establishment of an Air Force Academy, Nov 27, 1948, RG 340, Gen Corresp 1947–1948, File 12690, Aug 1948–Dec 1948, vol 1, NARA; memo, W. Stuart Symington to James V. Forrestal, subj: Memo from General Eisenhower Concerning Service Academy Training for Future Air Force Officers, Jan 17, 1949, RG 340, Gen Corresp 1947–1948, Files 408, Feb 1948, and 493, Apr 1949, NARA; intvw, W. Stuart Symington by author, Oct 21, 1981.

43. Memo, James V. Forrestal to Secys Army, Navy, and AF, Feb 3, 1948, RG 340, Reorg of the NME, Special Interest Files, Special File 4A, Roles and Missions, NARA; Hearings Before the Committee on Expenditures. *Executive Departments*, U.S. House of Representatives, 80th Cong, 1st sess (Washington, D.C.: GPO, 1948), p 102, copy in RG 340, Reorg of the NME, Special Interest Files, Special File 4C, Unification Flaws, NARA.

44. Cole et al, eds, *Department of Defense Documents*, pp 65–73; copy of Report of the Investigation on Unification and Strategy by the Committee on Armed Services, House of Representatives, RG 340, Reorg of the NME, Special Interest Files, Special File 4C, Unification Flaws, NARA.

45. Memo, W. Barton Leach to W. Stuart Symington, Jun 11, 1948, RG 340, Special Interest Files, Special File 9, OSD Chron File, NARA.

46. *Ibid.*

47. Memo, W. Stuart Symington to James V. Forrestal, subj: Recommended Changes in the National Military Establishment, Sep 14, 1948, RG 340, Special Interest Files, Special File 9, OSD Chron File, NARA.

48. Ltr, W. Stuart Symington to Ferdinand Eberstadt, Chmn, Ctee on Nat Security Org, Jun 30, 1948, RG 340, Reorg of the NME, Special Interest Files, Special File 4B, Hoover Commission, Box 5, NARA.

49. OSD press release no 38–48, Mar 26, 1948, subj: Secretary Forrestal Announces Results of Key West Conference, RG

340, Reorg of the NME, Special Interest Files, Special File 4A, Roles and Missions, NARA.

50. OSD press release no 140–48, Aug 24, 1948, subj: Newport Conference Discussed Before Senior Military Officers, RG 340, Special Interest Files, Special Files 60–70, Box 56, no 60, p 18A, NARA.

51. Walter Millis, ed, with E. S. Duffield, *The Forrestal Diaries* (New York: Viking Press, 1951), pp 475–78.

52. Memo, W. Stuart Symington to James V. Forrestal, Jan 29, 1948, RG 340, Special Interest Files, Special File 4A, Roles and Missions, NARA; ltr, William H. Strong, Asst to Ferdinand Eberstadt, to W. Stuart Symington, Oct 25, 1948, with notes on Symington's testimony before the Committee on Security Organization of the Commission of Organization of the Executive Branch of the Government, Oct 18, 1948, RG 340, Reorg of the NME, Special Interest Files, Special File 4B, Hoover Commission, Box 5, NARA;

53. Memo, W. Stuart Symington to James V. Forrestal, Mar 12, 1948, RG 330, Records of the Office of the Secretary of Defense, E199, CD 12–1–26, Box 64, NARA.

54. Memo, W. Stuart Symington to James V. Forrestal, Jun 9, 1948; copy of article published in the *Buffalo Evening News*, May 1, 1948; Richard Essex, "Naval Air Superiority to Land-Based Power Concealed by USAF," *Armed Forces Journal*, May 29, 1948, editorial; all sources from RG 340, Gen Corresp 1947–1948, File 000.7, NARA, also Special Interest Files, Special File 9, OSD Chron File, Symington to Forrestal Apr–Dec 1948, NARA.

55. Ltr, W. Stuart Symington to Ferdinand Eberstadt, Oct 25, 1948, RG 330, E199, CD 12–1–26, Box 64, NARA.

56. Ltr W. Stuart Symington to Ferdinand Eberstadt, Nov 1, 1948, Symington Papers, Box 5, Corresp, Eberstadt, HSTL

57. Memo, W. Stuart Symington to James V. Forrestal, Nov 22, 1948, Symington Papers, Box 4, Declassified Documents, HSTL.

58. Report of the Investigation on Unification and Strategy by the Committee on Armed Services, House of Representatives, pp 1–3, RG 340, Reorg of the NME, Special Interest Files, Special File 4C, Unification Flaws, NARA.

59. *Ibid.*

60. Memo, Pres Truman to W. Stuart Symington, May 13, 1948, RG 340, Gen Corresp 1947–1948, File 040, NARA; ltr, Pres Truman to James V. Forrestal, Jun 3, 1948, RG 340, Special Interest Files, Special File 4, Corresp Oct 1947–Nov 1948, NARA.

61. Memo, James V. Forrestal to Secys Army, Navy, and AF, and the JCS, Feb 4, 1948, RG 340, Gen Corresp 1947–1948, File 020, Secy AF, Executive, NARA.

62. *Ibid.*

63. *Ibid.*

64. Memo, W. Stuart Symington to James V. Forrestal, Jun 3, 1948, RG 340, Special Interest Files, Special File 4, OSD Chron File, Symington to Forrestal, Apr–Dec 1948, NARA.

65. *Ibid.*

66. *Ibid.*

67. *Ibid.*

68. Memo, W. Stuart Symington to Lt Gen Edwin W. Rawlings, Air Comptroller, Dec 17, 1947; memo, W. Stuart Symington to James V. Forrestal, Jan 26, 1948; both sources from RG 340, Special Interest Files, Special File 14, Corresp Oct 1947–Sep 1948, NARA.

69. Memo, W. Stuart Symington to James V. Forrestal, Jan 26, 1948; memo, W. Stuart Symington to Lt Gen Edwin W. Rawlings, Dec 17, 1947;

70. Ltr, W. Stuart Symington to James E. Van Zandt, U.S. House of Representatives, Mar 5, 1948, RG 340, Special Interest Files, Special File 14, Corresp Oct 1947–Sep 1948, NARA.

71. Arnold A. Rogow, *James Forrestal: A Study of Personality, Politics, and Policy* (New York: The Macmillan Co, 1963), pp 290–91.

72. Ltr, W. Stuart Symington to James Webb, Dir, Bur of the Budget, Dec 16, 1947, RG 340, Special Interest Files, Special File 14, Corresp Oct 1947–Sep 1948, NARA.

73. Remarks by W. Stuart Symington, Secretary of the Air Force, before the

Senate Armed Services Committee, Washington, DC, Mar 25, 1948, AFHRC, Maxwell AFB, Ala.

74. Remarks by W. Stuart Symington delivered off the record to a group of publishers, New York, New York, Apr 20, 1948; remarks by W. Stuart Symington at a meeting of executives, Chicago, Illinois, Apr 13, 1948; both sources from AFHRC, Maxwell AFB, Ala.

75. Paul Y. Hammond, "Super Carriers and B–36 Bombers: Appropriations, Strategy and Politics," *American Civil-Military Decisions: A Book of Case Studies*, ed Harold Stein (University of Alabama Press, 1963), p 473; Evan Luard, ed, *The Cold War: A Reappraisal* (New York: Frederick A. Praeger, Publishers, 1964), pp 23–24.

76. Ltr, W. Stuart Symington to John Taber, U.S. House of Representatives, Apr 15, 1948, RG 340, Special Interest Files, Special File 14, Budget Oct 1–Dec 31, 1948, Corresp, NARA; Chronological History of Statements and Events Concerning Air Force Programs, Mar 11, 1948–Apr 27, 1948, prepared by Brig Gen Ralph Stearley, USAF, Dir, Legis and Liaison Div, RG 340, Special Interest Files, Special File 4A, NARA.

77. Daniel Yergin, *Shattered Peace: The Origins of the Cold War and the National Security State* (Boston: Houghton Mifflin Co, 1977), p 358.

78. Hearings before the Committee on Armed Services, Universal. *Military Training*, U.S. Senate, 80th Cong, 2d sess (Washington, D.C.: GPO, 1948), pp 395–96; *New York Times*, Apr 16, 1948; *The Public Papers of Harry S. Truman*, no 77 (Washingtom, D.C.: GPO, 1964), p 216, the President's news conference of Apr 15, 1948.

79. Rogow, *James Forrestal*, p 294; memo, W. Stuart Symington to James V. Forrestal, Apr 21, 1948, Symington Papers, Box 4, Declassified Documents, HSTL.

80. Rogow, *James Forrestal*, p 295.

81. Memo, W. Stuart Symington to James V. Forrestal, Mar 31, 1948; memo, W. Stuart Symington to James V. Forrestal, Apr 21, 1948; both sources from Symington Papers, Box 4, Declassified Documents File, HSTL.

82. Statement by W. Stuart Symington, Secretary of the Air Force, before the Deficiencies Subcommittee of the Senate Appropriations Committee, Apr 27, 1948, CAFH.

83. Memo, W. Stuart Symington to James V. Forrestal, subj: Position of the Department of the Air Force with Respect to UMT Legislation, Oct 8, 1948, RG 340, Special Interest Files, Special File 9, OSD Chron File, Symington to Forrestal, Apr–Dec 1948, NARA.

84. *Ibid.*

85. Millis, *The Forrestal Diaries*, pp 462–63.

86. *Ibid*, p 463.

87. *Ibid.*

88. Intvw, W. Stuart Symington by Hugh N. Ahmann and Herman S. Wolk, May 2, 1978, Dec 12, 1978.

89. Memo, W. Stuart Symington to Chief of Staff, USAF, Dec 30, 1948, Symington Papers, Box 13, HSTL.

90. William H. Tunner, *Over The Hump*, (New York: Duell, Sloan, and Pearce, 1964), p 197.

91. *Ibid*, p 200.

92. *Time* magazine, Jan 19, 1948, pp 24–25.

Chapter 4

The Battle over the B–36

1. Robert H. Ferrell, ed, *The Eisenhower Diaries* (New York: Norton, 1981), p 152.

2. Chronology of the B–36 Program Prepared under Gen Counsel Brackly Shaw, 6th draft, May 31, 1949, RG 341, Records of Headquarters U.S. Air Force, DCS/Compt (73), Admin Div 1942–1953, File 452.1, Aircraft: B–36 Special Files, Box 207, NARA; memo for record by Gen Muir S. Fairchild, Vice Chief of Staff, USAF, Jun 25, 1948, RG 340, Special Interest

Files, Special File B, Congressional Inquiry of the B-36, Box 51, NARA.

3. W. Stuart Symington's personal recollections, undated, unsigned, dictated about Jun 16, 1949; NARA; ltr, W. Stuart Symington to John L. Sullivan, Jan 22, 1948; ltrs, Hugh L. Hanson, Nov 22, 1947, Dec 7, 1947, to Steven F. Leo; all sources from RG 340, Special Interest Files, Special File B, Congressional Inquiry of the B-36, Box 51, NARA.

4. Memo for record by Gen Muir S. Fairchild; Murray Green, "Stuart Symington and the B-36," PhD dissertation, American Univ, 1960, pp 78–79; memo for record by Arthur S. Barrows, subj: B-36 Discussion of May 22, May 24, 1948, RG 341, DCS/Compt (73) Admin Div 1942–1953, File 452.1, Aircraft: B-36 Special Files, Box 212, NARA.

5. Memo, W. Stuart Symington to James V. Forrestal, subj: Certification and Request for Release of Funds for 32 B-36B Aircraft and 7 RB-36B Aircraft, Jan 22, 1949; memo, W. Stuart Symington to James V. Forrestal, subj: The Air Force 48-Group Program, Feb 25, 1949; both sources from RG 340, Special Interest Files, Special File B, Congressional Inquiry of the B-36, Box 51; History of B-36 Procurement, presented to House Armed Services Ctee by Maj Gen Frederic H. Smith, Jr., (168.04–1 vol 1, vault), CAFH.

6. Ltr, Lt Gen Curtis E. LeMay, Commanding Gen, SAC, to Gen Hoyt S. Vandenberg, Chief of Staff, USAF, Feb 2, 1949, RG 341, File 452.1, Aircraft: B-36 Special Files, Box 212, NARA.

7. Document in CAFH files, Box 709 K168, 04–1, folder marked Miscellaneous Papers Pertaining to the B-36 Investigation.

8. NME-USAF press release no 161, Apr 5, 1949; ltr, Brig Gen H. A. Shepard, Chief, Procurement Div, AMC, to W. Stuart Symington, Mar 28,1949; both sources from RG 340, Special Interest Files, Special File B, Congressional Inquiry of the B-36, Box 51, NARA.

9. Memo, W. Stuart Symington to James V. Forrestal, Feb 16, 1949, RG 330, 199, CD 11–1–2, Box 61, NARA.

10. Hammond, "Super Carriers and B-36 Bombers," pp 494–95; Hearings before the House Armed Services Committee. *The National Defense Program: Unification and Strategy*, 81st Cong, 1st sess, (Washington, D.C.: GPO, 1949), pp 622–23; Steven L. Rearden, *History of the Office of the Secretary of Defense: The Formative Years, 1947–1950*, vol 1 (Washington, D.C.: Historical Office, Office of the Secretary of Defense, 1984), p 390.

11. Hammond, "Super Carriers and B-36 Bombers," pp 494–95; Hearings, *The National Defense Program: Unification and Strategy*, pp 622–23.

12. Hammond, "Super Carriers and B-36 Bombers," p 495; Green, "Symington and the B-36," pp 141–43.

13. Memo, Lt Gen Edwin W. Rawlings to W. Stuart Symington, subj: Analysis of Fiscal Year 1950, Budget Estimates, Jan 11, 1949, (no signature), Vandenberg Collection, Box 41, LC Manuscript Div.

14. Statement of James E. Van Zandt, MC, in the House of Representatives, May 26, 1949, RG 340, File 5214, Box 1564, vol 1, B-36: May 31, 1949–Aug 31, 1949; *Congressional Record*, U.S. House of Representatives (Washington, D.C.: GPO, May 26, 1949), pp 7028–29; Hearings before the Committee on Armed Services. *Investigation of the B-36 Bomber Program*, House of Representatives, 81st Cong, 1st sess (on HR 234) (Washington, D.C.: GPO, 1949), pp 11–15.

15. Statement of James E. Van Zandt, May 26, 1949; *Congressional Record*, pp 7028–29; Hearings, *Investigation of the B-36 Bomber Program*, pp 11–15; *Los Angeles Daily News*, Jul 27, 1949, Drew Pearson's column.

16. Statement of James E. Van Zandt, May 26, 1949; *Congressional Record*, pp 7028–29; Hearings, *Investigation of the B-36 Bomber Program*, pp 11–15; *Los Angeles Daily News*, Jul 27, 1949, Drew Pearson's column.

17. Hanson Weightman Baldwin, U.S. Navy (Ret.), *Reminiscences*, vol 2 (Annapolis: U.S. Naval Institute, 1976), pp 458–70.

18. Intvw, W. Stuart Symington and Stephen F. Leo by author, Aug 19, 1982, author's files.

19. Ltr, W. Stuart Symington to mem-

bers, House Armed Services Ctee (no date); memo, W. Stuart Symington to Arthur S. Barrows, Jun 2, 1949; both sources from RG 340, File 5214, Box 1564, vol 1, B-36: May 31, 1949–Aug 31, 1949, NARA;

20. Memo, W. Barton Leach to Gen Muir S. Fairchild, subj: Organization of Preparation for the B-36 Hearings, Jun 2, 1949, RG 340, DCS/Compt (73), Admin Div 1942–1953, File 452.1, Aircraft: B-36 Special File, Box 211, NARA.

21. Ltr, W. Stuart Symington to Carl Vinson, Chmn, Ctee on Armed Services, U.S. House of Representatives, Jun 2, 1949, RG 340, File 5214, Box 1564, vol 1, B-36: May 31, 1949–Aug 31, 1949, NARA (also printed in Hearings, *Investigation of the B-36 Bomber Program*, pp 7–8).

22. *Ibid.*

23. *Ibid.*

24. Hearings, *Investigation of the B-36 Bomber Program*, pp 20–57.

25. Ltr, Gen George C. Kenney to W. Stuart Symington, Jun 18, 1949, printed in Hearings, *Investigation of the B-36 Bomber Program*, pp 118–23.

26. Hearings, *Investigation of the B-36 Bomber Program*, p 124.

27. *Ibid*, pp 144-47.

28. *Ibid*, p 148.

29. *Ibid*, pp 171, 175, 196.

30. *Ibid*, p 209.

31. *Ibid*, p 210.

32. *Ibid*, p 220.

33. *Ibid*, p 242.

34. *Ibid*, p 279.

35. *Ibid*, pp 284–85.

36. *Ibid*, p 343.

37. *Ibid*, pp 524–25; intvw, Gen Joseph F. Carroll by Edward C. Mishler, Jan 12, 1983, History Ofc, AF Ofc of Special Investigations.

38. Hearings, *Investigation of the B-36 Bomber Program*, pp 610-11.

39. Paul Y. Hammond, "Background to the Second Phase of the Hearings: The Navy Finds Silence Impossible," *American Civil-Military Decisions*, ed Harold Stein, p 505.

40. Hammond, "Super Carriers and B-36 Bombers," pp 505-7.

41. *Ibid*, p 507.

42. Hearings, *Investigation of the B-36 Bomber Program*, pp 660–61.

43. *Ibid*, p 660.

44. Hammond, "Super Carriers and B-36 Bombers," p 517; Hearings, *The National Defense Program: Unification and Strategy*, pp 43, 45, 52.

45. Hearings, *The National Defense Program: Unification and Strategy*, p 400.

46. *Ibid*, p 401; Hammond, "Super Carriers and B-36 Bombers," p 532.

47. Hearings, *The National Defense Program: Unification and Strategy*, p 408.

48. *Ibid*, pp 407-08.

49. Hammond, "Super Carriers and B-36 Bombers," p 532; Hearings, *The National Defense Program: Unification and Strategy*, p 458.

50. Hearings, *The National Defense Program: Unification and Strategy*, p 459.

51. *Ibid*, p 462.

52. *Report of the Committee on Armed Services, Investigation of the B-36 Bomber Program*, U.S. House of Representatives, HR 234 (Washington, D.C.: GPO, 1949), pp 32–33.

53. *Report of Investigation by the Committee on Armed Services, Unification and Strategy*, 81st Cong, 2nd sess (Washington, D.C.: GPO, 1950), pp 53–58.

54. *Ibid.*

55. Ltr, W. Stuart Symington to W. Barton Leach, Apr 20, 1950, Symington Papers, Box 7, HSTL.

56. Speech by W. Stuart Symington before Chamber of Commerce, San Francisco, California, Apr 18, 1950; speech by W. Stuart Symington before Yale Alumni Assoc luncheon, New Haven, Connecticut, Feb 22, 1950; both sources from CAFH.

57. "The Baylor Speech," *Air Force Magazine*, Mar 1950, pp 26–29 (concerning a speech by W. Stuart Symington before the graduating class of Baylor University, Waco, Texas, Feb 1, 1950).

58. Ltr, W. Barton Leach to W. Stuart Symington, Mar 9, 1950, Symington Papers, Box 7, HSTL.

59. Ltr, W. Stuart Symington to Leverett Saltonstall, U.S. Senate, Feb 17, 1950, Symington Papers, Box 11, HSTL.

60. *Ibid.*

61. Memo, W. Stuart Symington to Secy Defense Louis A. Johnson, Mar 15,

1950, RG 340, Special Interest Files, Special File 9, OSD Chron File, Symington to Johnson, NARA.

62. Intvw, W. Stuart Symington by author, Oct 21, 1981, pp 53–55.

63. Ltr, W. Stuart Symington to Gen

Hoyt S. Vandenberg, Apr 24, 1950, Vandenberg Collection, Box 61, LC Manuscript Div.

64. Ltr, W. Barton Leach to W. Stuart Symington, Apr 7, 1950, Symington Papers, Box 7, HSTL.

Chapter 5

The Finletter Era (1950–1953)

1. Hearings before the Subcommittee of the Committee on Appropriations. *Military Public Works Appropriations for 1952*, U.S. House of Representatives, 82d Cong, 1st sess (Washington, D.C.: GPO, 1951), p 10; remarks by Asst Secy AF Eugene M. Zuckert before the Joint Orientation Conference, Apr 1950, RG 340, Asst Secy AF, Management, Chron File Jan 1950–Mar 1950, Box 186, NARA.

2. *Who's Who in America*, vol 29, p 842; *New York Times*, Apr 5, 1950, p 1, 9.

3. John A. Ballard, comp, " The Job of the Civilian Secretary," *Harvard University Defense Policy Seminar, 1956–1957*, serial no 93, Nov 8, 1956, excerpts from remarks by Thomas K. Finletter, former Secy AF, at the Defense Policy Seminar, Mar 29, 1955, p 6.

4. *New York Times*, Apr 5, 1950, p 30, Jun 7, 1950, p 23.

5. Robert J. Donovan, *Tumultuous Years: The Presidency of Harry S. Truman, 1949–1953* (New York: W. W. Norton & Company, 1982), p 265; Kent M. Beck, "The Dove as Realist: Thomas K. Finletter and the Cold War, 1945–1950," unpublished paper, Behrend College, Pennsylvania State Univ, p 1.

6. DOD, Ofc of Public Info, release no 728–50, Jun 15, 1950, "John A. McCone Sworn in As Under Secretary of the Air Force," RG 340, John A. McCone, Personal File, Box 57, NARA.

7. *Who's Who In America*, vol 29, p 2503.

8. Intvw, Roswell L. Gilpatric by Jerry N. Hess, Jan 19, 1972, pp 8–9, HSTL.

9. Ltr, Col William S. Steele to Thomas K. Finletter, Apr 10, 1951, RG 340, Box 695, NARA.

10. Intvw, Eugene M. Zuckert by author, Jan 24, 1984, pp 5–7, USAF Oral History Collection, AFHRC file K239.0512–1582, AFHRC, Maxwell AFB, Ala.

11. *Ibid.*

12. Intvw, Roswell L. Gilpatric by Jerry N. Hess, pp 22–23.

13. *Ibid*, p 23.

14. Intvw, Gen William F. McKee by author, Mar 20, 1984, USAF Oral History Collection, AFHRC file K239.0512–1588, AFHRC, Maxwell AFB, Ala.

15. Ltr, John A. McCone to Pres Truman, Oct 9, 1951, RG 340, Box 31, File 60A–1055, NARA.

16. Intvw, Roswell L. Gilpatric by Jerry N. Hess, pp 25–26; intvw, Eugene M. Zuckert by author, Jan 24, 1984, p 13.

17. Memos, Thomas K. Finletter to Chief of Staff, USAF, Feb 8, 1952, Jan 20, 1953, RG 340, Box 30, File 60A–1055, NARA; intvw, Gen William F. McKee by author, Mar 20, 1984, p 25.

18. Telephone intvw, Gen William G. Hipps by author, Aug 20, 1984, author's files.

19. Intvw, Gen William F. McKee by author, Mar 20, 1984, pp 31–32.

20. Ballard, comp, "The Job of the Civilian Secretary."

21. Memo, Stephen F. Leo to Eugene M. Zuckert, Apr 7, 1950; memo, Eugene M. Zuckert to Thomas K. Finletter, May 5, 1950; both sources from RG 340, Acces no A1749, Box 4/4, Ofc of the Admin Asst, folder marked Ofc of Info Services 1947–1961 Org, NARA.

22. Memo, Gen Hoyt S. Vandenberg to Thomas K. Finletter, subj: Consideration of National Defense Public Information Problems by the Joint Secretaries, Oct 30,

1950, RG 340, File 020, OSD 3374, Box 697, NARA.

23. Ltr, Gen George C. Stratemeyer to Gen. Hoyt S. Vandenberg, Stratemeyer Diary, Aug 22, 1950, CAFH.

24. *Ibid.*

25. Memo, OSAF Admin Asst John J. McLaughlin to Mr. Hill, Aug 1, 1952, RG 340, Acces no 60–A1055, Box 27, R. L. Gilpatric, SAFUS, Misc Files 1951–1953, folder marked Responsibilities Mr. Gilpatric, NARA.

26. Memo, OSAF Deputy Admin Asst Philip J. Curran to John J. McLaughlin, subj: Clarification of Responsibilities within OSAF, Nov 24, 1953, RG 340, Acces no 63–A1749, Box 3 of 4, folder marked 1949–1954, Org, Functional Overall, OSAF, NARA.

27. Memo, Eugene M. Zuckert to Under Secy AF John A. McCone, Dec 29, 1950, RG 340, Asst Secy AF (Management) Box unknown, NARA.

28. Telephone conversation, John A. McCone and Tom Morgan (Sperry), Feb 28, 1951, Daily Log-Telephone Conversations, RG 340, File 60A–1055, Box 31, NARA.

29. Intvw, Thomas K. Finletter by Jerry N. Hess, Jan 20, Feb 15, 1972, pp 22–27, HSTL; intvw, Thomas K. Finletter by Col Marvin Stanley, Feb 1967, p 14, USAF Oral History Collection, AFHRC file K239.0512–760, AFHRC, Maxwell AFB, Ala.

30. Harry S. Truman, *Memoirs*, vol 2, *Years of Trial and Hope* (Garden City, New York: Doubleday & Company, Inc, 1956), pp 332–40; *Public Papers of the Presidents of the United States: Harry S. Truman* (Washington, D.C.: GPO, 1965), pp 491–93, public messages, speeches, and statements, 1950.

31. Remarks by Thomas K. Finletter, Secretary of the Air Force, at the Commencement Exercises of the University of Pennsylvania, Philadelphia, Jun 14, 1950, vol 1 of 6, CAFH.

32. Remarks by Thomas K. Finletter before the Aviation Writers Group, Washington, D.C., Sep 21, 1950; remarks by Thomas K. Finletter on NBC Television's "Battle Report," Washington D.C., Sep 24,

1950; remarks by Thomas K. Finletter at the Herald Tribune Forum, New York, New York, Oct 25, 1950; all sources at CAFH under "Public Statements and Speeches by Thomas K. Finletter, Jan 26, 1950–Dec 20, 1950," vol 1 of 6, K168.76A; speech given by Under Secy AF John A. McCone before the Institute of Aeronautical Science, Cleveland, Ohio, Mar 16, 1951, RG 340, File 020, 1951, Box 695, NARA; George J. Nagy, "History, Assistant for Programming, Jul 1, 1950–Dec 31, 1950, p 13, CAFH, File 142.28, July 1950–Dec 1950.

33. Hearings, *Department of Defense Appropriations for 1952*, p 1254.

34. *Department of Defense Semiannual Report of the Secretary of Defense and the Semiannual Reports of the Secretary of the Army, Secretary of the Navy, and Secretary of the Air Force, January 1 to June 30 1951*, (Washington, D.C.: GPO, 1951), pp 197–99, CAFH, K160.04, 1951; memo, Thomas K. Finletter to Secy Defense George C. Marshall, Dec 30, 1950; memo, George C. Marshall to Thomas K. Finletter, Jan 5, 1951, RG 340, Special Interest Files, Special File 9, 1950, Secy AF to Secy Defense Corresp, Finletter to Johnson and Finletter to Marshall, NARA.

35. *New York Times*, Jan 30, 1951, p 6; intvw, Eugene M. Zuckert by author, January 24, 1984, p 24.

36. Charles J. Gross, *Prelude to the Total Force: Origins and Development of the Air National Guard, 1943–1969*, draft, pp 96–97, CAFH.

37. Telephone intvw, Gen William G. Hipps by author, Sep 27, 1984, author's files; *History of the Air Training Command, Jan 1, 1952–Jun 30, 1952*, (History Office, Air Training Command) p 117.

38. Paul Shnitzer, comp, under direction of E. A. Jensen, Historical Officer, "History, Assistant for Programming, Jul 1, 1951–Dec 31, 1951," part 2, History of Analysis Division, DCS/O, pp 1–2.

39. Remarks by Thomas K. Finletter before the Commercial Club of Cincinnati, Ohio, Jan 19, 1952, CAFH, File K168.76A, vol 4.

40. Remarks by Thomas K. Finletter before the Frank M. Hawks Memorial Award Dinner at American Legion Post

501, New York, New York, Jan 23, 1952, CAFH.

41. Remarks by Thomas K. Finletter before the National Industrial Conference Board, San Francisco, California, Mar 20, 1952, CAFH.

42. Stanley A. Blumberg and Gwinn Owens, *Energy and Conflict: The Life and Times of Edward Teller* (New York: G. P. Putnam's Sons, 1976), pp 288–89, 314–16; Phillip M. Stern, *The Oppenheimer Case: Security on Trial* (New York: Harper and Row, Publishers, 1969), pp 182–200; Kenneth Schaffel, *The Emerging Shield: The Air Force and the Evolution of Continental Air Defense, 1945–1960* (Washington, D.C.: Office of Air Force History, 1991), pp 169–96.

43. Edward A. Kolodziej, *The Uncommon Defense and Congress, 1945–1963* (Columbus: Ohio State University Press, 1966), pp 151–70.

44. Memo, Thomas K. Finletter to Secy Defense Robert A. Lovett, Feb 15, 1952, RG 340, File 60A–1055, Box 30, NARA.

45. Schnitzer, comp, "History, Assistant for Programming," part 2, Programming and Budgeting Cycle, projections for FY 1953, pp 6–12.

46. *Ibid*, p 3.

47. Ltr, Thomas K. Finletter to John C. Stennis, U.S. Senate, Apr 28, 1952, RG 340, Box 1066, NARA; memo, Edward F. McGinnis, to Thomas K. Finletter, subj: Questions for Legion-Sponsored Broadcast, Mar 20, 1952, RG 340, File 020, Confidential and Unclassified, 1952, Box 1061, NARA; Statement of Honorable Thomas K. Finletter, Secretary of the Air Force, to the Committee on Appropriations, U.S. Senate, Fiscal Year 1953 Budget Estimates, RG 340, File 110 (secret), Box 986, NARA.

48. Memo, Lt Gen Lawrence S. Kuter, Acting Vice Chief of Staff, USAF, to Thomas K. Finletter, Roswell L. Gilpatric and General Nathan F. Twining, Aug 11, 1952, with attachment, "New Phase: A Statement of Air Force Policy," Twining Collection, Top Secret File, Box 122, LC Manuscript Div.

49. Telephone conversation, John A. McCone and W. Stuart Symington, Feb 7, 1951, Daily Log-Telephone Conversations,

RG 340, 60A–1055, Box 31, NARA.

50. Thomas K. Finletter, *Power and Policy: U.S. Foreign Policy and Military Power in the Hydrogen Age* (New York: Harcourt, Brace and Company, 1954), p 247.

51. Memo, John A. McCone to Asst Secy AF Harold Stuart, Apr 19, 1951, RG 340, 60A–1055, Box 31, NARA; telephone intvw, Harold Stuart by author, Oct 16, 1987, author's files.

52. Memo, John A. McCone to Secy Defense George C. Marshall, Apr 19, 1951, RG 340, Box 109, NARS.

53. Ballard, comp, "The Job of the Civilian Secretary," p 8.

54. Ltr, John F. Kennedy, U.S. House of Representatives, to Thomas K. Finletter, Aug 26, 1952; ltr, Thomas K. Finletter to John F. Kennedy, Sep 5, 1952; both sources from RG 340, File 110, Confideential and Unclassified, 1952, NARA.

55. Hearings before the Subcommittee of the Committee on Appropriations. *Department of Defense Appropriations for 1953*, U.S. Senate, 82d Cong, 2d sess (Washington, D.C.: GPO, 1952), pp 384, 660–62.

56. Memo, John A. McCone to Thomas K. Finletter, Aug 10, 1950, RG 340, 60A–1055, Box 31, NARA.

57. *Ibid*.

58. Intvw, Thomas K. Finletter by Col Marvin Stanley, February 1967, pp 20–21; for a complete history of the USAF's missile program during the 1950's see Jacob Neufeld, *Ballistic Missiles in the United States Air Force, 1945–1960* (Washington, D.C.: Office of Air Force History, 1990).

59. Ballard, comp, "The Job of the Civilian Secretary," p 8.

60. Memo, Col Frederic H. Miller, Jr., in the absence of Brig Gen Robert B. L. Eaton, Dir, Legis and Liaison, to Thomas K. Finletter, Jul 31, 1952, with 5-page summary of the results of aircraft production hearings held by the Senate's Preparedness Investigating Subcommittee, RG 340, 60–A1055, R. L. Gilpatric, SAFUS, Miscell Files 1951–1953, Box 27, folder marked Johnson Subcommittee, Part I, through Nov 1952, NARA.

61. *Ibid*.

62. *Ibid.*

63. Cole et al, eds, *Department of Defense Documents*, pp 123–24.

64. Draft, "Headquarters USAF History, 1952–1953," K168.01–53, CAFH.

65. Hearings before the Committee on Armed Services. *Sundry Legislation Affecting the Naval and Military Establishments*, U.S. House of Representatives, 82d Cong, 1st sess (Washington, D.C.: GPO, 1951), p 26.

66. *Ibid*, p 34.

67. *Ibid*, p 45.

68. *Ibid*, p 115.

69. Air Force Organization Act of 1951, Conference Report, pp 3–5, part of *House Bills Histories, HR 1691–2275*, 82d Cong, vol 3, Pentagon Library.

70. "Headquarters USAF History," pp 15–16.

71. *Ibid*, p 17.

72. Barr O. Braman, *History of Military Supply Centralization, 1903–1957*, Historical Study No 345, Historical Research Division (Wright-Patterson AFB, Ohio: Air Force Logistics Command, Oct 1964), p 35; "Headquarters USAF History," pp 18–19; "Department of Defense Directive No 250.01–1, Title 250, Supply Management: Clarification of Department of Defense Policies and Assignment of Responsibility," Jul 17, 1951.

73. Ltr, Roswell L. Gilpatric to Herbert C. Bonner, Chmn, Inter-Govt Relations Subctee, U.S. House of Representatives, Mar 22, 1952, RG 340, File 60A–1055, Box 27, Bonner Subctee Trip to AMC, Tab H, NARA.

74. Memo, Lt Gen Orval R. Cook,

Deputy Chief of Staff, Materiel, to Dir, Legis and Liaison, subj: HR 8130, to Promote Economy and Efficiency through Certain Reorganizations and the Integration of Supply and Service Activities within and among the Military Departments, Jun 18, 1952, RG 340, File 60A–1055, Box 27, Bonner Subctee Trip to AMC, NARA.

75. Ltr, Robert A. Lovett to Carl Vinson, U.S. House of Representatives, Jul 2, 1952, RG 340, File 60A–1055, Box 27, Bonner Subctee Trip to AMC, NARA.

76. Charles J. Gross, *On Logistics Centralization*, Historical Study No 399 (Wright-Patterson AFB, Ohio: Office of History, Air Force Logistics Command, Oct 1981), p 23; Braman, *History of Military Supply Centralization*, pp 41–42; "Headquarters USAF History," pp 20–21.

77. Hearings of the Committee on Expenditures in the Executive Departments on Federal Supply Management. *Implementation of Military Supply Requirements*, U.S. House of Representatives, 82nd Cong, 2d sess (Washington, D.C.: GPO, 1952), pp 348–55; Braman, *History of Military Supply Centralization*, p 42; Gross, *On Logistics Centralization*, pp 23–24; "Headquarters USAF History," pp 21–22.

78. Statement by Roswell L. Gilpatric, Under Secretary of the Air Force, before the Inter-Governmental Relations Subcommittee of the House Committee on Government Operations, Dec 4, 1952, RG 340, File 60A–1055, Box 27, Bonner Subctee Trip to AMC, NARA.

79. *Ibid.*

80. Hewes, *From Root to McNamara*, pp 289–91.

Chapter 6

Talbott and Quarles (1953–1957)

1. Herman S. Wolk, "The New Look in Retrospect," *Air Force Magazine*, vol 57, no 3, Mar 1974, pp 48–51; Robert F. Futrell, *Ideas, Concepts, Doctrine: A History of Basic Thinking in the United States Air Force, 1907–1964* (Maxwell AFB, Alabama: Air University, 1971), p 211.

2. Herbert S. Parmet, *Eisenhower and the American Crusades* (New York: The Macmillan Company, 1972), pp 170–71.

3. Robert H. Ferrell, ed, *The Eisenhower Diaries* (New York: W. W. Norton & Company, 1981), pp 203–4; *Who's Who In America*, vol 29, p 2531; "New Faces in

the Pentagon," *Air Force Magazine*, vol 36, no 2, Feb 1953, p 37; "Pentagon Planners," *Air Force Magazine*, vol 36, no 5, May 1953, p 16.

4. Intvw, James H. Douglas, Jr., by Hugh N. Ahmann, Jun 13–14, 1979, USAF Oral History Collection, AFHRC file K239. 0512–1126, AFHRC, Maxwell AFB, Ala, pp 3–5.

5. *Who's Who in America*, vols 29 and 33; "Pentagon Planners", *Air Force Magazine*, p 16; memo, Harold E. Talbott to Pres Eisenhower, Oct 18, 1954, with 2-page biography of David S. Smith, RG 340, File 17/31, Corresp Control Div, 1953–1954, Talbott Chron Files 1953–1954, NARA.

6. Memo, Murray Green, Research and Analysis Div, to Gen Kinney, Aug 8, 1956, RG 340 acces no 60–A1283, Box 39, SAF Files for 1956, numerical, NARA.

7. "Symington on Talbott," *Aviation Week*, vol 63, no 4, Aug 8, 1955, p 11.

8. Hearings before the Subcommittee of the Committee on Appropriations on HR 5969, Part I. *Department of Defense Appropriations for 1954*, U.S. Senate, 83d Cong, 1st sess, (Washington, D.C.: GPO, 1953), pp 160–61, 218–19.

9. Intvw, Gen William F. McKee by author, Mar 20, 1984.

10. Address by Harold E. Talbott before the Air Force Association Convention, Statler Hotel, Washington, D.C., Aug 22, 1953, Twining Papers, Box 64, Chief of Staff 1953 SAF(2), LC Manuscript Div.

11. *Ibid.*

12. *Semiannual Report of the Secretary of the Air Force, January 1, 1955–June 30, 1955* (Washington, D.C.: GPO, 1955), p 253.

13. Memo, Harold E. Talbott to Secy Defense Charles E. Wilson, Mar 17, 1954; ltr, Harold E. Talbott to Homer E. Capehart, Chmn, Ctee on Banking and Currency, U.S. Senate, May 18, 1954; both sources from RG 340, acces no 60–A1055, Talbott Chron Files 1953–1954, NARA.

14. Ltr, Harold E. Talbott to J. S. Leach, Chmn of the Board, The Texas Co, RG 340, acces no 60–1055, Box 18, Talbott Chron Files 1954–1955, Quarles Chron Files 1955, NARA.

15. *Air Force Times*, vol 14, Jun 26, 1954, p 7.

16. *Army Navy Air Force Journal*, vol 91, Aug 28, 1954, pp 1569, 1590; "Praise for Talbott," *Aviation Week*, vol 62, no 15, Apr 11, 1955, p 11.

17. "Praise for Talbott," *Aviation Week*, p 11.

18. Ltr, Harold E. Talbott to Thomas K. Finletter, Feb 5, 1954, RG 340, acces no 60–A1055, File 17/31/OSAF, Corresp Control Div, 1953–1954, Talbott Chron Files 1953–1954, NARA.

19. Ltr, Harold E. Talbott to E. G. Grace, Chmn, Bethlehem Steel Co, Inc, May 6, 1953, RG 340, acces no 60–A1055, File 17/31/ OSAF, Corresp Control Div, 1954–1955, Talbott Chron Files 1953–1954, NARA.

20. Ltr, Harold E. Talbott to Thomas G. Lanphier, Jr, Vice Pres, Consolidated-Vultee Aircraft Corp, May 5, 1953, RG 340, acces no 60–A1055, File 17/31/OSAF, Corresp Control Div, 1953–1954, Talbott Chron Files 1953–1954, NARA.

21. Ltr, Harold E. Talbott to Lt Gen Harold L. George (Ret.), Vice Pres, Gen Mgr, Hughes Aircraft Co, May 5, 1953, RG 340, acces no 60–A1055, File 17/31/ OSAF, Corresp Control Div, 1953–1954, Talbott Chron Files 1953–1954, NARA.

22. "Services Outline Airpower Plans for Congress," *Aviation Week*, vol 62, no 18, May 2, 1955, p 15; "Talbott Clarifies Dispersal Policy," *Aviation Week*, vol 62, no 19, May 9, 1955, pp 13–15; William J. Coughlin, "Talbott Gives Dispersal Details," *Aviation Week*, vol 62, no 21, May 23, 1955, p 15.

23. Ltr, Harold E. Talbott to Donald W. Douglas, Pres, Douglas Aircraft Co, Inc., Jun 17, 1953, RG 340, acces no 60–A1055, File 17/31/OSAF, Corresp Control Div, 1953–1954, Talbott Chron Files 1953–1954, NARA.

24. Robert Hotz, "USAF Buying Test: Proved Performance," *Aviation Week*, vol 61, no 20, Nov 15, 1954, pp 13–15; "Services Outline Airpower Plans for Congress," *Aviation Week*, vol 62, no 18, May 2, 1955, p 15.

25. Memo, Harold E. Talbott to Charles E. Wilson, Mar 17, 1954, RG 340, acces no

60–A1055, File 17/31/OSAF, Corresp Control Div, 1953–1954, Talbott Chron Files 1953–1954, NARA.

26. *Ibid.*

27. Robert J. Donovan, *Eisenhower: The Inside Story* (New York: Harper & Brothers, 1956), pp 332–34; "Talbott Business Connections Questioned," *Aviation Week*, vol 63, no 4, Jul 25, 1955, pp 13–14.

28. "Talbott Quits Mulligan, Clings to USAF," *Aviation Week*, vol 63, no 5, Aug 1, 1955, p 13.

29. Katherine Johnson,"Talbott Quits Post Under Pressure," *Aviation Week*, vol 63, no 6, Aug 8, 1955, p 15.

30. *Ibid*; telephone intvw, Brig Gen William G. Hipps by author, Sep 25, 1984, author's files; Dwight D. Eisenhower, *Mandate For Change, 1953–1956* (New York: Doubleday & Company, Inc, 1963), pp 494; Johnson, "Talbott Quits Post Under Pressure," *Aviation Week*, p 15.

31. Johnson, "Talbott Quits Post Under Pressure," *Aviation Week*, p 15; "Talbott Praised and Criticized," *Aviation Week*, vol 63, no 8, Aug 22, 1955, p 16.

32. Written responses by Brig Gen William G. Hipps to questions submitted by author, author's files; intvw, James H. Douglas, Jr., by Hugh N. Ahmann, Jun 13–14, 1979, pp 24–25.

33. "Talbott Praised and Criticized," *Aviation Week*, p 16.

34. Intvw, James H. Douglas, Jr., by Hugh N. Ahmann, Jun 13–14, 1979, pp 29–30; telephone intvw, Brig Gen William G. Hipps by author, Sep 25, 1884; Johnson, "Talbott Quits Post Under Pressure," *Aviation Week*, p 15.

35. Memo, Harold E. Talbott to Charles E. Wilson, May 27, 1955, RG 340, acces no 60–A1055, File 17/ 31/OSAF, Corresp Control Div, 1953–1954, Talbott Chron Files 1953–1954, NARA.

36. *Ibid.*

37. Memo, Asst Secy AF Lyle S. Garlock to Deputy Asst Secys of Defense, Public Affairs, and Asst Secy of Defense, Legis and Public Affairs, Nov 7, 1955, RG 340, acces no 59–A–1818, Corresp Files 1955, 240.1–300.7, Box 29, NARA.

38. *United States Air Force Statistical Digest, Fiscal Year 1958*, p 331, CAFH.

39. Biographical sketch of Donald A. Quarles, DOD Ofc of Public Info, Press Branch, Twining Papers, Box 81, 1955 SAF(2), LC Manuscript Div; "Quarles Differs," *Aviation Week*, vol 63, no 9, Aug 29, 1955, p 11; "Quarles Choice Significant," *Aviation Week*, vol 63, no 10, Sep 10, 1955, p 110.

40. Intvw, Dudley C. Sharp by James C. Hasdorff, Jun 6–7, 1979, USAF Oral History Collection, AFHRC file K239. 0512–1128, AFHRC, Maxwell AFB, Ala.

41. *Air Force Times*, vol 16, Aug 20, 1955, p 3; biographical sketch of Trevor Gardner, Special Assistant for Research and Development, OSAF, Mar 22, 1953, RG 340, acces no 60–A1055, Box 18, Talbott Chron Files 1953–1954, Quarles Chron Files 1955, NARA.

42. Ltr, Harold E. Talbott to J. Edgar Hoover, Dir, Fed Bur of Investigation, Jul 6, 1955, with biographical sketch of Dudley C. Sharp, RG 340, acces no 60–A1055, Box 18, Talbott Chron Files 1953–1954, Quarles Chron Files 1955, NARA; "Sharp Is Appointed Successor to Lewis," *Aviation Week*, vol 63, no 4, Jul 25, 1955, p 15.

43. "Quarles Outlines Key Objectives in Talk to Foreign Air Attaches," *Air Force Times*, vol 16, Sep 10, 1955, p 31.

44. "U.S. Striking Power Leads Quarles Says," *Air Force Times*, vol 16, Nov 16, 1955, p 39.

45. "Quarles Outlines Key Objectives in Talk to Foreign Air Attaches," *Aviation Week*, p 31; "Quarles' Policy," *Aviation Week*, vol 63, no 12, Sep 19, 1955, p 150.

46. Ltr, Trevor Gardner to Donald A. Quarles, Aug 30, 1955, Twining Papers, Box 81, 1955 SAF(2), LC Manuscript Div; Parmet, *Eisenhower and the American Crusades*, pp 498–99.

47. Ltr, Trevor Gardner to Donald A. Quarles, Aug 30, 1955; Parmet, *Eisenhower and the American Crusades*, pp 498–99.

48. "Quarles Outlines Defense Views on Industrial Dispersal Policy," *Air Force Times*, vol 16, Dec 3, 1955, p 3.

49. Neufeld, *USAF Ballistic Missiles*, pp 242–44; "Gardner Quits, Starts USAF R&D Fight;" "Change in Quarles' Thinking Seen in Emphasis on Skilled Personnel;" both articles in *Aviation Week*, vol 64 no

7, Feb 13, 1956, pp 28–29; Kolodziej, *Uncommon Defense and Congress*, pp 232–33.

50. "White Warns of Red R&D, Production," *Aviation Week* vol 64, no 8, Feb 20, 1956, p 31.

51. *Ibid.*

52. *Ibid.*

53. "Russians Outpacing U.S. in Air Quality, Twining Warns Congress," *Aviation Week*, vol 64, no 9, Feb 27, 1956, pp 26–27.

54. *Ibid.*

55. *Ibid*; *Washington Post & Times Herald*, Mar 7, 1956, column by Joseph Alsop and Stewart Alsop, p 11, copy from Twining Papers, Box 90, 1956 Secy AF(2), LC Manuscript Div.

56. Kolodziej, *Uncommon Defense and Congress*, p 233; Futrell, *Ideas, Concepts, Doctrine*, p 229.

57. Intvw, Dudley C. Sharp with James C. Hasdorff, Jun 6–7, 1979.

58. Memo, Donald A. Quarles to Gen Nathan F. Twining, Chief of Staff, USAF, Aug 18, 1955, Twining Papers, Box 81, LC Manuscript Div.

59. Memo, Donald A. Quarles to Asst Secys AF (Research and Development), (Financial Management), and (Materiel), and Chief of Staff, USAF, subj: Establishment of the Air Force Ballistic Missiles Committee, RG 340, acces no A59–1818, Box 11, Corresp Files 1955, 471.6–684, NARA.

60. *Ibid.*

61. Neufeld, *USAF Ballistic Missiles*, p 248.

62. Donald A. Quarles, "How Much is Enough?" *Air Force Magazine*, vol 39, Sep 1956, pp 51–53; Hearings before the Subcommittee of the Committee on Armed Services. *A Study of Air Power*, U.S. Senate, 84th Cong, 2d sess, Jun 19, 1956, Part XX (Washington, D.C.: GPO, 1956), pp 1544–45; Samuel P. Huntington, *The Common Defense: Strategic Programs In National Politics* (New York: Columbia University Press, 1961), pp 100–101.

63. "Quarles Denies LeMay Testimony; Says U.S. Will Retain Superiority," *Aviation Week*, vol 65, no 1, Jul 2, 1956, p 31; Hearings, *A Study of Airpower,* Putt testimony, pp 554–58, LeMay testimony, pp 212–15.

64. "Senate Votes Boost in Air Force Budget," *Aviation Week*, vol 65, no 1, Jul 2, 1956, pp 31–32.

65. Robert Hotz, "Wilson on Russia, "*Aviation Week*, vol 65, no 4, Jul 23, 1956, p 21.

66. "Gardner Warns Russia is Ahead on IRBM, Blames U.S. Rivalries," *Aviation Week*, vol 65, no 4, Jul 23, 1956, p 31.

67. *Ibid.*

68. "Air Force Assn Demands Single Service," *Aviation Week*, vol 65, no 7, Aug 13, 1956, p 29.

69. "Superiority and Security," *Aviation Week*, vol 65, no 11, Sep 10, 1956, p 25.

70. "AFA Riles Wilson,"*AviationWeek*, vol 65, no 7, Aug 13, 1956, p 25.

71. "Symington Report Urges Airpower Boost," *Aviation Week*, vol 66, no 5, Feb 4, 1957, pp 32–33; "The Senate Airpower Report," *Aviation Week*, vol 66, no 6, Feb 11, 1957, p 21; Hearings, *A Study of Air Power*, pp 1–1869.

72. "Quarles Slows Bid for Boost in Budget," *Aviation Week*, vol 66, no 9, Mar 4, 1957, p 28.

Chapter 7

The Air Staff and the OSAF

1. Falk and Yoshpe, *The Economics of National Security*, pp 49–50.

2. *Ibid*, pp 46–51; Cole et al, eds, *Department of Defense Documents*, pp 175–88.

3. John D. Glover and Paul R. Lawrence, *A Case Study of High Level Administration in a Large Organization* (Boston: Harvard University Division of Research, School of Business Administra-

tion, 1960), pp 44–45.

4. John J. McLaughlin, "Organization of the Air Force," *Air University Quarterly Review*, vol 13, no 3, spring 1962, pp 4–5; Falk and Yoshpe, *The Economics of National Security*, p 36;

5. Memo, John J. McLaughlin to Eugene M. Zuckert, Jan 5, 1952, RG 340, acces no 68–A269, Box 5, McLaughlin Chron Files 1947–1952, NARA.

6. Memo, John J. McLaughlin to Mr. White (presumably H. Lee White), May 4, 1953; ltr, John J. McLaughlin to Lt. Col Thomas A. Miller, Apr 25, 1953; both sources from RG 340, acces no 68–A269, Box 6, McLaughlin Chron Files 1953, 1958–1962, NARA.

7. Memo, John J. McLaughlin to Mr. White, May 4, 1953.

8. Memo, James H. Douglas, Jr., to Asst Secys AF Garlock, Smith, Sharp, and Horner, May 14, 1956, RG 340, acces no 72–A6888, Box 8, Admin Asst, Misc Corresp, OSAF-Air Staff Relationship Study, NARA.

9. *The Secretary of the Air Force-Air Staff Relationship Study* (hereafter, *OSAF-Air Staff Study*), Oct 4, 1956, pp 1–4, RG 340, acces no 72–A6888, Box 8, Admin Asst, Misc Corresp, OSAF-Air Staff Relationship Study; NARA.

10. Intvw, Malcolm A. MacIntyre by author, Sep 26, 1985, pp 3–4, AFHRC file K239.0512–01683, AFHRC, Maxwell AFB, Ala.

11. *Ibid*.

12. *OSAF-Air Staff Study*, pp 1–4.

13. *Ibid*, pp 4–5.

14. Memo, Harold E. Talbott to Deputy Secy Defense, subj: Assignment of Responsibility within the Department of Defense for Base Rights Negotiations, Mar 19, 1953, RG 340, acces no 60–A1055, Box 18, Talbott Chron Files 1954–1955, NARA.

15. Memo, Gen Nathan F. Twining to Harold E. Talbott, Sep 16, 1954, subj: Organization Directives for the Office of Secretary of Defense, Twining Collection, Box 72, SAF(1), Corresp between General Twining and Secy AF only, LC Manuscript Div.

16. *OSAF-Air Staff Study*, pp 5–6.

17. Memo, Harold E. Talbott to Charles E. Wilson, Jul 30, 1955, subj: Hoover Commission Report on Business Organization of the Department of Defense, RG 340, acces no 60–A1055, Box 18, Talbott Chron Files 1954–55, Quarles Chron Files 1955, NARA.

18. Intvw, Robert E. Hampton by Maclyn Burg, Feb 6, 1975, p 34 (Hampton worked for Asst Secy AF (Manpower and Personnel) David S. Smith between 1955 and 1957), no 485, Dwight D. Eisenhower Library, Abilene, Kansas.

19. *OSAF-Air Staff Study*, pp 6–7.

20. *Ibid*, pp 8–9.

21. Memo, John J. McLaughlin to Under Secy AF Malcolm A. MacIntyre, subj: Work Relationships Study, OSAF-Air Staff, Feb 7, 1958, RG 340, acces no 72–A6888, Box 8, Admin Asst, Misc Corresp, OSAF-Air Staff Relationship Study, NARA.

22. *Ibid*; memo, John J. McLaughlin to Malcolm A. McIntyre, subj: Organization of the Secretariat: Work Relationships between OSAF and the Air Staff; Present Status of Communications Media as they Exist within OSAF, and between OSAF and the Air Staff, Jan 1958 (no day indicated), RG 340, acces no 63–A1521, Box 16, OSAF-Air Staff Relationship Study, folder marked 107–58, NARA.

23. Memo, John J. McLaughlin to Malcolm A. MacIntyre, subj: Work Relationships Study, OSAF-Air Staff, Feb 7, 1958, RG 340, acces no 72–A6888, Box 8, Admin Asst, Misc Corresp, OSAF-Air Staff Relationship Study, NARA.

24. Memo, Malcolm A. MacIntyre to Maj Gen Jacob E. Smart, Asst Vice Chief of Staff, USAF, Mar 18, 1958, RG 340, acces no 63–A1521, Box 16, OSAF-Air Staff Relationship Study, folder marked 107–58, NARA.

25. "The Office of the Secretary of the Air Force, Its Organizational Development, Growth, and Costs," Aug 5, 1947, RG 340, acces no 72–A4815, Box 7, NARA.

26. Robert Hotz, "Cleaning Up the Pentagon," *Aviation Week*, vol 67, no 7, Aug 19, 1957, p 21.

Chapter 8

Douglas and Sharp (1957–1961)

1. Dwight D. Eisenhower, *Waging Peace, 1956–1961: The White House Years* (Garden City, New York: Doubleday & Company, Inc, 1965), p 206.

2. Intvw, James H. Douglas, Jr., by Hugh N. Ahmann, Jun 13–14, 1979, pp 32–35.

3. "Good Air Force Appointments," *Aviation Week*, vol 66, no 13, Apr 1, 1957, p 21; "Douglas as USAF Secretary," *Aviation Week*, vol 65, no 11, Sep 11, 1956.

4. "Hope for Science," *Aviation Week*, vol 66, no 18, May 6, 1957, p 25.

5. Memo, Col Robert L. Petit to Maj Gen Gen Joe W. Kelly, Dir, Legis and Liaison, OSAF, Jun 14, 1957, RG 340, acces no 61–A1674, Box 24, OSAF Corresp, (871–57), NARA.

6. Biographical sketch of Malcolm A. MacIntyre, Ofc of Info Service, Public Info Div, Jul 1957, CAFH.

7. Memo, James H. Douglas, Jr., to Asst Secy Defense (Comptroller), subj: Reduction of Direct Obligations for FY 1957, May 13, 1957, RG 340, acces no 65A–3152, Box 33, NARA.

8. Memo, James H. Douglas, Jr., to Charles E. Wilson, subj: FY 1958 Expenditure Ceilings, Jun 12, 1957, RG 340, acces no 65A–3152, Box 33, NARA.

9. Memo, Gen Thomas D. White, Chief of Staff, USAF, to James H. Douglas, Jr., subj: Air Force Procurement Program, Jul (no day indicated) 1958, RG 340, acces no 65A–3152, Box 7, NARA.

10. Memo, James H. Douglas, Jr., to Charles E. Wilson, subj: Expenditure Control Actions Taken and Pending, Jul 18, 1957, RG 340, acces no 65A–3152, Box 33, NARA.

11. Ltr, James H. Douglas, Jr., to William E. Hess, U.S. House of Representatives, Jul 17, 1957, RG 340, acces no 65A–3152, Box 33, NARA.

12. Memo, James H. Douglas, Jr., to Charles E. Wilson, subj: FY 1958 Military Construction Appropriation Program, Jun 20, 1957, RG 340, acces no 65A–3152, Box 33, NARA.

13. Ltr, James H. Douglas, Jr., to Carl Vinson, House of Representatives, Aug 9, 1957, RG 340, acces no 65A–3152, Box 33, NARA; ltr, James H. Douglas, Jr., to Clarence Cannon, Chmn, Ctee on Appropriations, U.S. House of Representatives, Dec 13, 1957, RG 340, acces no 65A–3152, Box 19, Douglas Chron Files 1957–1959, NARA.

14. Statement by James H. Douglas, Jr., at the National Security Council meeting, Nov 14, 1957, RG 340, acces no 61–A1674, Box 40, AF Budget, vol 4, pp 57–60, NARA.

15. Remarks by Malcolm A. MacIntyre before the Advertising Club of Washington, D.C., Presidential Arms, Sep 24, 1957, RG 340, acces no 65–A3152, Box 7, NARA.

16. *Ibid.*

17. Memo, Malcolm A. MacIntyre to Secy Defense Neil H. McElroy, Apr 1, 1958; memo, Malcolm A. MacIntyre to Deputy Secy Defense, Apr 7, 1958; both sources from RG 340, acces no 65–A3152, Box 7, MacIntyre Chron Files, NARA.

18. Eisenhower, *Waging Peace*, p 206.

19. Hearings before the Subcommittee of the Committee on Appropriations. *Department of Defense Appropriations for 1959*, U.S. Senate, 85th Cong, 2d sess, on HR 12738 (Washington, D.C.: GPO, 1958), pp 377; Herman S. Wolk, "Independence and Responsibility: USAF in the Defense Establishment," *Evolution of the American Military Establishment Since World War II*, ed Paul R. Schratz (Lexington, Virginia: The George Marshall Research Foundation Publications, 1978), pp 62–63.

20. Hearings, *Department of Defense Appropriations for 1959*, p 392.

21. *Ibid*, pp 388, 392–94, 396, 401.

22. Intvw, James H. Douglas, Jr., by T. H. Baker, Oct 23, 1972, pp 28–29. Dwight D. Eisenhower Library, Abilene, Kansas.

23. *Ibid*, pp 17–18.

24. Hearings before the Subcommittee of the Committee on Appropriations. *Department of Defense Appropriations for 1961*, U.S. Senate, 86th Congress, 2d sess,

on HR 11998 (Washington, D.C.: GPO, 1960), pp 184–87.

25. Ltr, James H. Douglas, Jr., to George Mahon, Chrmn, Ctee on Appropriations, U.S. House of Representatives, Aug 7, 1957, RG 340, acces no 65–A3152, Box 33, NARA.

26. Intvw, James H. Douglas, Jr., by T. H. Baker, Oct 23, 1972, p 38.

27. *Ibid.*

28. *Ibid*, pp 39.

29. Ltr, James H. Douglas, Jr., to John T. O'Rourke, Jul 29, 1958, RG 340, acces no 65–A3152, Box 19, Douglas Chron Files 1957–1958, NARA.

30. U.S. Comptroller General, *Report to the Congress of the United States: Examination of the Programs for Constructing and Equipping the Air Force Academy, Colorado Springs, Colorado,* Apr 1959, pp 1–17; ltr, James H. Douglas, Jr., to Carl Vinson, U.S. House of Representatives, May 15, 1959, RG 340, acces no 65A, Box 19, Douglas Chron Files 1957–1959, NARA.

31. Robert Hotz, "The Critical Role of ARPA," *Aviation Week*, vol 68, no 4, Jan 27, 1958.

32. Memo, James H. Douglas, Jr., to Neil H. McElroy, subj: Draft Directive Establishing an Advanced Research Project Agency, Dec 14, 1957, RG 340, acces no 65–A3152, Box 19, Douglas Chron Files 1957–1959, NARA.

33. PL 85–658, The National Aeronautics and Space Act of 1958, Jul 29, 1958.

34. Futrell, *Ideas, Concepts, Doctrine*, p 298.

35. Memo, James H. Douglas, Jr., to Dr. Glennan, Oct 9, 1958, RG 340, acces no 65–A3152, Box 19, Douglas Chron Files 1957–1959, NARA.

36. Memo, James H. Douglas, Jr., to Gen Thomas D. White, subj: Terms of Reference for Civilian-Military Liaison Committee to the NASA and the DOD, Oct 16, 1958, RG 340, acces no 65–A3152, Box 19, Douglas Chron Files 1957–1959, NARA.

37. Ltr, Acting Secy AF Malcolm A. MacIntyre to Chmn, Subctee on Govt Org for Space Activities, Senate Ctee on Aeronautical and Space Sci, U.S. Senate, May

6, 1959, RG 340, acces no 65–A3152, Box 7, NARA.

38. Futrell, *Ideas, Concepts, Doctrine*, pp 298–301.

39. Memo, Malcolm A. MacIntyre to Dir, Defense Research and Engineering, OSAF, subj: Relationship of NASA Program to Related Department of Defense Programs, May 19, 1959, RG 340, acces no 65–A3152, Box 7, NARA.

40. Memo, James H. Douglas, Jr., to Gen Thomas D. White, subj: Airlift, Apr 17, 1959, RG 340, acces no 65–A3152, Box 19, Douglas Chron Files 1957–1959, NARA.

41. Memo, James H. Douglas, Jr., to Deputy Secy Defense, subj: Production Sharing with Canada, Jan 5, 1959, RG 340, acces no 65–A3152, Box 19, Douglas Chron Files 1957–1959, NARA.

42. Intvw, Dudley C. Sharp by James C. Hasdorff, Jun 5–6, 1979.

43. Ltr, Dudley C. Sharp to Richard B. Russell, Chmn, Ctee on Armed Services, U.S. Senate, Feb 15, 1960, RG 340, acces no 66–A3655, Box 18, Sharp Chron Files, NARA.

44. Memo, James H. Douglas, Jr., to Secy Defense Charles E. Wilson, subj: Air Defense, Jun 13, 1957, RG 340, acces no 65–A3152, Box 33, NARA.

45. Memo, Dudley C. Sharp to Secy Army, subj: The United States Air Force Ballistic Missile Construction Program, RG 340, acces no 66–A3655, Box 18, Sharp Chron Files, NARA.

46. *Ibid.*

47. Ltr, James H. Douglas, Jr., to Dr. Laurence A. Hyland, Gen Mgr, Hughes Aircraft Corp, Sep 3, 1959, RG 340, acces no 65–A3152, Box 19, Douglas Chron Files 1957–1959, NARA.

48. Ltr, James H. Douglas, Jr., Jun 12 1959, no addressee, RG 340, acces no 65–A3152, Box 19, Douglas Chron Files 1957–1959, NARA.

49. Ltr, James H. Douglas, Jr., to Richard B. Russell, U.S. Senate, Jul 18, 1959, RG 340, acces no 65–A3152, Box 19, Douglas Chron Files 1957–1959, NARA; Hearings, *Department of Defense Appropriations for 1961*, p 196.

50. Comments for Commanders Con-

ference by Dudley C. Sharp, Jan 11, 1960, RG 340, acces no 66–A3655, Box 18, Sharp Chron Files 1959–1961, NARA.

51. Ltr, Col John W. Baer, Exec Asst to Secy AF, to Robert M. DeHaven, Chmn, Awards Banquet Ctee, Society of Experimental Test Pilots, Sep 30, 1960; memo for record from Col John R. Kullman, Deputy Exec Asst to Secy AF, Oct 3, 1960; both sources from RG 340, acces no 66–A3655, Box 18, Sharp Chron Files 1959–1961, NARA.

52. Intvw, Dudley C. Sharp by James C. Hasdorff, Jun 5–6, 1979, pp 55–56.

53. Comments for Commanders Conference by Dudley C. Sharp; *Department of Defense Appropriations for 1961*, p 185.

54. Intvw, Dudley C. Sharp by James C. Hasdorff, p 119.

55. Ltr, David S. Smith to the James H. Douglas, Jr., Jan 26, 1959, RG 340, acces no 65–A3152, Box 12, David S. Smith Chron Files, NARA.

56. Ltr, John J. McLaughlin to J. Edgar Hoover, Dir, Fed Bur of Investigation, Feb 5, 1960; ltr, Thomas S. Gates to the President Feb 9, 1960; both sources from RG 340, acces no 66–A3655, Box 17, NARA.

57. Biographical sketch of Asst Secy AF (Materiel) Philip B. Taylor, Ofc of Info Service, Public Info Div, USAF, CAFH; Hearings, *Department of Defense Appropriations for 1961*, p 1668.

58. Ltr, Dudley C. Sharp to U.S. Comptroller Gen, Apr 1, 1958, RG 340, acces no 66–A3655, Box 18, Sharp Chron Files, NARA.

59. *Ibid.*

60. *Ibid.*

61. Ltr, Dudley C. Sharp to U.S. Comptroller Gen, Oct 28, 1960, RG 340, acces no 66–A3655, Box 18, Sharp Chron Files, NARA.

62. *Ibid.*

63. Hearings, *Department of Defense Appropriations For 1961*, p 352.

64. Ltr, Dudley C. Sharp to John W. McCormack, U.S. House of Representatives, Aug 11, 1960, RG 340, acces no 66–A3655, Box 18, Sharp Chron Files 1959–1961, NARA.

65. Ltr, Dudley C. Sharp to James C. Davis, Chmn, Subctee on Manpower Utilization, Ctee on Post Ofc and Civil Service, U.S. House of Representatives, Aug 18, 1960, RG 340, acces no 66–A3655, Box 18, Sharp Chron Files 1959–1961, NARA.

66. Memo, Dudley C. Sharp to Secy Defense Thomas S. Gates, Jr., Jul 14, 1960, subj: Air Force Position on Reductions to Rated Inventory, RG 340, acces no 66–A3655, Box 18, Sharp Chron Files 1959–1961, NARA.

67. Memo, Dudley C. Sharp to Thomas S. Gates, Jr., Jul 18, 1960, subj: Proposed Presidential Memorandum Relating to the Administration of Overseas Activities, RG 340, acces no 66–A3655, Box 18, Dudley C. Sharp Chron Files, 1959–1961, NARA.

68. Memo, Dudley C. Sharp to Secy Defense Thomas S. Gates, Jr., subj: Congressional Add-Ons, Jul 18, 1960, RG 340, acces no 66–A3655, Box 18, Sharp Chron Files 1959–1961, NARA.

69. *Chicago Sun-Times*, Dec 7, 1960, p 13; *Chicago Sun-Times*, Dec 11, 1960, p 16; Eugene M. Zuckert, "The Service Secretary: Has He A Useful Role?" *Foreign Affairs*, Apr 1966, p 462.

70. Hearings, *A Study of Airpower*, p 1505.

71. *Cincinnati Enquirer*, Dec 8, 1960, p 22; *New York Times*, Dec 6, 1960, pp 1F–3F; Falk and Yoshpe, *The Economics of National Security*, pp 60–62.

72. *Washington Post*, Dec 22, 1960, p 7F.

73. Intvw, Dudley C. Sharp by Joseph W. Angell, Jr., and Alfred Goldberg, Jan 19, 1961, pp 3–4, USAF Oral History Collection, AFHRC file K239.0512–711, AF HRC, Maxwell AFB, Ala.

74. *Ibid*, p 3.

75. Ltr, Dudley C. Sharp to Lewis S. Thompson, Spec Asst, Manpower, Personnel, and Reserve Forces, OSAF, Jan 19, 1961; ltr, Dudley C. Sharp to Asst Secy AF (Materiel) Philip B. Taylor, Jan 19, 1961; both sources from RG 340, acces no 66–A3655, Box 18, Sharp Chron Files 1959–1961, NARA.

Chapter 9

The Zuckert Era (1961–1965)

1. Ford Eastman, "Defense Reorganization Will Await McNamara's Study of the Pentagon," *Aviation Week*, vol 73, no 25, Dec 19, 1960, p 28.

2. James M. Roherty, *The Decisions of Robert S. McNamara: A Study of The Role of the Secretary of Defense* (Miami: University of Miami Press, 1970), pp 65–67; Henry L. Trewhitt, *McNamara: His Ordeal in the Pentagon* (New York: Harper and Row, 1971), pp 6, 8–9;

3. Eastman, "Defense Reorganization," *Aviation Week*, p 28; Trewhitt, *McNamara: His Ordeal*, p 83.

4. Roherty, *Decisions of McNamara*, p 68.

5. Zuckert, "The Service Secretary," *Foreign Affairs*, p 464; Ford Eastman, "Kennedy Orders Defense Review, Boost in Airlift, Missile Programs," *Aviation Week*, vol 74, no 6, Feb 6, 1961, p 31; Ford Eastman, "McNamara Will Oppose Spending Any Additional SAC Bomber Funds," *Aviation Week*, vol 74, no 23, Jun 5, 1961, p 23; Col William G. McDonald, "The Changing Management Role of the Military Departments," *Air University Review*, vol 13, no 4, summer 1962, p 48; Roherty, *Decisions of McNamara*, p 69.

6. Intvw, Eugene M. Zuckert by author, Dec 4–6, 9, 1986; Ofc of Info Service, Public Info Div, USAF, biographical sketches of Robert H. Charles, Joseph S. Imirie, Brockway McMillan, Leonard Marks, Jr. and Joseph V. Charyk; memo, Neil E. Harlan to Eugene M. Zuckert, Dec 28, 1961, RG 340, acces no 66–A3655, Box 3, NARA; ltr, Joseph S. Imirie to Pres Kennedy Aug 28, 1963, Zuckert Collection, microfilm roll no 30161, IRIS no 1001752, frame no 115; memo, Eugene M. Zuckert to Secy Defense Robert S. McNamara, Apr 15, 1963, Zuckert Collection, microfilm roll no 30161, IRIS no 1001753; both Zuckert Collection sources from AFHRC, Maxwell AFB, Ala.

7. Intvw, Eugene M. Zuckert by author, Dec 4–6, 9, 1986.

8. Intvw, Eugene M. Zuckert by John Frisbee, Sep 1, 1965, USAF Oral History Collection, AFHRC file K239.0512–763, microfilm roll no 1000320–323, frame nos 1097–194, AFHRC, Maxwell AFB, Ala, pp 13–14; intvw, Eugene M. Zuckert by author, Dec 4–6, 9, 1968.

9. Intvw, Eugene M. Zuckert by John Frisbee, Sep 1, 1965, pp 19–20; intvw, Eugene M. Zuckert by author, Dec 4–6, 9, 1986.

10. Intvw, Eugene M. Zuckert by John Frisbee, Sep 1, 1965, pp 21–22; Claude Witze, "U.S. Air Force's New Chief of Staff: Man With a Mission," *Air Force Space Digest*, vol 48, no 2, Feb 1965, pp 32–34.

11. Ltr, Eugene M. Zuckert to William A. Blakley, U.S. Senate, Feb 16, 1961, Zuckert Collection, microfilm roll no 30155, IRIS no 100172, frame no 310, AFHRC, Maxwell AFB, Ala; Intvw, Eugene M. Zuckert by author, Dec 4–6, 9, 1986.

12. Intvw, Eugene M. Zuckert by author, Dec 4–6, 9, 1986.

13. Zuckert, "The Service Secretary," *Foreign Affairs*, p 464–66.

14. Intvw, Eugene M. Zuckert by author, Dec 4–6, 9, 1986.

15. Trewhitt, *McNamara: His Ordeal*, pp 18–19,88.

16. Thomas M. Coffey, *Iron Eagle: The Turbulent Life of General Curtis LeMay* (New York: Crown Publishers, Inc, 1986), pp 369–73.

17. Intvw, Lt Gen Glen W. Martin by Lt Col Vaughn H. Gallacher, Feb 6–10, 1978, USAF Oral History Collection, AFHRC file K239.0512–982, AFHRC, Maxwell AFB, Ala, p 431, 438.

18. "Washington Roundup," *Aviation Week*, vol 74, no 21, May 22, 1961, p 21; "Washington Roundup," *Aviation Week*, vol 75, no 24, p 25; intvw, Eugene M. Zuckert by John Frisbee, Sep 1, 1965, pp 11–12; intvw, Lt Gen Glen W. Martin by Col Vaughan H. Gallacher, Feb 6–10, 1978, p

432.

19. Memo, Eugene M. Zuckert to Gen Curtis E. LeMay, Chief of Staff, USAF, Feb 16, 1963, microfilm roll no 30162, IRIS no 1001756, frame no 127, AFHRC, Maxwell AFB, Ala.

20. Intvw, Eugene M. Zuckert by author; memo, Eugene M. Zuckert to Gen Thomas D. White, Chief of Staff, USAF, Feb 15, 1961, Zuckert Collection, microfilm roll no 30155, IRIS no 1001725, frame no 325, AFHRC, Maxwell AFB, Ala.

21. Coffey, *Iron Eagle*, p 366.

22. Robert Hotz, "A Dismal Pattern," *Aviation Week*, vol 75, no 19, Nov 6, 1961, p 21.

23. Memo, Eugene M. Zuckert to Gen Frederic H. Smith, Jr., Vice Chief of Staff, USAF, Dec 1, 1961, Zuckert Collection, microfilm roll no 30157, IRIS no 1001737, frame no 1352, AFHRC, Maxwell AFB, Ala.

24. Memo, Eugene M. Zuckert to Gen Thomas D. White, May 1, 1961, Zuckert Collection, microfilm roll no 30156, IRIS no 1001730, frame no 498; memo, Col John R. Kullman to exec assts, Jun 14, 1961 Zuckert Collection, microfilm roll no 30156, IRIS no 1001731, frame no 744; both sources from AFHRC, Maxwell AFB, Ala.

25. Memo, Eugene M. Zuckert to Gen Frederic H. Smith, Jr., USAF, subj: Study of Management Practices in the Air Staff, Nov 1, 1961, Zuckert Collection, microfilm roll no 30157, IRIS no 1001736, frame no 988, AFHRC, Maxwell AFB, Ala.

26. Memo, author not indicated, subj: Improvement of Operational Analysis and Studies, as of 1 March, 1964, Zuckert Collection, microfilm roll no 30164, IRIS no 1001768, frame no 750, AFHRC, Maxwell AFB, Ala.

27. Memo, Eugene M. Zuckert to Asst Secy Defense (Internat Security Affairs), subj: Assistance in the Decisionmaking Process, Jun 2, 1961, Zuckert Collection, microfilm roll no 30154, IRIS no 1001724, frame no 925, AFHRC, Maxwell AFB, Ala.

28. Memo, Eugene M. Zuckert to Asst Secy Defense, Internat Security Affairs, subj: Non-Military Emphasis of Future Military Assistance to Africa, Jun 27, 1961,

Zuckert Collection, microfilm roll no 30 154, IRIS no 1001724, frame no 879, AFHRC, Maxwell AFB, Ala.

29. Ltr, Eugene M. Zuckert to Secy Defense Robert S. McNamara, Jun 23, 1961, Zuckert Collection, microfilm roll no 30154, IRIS no 10001724, frame nos 888–89; memo, Eugene M. Zuckert to Gen Thomas D. White, subj: Status of USAF Ballistic Missile Program, Jan 30, 1961, Zuckert Collection, microfilm roll no 30 155, IRIS no 1001726, frame no 10, AF HRC, both sources from AFHRC, Maxwell AFB, Ala.

30. *Ibid.*

31. Memo, Eugene M. Zuckert to Gen Thomas D. White, Apr 20, 1961, Zuckert Collection, microfilm role no 30155, IRIS no 1001729, frame nos 1391–93, AFHRC, Maxwell AFB, Ala.

32. Memo, Eugene M. Zuckert to Deputy Secy Defense, subj: DOD-NASA Negotiations Re Range Joint Venture, Aug 24, 1961, Zuckert Collection, microfilm roll no 30154, IRIS no 1001725, frame no 1417, AFHRC, Maxwell AFB, Ala.

33. "New Flow Shocks McNamara; He Will Re-educate Contractors," *Aviation Week and Space Technology*, vol 74, no 7, May 14, 1961, p 39.

34. Memo, Gen Curtis E. LeMay to Eugene M. Zuckert, Mar 2, 1961, Zuckert Collection, microfilm roll no 30154, IRIS no 1001724, frame 1764, AFHRC, Maxwell AFB, Ala; "Washington Roundup," *Aviation Week*, vol 74, no 24, Jun 12, 1961, p 25.

35. Memo, Eugene M. Zuckert to Deputy Secy Defense, subj: Revised Directive for Public Affairs, Apr 29, 1961, Zuckert Collection, microfilm roll no 30154, IRIS no 1001724, frame no 1009, AFHRC, Maxwell AFB, Ala.

36. *Ibid.*

37. "Washington Roundup," *Aviation Week*, vol 75, no 19, Nov 6, 1961, p 25.

38. Ltr, Eugene M. Zuckert to John W. Macy, Jr, Chmn, U.S. Civil Service Commis, Mar 5, 1961, Zuckert Collection, microfilm roll no 30154, IRIS no 1001724, frame no 1178, AFHRC, Maxwell AFB, Ala.

39. "Washington Roundup," *Aviation*

Week, vol 76, no 6, Feb 5, 1962, p 25.

40. "Single Defense Information Office Urged," *Aviation Week and Space Technology*, vol 79, no 25, Dec 16, 1963, p 36.

41. Memo, Eugene M. Zuckert to Robert S. McNamara, Aug 2, 1961, Zuckert Collection: microfilm roll no 30154, IRIS no 1001725, frame no 1474; memo, Eugene M. Zuckert to Asst Secy Defense, Public Affairs, Arthur Sylvester, Oct 19, 1961, Zuckert Collection, microfilm roll no 30154, IRIS no 1001725, frame no 1331; both sources from AFHRC, Maxwell AFB, Ala.

42. Memo, Eugene M. Zuckert to Secy Defense Robert S. McNamara, subj: Establishment of a Defense Intelligence Agency, Jul 19, 1961, Zuckert Collection, microfilm roll no 30154, IRIS no, 1001725, frame no 1514, AFHRC, Maxwell AFB, Ala.

43. *Ibid.*

44. Memo, Eugene M. Zuckert to Secy Navy Fred Korth, Jan 31, 1963; ltr, Eugene M. Zuckert to Fred Korth Jan 31, 1963; both sources from Zuckert Collection, microfilm roll no 30161, IRIS no 1001754, frame nos 1225–27, AFHRC, Maxwell AFB, Ala.

45. Memo, Eugene M. Zuckert to Cost Reduction Prog Mgr, USAF, Sep 21, 1965, subj: Air Force Cost Reduction Program, Zuckert Collection, microfilm roll no 30172, IRIS no 1001796, frame no 1099, AFHRC, Maxwell AFB, Ala; Statement of Honorable Eugene M. Zuckert, Secretary of the Air Force, before the Committee on Armed Services, House of Representatives, on Military Posture, Feb 1964, extracted from Air Force Information Policy Letter Supplement for Commanders, Feb 1964.

46. Ltr, Eugene M. Zuckert to J. Glenn Beall, U.S. Senate, Mar 31, 1961, Zuckert Collection, microfilm roll no 30155, IRIS no 1001728, frame nos 707–8, AFHRC, Maxwell AFB, Ala.

47. Intvw, Eugene M. Zuckert by author, Dec 4–6, 9, 1986; memo, Eugene M. Zuckert to Gen Bernard A. Schriever, Sep 24, 1965, Zuckert Collection, microfilm roll no 30172, IRIS no 1001796, frame no 1185, AFHRC, Maxwell AFB, Ala.

48. Hearings before the Subcommittee on Appropriations. *Department of Defense Appropriations for 1962*, U.S. Senate, 87th Cong, 1st sess, on HR 7851 (Washington, D.C.: GPO, 1962), pp 17, 84, 864–65, 1683, 1709.

49. Hearings, *Department of Defense Appropriations for 1962*, pp 396, 397; Zuckert, "The Service Secretary," *Foreign Affairs*, p 470.

50. Hearings, *Department of Defense Appropriations for 1962*, pp 273–75, 1543–44.

51. Zuckert, "The Service Secretary," *Foreign Affairs*, p 472.

52. *Ibid.*, p 473; Intvw, Eugene M. Zuckert by John Frisbee, Sep 1, 1965, pp 36–37.

53. Robert J. Art, *The TFX Decision: McNamara and the Military* (Boston: Little, Brown and Company, 1968), p 6, 78; Trewhitt, *McNamara: His Ordeal*, pp 137–39; Hearings before the Permanent Subcommittee on Investigations of the Committee on Government Operations. *TFX Contract Investigation*, U.S. Senate, 88th Cong, 1st sess (Washington, D.C.: GPO, 1963), p 429, 1900–1975; George C. Wilson, "F–111A Program Posts Several Aeronautical and Political Firsts," *Aviation Week and Space Technology*, vol 81, no 16, Oct 19, 1964, pp 27–28.

54. Intvw, Gen Curtis E. LeMay by Herman S. Wolk, Nov 14, 1974, interviewer's files, CAFH.

55. Intvw, Eugene M. Zuckert by author, Dec 4–6, 9, 1986; Coffey, *Iron Eagle*, p 396; Hearings, *TFX Contract Investigation*, p 757.

56. Trewhitt, *McNamara: His Ordeal*, pp 138-39; Intvw, Gen William F. McKee by James C. Hasdorff, Mar 13–14, 1979, USAF Oral History Collection, AFHRC file K239.0512–1118, AFHRC, Maxwell AFB, Ala, pp 139–41; George C. Wilson,"TFX Probe to Focus on Possible Conflict in Gilpatric, Force Roles," *Aviation Week and Space Technology*, vol 79, no 11, Sep 9, 1963, p 27; memo for record by Eugene M. Zuckert, subj: TFX Investigation: Interview with McClellan Subcommittee Investigators, Dec 31, 1962, Zuckert Collection, microfilm roll no 30160, IRIS no 1001750, frame no 345, AFHRC, Maxwell AFB, Ala.

57. Memo for record by Eugene M.

Zuckert, subj: General Accounting Office Interview on TFX, Apr 24, 1963, Zuckert Collection, microfilm roll no 30162, IRIS no 1001758, frame no 887, AFHRC, Maxwell AFB, Ala.

58. Hearings, *TFX Contract Investigation*, p 695.

59. *Ibid.*, p 758; Art, *The TFX Decision*, pp 119–23.

60. Hearings, *TFX Contract Investigations*, pp 428–37, 1979–80; Michael H. Gorn, *The TFX: Conceptual Phase to F-11B Termination, 1958–1968* (Washington, D.C.: Office of History, Air Force Systems Command, 1985), pp 29–31.

61. Hearings, *TFX Contract Investigation*, pp 1982–88.

62. *Ibid.*, p 1991; "Zuckert TFX Judgment Changed," *Aviation Week and Space Technology*, vol 79, no 7, Aug 12, 1963, p 29.

63. Hearings, *TFX Contract Investigation*, p 1995; *Aviation Week and Space Technology*, vol 79, no 5, Jul 29, 1963, p 19.

64. Coffey, *Iron Eagle*, p 412; intvw, Eugene M. Zuckert by author, Dec 4–6, 9, 1986; Zuckert, "The Service Secretary," *Foreign Affairs*, p 474; Wilson, "F–111A Program," *Aviation Week and Space Technology*, pp, 28–29; Edward H. Kolcum, "President's Role in TFX Award Disclosed," *Aviation Week and Space Technology*, vol 79, no 9, Aug 26, 1963, p 34.

65. Intvw, Eugene M. Zuckert by author, Dec 4–6, 9, 1986; intvw, Eugene M. Zuckert by John Frisbee, Sep 1, 1965, pp 34–35.

66. Trewhitt, *McNamara: His Ordeal*, p 175.

67. Intvw, Eugene M. Zuckert by author, Dec 4–6, 9, 1986.

68. *Aviation Week and Space Technology*, vol 78, no 1, Jan 7, 1963, pp 29–30.

69. *Ibid.*

70. Intvw, Eugene M. Zuckert by author, Dec 4–6, 9, 1986; memo, Eugene M. Zuckert to Gen William F. McKee, May 21, 1963, Zuckert Collection, microfilm roll no 30162, IRIS no 1001759, frame no 1365; ltr, Eugene M. Zuckert to Gen Bernard A. Schriever, Jul 9, 1963, microfilm roll no 30163, IRIS no 1001761, frame nos 314–15; briefing on Project Forecast, May 1, 1964,

microfilm roll no 30164, IRIS no 1001768, frame no 697; all Zuckert Collection sources from AFHRC, Maxwell AFB, Ala.

71. Memo, Eugene M. Zuckert to Under Secy AF and Asst Secys AF, Apr 10, 1965, Zuckert Collection, microfilm roll no 30171, IRIS no 1001791, frame no 295, AFHRC, Maxwell AFB, Ala; "Zuckert Gives Views on Aerospace Issues," *Aviation Week and Space Technology*, vol 80, no 9, p 72.

72. Memo, Eugene M. Zuckert to the Chief of Staff, USAF, May 10, 1965, Zuckert Collection, microfilm roll no 40171, IRIS no 1001792, frame no 659, AFHRC, Maxwell AFB, Ala; "Washington Roundup," *Aviation Week and Space Technology*, vol 80, no 21, May 25, 1964, p 21.

73. Memo, Eugene M. Zuckert to Gen John P. McConnell, Chief of Staff, USAF, Aug 25, 1965, Zuckert Collection, microfilm roll no 30172, IRIS no 1001795, frame no 546, AFHRC, Maxwell AFB, Ala.

74. Intvw, Eugene M. Zuckert by author, Dec 4–6, 9, 1986; intvw, Brig Gen Brian S. Gunderson by author, Nov 1986, author's files.

75. Eugene M. Zuckert, "Keeping the Organizational Engine in Tune," *Air Force*, Oct 1964, pp 37–38; intvw, Eugene M. Zuckert by author, Dec 4–6, 9, 1986; Air Force Information Policy Letter Supplement for Commanders, no 112, Oct 1962, p 4; Eugene M. Zuckert, "A Parting Message," *Air Force*, Sep 1965, p 41.

76. Air Force Information Policy Letter Supplement for Commanders, no 11, Oct 1964; remarks by Eugene M. Zuckert before the Air Force Association luncheon, Washington, D.C., Sep 11, 1964.

77. Zuckert, "The Service Secretary," *Foreign Affairs*, p 479.

78. *Ibid.*

79. "Eugene Zuckert: The Man and the Manager," *Airman*, Oct 18, 1965, p 12.

80. Zuckert, "A Parting Message," *Air Force*, p 40.

81. *Air Force*, vol 48, no 11, Nov 1965, pp 34–35.

82. Trewhitt, *McNamara: His Ordeal*, p 165; Coffey, *Iron Eagle*, p 396;

83. "Washington Roundup," *Aviation Week and Space Technology*, vol 80, no 17,

Apr 27, 1964, p 25.

84. *Ibid.*

85. "Washington Roundup," *Aviation Week and Space Technology*, vol 82, no 6, Feb 8, 1965, p 15.

86. *Ibid.*

87. *Congressional Record*, U.S. Senate, 89th Cong, 1st sess, vol 3, no 140, p 18290.

88. "Eugene Zuckert: The Man and the Manager," *Airman*, p 12.

89. Ltr, Eugene M. Zuckert to Frank E. Moss, U.S. Senate, Aug 18, 1965, Zuckert Collection, microfilm roll no 30172, IRIS no 1001785, frame no 631, AFHRC, Maxwell AFB, Ala.

Bibliographic Note

Bibliographic Note

Governmental Sources

National Archives and Records Administration

Major sources for *The Office of The Secretary of the Air Force, 1947–1965* are filed in Record Group 107, the records of the Office of the Secretary of War, and in Record Group 340, the records of the Office of the Secretary of the Air Force. Record Group 107 is located at the National Archives and Records Administration in Washington, D.C. Record Group 340 is located at the Modern Military Branch of the National Archives and Records Administration's Federal Records Center in Suitland, Maryland. More than one hundred boxes of documents from Record Group 107 form a section on the Office of the Assistant Secretary of War for Air and focus on Robert A. Lovett. They contain letters, memoranda, notes, and charts which shed light on Lovett's dealings with such war time personages as Secretary of War Henry L. Stimson, General George C. Marshall, Chief of Staff of the U.S. Army, and General Henry H. Arnold, Commander of the U.S. Army Air Forces.

Approximately 1,530 feet of documents from Record Group 340 cover the period 1947 through 1954. Pre-1954 records are the property of the National Archives. They have been inventoried, distributed within labeled Hollinger boxes, shelved, and preliminarily indexed by Dr. Gibson Bell Smith. Post-1954 records are owned by the Office of the Secretary of the Air Force but are retained at the Federal Records Center, as yet unserviced and unsurveyed by professional archivists. Their only finding guides are standard government forms (SF 135s) filled out at the Office of the Secretary of the Air Force and bound in notebooks. These forms are only superficial indicators of the contents of each square foot box.

Record Group 340 includes nearly twenty-four feet of topically and chronologically arranged Special Interest Files that were kept separately by W. Stuart Symington. These files consist of his correspondence with Secretary of Defense James V. Forrestal and others, reports, telegrams, memoranda, and press releases dealing with such key issues as service roles and missions, budgeting of programs, the establishment of an Air Force Academy, and housing shortages. Unfortunately, Special Interest Files were not maintained by later Secretaries of the Air Force.

The most valuable find among Record Group 340's thousands of documents, a study ordered by Donald A. Quarles in 1956, provides an analysis of the relationship between the Office of the Secretary of the Air Force and the Air Staff and became the basis of Chapter 7 in this book. The most useful documents to my research at the Federal Records Center were organized under the following accession numbers: 60A–1055, 59A–1818, 72A–6888, 63A–1743, 61A–1614, 61A–1674, 72A–4814, 72A–4815, 60A–1283, 67A–5143, 70A–3652, 63A–1521, 69A–3338, 68A–4494, 68A–4994, 65A–3152, 68A–3187, 66A–3655.

I also consulted Record Group 341, the records of the USAF Chief of Staff at the National Archives in Washington.

Library of Congress

The Manuscript Division of the Library of Congress in Washington, D.C., maintains well-indexed papers of the USAF Chiefs of Staff. Correspondence is arranged alphabetically; topics are arranged chronologically. In some collections folders are specifically labeled as OSAF correspondence. The views of the Air Force Secretaries and the Chiefs of Staff at times differed sharply. Papers of the following officers clarify Air Staff positions on such subjects as the B-36, the B-70, and missiles:

General Henry H. Arnold, Commander, U.S. AAF
    110 ft. of records, 85,000 items
General Ira C. Eaker, Deputy Commander, U.S. AAF
    287 ft. of records, 30,000 items
General Carl A. Spaatz, Chief of Staff, USAF (1947–1948)
    143 ft of records, 115,150 items
General Muir S. Fairchild, Vice Chief of Staff, USAF (1948–1950)
    2 ft of records, 1,400 items
General Hoyt S. Vandenberg, Chief of Staff, USAF (1948–1953)
    47 containers, 85,000 items
General Nathan F. Twining, Chief of Staff, USAF (1953–1957)
    31 ft. of records, 40,000 items
General Thomas D. White, Chief of Staff, USAF (1957–1961)
    23 ft. of records, 20,000 items
General Curtis E. LeMay, Chief of Staff, USAF (1961–1965)
    98 ft. of records, 250,000 items

Harry S. Truman Library

The Harry S. Truman Library in Independence, Missouri, houses the papers of W. Stuart Symington, Thomas K. Finletter, and James T. Hill, General Counsel of the Air Force from 1950 to 1952 and Assistant Secretary of the Air Force from 1952 to 1953. Symington's papers offer excellent material on his tenure as Secretary of the Air Force. Finletter's papers scarcely mention his time in offfice. Hill's detailed appointment diary and telephone log contain little of the substance of meetings and conversations. President Truman's papers proved, for my purposes, as unfruitful as Finletter's and Hill's. Many of Symington's aircraft procurement messages are duplicates of originals in his Special Interest Files at the Federal Records Center in Maryland. The Truman Library also maintains oral history files on members of the Truman administration. Interviews of Roswell L. Gilpatric, Thomas K. Finletter, and Eugene M. Zuckert were quite informative.

USAF Historical Research Center

Many documents available at the USAF Historical Research Center at Maxwell Air Force Base in Montgomery, Alabama, are filed on microfilm at the Center for Air Force History at Bolling Air Force Base in Washington, D.C. Few original sources from the Office of the Secretary of the Air Force are stored within USAF repositories; nearly all have been retired to the National Archives and Records Administration.

The Historical Research Center has acquired the personal and professional papers of USAF members of every rank. The papers of Brig. Gen. George A. Brownell, Robert A. Lovett's executive officer during World War II, detail many of the Air Secretary's interactions with Stimson, Marshall, and Arnold, convey some sense of his office routine, and indicate that his authority and duties were, at best, ill-defined.

Center for Air Force History

The Center for Air Force History at Bolling Air Force Base in Washington, D.C., also houses the speeches of W. Stuart Symington and Thomas K. Finletter. These reveal how both men attempted to project Air Force needs and policies. Key speeches of other Secretaries of the Air Force are scattered throughout Record Group 340 and are reproduced in various newspapers and aviation journals, such as *Aviation Week* and *Air Force Magazine*.

An early attempt by the Secretary of the Air Force's administrative assistant to prepare an annual history of the Secretariat lasted only until 1953. The products of this effort, filed at the Center for Air Force History, provide little insight into how Secretaries Symington and Finletter interacted with the Air Staff. They merely list the names of office holders and contain marginal treatment of a few major issues.

Reports

Reports of the Secretaries of the Air Force and the Secretaries of Defense for the years 1948 through 1965 contain the fullest, and on some issues virtually the only, individual policy statements I found. These reports enabled me to balance official policies against views articulated in press assessments, interviews, and other sources.

Annual Report of the Secretary of the Air Force, Fiscal Year 1948. Washington, D.C.: Government Printing Office, 1948.
through
Annual Report of the Secretary of the Air Force, Fiscal Year 1965. Washington, D.C.: Government Printing Office, 1965.

SECRETARIES OF THE AIR FORCE

Survival in the Air Age: A Report by the President's Air Policy Commission. Washington, D.C.: Government Printing Office, 1948.

First Report of the Secretary of Defense, 1948. Washington, D.C.: Government Printing Office, 1949.

through

Annual Report of the Secretary of Defense, July 1, 1964 to June 30, 1965. Washington, D.C.: Government Printing Office, 1967.

Interviews

I was able, fortunately, to interview several key participants in and witnesses to events discussed in this book. Senator Stuart Symington gave most graciously of his time on several occasions, as did his former special assistant and information director, Mr. Stephen F. Leo. Mr. Leo described the workings between the Air Secretariat and the Air Staff and recalled the extraordinary abilities that earned the first Secretary of the Air Force the enduring respect of his staff. Mr. Eugene M. Zuckert kindly allowed three interviews during which I was able to cover his affiliation with the Office of the Secretary of the Air Force in depth. Brig. Gen. Turner A. Sims, USAF (Ret.), executive officer to Mr. Symington; Brig. Gen. William G. Hipps, USAF (Ret.), executive officer to Air Secretaries Finletter and Talbott; and Gen. William F. McKee, USAF (Ret.), Assistant Vice Chief of Staff, USAF, under Mr. Symington and later Vice Chief of Staff, USAF, under General LeMay provided military impressions of the Office of the Secretary of the Air Force. Another of Mr. Symington's executive officers, Gen. Glen W. Martin, USAF (Ret.), answered my inquiries by letter and Mr. Harold C. Stuart spoke to me by telephone of his tenure as former Assistant Secretary of the Air Force (Civil Affairs).

Transcripts of interviews with the following individuals were very useful (copies are available through the USAF Historical Research Center's Oral History Collection and the Center for Air Force History):

Joseph V. Charyk
James H. Douglas, Jr.
Lt. Gen. Ira C. Eaker
Thomas K. Finletter (also available at the Harry S. Truman Library)
Lt. Gen. Barney M. Giles
Roswell L. Gilpatric (also available at the Harry S. Truman Library)
Maj. Gen Leon W. Johnson
Maj. Gen. Hugh J. Knerr
Gen. Laurence S. Kuter
Gen. William F. McKee
Lt. Gen Glen W. Martin
Dudley C. Sharp
Gen. Carl A. Spaatz
W. Stuart Symington
Eugene M. Zuckert (also available at the Harry S. Truman Library)

Congress

Congressional hearings provide a forum within which Air Force Secretaries and Chiefs of Staff annually defend their proposed budgets and discuss Air Force policies. Transcripts of hearings covering the period 1940 through 1965 were very helpful, particularly those on the B-36, the B-70, and the TFX:

House. Hearings before the Select Committee on Post-War Military Policy. *Proposal to Establish a Single Department of Armed Forces.* 78th Cong., 2d sess. Washington, D.C.: Government Printing Office, 1944.

House. Hearings before the Committee on Armed Services. *Unification and Strategy.* 81st Cong., 1st sess. Washington, D.C.: Government Printing Office, 1950.

House. Hearings before the Committee on Armed Services. *Investigation of the B-36.* House Resolution 234. 81st Cong., 1st sess. Washington, D.C.: Government Printing Office, 1949.

House. Hearings before the Subcommittee of the Committee on Appropriations. *Military Public Works Appropriations for 1952.* 82d Cong., 1st sess. Washington, D.C.: Government Printing Office, 1951.

House. Hearings before the Committee on Expenditures in the Executive Department of Federal Supply Management. *Implementation of Military Supply Requirements.* 82d Cong., 2d sess., Washington, D.C.: Government Printing Office, 1952.

House. Hearings before the Committee on Armed Services. *Reorganization of the Department of Defense.* 85th Cong., 2d sess. Washington, D.C.: Government Printing Office, 1958.

House. Hearings before the Subcommittee of the Committee on Appropriations. *Department of Defense Appropriations for 1961.* Policy Statements of the Secretaries and the Chiefs of Staff. 86th Cong., 2d sess. Washington, D.C.: Government Printing Office, 1960.

House. Hearings before the Subcommittee of the Committee on Appropriations. *Department of Defense Appropriations for 1964.* Chairman, Joint Chiefs of Staff, Overall Financial Statements, Service Secretaries and Chiefs of Staff, Part 2. 88th Cong., 1st sess. Washington, D.C.: Government Printing Office, 1963.

House. Hearings before the Committee on Armed Services. *Statement of Honorable Eugene M. Zuckert on Military Posture.* Washington, D.C.: Government Printing Office, 1964.

Senate. Hearings before the Subcommittee of the Committee on Appropriations. *Department of Defense Appropriations for 1952.* 82d Cong., 1st sess. Washington, D.C.: Government Printing Office, 1951.

Senate. Hearings before the Subcommittee of the Committee on Appropriations. *Department of Defense Appropriations for 1954.* House Resolution 5969, Part 1. 83d Cong., 1st sess. Washington, D.C.: Government Printing Office, 1953.

Senate. Hearings before the Subcommittee of the Committee on Armed Services. *A Study of Air Power*. 84th Cong., 2d sess. Washington, D.C.: Government Printing Office, 1956.

Senate. Hearings before the Committee on Armed Services. *Department of Defense Reorganization Act of 1958*. 85th Cong., 2d sess. Washington, D.C.: Government Printing Office, 1958.

Senate. Hearings before the Subcommittee of the Committee on Appropriations. *Department of Defense Appropriations for 1959*. 85th Cong., 2d sess. Washington, D.C.: Government Printing Office, 1958.

Senate. Hearings before the Subcommittee of the Committee on Appropriations. *Department of Defense Appropriations for 1961*. 86th Cong., 2d sess. Washington, D.C.: Government Printing Office, 1960.

Senate. Hearings before the Subcommittee of the Committee on Appropriations. *Department of Defense Appropriations for 1962*. 87th Cong, 1st sess. Washington, D.C.: Government Printing Office, 1962.

Senate. Hearings before the Permanent Subcommittee on Investigations of the Committee on Government Operations. *TFX Contract Investigation*. 88th Cong., 1st sess. Part 1. Washington, D.C.: Government Printing Office, 1963.

Books

Cole, Alice C., Alfred Goldberg, Samuel A. Tucker, and Rudolph A. Winnacker, eds. *The Department of Defense: Documents On Establishment and Organization, 1944–1978*. Washington, D.C.: Office of the Secretary of Defense, Historical Office, 1978.

Condit, Kenneth W. *The History of the Joint Chiefs of Staff: The Joint Chiefs of Staff and National Policy, 1947–1949*. Vol. 2. Washington, D.C.: Historical Division, Joint Secretariat, Joint Chiefs of Staff, 1977.

Craven, Wesley F., and James L. Cate, eds. *The Army Air Forces in World War II*. 7 vols. Chicago: University of Chicago Press, 1948–1958. (Reprinted in 1983 by the Office of Air Force History.)

Futrell, Robert F. *Ideas, Concepts, Doctrine: A History of Basic Thinking in the United States Air Force, 1907–1964*. Maxwell Air Force Base, Alabama: Air University, 1974.

———. *The Advisory Years to 1965: The United States Air Force In Southeast Asia*. Washington, D.C.: The Office of Air Force History, 1981.

———. *The United States Air Force in Korea, 1950–1953*. Washington, D.C.: Office of Air Force History, 1983, revised edition.

Gorn, Michael H. *The TFX: Conceptual Phase to F-111B Termination, 1958–1968*. Washington, D.C.: Air Force Systems Command, 1985.

Gropman, Alan L. *The Air Force Integrates, 1945–1964*. Washington, D.C.: Office of Air Force History, 1978.

Gross, Charles J. *Prelude to the Total Force: The Air National Guard, 1943–1969*. Washington, D.C.: Office of Air Force History, 1985.

Hewes, James E., Jr. *From Root To McNamara: Army Organization and Administration, 1900–1963*. Washington, D.C.: U.S. Army Center of Military History, 1975.

Holley, Irving Brinton, Jr. *Buying Aircraft: Materiel Procurement for the Army Air Forces. United States Army in World War II*. Washington, D.C.: Office of the Chief of Military History, Department of the Army, 1964.

Hopkins, J.C. *The Development of Strategic Air Command, 1946–1981*. Office of the Historian, Headquarters Strategic Air Command, 1981.

Knaack, Marcelle S. *Encyclopedia of U.S. Air Force Aircraft and Missile Systems. Vol. I: Post-World War II Fighters, 1945–1973*. Washington, D.C.: Office of Air Force History, 1978.

Neufeld, Jacob. *Ballistic Missiles in the United States Air Force, 1945–1960*. Washington, D.C.: Office of Air Force History, 1990.

Rearden, Steven L. *History of the Office of the Secretary of Defense: The Formative Years, 1947–1950*. Vol. I. Washington, D.C.: Historical Office, Office of the Secretary of Defense, 1984.

Schaffel, Kenneth. *The Emerging Shield: The Air Force and the Evolution of the Continental Air Defense, 1945–1960*. Washington, D.C.: Office of Air Force History, 1991.

Stanley, Dennis J., and John J. Weaver. *An Air Force Command for R&D, 1949–1976: The History of ARDC/AFSC*. Andrews Air Force Base, Maryland: Office of History, Headquarters, Air Force Systems Command, 1977,

Sturm, Thomas A. *The USAF Scientific Advisory Board: Its First Twenty Years, 1944–1964*. Washington, D.C.: USAF Historical Division Liaison Office, 1967.

Watson, Mark Skinner. *Chief of Staff: Prewar Plans and Preparations, The United States Army in World War II*. Washington, D.C.: U.S. Army Historical Division, 1950.

Watson, Robert J. *The History of the Joint Chiefs of Staff: The Joint Chiefs of Staff and National Policy, 1953–1954*. Vol V. Washington, D.C.: Historical Office, Joint Chiefs of Staff, 1986.

Wolk, Herman S. *Planning and Organizing the Postwar Air Force, 1943–1947*. Washington, D.C.: Office of Air Force History, 1984.

Yoshpe, Harry B., and Stanley L. Falk. *The Economics of National Security: Organization for National Security*. Washington, D.C.: Industrial College of the Armed Forces, 1963.

Non-Governmental Sources

Books

Albion, Robert Greenhalgh, and Robert Howe Connery. *Forrestal and the Navy*. New York: Columbia University Press, 1962.

Arnold, Henry H. *Global Mission*. New York: Harper & Brothers, 1949.

Art, Robert J. *The TFX Decision: McNamara and the Military*. Boston: Little, Brown and Company, 1968.

Ballard, John A., ed. *Harvard University Defense Policy Seminar, 1956–1957: The Job Concept of the Civilian Secretary*. Boston: Harvard University, 1956.

Blumberg, Stanley A., and Gwinn Owens. *Energy and Conflict: The Life and Times of Edward Teller*. New York: G.P. Putnam's Sons, 1976.

Clifford, Clark M., with Richard Holbrooke. *Counsel to the President: A Memoir*. New York: Random House, 1991.

Coffey, Thomas M. *Iron Eagle: The Turbulent Life of General Curtis LeMay*. New York: Crown Publishers, Inc., 1986.

Donovan, Robert J. *Tumultuous Years: The Presidency of Harry S. Truman, 1949–1953*. New York: W.W. Norton & Company, 1982.

Eisenhower, Dwight D. *Mandate for Change, 1953–1956*. New York: Doubleday and Company, Inc., 1963.

———. *Waging Peace, 1956–1961: The White House Years*. New York: Doubleday and Company, Inc., 1965.

Ferrell, Robert H. *The Eisenhower Diaries*. New York: W.W. Norton & Company, 1981.

Finletter, Thomas K. *Power and Policy: U.S. Foreign Policy and Military Power in the Hydrogen Age*. New York: Harcourt, Brace and Company, 1954.

Forrestal, James. *The Forrestal Diaries*. Edited by Walter Millis. New York: The Viking Press, 1951.

Glover, John D., and Paul R. Lawrence. *A Case Study of High Level Administration in a Large Organization*. Boston: Harvard University, 1960.

Hammond, Paul Y. *Organizing for Defense: The American Military Establishment in the Twentieth Century*. Princeton: Princeton University Press, 1961.

Hinton, Harold B. *Air Victory: The Men and Machines*. New York: Harper Brothers, 1948.

Hitch, Charles J., and Roland N. McKean. *The Economics of Defense in the Nuclear Age*. Cambridge: Harvard University Press, 1960.

Holley, Irving Brinton, Jr. *Ideas and Weapons*. New Haven: Yale University Press, 1961.

Huntington, Samuel P. *The Common Defense: Strategic Programs In National Politics*. New York: Columbia University Press, 1961.

Issacson, Walter, and Evan Thomas. *The Wisemen: Six Friends and The World They Made: Acheson, Bohlen, Harriman, Lovett, McCloy*. New York: Simon & Schuster Inc., 1986.

Kaufmann, William W. *The McNamara Strategy*. New York: Harper & Row, 1964.

Kolodziej, Edward A. *The Uncommon Defense and Congress: 1945–1963*, Columbus: Ohio State University Press, 1966.

Lash, Joseph P. *Roosevelt and Churchill, 1939–1941: The Partnership that Saved the West*. New York: W.W. Norton & Company, 1976.

LeMay, Curtis E., and MacKinlay Kantor. *Mission With LeMay: My Story*. Garden City, New York: Doubleday & Co, 1961.

Luard, Evan, ed. *The Cold War: A Reappraisal*. New York: Frederick A. Praeger, 1964.

Morison, Elting E. *Turmoil and Tradition: A Study of the Life and Times of Henry L. Stimson*. Boston: Houghton Mifflin Company, 1960.

Parmet, Herbert S. *Eisenhower and the American Crusades*. New York: The Macmillan Company, 1972.

Pogue, Forrest C. *George C. Marshall: Ordeal and Hope, 1939–1942*. New York: Viking Press, Inc, 1965.

Rogow, Arnold A. *James Forrestal: A Study of Personality, Politics, and Policy*. New York: The Macmillan Company, 1963.

Roherty, James M. *The Decisions of Robert S. McNamara: A Study of the Role of the Secretary of Defense*. Coral Gables, Florida: The University of Miami Press, 1970.

Stein, Harold, ed. *American Civil-Military Decisions: A Book of Case Studies*. University of Alabama Press, 1963.

Stern, Phillip M. *The Oppenheimer Case: Security on Trial*. New York: Harper and Row, 1969.

Stimson, Henry L., and McGeorge Bundy. *On Active Service in Peace and War*. New York: Harper Brothers, 1948.

Trewhitt, Henry L. *McNamara: His Ordeal in the Pentagon*. New York: Harper and Row, 1971.

375

Truman, Harry S. *Memoirs*. Vol. II: *Years of Trial and Hope*. Garden City, New York: Doubleday & Company, 1956.

Truman, Margaret. *Harry S. Truman*. New York: William Morrow & Co, 1973.

Tunner, William H. *Over The Hump*. New York: Duell, Sloan, and Pearce, 1964.

Wellman, Paul I. *Stuart Symington: Portrait of a Man with a Mission*. New York: Doubleday and Company, Inc., 1960.

Who's Who in America, 1950–1951. Vol. 26. Chicago: The A.N. Marquis Company; 1950.

Who's Who in America, 1955–1956. Vol. 29. Chicago: The A.N. Marquis Company, 1957.

Yergin, Daniel. *Shattered Peace: The Origins of the Cold War and the National Security State*. Boston: Houghton Mifflin Co, 1977.

Articles

"AFA Riles Wilson." *Aviation Week*. Vol. 65, No. 7, August 13, 1956.

"Air Force Association Demands Single Service." *Aviation Week*. Vol. 65. No. 7, August 13, 1956.

The Army Navy Air Force Journal. Vol. 91, August 28, 1954, pp. 1569, 1590.

"The Baylor Speech." *Air Force Magazine*. March 1950.

"Change in Quarles's Thinking Seen in Emphasis on Skilled Personnel." *Aviation Week*. Vol. 64, No. 7, February 13, 1956.

Coughlin, William J. "Talbott Gives Dispersal Details." *Aviation Week*. Vol. 62, No. 21, May 23, 1955.

"Douglas as USAF Secretary." *Aviation Week*. Vol. 65, No. 11, September 11, 1956.

Eastman, Ford. "Defense Reorganization Will Await McNamara's Study of the Pentagon." *Aviation Week*. Vol. 73, No. 25, December 19, 1960.

"Eugene Zuckert the Man and the Manager." *Airman*. October 18, 1965.

"Gardner Quits, States USAF R&D Fight." *Aviation Week*. Vol. 64, No. 7, February 13, 1956.

"Gardner Warns Russia Is Ahead on IRBM, Blames U.S. Rivalries." *Aviation Week*. Vol. 65, No. 4, July 23, 1956.

"Good Air Force Appointments." *Aviation Week*. Vol. 66, No. 13, April 1, 1957.

"Hope for Science." *Aviation Week*. Vol. 66, No. 18, May 6, 1957.

Hotz, Robert. "USAF Buying Test: Proved Performance." *Aviation Week.* Vol. 61, No. 20, November 15, 1954.

———. "Wilson on Russia." *Aviation Week.* Vol. 65, No. 4, 23 July 1956.

———. "Cleaning Up the Pentagon." *Aviation Week.* Vol. 67, No. 7, August 19, 1957.

———. "The Critical Role of ARPA." *Aviation Week.* Vol. 68. No. 4, January 27, 1958.

———. "Kennedy Orders Defense Review, Boost in Airlift, Missile Programs." *Aviation Week.* Vol. 74, No. 6, February 6, 1961.

———. "A Dismal Pattern." *Aviation Week.* Vol. 75, No. 19, December 6, 1961.

Johnson, Katherine. "Talbott Quits Mulligan, Clings to USAF." *Aviation Week.* Vol. 63, No. 6, August 8, 1955.

Kolcum, Edward H. "President's Role in TFX Award Disclosed." *Aviation Week and Space Technology.* Vol. 81, No. 16, October 19, 1964.

Lewis, Flora. "The Education of A Senator." *The Atlantic Monthly.* December 1971.

McDonald, William G. "The Changing Management Role of the Military Departments. *Air University Review.* Vol. 13, No. 4, Summer 1962.

McLaughlin, John J. "Organization of the Air Force." *Air University Quarterly Review.* Vol. 13, No. 3, 1962.

"McNamara Will Oppose Spending Any Additional SAC Bomber Funds." *Aviation Week and Space Technology.*, Vol. 74, No. 23, June 5, 1961.

"New Faces in the Pentagon." *Air Force Magazine.* Vol. 36, No. 2, February 1953.

"New Flow Shocks McNamara; He Will Re-educate Contractors." *Aviation Week and Space Technology.* Vol. 74, No. 7, May 14, 1971.

"Pentagon Planners." *Air Force Magazine.* Vol. 36, No. 5, May 1953.

"Praise for Talbott." *Aviation Week.* Vol. 62, No. 15, April 11, 1955.

"Quarles Choice Significant." *Aviation Week.* Vol. 63, No. 10, September 10, 1955.

"Quarles Denies LeMay Testimony; Says U.S. Will Retain Superiority." *Aviation Week.* Vol. 65. No. 1, July 2, 1956.

"Quarles Differs." *Aviation Week.* Vol. 63, No. 9, August 29, 1955.

Quarles, Donald A. "How Much is Enough?" *Air Force Magazine.* Vol. 39, September 1956.

"Quarles Policy." *Aviation Week.* Vol. 63. No. 12, September 19, 1955.

"Quarles Slows Bid for Boost in Budget." *Aviation Week.* Vol. 66. No. 9, March 4, 1957.

"Russians Outpacing U. S. in Air Quality, Twining Warns Congress." *Aviation Week.* Vol. 64, No. 9, February 27, 1956.

"Senate Votes Boost in Air Force Budget." *Aviation Week.* Vol. 65, No. 1, July 2, 1956.

"Services Outline Airpower Plans for Congress." *Aviation Week.* Vol. 62, No. 18, May 2, 1955.

"Sharp is Appointed Successor to Lewis." *Aviation Week.* Vol. 63, No. 4, July 25, 1955.

"Single Defense Information Office Urged." *Aviation Week and Space Technology.* Vol. 79, No. 25, December 16, 1963.

"Superiority and Security." *Aviation Week.* Vol. 65, No. 11, September 10, 1956.

"Symington on Talbott." *Aviation Week.* Vol. 63, No. 4, August 8, 1955.

"Symington Report of Airpower." *Aviation Week.* Vol. 66, No. 5, February 4, 1957.

"Symington Report Urges Airpower Boost." *Aviation Week.* Vol. 66, No. 5, February 4, 1957.

"Talbott Business Connections Questioned." *Aviation Week.* Vol. 63, No. 4, July 25, 1955.

"Talbott Clarifies Dispersal Policy." *Aviation Week.* Vol. 62, No. 19, May 9, 1955.

"Talbott: Praised and Criticized." *Aviation Week.* Vol. 63, No. 8, August 22, 1955.

Time Magazine. January 19, 1948.

"Washington Roundup." *Aviation Week.* Vol. 74, No. 21, May 22, 1961.

"Washington Roundup." *Aviation Week.* Vol. 74, No. 24, June 12, 1961.

"Washington Roundup." *Aviation Week.* Vol. 75, No. 19, November 6, 1961.

"Washington Roundup." *Aviation Week.* Vol. 76, No. 6, February 5, 1962.

"Washington Roundup." *Aviation Week and Space Technology.* Vol. 80, No. 17, April 27, 1964.

"Washington Roundup." *Aviation Week and Space Technology.* Vol. 80, No. 21, May 25, 1964.

"Washington Roundup." *Aviation Week and Space Technology.* Vol. 82, No. 6, February 8, 1965.

"White Warns of Red R&D Production." *Aviation Week.* Vol. 64, No. 8, February 20, 1956.

Wilson, George C. "F-111A Program Posts Several Aeronautical and Political Firsts." *Aviation Week and Space Technology.* Vol. 81, No. 16, October 19, 1964.

―――. "TFX Probe to Focus on Possible Conflict in Gilpatric, Force Roles." *Aviation Week and Space Technology.* Vol. 79, No. 11, September 9, 1963.

Wolk, Herman S. "The New Look in Retrospect." *Air Force Magazine.* Vol. 57, No. 3, March 1974.

Zuckert, Eugene M. "Keeping the Organizational Engine in Tune." *Air Force.* October 1964.

―――. "A Parting Message." *Air Force.* September 1965.

―――. "The Service Secretary: Has He a Useful Role?" *Foreign Affairs.* April 1966.

"Zuckert Gives Views on Aerospace Issues." *Aviation Week and Space Technology.* Vol. 80, No. 9.

"Zuckert TFX Judgement Changed." *Aviation Week and Space Technology.* Vol. 79, No. 7, August 12, 1963.

Newspapers

Air Force Times. Vol. 14, June 26, 1954, p. 7.

Air Force Times. Vol. 16, December 3, 1955.

Air Force Times. Vol. 16, September 10, 1955.

Air Force Times, Vol. 15, Vol. 16, August 20, 1955, p. 3.

Air Force Times, Vol. 16, November 16, 1955.

The *Chicago Sun-Times,* December 7, 1960, p. 13.

The *Chicago Sun-Times,* December 11, 1960, p. 16.

The *Cincinnati Enquirer,* December 8, 1960, p. 22.

The *Evening Star* (Washington, D.C.), March 18, 1949.

The *New York Times,* April 5, 1950, p. 30.

The *New York Times,* June 7, 1950, p. 23.

The *New York Times,* January 30, 1951, p. 6.

The *New York Times,* December 6, 1960, pp. 1F–3F.

SECRETARIES OF THE AIR FORCE

Ph.D. Dissertations

Two Ph.D dissertations were especially helpful:

Fanton, Jonathan Foster. "Robert A. Lovett: The War Years." Yale University, 1978.

Green, Murray. "Stuart Symington and the B-36." American University, 1960.

Fanton's dissertation is the best single source I found on Robert A. Lovett. It describes several of Lovett's influential contacts from industry and publishing who helped him throughout his tenure as Assistant Secretary of War for Air. It reveals much about Lovett's operations with Secretary of War Stimson and the Air Staff and thus the extent of his influence on W. Stuart Symington and succeeding Secretaries of the Air Force.

Green's dissertation is one of the most detailed accounts available on Symington's role in the B-36 controversy.

Index

Index

385